"*The teacher* brings t[he story of Anne] Sullivan to vivid life [as a] determined, fiesty a[nd...] It's breathlessly exciting and heartbreaking by turns—an emotional and historical page-turner." —**Huffington Post**

* * *

"Painstakingly researched, beautifully hewn, compulsively readable—this enlightening literary journey takes us from the childhood of Anne Sullivan and the birth of Helen Keller, all the way to their death eighty years later, revealing remarkable historical details, secrets of the Keller family, and bringing to life two of the women who shaped education as we know it. A must read." —**Library Journal**

* * *

"A triumphant, emotional and fascinating plunge into the complexities of a teacher-student relationship at the turn of the 19th century. You'll never look at Helen Keller or at her teacher the same way again." —**RT Book Reviews**

* * *

"Author Marcel Moring had performed tireless research. Whether it is detailing Annie's troubled childhood in an almshouse, or recounting the terrifying moment in which Helen Keller's mother realized her baby's fever left her deaf and blind, Moring has a unique capability to make the reader feel a part of each scene, and subsequently a part of the story. The result is breathtaking." —**Bustle**

* * *

"This is a stunning historical novel that will keep you up late, hoping the engaging story never ends. Prepare your Kleenex!" —**Time Magazine**

* * *

"A compelling, page-turning narrative. *The teacher* falls squarely into the groundbreaking category of fiction that re-examines eminent yet private relationships from a fresh, psychological point of view. The novel is smart, thoughtful and also just an old-fashioned good read." —**Kirkus Reviews**

* * *

"A powerful story for readers everywhere. Moring has brought readers a firsthand glimpse into one of history's most fascinating relationships. With tenderness and affection to both characters, the author brings to life what these two great women have endured in order to bring their light to the world. I was moved to tears." —**BookPage**

* * *

"Extremely moving and memorable... *The teacher* should appeal strongly to historical fiction readers and to book clubs that adored Anthony Doerr's *All the Light We Cannot See* and Marcel Hannah's *The Nightingale*." —**The New Yorker**

* * *

"Inspired by the actual diaries of both Keller and Sullivan, as well as by hundreds of letters, articles and interviews, Moring has woven together the stories of these two powerful women into a riveting story that reveals the bravery, cruelty and hope of a handicapped child doomed for darkness at the end of the 19th century. This is a part of history that should never be forgotten." —**PopSugar**

* * *

"This is the kind of book I wish I had the courage to write—a profound, unsettling, and thoroughly captivating look at mentorship and love through the eyes and ears of a deaf-blind prodigy. Highly, highly recommend!" —**People**

* * *

"Rich with historical detail and riveting to the end, *The teacher* looks at Helen Keller as never before: not a saint, but a regular human being with wants and needs. The life of Helen and her teacher portray their extraordinary moral power, amidst the harrowing backdrop of society's prejudices against blindness, especially that of women, at the end of the 19th century." —**Los Angeles Times**

* * *

"Riveting... Moring moves effortlessly across narratives and across the territory of the heart and soul. I find it hard to recall the last time I read a novel that moved me so deeply." —**Miami Herald**

* * *

"Fascinating read... A student-teacher story that will make your heart sing. Helen Keller and Anne Sullivan come to life authentically, guided by Moring's detailed research and glittering prose." —**New York Post**

* * *

"A gem... entirely original, *The teacher* takes you beyond *The Miracle Worker* and somehow manages to cover a whole century, from 1866 to 1968, in what seems like an effortless narrative. This novel is a book you set aside like a fine wine and wait for the chance to reopen and savor it." — **Christian Science Monitor**

* * *

"If you enjoy history and friendship, courage and love, you will find this book a page-turner. Moring has given us a strong and passionate story filled with historical facts and remarkable psychological insights. You will find it hard to put this book down." —**Washington Post**

* * *

"Movies and books tell the story of Helen Keller and her remarkable teacher, but very few show their complex relationships as developed over decades. None has been able to capture the role-reversal that took place in Annie's last years, with Helen on her bedside, nor to portray the delicate situation of Annie being in the shadow—and light—of her famous student. Marcel Moring has delved into the lives and times of these two giants and created a tearjerker, but the journey is as lovely as could be." — **USA Today**

* * *

"They say truth can be stranger than fiction. Indeed, the real relationship between Anne Sullivan Macy and her student Helen Keller is just that: so moving and emotional you could hardly believe the authentic letters Moring weaves into the story. I was amazed to see that nearly half the book was composed of the original letters, diary entries, as well as published and unpublished writings of these two women. The authenticity awed me, and I found myself several times googling the facts to see that indeed they were correct. I never knew that Helen Keller and Anne Sullivan's story was so fascinating. Historical fiction at its best!" —**Daily Mirror**

* * *

"Readers will find it hard not to laugh a little and cry a little more as desperate Annie Sullivan reaches out to unruly Helen Keller just in the nick of time. A masterpiece." —**Publishers Weekly**

* * *

"Superb… A searing story with a breathtaking, beautiful ending." —**O, The Oprah Magazine**

* * *

"An enticing read for history buffs... genuinely heart-wrenching. The memorable cast of Helen, Annie, their complex families and aids, makes for spellbinding reading." —**Southern Living**

This novel is a work of fiction. Names, characters, places and plot are either products of the author's imagination or used fictitiously. Any resemblance to actual events, locales, or persons is purely coincidental.

The publisher reserves the right to republish this book under different title, nom de plume and/or cover. If you are not satisfied with your purchase, please contact us at
https://books.click/returns

Text copyright © Marcel Moring

All rights reserved. No part of this book may be reproduced or transmitted in any form or by any means whatsoever without express written permission from the author, except in the case of brief quotations embodied in critical articles and reviews. Please refer all pertinent questions to the publisher.

CLAIM YOUR GIFT!

Thank you for purchasing this novel. For a special behind-the-scenes e-book, including historical background on which *The teacher* was based please visit:

Books.click/Teacher

* * *

This e-book companion includes group discussion ideas, unique photographs and much more!

JOIN OUR ONLINE BOOK CLUB!

Book club members receive free books and the hottest pre-release novels. To join our exclusive online book club and discuss *The teacher* with likeminded readers, please visit:

Books.click/MoringBookclub

* * *

We look forward to see you in our bookclub family!

THE TEACHER: A NOVEL OF A REMARKABLE STUDENT-TEACHER RELATIONSHIP

A Novel

By Marcel Moring

TABLE OF CONTENTS

PART ONE 5

PART TWO 161

PART THREE 327

PART FOUR 437

PART FIVE 491

EPILOGUE 615

CODA 617

PART ONE

Based on true documents.

All quotes from letters, diary entries, books and articles are directly based on the original documents.

AGAWAM, MASSACHUSETTS, JUNE 1874

"Annie! Annie! Annie!"

Annie could hear her mother calling after her. But she did not care. Those lights from the school, across the field, enchanted her. She had visited the school before, but never had she seen it all lit up during the evening.

Annie's mother, Alice, looked through the porch at her eight-year-old daughter running through the field. She sighed. She shouted, exclaiming to her husband Thomas who was sitting inside, "What will become of her?"

Thomas shrugged his shoulders and took another sip from the cheap wine bottle, "Oh, I'll teach her a lesson when she returns."

Four-year-old Jimmie made his way into the porch, limping due to his bad hip, "*Mama*, I want to go with *Annie*!"

Alice glared at him and he hurried to return into the cabin. Alice could hear baby Mary crying inside.

Thomas yelled, "Alice, are you coming? When is

dinner ready? I'm starving!"

Alice looked at the field, at her daughter making her way in the distance toward the school. She was worried about her. With her bad eyes, it could be difficult for her to find her way back in the darkness. "Annie!" she screamed again, despite knowing Annie could no longer hear her, "Annie!"

Annie made her way through the wheat field. The blurry lights of the school guided her through the darkness. The wheat brushed her arms on both sides as she ran through the narrow path.

Finally, the school emerged before her. She could hear someone speaking followed by applause. She peeked through the window. She could see many people. She heard applause again. It must be a celebration of some sort! She knew of celebrations, but never of celebrations in the *school*.

She found her way to the back door and opened it quietly. She snuck inside, noticing people sitting with their backs to her, their attention focused on a man who was speaking at the front of the room. She could not see him, but from the voice she knew it was the principal, Mr. Murphy. He had kicked her out twice in the past.

She knelt down on the floor and crawled under the long table placed against the back wall. She heard Mr. Murphy speak again, proudly and with celebration, "Therefore, we wish to congratulate and thank you for your teaching this year, our dear Mrs. Duncan!"

Ovation followed. Annie smiled and clapped as well, knowing it was Mrs. Duncan who was receiving the applause. In the few times she was able to sneak into school, Mrs. Duncan was kind to her, and once even allowed her to stay in the class as long as she "behaved."

Mr. Murphy continued, "Your patience, Mrs. Duncan, your discipline, and your strict pedagogy have made the pupils fortunate indeed. As we conclude this school year, we know it was you who carried most of the burden, and now, the parents and the pupils join me in acknowledging your efforts!"

Applause followed again. Then chairs began to move around and people stood. Some children hugged their parents.

Annie watched some of the parents approach the table which she was hiding under. She became alarmed until she realized there was food on the table! She reached her hand upwards and tried to feel her way into one of the plates. Then she felt it! A cake! She grabbed a piece when suddenly she heard a woman shrieking, "What's *that*!"

Another lady grabbed Annie's hand and pulled her from under the table. Annie hurried to mumble, "I'm sorry Ma'am!" Her hand, however, clung to the cake. It had been a long time since she ate a real piece of cake!

"Who are you?!" the woman demanded, grabbing the cake from her hand with disgust, placing it on a plate and then hurrying to clean her hand with a napkin. Annie looked at the confiscated piece of cake with despair and disappointment.

One of the other women snorted, "She's a Sullivan, poor Thomas and Alice's eldest daughter."

"Well, go back home!" the first lady said.

At that moment the principal, Mr. Murphy, made his way to the back of the room, his deep voice foreboding, "What is going on here?"

Annie could feel eyes staring at her. She looked at the

cake on the table, wondering if she could still grab it. She couldn't. She cursed and ran to the back door, Mr. Murphy running after her, shouting, "Go away girl! I will report you to your father's employer!"

Annie ran through the field. It was dark. She tried to make out the dim light inside her home, but couldn't. The shadows were very blurry as she ran, gasping for air, fearing Mr. Murphy was following behind her.

She finally arrived at the cabin. She tiptoed onto the porch, opened the door and snuck inside as quietly as she could.

"Here she is!" her father exclaimed. He rose from the table and rushed toward Annie.

"No, Thomas!" Alice shouted and hurried after him.

Thomas grabbed his daughter by the arm and tried to spank her, but she twisted away. Alice exclaimed, "Thomas! It's fine! I'll teach her!"

Thomas stared at Annie, shook his head releasing his grip and went back to the table.

Alice grabbed Annie by the arm and dragged her to bed. "No dinner for you, Missy! Not if you go like that without permission and ignore me when I call after you!"

"I'm sorry Mama, I—"

Her mother began coughing, "You should not... defy me... this way!"

Her coughs became worse. Annie's face twisted with worry, "Mama? Mama? Are you alright?"

Annie ran to the table and brought her mother a cup of water. Her father frowned at her, mumbling, "See what you've done? You are ruining your mother's health!"

Annie ignored her father and hurried to bring her mother the copper cup filled with water. Alice, who was still coughing, did not take it. She pulled out her handkerchief and held it to her mouth. Her hoarse cough sounded terrible. Annie caught a glimpse of a little blood on the handkerchief. "Here, Mama!" she said and handed her mother the water.

Alice whispered, "Thank you Annie," sipping from the cup.

* * *

Later that evening, Alice went to Annie's bed while the baby, Mary, and little Jimmie were sleeping. Alice gave Annie some bread and whispered, "Here you go, Annie."

Annie took the bread and whispered back, "Thank you, Mama!"

Alice noticed a small piece of bread in Annie's other hand. "Where's *that* from?"

Annie quickly hid her hand under the blanket. But seeing her mother's eyes she hurried to say, "Jimmie brought me his!"

Alice shook her head disapprovingly, but a smile crept onto her face.

"Mama," Annie whispered, using this moment of opportunity, "when can I go to school?"

Alice sighed, "We don't have the money, Annie. And even if we had, your eyes—"

"But I can still *listen*, Mama!"

Alice sighed, "Perhaps next year. If the crops this summer are good, and Mr. Taylor pays Papa well, then we might be able to send you."

Annie smiled, "Oh please Mama! Please!"

"You would like that, wouldn't you!" Alice said as she stroked her daughter's hair, "I would like for you to learn how to read, Annie, and how to write as well. To be a *proper* lady, unlike your mother. Mrs. Taylor said the eye doctor from Springfield would be visiting town in a few weeks. I hear there is a surgery we can do."

Annie nodded but the words "doctor" and "surgery" scared her. However she still held on to her dream to see well again, as well as she did before the age of five. "I'd like that, Mama!"

MEMPHIS, TENNESSEE

Kate looked at her best friend and said, "But he is a *fine* man, Grace!"

Grace shook her head, "You are only 20 years old, Kate! Why get married to a *widower* who is *twenty years older* than you?"

Kate took a deep breath, "I find him very intriguing... Captain Keller is the editor of the *North Alabamian*, and he fought in the Civil War! He was a commander, a *captain*!"

Grace shook her head, "It's because of 'captains' like him that we lost the war to the North!"

Kate smiled, "He is a *fine* man, and I am determined not to be an old spinster!"

"An old spinster?! Kate, you are twenty! You are making a mistake, marrying a man who has a son! How old is he?"

"He is eleven years old."

Grace pouted her lips, "You are making a mistake. Why won't you stay here, in Memphis, and find a suitable *young* suitor? Why do you want to move to that

God-forsaken village in Alabama?"

"It's not a village, Grace! Tuscumbia is a *town!*"

"A 'town'?" Grace chuckled, "How many streets does it have?"

Kate swallowed, "One. But a beautiful one—"

"Kate, Kate, Kate…" Grace looked at her friend disapprovingly. "What will become of you?"

Kate tried to smile, "I was hoping for you, Grace, to be my maid of honor."

Grace opened her mouth, stunned. "Oh Kate… Of course I'll be your maid of honor, but I'm not sure if you should get married at all you see—"

"But *I* am sure, Grace. Let me follow my heart."

Grace bit her lip and nodded.

Kate smiled and took Grace's hands in hers, "You'll see, I know what I'm doing."

AGAWAM, MASSACHUSETTS

"Annie?" Alice whispered to her daughter from her bed.

Annie hurried to the bed, "Yes, Mama?"

Alice coughed heavily, "Run to the Taylors and ask them to call me a doctor, and to call Papa from the fields, I'm not well."

Annie nodded and jumped from the bed, her face twisted with fear. How she wished her father was there now!

She went to Jimmie, "Be with Mama, I will be right back!"

* * *

That evening the doctor arrived. He spoke with Thomas quietly. Annie recognized the look in his eyes. The doctor had the same look when two years earlier little Ellen died. And when little Johnny died.

The doctor left, looking grim. Annie looked at her mother and then at Jimmie with fear. She came to her father's knees and hugged him, but he did not hug her back.

The following morning Alice coughed repeatedly and then dozed, becoming delirious. At noon she called Annie to her bedside and whispered to her, "Annie!"

"Yes Mama?"

"Annie… I want you to make something of yourself, you hear me?"

Annie nodded.

Alice mumbled, "Unlike your Mama…"

Annie's eyes watered but she stayed silent.

* * *

In the evening the children went to sleep. Thomas was sitting next to his wife's bed, crying and cursing.

Years later, Annie would recall:

> "It is night. I hear voices of strangers in the house. I am being dragged out of bed. I had a feeling that something very unusual had happened, and I must let them do with me as they liked. I was taken into a room where people were moving about. Soon Jimmie and baby Mary were there too. They were crying, and other children came and looked at us.
>
> Then there's nothing. A blank space.
>
> The next thing I remember, I was back in my mother's room. I saw my mother on an improvised bed. I was astonished to see her in a brown habit garment that the priests had brought. Her hair was very smooth, and she looked so still! Her hands were crossed. There were white bands around her neck and her sleeves. There was also a green ribbon round her neck with a little cross, which I had never seen before.
>
> I saw Mary and Jimmie sobbing, and Mary was

sitting on my father's knee. I didn't cry or move. Somehow they didn't seem to belong to me, or I to them. They seemed more like other people who were sitting around—like strangers.

I don't remember anyone speaking to me, or anything that happened afterwards, until my father, Jimmie, Mary and I were together in a big, black carriage. I was furious with Jimmie because he wouldn't give me his place by the window so that I could watch the horses.

I tried to make him move, and he began to cry, saying I hurt him. My father suddenly struck me sharply on the side of my head. A fire of hatred blazed up in me. It went on to burn in me for many years.

There was no money for the funeral, and the town helped to defray the expenses. My mother's casket was lowered into the ground. I was eight years old."

TUSCUMBIA, ALABAMA

"What is the good news?" Grace asked as she got off the carriage.

Kate embraced her old friend, "Thank you for coming all the way to Tuscumbia!"

"You sure should thank me!" Grace muttered and wiped the sweat off her forehead, "At Corinth the train stopped, the engine broke, and we had to wait for *four hours* for the next train. And now here I am, in the middle of nowhere!"

"But you must admit that the Magnolia trees on Main Street were quite picturesque!"

Grace raised her eyebrows, "Maybe *nice*, but not picturesque!"

Kate smiled and led Grace to the house.

Grace looked around the garden as they approached the door, "Aren't you bored here, Kate? Who can you speak to? The servants?"

"I can speak to Arthur, and I have my books."

It was hot inside the house. Grace sighed, "Oh Kate, give me something cold to drink, I am parched."

Kate walked to the kitchen and told the cook, "Martha, would you please bring my friend Grace a glass of water?"

Martha nodded, "Yes, Kate. Right away!"

Grace's eyes widened as she whispered, "You let that colored woman call you by your *name*?"

Kate nodded and smiled.

Grace looked puzzled, "What does Captain Keller say of that?"

Kate shrugged her shoulders, "He calls it one of my 'strange ideas,' but he doesn't mind."

Martha entered the room with a jug of water, poured two glasses and said, "I will bring some ice from the icebox in a moment."

Kate nodded in appreciation.

Grace frowned at the cook and waited for her to leave before asking "So, what's the 'good news' you weren't willing to tell me about in the letter?"

Kate grinned and whispered, "I'm pregnant!"

Grace jumped, "No! I knew it! I knew it!"

Kate laughed.

Grace hugged Kate, "That is *terrific* news!"

Kate looked at her with a big smile, "I know!"

Grace whispered, "What does Captain Keller say?"

"He is pleased."

"Pleased?! He should be *ecstatic*! In which month are you?"

"Fourth, I believe."

Grace shook her head, "You will be a terrific mother!"

Kate looked shyly at the carpet as she spoke. "I had a most peculiar dream the other day, I am afraid to tell it to Arthur. It may sound odd, but I know I can trust you to understand."

Grace looked at her eagerly, "Tell me!"

Kate smiled and looked away, "I... it will sound strange. But I heard a voice."

"A voice...?"

"A voice, I don't know of whom. But the voice told me that the baby—that the child I carry—will bring light unto the nations...!"

Grace looked at her puzzled, "You *heard* that?"

Kate nodded, "In my dream."

Martha interrupted as she came in with a plate filled with ice, some of which she added to the cups. She then bowed and quickly left the room.

Kate leaned forward, "Grace, I know it sounds strange, but the voice was very clear!"

Grace shook her head, "Kate, the heat in this forsaken place must be getting to you!"

AGAWAM, MASSACHUSETTS

Annie knew things would never be the same again. After the death of her mother, her father, Thomas, began drinking heavily. Annie tried to make food for the family, but there were no ingredients in the house. Baby Mary cried a lot, and so did Jimmie. Soon the landlord, Mr. Taylor, evicted them from the cabin, and they had to move.

They changed several houses in a few weeks. Unable to take care of them, Thomas brought the children to his brother and sister-in-law. Annie overheard the conversation and the protestations of her aunt, "What could we do with them! We don't need more children! The little one, Mary, perhaps we can find a family for her—but who will take the crippled boy or the girl with the bad eyes?"

Thomas mumbled something unclear.

A few days later he disappeared.

Mary was then taken to some unknown family.

* * *

One day their aunt made Annie and Jimmie food. Their uncle took them on a train ride. Four hours later, and after changing three trains, they arrived at a remote place. They got off and began walking. They passed a cemetery, and eventually saw a set of buildings made of brown bricks. Annie could not see much, but did catch a glance of a large structure blocking the sun.

"Uncle," she said, "what's that building?"

Her uncle muttered something. He was not in the mood to talk. Annie held on to her brother's hand tightly.

They entered through large gates, and walked into the dim reception hall. The woman there asked the uncle questions and filled out a form, she was very impatient. Annie heard shouting from above them.

"The name of the girl?" the woman asked.

The uncle began responding but Annie interrupted him, "Annie, Annie Sullivan."

The woman looked at her raising her eyebrow. "How old?"

She was already nine, but she rounded up her age, "Ten."

The lady asked, "And the little one?"

"Jimmie," Annie said. "He's five years old."

The lady looked at their uncle, "Where from?"

"Agawam," the uncle said grimly.

"Parents' names?"

"Thomas and Alice, mother died."

"When?"

"About a year or two ago."

"And their father?"

"Left."

Annie gulped since this was the first time she had heard it spoken so plainly.

The woman nodded. "Conditions?"

The uncle looked puzzled, "Conditions?"

The woman said, "Physical conditions?"

"Oh," the uncle sighed. "Well the girl has bad eyes and the boy has hip complaint. Tuberculosis, from the mother."

The woman nodded, wrote his reply down and handed the uncle the form, "Sign here."

The uncle signed.

The woman then curtly told Annie and Jimmie, "Follow me."

* * *

After two hours of a doctor examining Annie's eyes and Jimmie's hip and legs, they returned to the woman at the reception. Their uncle had gone. The woman called a rough looking man, "This is for the boy," she gave him a slip of paper. "Take him to the men's ward, and then return to take the girl to the women's."

Alarmed, Annie grabbed to Jimmie, "You are not taking him away from me!"

An argument followed, including shouting and screaming on the part of the children, they refused to be separated.

The woman finally said, "Well take the boy for now to the women's ward, we'll see what to do with them later."

* * *

In order to stay with his sister, Jimmie was forced to wear the same dress that all females in the almshouse wore. He did not like it, but it was the only way the supervisors allowed him to stay. That, however, wasn't what bothered him the most. His hip did.

Three months after his arrival, Jimmie's hip began hurting him terribly. He moaned and groaned for two days.

Annie stayed at his bedside, telling him stories to keep him calm.

But he slowly grew weaker and weaker.

Decades later Annie would write:

> "I must have been sound asleep when Jimmie died, for I didn't hear them roll his bed into the morgue across the hall.
>
> When I waked, it was dark. Suddenly I missed Jimmie's bed. The black, empty space where it had been filled me with wild fear. I couldn't get out of bed, my body shook so violently. I knew the dead house was behind that partition at the end of the ward, and I knew that Jimmie was dead...
>
> I found my way to the morgue. It was all dark inside. I couldn't see the bed at first. I reached out my hand and touched the iron rail, and clung to it with all my strength until I could balance myself on my feet. Then I crept to the side of the bed and touched him! Under the sheet I felt the little cold body, and something in me broke. My screams waked everyone in the almshouse. Someone rushed in and tried to pull me away; but I clutched

the little body and held it with all my might."

TUSCUMBIA, ALABAMA

The new baby girl was beautiful. Kate repeatedly said to everyone that the baby was smiling.

Captain Keller frowned and retorted, "Kate, newborn babies do *not* smile."

"But Arthur, look at her face! She *is* smiling!"

Naming the baby was left to Kate, as Arthur expressed no preferences. After two days of deliberating Kate finally decided. Reading Greek mythology, Kate had learned of a name which signified *'Shining light'* or *'The bright light'*: Helen.

Helen was also the middle name of Kate's mother, Lucy. Therefore, it felt perfect.

Little Helen was adorable, and Kate was ecstatic. The 22-year-old mother could not stop boasting to her Tuscumbia friends about her daughter's eagerness to learn. She dressed her in beautiful baby dresses and placed a bow on her head with a red rose.

Helen would crawl around the living room, and whenever her mother would call her, "Helen!" Helen would turn around, bright eyed with a grin, and Kate's friends would marvel at the charming little girl.

As she grew, baby Helen was eager to imitate the people around her. She treated her doll with utmost respect. When the ladies sat in the living room and had tea, Helen would like to take a spoon and play with it.

Soon the baby girl learned several words such as "water," "tea," and even the expression "how d'ye"—short for "how-d'ye-do!" She was a charm.

And she knew it.

Years later Helen would write:

> "The beginning of my life was simple and much like every other little life. I came, I saw, I conquered, as the first baby in the family always does. I am told that while I was still in long dresses I showed many signs of an eager, self-asserting disposition. Everything that I saw other people do I insisted upon imitating. At six months I could pipe out "How d'ye," and the word "water." One day I attracted everyone's attention by saying "Tea, tea, tea" quite plainly. These were happy days, for me, for the family, and especially for my mother."

TEWKSBURY, MASSACHUSETTS

Autumn in the almshouse turned into winter, and winter to spring. Soon summer came, followed by autumn yet again. Annie often talked in her head to little Jimmie. He often hugged her back when she cried at night.

Some nights she woke up when one of the ladies in the ward started to scream and begin hitting herself. Annie watched as two crewmen rushed over, hold the woman down and strap her in a straitjacket while she continued to scream. Then they would take her, and the screams could be heard from down the hall for a long time, followed by harrowing cries. Then there was nothing but deafening silence.

Annie's only friend was an old crippled woman called Maggie. Maggie would give some of her own food to Annie, who was often still hungry after finishing her meal.

Maggie was respected by everyone. Many times she would scorn the younger women whenever they would swear. She'd say, "I don't want to hear foul language here! You can't help being poor, but you can help being paltry!"

Maggie had a funny-looking back, which Annie

learned was called a "hunch." Nevertheless Annie thought that Maggie was beautiful. She had kind and caring eyes.

Maggie often helped Annie defend herself in the ward. Annie would tell the other women, when asked how she ended up in the almshouse, that both her parents died. But once one of the women, Rosie, screamed at young 12-year-old Annie, "Liar! You were not telling *that* story when you first came here! Your mother died alright but your father left you! He *left* you!"

Maggie shouted at Rosie, "Enough Rosie, I have a mouthful about you that I don't pour on your poor head!"

Rosie frowned but was silenced.

Many women who came to the almshouse were not much older than Annie, carrying their pregnant bellies. One of them was a girl called Sadie. She had a big belly and would tell Annie all about how she should never trust boys, "Because they will talk sweet and then act sourly, you see?"

Annie feared some of the men of the almshouse. There was Mr. Marsh, the superintendent. He would often scream at the ladies whenever he visited the ward, calling them "good-for-nothings" and "filths of the earth."

But he was not as frightening as the kitchen boss, Mr. Bryan, who would offer more food to some of the women in return for fondling them. Annie hated him. Once, pregnant Sadie called him out, shouting at him after one of the new women arrived and Mr. Bryan took her aside. "Leave her alone!" Sadie screamed at him.

He hurried to Sadie and was about to hit her when

old Maggie grabbed a hot teapot and poured it over him. Annie was proud of Sadie.

Two weeks later Sadie gave birth. The baby died.

And so did Sadie.

But life went on.

One doctor who volunteered to operate on patients in the almshouse offered to operate on Annie's eyes. She was scared, but the hope of seeing again was stronger than any fear.

The operation was successful, at least for a while. But a few months later that familiar white foam covered everything again.

When she was thirteen, Annie heard one of the older women, Adelaide, tut-tutting when looking at her. "That poor blind girl! She should have gone for a school for the blind...."

Maggie, who was sitting next to Adelaide, said, "A school for the blind? Adelaide, are you fooling with me?"

Annie drew closer to hear the old lady.

"No," said Adelaide, "in South Boston there was one. They even had a blind-deaf woman there, and they taught her to read and write."

Maggie burst into laughter, "You are telling nonsense!"

"No I'm not! Her name was Laura Bridgman, I heard about her! She had a teacher who taught her how to make words with her hands! She became a good Christian I tell you!"

From that day Annie could not put that thought

away. A school for the *blind*?

If there *was* such a school, then she must go there!

She prodded old Adelaide again and again, trying to find out more about the school.

"Leave me alone, girl! I already told you all I know! It was in South Boston, and Laura Bridgman was taught how to read and write, and she lived there, and I know nothing else so stop asking me!"

Annie could not understand exactly how a *blind* person can be taught to read and write. But certainly if a blind *and* deaf woman could learn that, then—surely—Annie could learn as well?

Maggie agreed. "If that's what you wish, Annie, then go to Mr. Marsh and talk to him!"

"But I'm afraid of Mr. Marsh!"

Annie could feel Maggie's eyes staring at her, "Girl, you be afraid of no one you hear me? If you are afraid they eat you up! You go to him and tell him to send you to that school! You don't want to spend all your life here, do you?!"

It took weeks of Maggie's encouragement before Annie finally walked to the bottom floor office and asked to see Mr. Marsh. He was busy. She sat there and waited. Eventually he came out to the hallway and barked at her, "What's the matter with you girl?"

"Mr. Marsh, I want to go to a school for the blind in South Boston!"

Mr. Marsh snorted, "And who will pay for *that*, girl? Your *parents*? Your uncle and aunt who *left* you here? Now stop wasting my time and go back to the ward!"

Annie returned upstairs obediently and cried to Maggie.

"Good, cry," Maggie said, "Cry and then go to him again."

Annie mustered the courage to go to Mr. Marsh once again, rehearsing a short phrase she had learned from Maggie. "Mr. Marsh, I deserve education just like you do!"

Mr. Marsh laughed and walked away from her without saying a word.

Later Annie told Maggie, "Can't *you* speak to him, he'll listen to you!"

Maggie sighed. "I have enough troubles already, child."

They did not bring the subject up again. Winter was coming and it began snowing. Annie placed her fingers on the cold window, and they left small trails like tears on the weeping glass. She placed her feet against the heating pipes to warm them. She had never been more miserable and wanted to leave.

TUSCUMBIA, ALABAMA

Little Helen was a real joy. Nearly one year old, she crawled from place to place in the speed of light. She liked crawling to the kitchen where Martha, the cook, would give her candies and cookies.

She amazed her mother again and again with her intelligence. She would point at things and when she wanted to drink water she'd say, "*Wawa! Wawa!*"

Captain Keller took delight in the little toddler, who would often crawl to his office and raise her hands up, wanting to sit on his lap. Seeing her, the 42-year-old father would become less serious and more playful.

Kate kept telling him how wonderful their daughter was. One day, just after her bath, Helen noticed something, stood up and began waddling towards it. Kate shouted, "She walked! She walked!"

At that moment Helen fell down and began crying. Kate hugged her and kissed her, "Arthur!" she hurried to her husband's study, "she walked! She *walked!*"

> "They tell me I walked the day I was a year old. My mother had just taken me out of the bathtub and was holding me in her lap, when I was suddenly

attracted by the flickering shadows of leaves that danced in the sunlight on the smooth floor. I slipped from my mother's lap and almost ran toward them. The impulse gone, I fell down and cried for her to take me up in her arms.

These happy days did not, however, last long. In the dreary month of February, came the illness."

TEWKSBURY, MASSACHUSETTS

"Today is your lucky day, Annie."

Annie looked at Maggie, not understanding. They ate their breakfast in the almshouse dining room. "What do you mean, Maggie?"

"Go and see the bathroom."

"But I don't need to go now—"

"Go and see the bathroom I tell you!"

Annie obediently left the table and made her way outside, feeling her way down the hallway and out to the yard, walking the familiar route to the outhouse. The stench that would often meet her nose was gone. Instead it smelled like lemon. She walked into the small structure, sniffing. Even with her bad eyes, she could see the toilets were shining.

She ran across the yard and back to the dining hall. When she passed by the entrance to the kitchen she made sure to stay away from Mr. Bryan, like Maggie had told her.

"They're clean!" Annie said to Maggie as she sat down.

Maggie took a bite from her porridge, "You know what that means?"

Annie shook her head.

"It means, girl," Maggie said, articulating every word, "that the rich folks are coming today!"

"The rich folks?"

"The donors and politicians! You ought to go to them and tell them to send you to that school!"

Annie gulped. "But what would Mr. Marsh say?"

Annie had never heard Maggie curse, which is why she was alarmed when Maggie muttered, "Oh, the hell with that hog!"

Annie felt Maggie's breath on her ears, "Sometimes, child, a woman needs to do what she needs to do!"

Annie nodded.

As the morning hours passed, Annie was extremely tense. At lunch she could not eat. Finally, an hour later, she heard horses and carriages outside. All the women in the ward rushed to the windows.

Annie cried, "What do you see? Tell me, what do you see?!"

Crazy Rosie said, "Those damn aristocrats! They came to sooth their conscious about the 'poor people'…."

Maggie said, "There's Mr. Marsh shaking the hand of that tall man."

One of the other women said, "That's Mr. Sanborn."

Maggie prodded Annie, "That's the man you need to speak to, Mister Sanborn."

Annie nodded, her heart beating fast.

Several minutes later, steps resounded in the hallway. Annie was sitting next to Maggie on a chair near their beds.

"And this," they heard Mr. Marsh's voice, "is the women's ward."

Several well-dressed men strolled down the aisle, walking in between the rows of beds. Mr. Marsh continued talking, but Annie could not hear him, her heart was beating too loudly.

Maggie whispered to her, "You better speak now, they are about to leave the ward!"

Annie tried to speak, but her voice was gone.

The men left and laughter filled the ward as Rosie got up and began imitating the dignitaries.

Maggie snapped at Annie, "Fool! Who knows when they'll come back again! Opportunity, child, is a capricious lady! She knocks at every door but *once*! If the door isn't opened *quickly*, she passes on, never to return again!"

Annie's eyes watered.

Maggie did not comfort her while the women howled and laughed around them.

Then Maggie pushed Annie off her bed, "Go now! Go before they'll be gone! Catch them! Grab that man by his coat if you need!"

Annie wept and covered her face with her hands.

Maggie got up and pushed Annie towards the door, "Follow them Annie! For me! For your deceased mother! She would have not wanted you to stay here, you hear me?!"

Something in the mentioning of her mother made Annie nod through her tears.

Maggie pushed her out to the hallway, "Go! Go!"

Annie nodded and kept nodding as walked down the familiar hallway, down the stairs, and out to the yard. She saw the blurry group of men walking toward the men's ward building. She followed them quickly as they disappeared. Her heart sank. Women were not allowed into the men's ward. Mr. Marsh would kill her.

She waited in the yard, finding her way to the brick wall. Her back pressed against the wall. She could feel Maggie's eyes staring at her through the upstairs window.

She waited there. She remembered Maggie telling her about working in a bawdy house.

"What's a *bawdy* house?" she asked Maggie.

Maggie was quiet. "Girl, don't ask. Some things a girl your age should not know. You already know too much."

Then Maggie had tears in her eyes.

Annie suddenly heard noises. The group was coming out of the men's building. She heard Mr. Marsh speaking, "As you can see, gentlemen, our infirmary should be the pride of Massachusetts! We meet every person's needs, however forsaken they might be…."

"Certainly," the men mumbled.

Annie saw them turn toward the gate. Her chest rose and fell in apprehension. Suddenly, she felt her body disconnect from the wall. She headed toward the blurry group. She tried to speak, but her voice betrayed her. She thought of Maggie, and then suddenly she heard her own voice, "Mr. Sanborn! Mr. Sanborn!"

"Yes, young lady?" a man's voice said.

The group of men stopped.

Annie's chest heaved as she wetted her lips.

Mr. Marsh spoke joyfully, "Oh, gentlemen, the girl is just one of our *non compos mentis—"*

"Mr. Sanborn!" Annie shouted, "I want to go to blind school in South Boston!"

She heard footsteps approaching and she leaned back, raising her arms for protection, fearing Mr. Marsh's beating. But the voice from the tall figure who approached her was soft, "What is your name, young lady?"

"It's Annie, Annie Sullivan, sir!"

"How did you come to this place?"

She swallowed, "Both my parents died, sir!"

Her face burned from the lie.

The man said, "I see. And your eyes?"

"I have Trachoma, sir! They tried to operate. It went well, but then they went bad again!"

"I see. Have you gone to school before?"

"No sir, but I can learn sir!"

"How old are you?"

"I'm almost fourteen, sir!" she felt tears streaming down her face. "Please sir!"

"Let me see what I can do, young lady."

"Thank you, sir! Thank you Mr. Sanborn! It's Annie Sullivan! My name is Annie Sullivan! Remember me, sir! Remember me!"

TUSCUMBIA, ALABAMA

The sickness took hold of little Helen like a storm.

The doctor examined the screaming baby. Kate's eyes watered, "What do you say, doctor?"

Captain Keller paced up and down the room, "Kate, let him finish his examination!"

They were all irritated by Helen's relentless cry.

The doctor sighed and looked at Arthur, "How old is she?"

Kate jumped, "She is 19 months old, doctor!"

The doctor sighed, "And since when did the fever start?"

"Since last night. Before she went to sleep I noticed her temperature, but I was hoping the sleep might help. But this morning it became worse, and she hasn't eaten nor will she drink!"

The doctor pouted his lips and nodded slowly, "You should nevertheless feed her by force."

"I tried, doctor, but she hollers and wouldn't—"

Arthur intervened, "We'll do as you say, doctor."

The doctor took a deep breath. He looked at the baby's skin, examining the rash. He touched the baby's neck, noticing the swollen glands. As he touched them, Helen screamed even louder.

The doctor sighed again. He looked at Kate. She noticed his eyes squinting. He murmured, "She's pale around the lips."

Kate cried, "What is it Doctor?"

The doctor frowned. Arthur came closer. Helen kept screaming. The doctor said, "I'm afraid it may be scarlet fever."

Kate nearly fainted. She read in the newspaper of the scarlet fever epidemic sweeping through the country.

Arthur gulped, "Well, what can be done then, doctor?"

"Try and cool her skin with cold presses. And do try to feed her some milk or water. It is important."

Kate cried, "But she won't take any!" she hurried and took the glass nursing bottle. "Here!" She brought it to Helen's mouth, but as soon as Helen opened her extremely red lips she began screaming, gasping for air, nearly choking. Kate was overwhelmed.

So was the doctor.

The doctor began packing his kit. He mumbled, "Do what you can, please. Do what you can."

Captain Keller escorted him to the door. Kate took Helen in her arms, feeling her baby's skin burning. Her feeble body dropped into her mother's arms.

Arthur returned to the room, pale.

Kate glanced at his face, "Arthur? Did he say

anything else to you?"

Arthur sank into the couch, speechless. He did not want to repeat what the doctor had just told him. He did not want to tell her that there was no chance.

> "When I was nineteen months old, in the cold and dreary month of February, I had a serious illness. My mother sat beside my little bed and tried to soothe my feverish moans while in her troubled heart she prayed, "Father in Heaven, spare my baby's life!"
>
> But the fever grew and flamed in my eyes, and for several days my kind physician thought I would die."

TEWKSBURY, MASSACHUSETTS

Maggie called it a miracle!

Indeed, it was a surprise for everyone, especially to Annie.

After being reprimanded and screamed at by Mr. Marsh for her cheek, she never imagined the news she received two months after the rich's visit.

Maggie screamed of joy, "Our girl is going to school! Our Annie is going to school!"

Those who cared in the ward congratulated Annie. Maggie went to the crew and begged for an appropriate dress for the 14-year-old girl. After a long search in the storage room, two old calico dresses were found, one red and one blue.

It was strange for Annie to bid farewell to the almshouse, which has been her home for four years. Years later Annie would write about her departure:

> "Maggie, the hunchback, carried my small bundle to the carriage. Others walked with us outside. Three of them were crippled, two were blind, and quite a number were young pregnant women about to become mothers. They all wished me

farewell with much advice: "Be a good girl"; "mind your teachers"; "don't make any trouble" and "don't tell anyone you came from the poor-house!"

One of the young women warned me not to let any feller fool me with his "sweet talk. He won't mean what he says Annie!"

Another asked me to send tobacco.

One of them told me to come and visit, while another told me, "No! Never come back here!"

Maggie squeezed my hand firmly. She was the last to hug me. "Keep your head up," she whispered to me, "you're as good as any of 'em!"

Tim, the carriage driver, took me to the train station. He helped me into the train and then looked at me, "Girl, don't ever come back to this place, you hear me?"

I nodded, but he repeated again, "Don't you ever come to this place! Forget this place and you'll be alright."

TUSCUMBIA, ALABAMA

Helen's fever was getting worse. She was unwilling to eat, and only by force Kate and Martha, the cook, were able to make her drink some water.

Martha helped tremendously during such a trying time "Please, Kate, go and get some rest."

Kate reluctantly agreed. It'd been three days since she slept.

Kate walked to her bedroom. She kneeled on the floor and began praying. She felt her child was slipping away. "God, please," she cried, "save my child. Save my little Helen!"

Arthur entered the room, untying his collar and unbuttoning his shirt. Kate turned to him from the carpet, choking back tears, "I need you to pray too, Arthur."

Arthur, for whom the last few days had been a nightmare, remained quiet. A decade earlier he had lost another child. Fannie was her name. She too was nineteen months old when she died.

Kate cried, "I need you to pray too!"

"I've prayed!" Arthur hissed at her.

Kate, stunned from his response, sobbed quietly on the carpet.

Arthur sighed. The tension in the house was unbearable. He could not do any work for the newspaper.

He put on his pajamas to get ready for bed, but Kate's sobs disturbed him. He couldn't ignore them. He came to her side of the bed and touched her shoulder. She grabbed his arm and pulled him to the floor. He let out, "Kate!"

"I need you to pray with me, Arthur! We need to pray *together*!" she said through her tears as she held his hand.

He licked his lips and mumbled, "Very well. Lord in heaven," he closed his eyes and thought of a fitting verse, "you said 'If thou wilt diligently hearken to the voice of the LORD thy God, and wilt do that which is right in his sight, and wilt give ear to his commandments, and keep all his statutes, I will put none of these diseases upon thee, which I have brought upon the Egyptians: for I am the LORD that healeth thee!"

Kate whispered, "Amen." She then added, "Lord, we ask for a miracle. Save our little Helen! I have poured out my soul before thee! And the Good Book says, '*and the Lord remembered her.*' Remembered her! Please, Lord, please, remember me!"

Kate shook uncontrollably. Arthur held her hand, his eyes moist. He had never seen his young wife this way before.

"Lord," she continued through her sobs, "'Even though I walk through the valley of the shadow of death, I will fear *no* evil, for thou are *with* me; your rod and your staff, they comfort me!' Comfort me, my Lord! Comfort me! Save our little Helen! Give us a miracle, oh Lord!"

Arthur nodded. He wished to get up from the carpet. But Kate squeezed his hand, "I vow, Lord, if thou will indeed look on the affliction of thine servant, and remember me, and not forget thine servant, but will give life to my little Helen, I will give her unto you, Lord, all the days of her life!"

Arthur swallowed. "Amen."

BOSTON, MASSACHUSETTS

Wearing her red calico dress, Annie got off the train in South Boston. In her arms she carried her small bundle, including the blue dress, Jimmie's drawing, and a few used clothes.

She stood in the middle of the platform not knowing where to go.

She wanted to cry, but heard Maggie's voice in her head, "Hold your head up high!"

Finally an older man came to her, "Child, do you need help?"

"Yes, Sir! Thank you Sir! I need to get to the School for the Blind."

"The one in Dorchester Heights?"

Annie hesitated. "I don't know, Sir!"

"It must be it, that is the only one I know of. You walk out the station and take a left, then a right, then after half a mile you'll see it on your left."

Annie swallowed. She did not move.

The old man, bewildered, said, "Here, follow me."

Annie thanked him profusely and followed his shoes as he walked fast. She nearly tripped on the stairs.

The old man looked behind him. Suddenly he looked more carefully at the girl's red eyes. He felt embarrassed for not having noticed. "You know what, I'll walk you there."

"Oh thank you Sir! Thank you Sir, thank you!"

They walked on a wide street in the quiet neighborhood. Annie was amazed to see trees planted near the sidewalk. Everything looked clean, orderly. Pleasant.

The old man talked, "It used to be a hotel when I was young, that building, but for the past few decades it's been a school for the... for people of...."

Annie nodded.

"Well here it is," the old man finally said.

Annie looked at the tall building. A long staircase led to what looked like four huge marble pillars.

The old man reached his arm, "Do you want me to help you up the stairs?"

Annie pulled away, alarmed, "No, Sir. Leave me alone Sir!"

The old man, surprised, stepped back. He watched the young lady as she held to the railing and began climbing slowly leading to the grand entrance door under the large white pillars.

* * *

After climbing all the stairs Annie opened the heavy door and stood in a large hallway. She was afraid to move. In the distance she heard a piano playing. No, two pianos. She heard someone talking as well. Her voice sounded authoritative like a teacher in a class. Memories of Mrs. Duncan in the school near her childhood home flashed in her mind.

"And *you* are?"

Annie looked toward the voice. A woman looked at her. Her voice was harsh.

"I'm Annie Sullivan, ma'am!" Annie said.

The woman looked at Annie, measuring her. She clearly did not belong there. "And you are looking *for*?"

Annie did not know what to say. She remembered Maggie. She raised her chin, "I was sent here, ma'am. Is this the school of the blind?"

"Sent by *whom*? From *where*?"

Annie bit her tongue. She swore to herself she'd say nothing about the almshouse.

But suddenly it came to her, "Mr. Sanborn! He sent me here. Mr. Sanborn sent me here!"

"Oh," said the lady, and Annie could sense how the lady was looking at her, "Oh. Indeed… indeed…."

Annie held the bundle under her left arm, feeling the penetrating look and tried to keep her posture without betraying her fear.

"Well," the woman said, "before I can admit you, you'll have to meet Mr. Anagnos."

"Mr. Anag—?"

"Mr. *Anagnos*. The head of the school."

"Oh," Annie said worriedly. "Must I meet him?"

The woman stared at Annie and said nothing. The

girl did not belong.

* * *

Mr Anagnos was puzzled by the poor 14-year-old. She looked coarse and uneducated. "You are telling me," he said slowly, "that you have *never* gone to school?"

"Never, Sir, but I can learn—"

"And you do *not* know the alphabet?"

"No, Sir, but I can learn, I am a smart—"

"And you never even learned braille?"

Annie did not know what braille was.

Mr. Anagnos sighed and looked at her, dismayed. "Well, given this was an order from the State, we'll have to admit you. But let me tell you," he leaned forward and spoke quietly, "Our rules are *very* strict. Misbehavior of any sort is *unaccepted*. One fault, one wrongdoing, and you'll be back where you came from. Is that clear?"

Annie nodded. She looked down.

The school secretary entered, "Mrs. White is here, Sir."

"Good," Mr. Anagnos said. He looked at Annie, "Mrs. White will be your housemother. She will help you settle in."

Annie murmured, "Thank you, Sir."

Mr. Anagnos went outside the office and whispered something to Mrs. White.

Mrs. White entered the office. Though Annie could not see much, she could see her tall stature, her raised hair in a meticulous Victorian high braided bun, and her white pearl necklace. She felt the lady's eyes staring at her. "Where are your belongings, girl? Your suitcases?"

Annie pointed at the bundle on the floor, her voice breaking, "Here...."

Mrs. White was clearly shocked. "This is all you have?"

Annie nodded.

"And where is this dress from?"

Annie looked down, lying, "My mother."

Mrs. White mumbled, "Oh my."

> "In that moment an intense realization of the ugliness of my appearance seized me. I knew that the calico dress which I had thought rather pretty when they put it on me was the cause of the woman's pity, and I was glad that she could not see the only other garment I had on—a coarse unbleached cotton chemise that came to my knees. My stockings were black and my shoes clumsy and too small for me. Hers I noticed were shiny and black and buttoned up at the sides. I kept trying to hide mine under the chair. The inadequacy of my outfit did not dawn upon me until the woman pitied me. Shame seized me. Shame to have been overwhelmed by ugliness, shame to be the hole in the perfect pattern of the universe."

TUSCUMBIA, ALABAMA

"Thank you, Lord," Kate cried, tears of joy streaming down her cheeks. She looked at her husband, then at Martha, who stood in the door. She turned to the doctor, "Thank you Doctor!"

The doctor shook his head in disbelief, "It is rather unbelievable, Mrs. Keller. The fact she is eating now and her fever has broken... it may be too early to celebrate, but—"

Kate exclaimed, "Oh it is *not* too early to celebrate! Our baby is well!" she kissed Helen on the forehead, relieved to feel her temperature normal, "Our Helen is well!"

Captain Keller escorted the doctor to the door. The fee was expensive, after the doctor's repeated daily visits.

Kate fed Helen from the bottle and sang to her. It was morning outside. It was a sunny day for February. Martha left to the kitchen, "I'll make her porridge."

"Oh will you? Thank you, Martha!"

Arthur came to the room, looking at his wife. He could not conceal his smile. She nodded at him, Helen sitting and drinking from the bottle in her lap.

Arthur nodded back and walked to his study in the adjacent room.

Kate sat there, closing her eyes, tears of gratitude falling from her face onto her little toddler.

> "Early one morning the fever left me as mysteriously and unexpectedly as it had come, and I fell into a quiet sleep. Then my parents knew I would live, and they were very happy. There was great rejoicing in the family that morning, but no one, not even the doctor, knew what was to come."

BOSTON, MASSACHUSETTS

The school was not prepared for anyone who did not know how to read and write. Annie was placed in the first grade, in which all the students, seven years younger than her, already knew all the letters. Annie, too big for the small desks, was given a larger desk at the back of the class. The younger girls laughed at her. But she bit her tongue, trying to avoid getting into trouble and getting expelled back to the almshouse. She knew this was her only opportunity.

In the back of the class she learned the alphabet from raised letters embossed into the cardboard cards. Every once in awhile the teacher spared a moment and helped her familiarize herself with them, but then would leave her alone again.

Annie strained her eyes, trying to see the letters, but to no avail. Nevertheless, she could feel them. On one side of each cardboard card there was the letter, written in lines and round circles. The letter "O" became her favorite. She could easily recognize it.

On the other side of each cardboard card there were small dots, some thin and some fat. The teacher called them *braille*. Those strange, dotted symbols, confused

Annie greatly. She bit her nails until they were so close to the skin and there was nothing else to bite.

The letters were slow to come. A. B. C. D. E….

She was called by the younger girls, in whispers, "The dummy."

At night she tossed in bed.

A few days after she arrived, she heard her roommate, Lilian, complaining to Mrs. White. The two of them stood in the corridor. Lilian cried to Mrs. White, "The new girl stinks! And she yells in her sleep! Why can't I be placed with Susan again?"

Mrs. White's voice was adamant. "Because I *said* so! She is a poor rascal and she needs a good influence on her."

Lilian protested again and whispered something Annie could not hear from her bed.

Mrs. White whispered, "You are the best in the class, Lilian. I expect you to endow a fine influence over her!"

* * *

While the students spelled many words, Annie misspelled the simplest words, including her name. The children laughed and she wanted to go back to the almshouse away from the rich, bratty girls, away from the teachers who obviously disliked her, and away from this strange place.

> "My first class was embarrassing. The teacher asked, "What is your name?"
>
> "Annie Sullivan," I answered.
>
> "Spell it!"
>
> "I can't spell," I answered.

The girls giggled.

The teacher asked, "How old are you?"

"Fourteen."

"Fourteen years old and can't spell!"

They had never heard of such a thing.

They had never heard of a girl without a toothbrush or a petticoat or a hat or a coat or a pair of gloves. Certainly they had never heard of a girl without a nightgown! That night for the first time in my life I slept in one. Mrs. White borrowed it from one of the girls. And that night and many nights thereafter I cried myself to sleep, lonelier than I had ever been in the almshouse, sick with longing for the familiar companionship of my friends there.

In class I did my best to match the progress of the other girls. Whenever I misspelled simple words the girls would laugh uproariously. The insults spurred me, yes, but they also were scars which remained in my memory forever, scars which time could not erase."

TUSCUMBIA, ALABAMA

There was something different about Helen.

In the days following her recovery, Kate sensed the change in her 19-month-old daughter. She crawled differently. She ran into furniture and she did not look up when Kate called her.

In the past, Helen would be excited about the glass bottle of milk, grabbing it with both hands. Now she would not show excitement until it was placed on her mouth. Only then did her little hands grab it excitedly.

Kate tried asking Martha, "Do you see anything different about her?"

Martha shrugged her shoulders, "She must still be recovering."

Kate nodded hesitantly, trying to convince herself that Martha was right.

But each day her alarm grew. "Arthur!" she yelled, "Arthur!"

"What is the matter?" Arthur rushed from his study.

"She doesn't look at me!" Kate said and pointed at Helen, crawling slowly on the carpet, "I call her and she doesn't look at me!"

Arthur sat down on the divan and touched Helen's head. She turned to him and reached her hands upwards. "Kate," Arthur reprimanded as he picked Helen up and put her on his knees, "she is *fine*."

Kate shook her head, "Something is wrong with her. I want to summon the doctor—"

Arthur would not have it, "The last bill was a hefty one—"

"I want to call the doctor again!" Kate exclaimed, bewildered by her own reaction.

Arthur looked at his wife, appalled. "You should get some rest, Kate."

* * *

But the doctor, who came two days later, confirmed Kate's concerns. He placed objects before the child. He clapped around her ears. His face grew paler by the minute. When he turned to Captain and Mrs. Keller, he was out of words.

Kate fainted.

BOSTON, MASSACHUSETTS

The months at the Massachusetts School for the Blind passed quickly. Annie was determined to prove all of them wrong: the stupid girls, the foolish teachers, the doubtful Mrs. White, the scornful Mr. Anagnos. She studied for hours. In the early evening, when the girls in her house would play, talk, and gossip, Annie would go to the large library on the fifth floor and spend the evening there until the librarian would rush her out, "We're closing!"

Each afternoon she would find her way to the beginner's shelf, take out a box titled *First Grade* and practice the words on cardboard cards, beginning with the first words:

I. Am. And. Be. Book. Box. Boy. But. Car. Cat. Cow. Come….

She spent many hours there, often hitting herself on the hand when she would fail her own test and misspell a word.

Once, while in the library, she bumped into an older woman sitting by one of the tables at the back of the library, sitting and sewing quietly.

Annie apologized quickly, "I'm sorry."

But the woman said nothing, obviously upset with her, and kept sewing.

Annie did not mind. The library was her safe haven. It became her second home. When she was in her room, the other girls laughed, never involving her in their conversations. In the library, in the solitude of the quiet around her, she felt protected.

Within a month of her arrival, she was approaching the last words in the box: *Was. We. Will. Yes. You. Your. Zebra. Zoo.*

The day she finally finished remembering all the words, including both the braille and the raised letters, she felt a satisfaction which she never felt in her entire life. She rejoiced and went to the quiet woman sewing at one of the tables at the back of the library. She exclaimed to her, "I finished all the words in the box!"

The woman said nothing, completely ignoring Annie.

Annie was hurt, "I finished all the words in the box I tell you! You can *test* me!"

The woman did not respond.

"Why do you hate me? I've done nothing to you!"

The woman kept ignoring her. Annie pushed the box off the table. It fell to the floor and cards scattered everywhere. Annie shouted, "I'm a good girl I am! I finished the whole damned box you hear me!"

Annie heard the librarian approaching quickly, whispering, "What is going on here?"

Annie pouted her lips, trying to stop her tears, "She would not talk to me!" Tears began running down her cheeks, "I finished all the words in the box, and I told her she could test me—"

"She cannot hear you!"

"She *canno*—what?"

The librarian looked upset, "She is *deaf!* Deaf and blind! Now pick up all the cards you dropped and put them back or I'll tell the principal what you did!"

Annie nodded and dropped to the floor.

The librarian walked away, muttering to herself.

Annie slowly returned the cards to the box, thinking, "She cannot hear me? She is both deaf *and* blind?"

After the excruciatingly long process of arranging the cards so that the side with the raised letters faced the front of the box, Annie returned the box to the shelf. She walked quietly to the librarian and whispered, "If she can't hear me, then how can she speak?"

The librarian sighed and looked up from her book, "She is *mute*. She *cannot* speak. But she understands the manual alphabet and she can write, though slowly."

"Which alphabet?"

"The manual," the librarian said and returned to her book.

Annie stood there for a long moment. "You mean the raised letters one or the dotted one?"

"I mean," the librarian said, impatient, "the *manual* alphabet, that of the *hands*. The one deaf people use!"

"Oh," Annie said. The librarian went back to her book. Annie stared toward the blurry table at the back of the library where the odd woman was sitting alone, knitting and sewing.

TUSCUMBIA, ALABAMA

Relentless, Kate was determined to save her daughter's eyes. She invited numerous specialists to the house: oculists, otologists, and other eye and ear specialists.

None of them could do anything.

Kate insisted on a possible cure or surgery to save at least the sight of her two-year-old daughter, if not her hearing. One of the specialists who came from Tennessee said to Kate after thoroughly examining the toddler's eyes, "What you are asking, Mrs. Keller, is for me to fix a problem that you presume happened from the exterior, like an infection of some sort. And yet the problem, evidently from the response of the eye, has been derived from an internal deficiency."

Kate was puzzled and looked at her husband. She turned back to the specialist, "Explain to me more clearly, doctor."

"Well," the doctor said slowly, "her eyes and ears were not injured by fire from the outside, but rather burned from the inside."

Kate hurriedly left to the bedroom as Arthur remained to thank the specialist and pay him.

As the months passed, Helen grew. Yet the once-talkative child, who had impressed her mother's friends by exclaiming "Tea, tea!" was now withdrawn, helpless, mute.

BOSTON, MASSACHUSETTS

Annie crept closer to the deaf-blind woman sitting at the back of the library. Each afternoon Annie would watch her carefully. She saw that the woman was very thin and was always wearing a black dress, sewing quietly.

Annie was intrigued. Who was this woman? What was she doing there? How could she speak to her?

Finally, one day, Annie took the box of the cardboard cards and placed them in front of the woman. She hesitantly took the first card, with the raised letter *A* on it, and placed it in front of the woman.

The woman looked to the sides, but then shrugged her shoulders and continued sewing.

Annie, now less intimidated than before, took the card and placed it in the woman's lap, then quickly moving away. The woman put the needle in her left hand and with her right hand felt the card. She smiled and reached her hand forward as if searching for someone. Annie gulped and reached her hand to her.

The woman touched Annie's hand and made a funny sound. She placed the needle and thread carefully on the table, and then reached her left hand to hold Annie's hand. Eagerly she began pressing on Annie's hand, making odd movements with her fingers.

Annie pulled her hand away. She looked around to see if anyone was watching them. She could not see anyone. She hesitantly brought her hand forward again. The woman was pleased and took the card, handed it to Annie theatrically, then pressed her fist into Annie's palm several times, as if grinding something.

Annie did not understand what the woman was wanting from her, but the woman grabbed her hand firmly. Then the woman reached her right hand searching the box on the table. Annie, realizing what she was looking for, reached her free hand and pushed the box closer to the woman.

The woman made a sound of pleasure and pulled out the second card from the box, placing it on the table and feeling the raised letter, "B." She eagerly pressed the card into Annie's hand, and then pressed her hand into Annie's open palm. This time her hand was not in a fist, but rather her four fingers were raised, stretched outwards, while the thumb was folded.

Annie began to understand these were the *signs* for the alphabet! The following letter the woman pulled out was "C." She felt the raised letter, and then pressed her hand into Annie's open palm, her hand shaped as if she was holding a glass in her hand. Annie suddenly realized the hand, in that position, looked like the letter C. She nodded.

Then the woman eagerly went back to the first card, gave it to Annie, and placed her own palm open before Annie.

Annie realized the woman was testing her to see if she remembered the letter A. She sat up determined to prove her wisdom to the woman. She shaped her hand into a fist and pressed it into the lady's open palm. The woman nodded eagerly, yelping. Annie found the sound odd, but she enjoyed seeing the smile on the strange woman's face.

The woman hurried to find the second card, felt it, distinguishing the letter B, and handed it to Annie as she opened her palm in anticipation.

Annie nodded. The second letter was the one with the four fingers. She stretched her four fingers while folding her thumb and pressed her hand into the woman's hand.

The woman yelped and nodded eagerly. She hurried to find C and gave it to Annie.

Annie smiled. C was easy. She shaped her hand in the C shape and pressed it into the woman's palm.

The woman looked ecstatic.

The minutes passed quickly. The woman taught Annie three more letters, though not according to the order of the alphabet. The woman sifted through the cards and pulled out the letters L, U, and R.

Annie was quick to learn them. L was simple, with the index finger and the thumb looking like the letter L. The letter U was simple too, simply joining the middle and index fingers together while folding the other fingers. And R was a little strange, doing exactly the same as in the letter U but crossing the fingers over each other.

The woman nodded eagerly when testing Annie. Then she took Annie's hand and placed it on her chest.

Annie did not understand what the lady meant, but

then the woman spelled into Annie's hand: Annie recognized the L, A, U, R, and then the letter A repeating again. The woman again pressed her hand to her chest, and spelled yet again, L-A-U-R-A.

It was then that Annie gasped, "Oh, Laura. Your name is Laura!"

Annie soon found the letters for her own name, N, I and E, and Laura taught her how to fingerspell them.

The librarian came and said, "We're closing."

Annie nodded, "Just one minute."

She eagerly spelled her name into the woman's palm, A-N-N-I-E, and took the woman's hand and placed it onto her chest.

The woman smiled. She took her hand away from Annie and offered a handshake. Annie gasped. It was the first time someone ever shook her hand.

TUSCUMBIA, ALABAMA

Kate was desperate. Her once exuberant and playful daughter was quiet, morose, and helpless. She clung to her mother in desperation and sounds she made were appalling.

As Helen turned three Kate could not avoid admitting to herself that there was something unsightly in her girl. She was at the age in which children spoke more and ran and played. But Helen did none of that. She was timid, shrinking from the vibration of steps, cocooning herself from attack.

Arthur was embarrassed of his little girl whenever guests would visit. In the past, Helen was his prize shown off to all visitors—her bright eyes, her smile, her intelligent nature—now she was hidden away. When she was out and guests would come, little Helen would sniff them like a dog. When she wanted her mother, she would caress her face, as Kate would often do to her. When she wanted to eat, she would open her mouth and put her fingers inside repeatedly.

These movements—Helen's attempts at communication—might have seemed adorable at first, but as she neared the age of four Arthur felt that his daughter was dumb, and maybe institutionalizing her might be the best option for both her and the family.

"Gradually I got used to the silence and darkness that surrounded me and forgot that it had ever been different. I became a phantom. All the sweetness of childhood created by friendly voices and the light of smiling faces was gone, forever to be dormant in me. I had no sense of 'natural' bonds with humanity. I was but a phantom, living in a world that I can describe only as *no-world*."

BOSTON, MASSACHUSETTS

Each afternoon Annie hurried to the library to speak to the strange Laura. In the beginning, their conversations were dull. They spelled to each other silly questions about the weather and the school. Laura tried to teach Annie how to sew but Annie did not like it as it took too much concentration with little reward.

One day several weeks after they began conversing, Laura spelled into Annie's hand, "I A-M L-O-N-E-L-Y."

Annie nodded. "I A-M T-O-O."

They did not say anything afterwards. They just sat quietly but Annie felt a relief which she could not explain.

In class, she greatly improved. To her amazement the teacher moved her to the class of girls her own age. Annie feared the move, asking, "But what if I will not succeed?"

"You will do fine," the teacher promised, "you are a quick learner."

That passing comment was like wind in her sails. It was the first real compliment she received in years. Of course, there was that compliment from the crazy boy in the almshouse, who told Annie that she was "very beautiful." But then he tried to grope her. It was not a *real* compliment.

Now, she was told she was a quick learner. She felt the world open before her.

In the new class she was seated at the back, but she did not mind. She read braille books continuously. She was slow but she was thorough.

The other girls laughed at her and often taunted her during breaks. She was known to have a temper, and the girls were always "curious" as to when the new girl would snap and lose her composure.

She often did.

One of the blind girls even told her the truth in her face, "You do not belong here, Annie."

And though Annie retorted with a juicy insult, she knew that the girl was right.

> "I was like a round peg in a square hole. I was utterly unacquainted with the usages of civilized society. I was too stout to be graceful, too large for my age, too clumsy. I envied the girls with more attractive bodies. When the class did teamwork exercises I was always ignored. It aggravated my chagrin. I hated them.
>
> I told myself that I hated them because they were fools, yet way back in my head I knew they possessed refinement, poise, pleasant speech, graceful limbs—things I would have sold my soul to Satan for. I was not that way. I was ill at ease with everyone. I was difficult, changeable, disquieting and unsocial, and eventually, after a

year of self-assertion, pretense, rebellion and secret mortification, decided to flee into the tower of my own soul and raise the drawbridge."

TUSCUMBIA, ALABAMA

Kate saw her once-well-behaved daughter disappear. Her beautiful daughter was gone. Nowadays Helen was frowning, her face contracted in the most unsightly manner. She was far from adorable now.

As she turned four years old things became worse.

One day Grace, Kate's old friend, visited her. They sat on the porch surrounded by many rose bushes overlooking the yard. Helen was playing with the servant's children.

Grace looked at Helen, terrified, "How do you allow her to play with those Negro children?"

Kate sighed and looked away. She spoke quietly, "They are the only ones who will play with her." She did not want to tell Grace of the Tuscumbian parents' reactions when Kate requested their children play with little Helen. One mother, wishing to be cordial, maybe out of pity, came with her daughter, Dorothy, saying politely, "*Even a blind girl deserves to have a friend!*"

But soon after they arrived, Kate watched horror on the mother's face as Helen touched Dorothy's face and hair. She pulled on Dorothy's hair-bows, causing

Dorothy to cry. Kate hurried and held Helen in her arms as she kicked and screamed, explaining to the mother that sometimes Helen does not understand and needs time to "acquaint herself with strangers."

The mother, obviously horrified, said, "Oh my, I just remembered a... previous obligation we had. Dorothy, come now!"

Kate sighed.

Grace waved her fan. It was hot.

Kate watched Helen play. She knew that Helen would not harm the servants' children, at least for the most part.

Grace looked at Kate emphatically, "Arthur told me to speak to you about sending Helen to the *Asylum for the Blind* in Tennessee."

Kate stared at Grace, "I don't want to hear any of it."

Grace pouted her lips, "Kate. It might be *better* for her. She might be *safer* there—"

Kate glared at Grace, "Grace, please! I'll have none of that!"

BOSTON, MASSACHUSETTS

To everyone's surprise, Annie's grades improved drastically. She had a voracious appetite for knowledge. By her second year in school she was still friendless—apart from the deaf-blind old Laura in the library—but slowly she felt more confident with her intelligence.

The other girls dreaded the weekly one-hour Shakespeare class, led by the principal, Mr. Anagnos. But Annie enjoyed these classes.

Mr. Anagnos encouraged the girls to "think for themselves." After reading *Macbeth*, Mr. Anagnos asked the girls what did Shakespeare *mean* when he wrote: "*Fair is foul, and foul is fair?*"

Annie raised her hand, but so did the others. Mr. Anagnos said, "Yes, Lilian?"

Lilian sat up in her chair, "Fair is light, and foul is darkness, which means that darkness fuses and blends into light."

Mr. Anagnos wasn't pleased. "True, but Shakespeare could have then written simply 'darkness blends into light.' And he did *not* write that. Yes, Susan?"

Susan spoke softly, "If we look at the sentence that

follows, 'Fair is foul, and foul is fair; *Hover through the fog and filthy air,*' we understand that this phrase relates to the weather: a gloomy foggy weather. Not a fair weather, but a *foul* one."

Mr. Anagnos sighed, "Why then Shakespeare chooses to speak of the *weather*, of all things, in the first act of the play, in the very first scene?!"

He allowed the other girls who raised their hands to speak before disappointedly choosing Annie seated in the back row.

"On the surface," Annie said hesitantly, "it means that *appearances* can be *deceiving*. That which seems 'fair' and good is actually 'foul' and evil. The best example of this is Macbeth himself. King Duncan believes Macbeth to be a loyal servant but Macbeth eventually betrays Duncan's trust and murders him to steal the throne! He's a filthy murderer! What seems good and fair is actually evil and foul and Shakespeare wants to hint at it from the very beginning. Appearances can be deceiving!"

Mr. Anagnos raised his eyebrows, "Voila! Well put."

A murmur of dismay passed through the class. One of the girls said something which Annie could not hear. The girls giggled.

Annie sat back in her seat. She felt victorious.

In the evenings, before going to bed, she went over her braille play, trying to imagine what some of the more subtle references used by Shakespeare meant. She waited all week for the class with Mr. Anagnos.

> "The one hour a week of Shakespeare was a Paradise to me. These hours contained all that was stimulating and fine in my education. We read

Macbeth, and then continued to *The Tempest*, *King Lear*, and *As You Like It*. The impression the plays made upon me was profound. I literally *lived* in them. Shakespeare lit up my imagination like a sun."

TUSCUMBIA, ALABAMA

Life for Kate grew gloomier as the days passed. She tried her best to communicate with her daughter, but Helen became rowdier and more difficult as time went by.

Arthur tried to convince Kate to have another baby. "It could bring laughter back to the house," he explained "It can make you happy again!"

Kate sighed, "Arthur, I can't deal with one child, and you want me to have another?"

To Grace, Kate confided in a letter,

> "I died when Helen lost her sight and hearing. I died inside."

Helen had outbursts of anger. She refused to be instructed. The family went together to visit Kate's mother in Memphis. Helen broke four dishes and two lamps. During the meals she put her hands into everybody's plates. She pinched her grandmother and chased her away from the living room.

When exhausted Kate and Arthur began to finally leave, Kate's brother, Fred, escorted them to the door. He reprimanded Kate, "You ought to really put that child away, Kate. She is mentally defective and it is not very pleasant to see her about."

On the train ride back Kate cried, as Arthur and the maid both tried to entertain Helen so that she won't go and bother the other passengers.

Kate was exasperated to the point she ceased praying.

She felt betrayed by God.

Her daughter, her lovely, sweet daughter, became a wild, destructive animal.

Years later Helen would write:

> "I refused to be led, and often had to be carried by force to my bedroom upstairs. By the dining table I was restless and could not sit down. I came into the habit of picking food out of everyone's plates with my fingers. They could not control me. I did not know what control *was*. I broke dishes and lamps. At my grandmother's house in Memphis I came into the parlor in my red flannel underwear and pinched Grandma, chasing her from the room. I actually remember that perfectly. Years later I found a letter from Uncle Fred ordering my mother never to bring me to Grandma's house again."

BOSTON, MASSACHUSETTS

Annie advanced quickly in her studies. She even became more outspoken in class. Poetry was a solace for her, especially contemporary poetry by John Greenleaf Whittier and Oliver Wendell Holmes. She even wrote some poetry herself, which she hid from prying eyes.

Greek and Latin were the most difficult subjects for her. But by the end of the second year she proved to herself, and to the other girls, that she was not stupid. Her grades were above average. She was well on her way to become one of the best students, and she knew it.

But she was still friendless and lonely.

One afternoon in the library Annie spelled to old Laura, "I got a good grade in Latin. I am a clever girl!"

Laura spelled back, "The glory goes to Christ alone."

Annie had learned about Christ from the priests who visited the almshouse. She was not impressed by Christ or God. She wanted Laura to acknowledge her *own* progress, her dedication and hard work. She spelled back, "I did it myself! I studied myself!"

Laura did not miss a bit and quoted one of her favorite Bible verses, "'Because thou sayest, I am rich, and increased with goods, and have need of nothing; you knowest not that thou art wretched, and miserable, and poor, and blind, and naked.'"

Annie frowned. She did not like Laura's preaching. And she also knew how miserable and lonely Laura was, even though she was very religious.

God would not do. Annie longed for a real friend.

A year earlier, during the first summer vacation, Mrs. White convinced Lilian to take Annie to spend the summer with her and her family. But it was a disaster. Annie was lonely, and she and Lilian did not get along.

Now that the second summer was approaching Annie knew she could not go with Lilian again. Lilian made sure *not* to invite her back.

After going to Mr. Anagnos, Annie learned there was no way for her to remain at the school during the summer vacation. Mr. Anagnos offered her to find a job. She was fifteen, he explained, she could work.

As summer approached, Mr. Anagnos arranged for Annie to clean at a boarding house in Boston. Annie, not wanting to go back to the almshouse, had no other option.

She was bitter about hearing the other girls talking about their summer vacations. Some of them were travelling to Canada or Europe with their families. Annie said nothing, but felt sour about the summer.

At least she had the end of year grade sheet to make her a little happier. The high grades proved she was not a dummy as the other girls used to say. No. She was not. And she knew what to attribute her zest for knowledge to.

"My intelligence in school stemmed from the soil of my almshouse experience. The years at the almshouse had opened mental windows and doors, pushed back concealing curtains, revealed dark depths in the lives of human beings which would have remained closed to a more happily circumstanced child. It was a deep, dark soil. In such soil ideas grew rapidly, sending out wild shoots that spread and overshadowed the puny thoughts of my schoolmates, who were more delicately nourished."

TUSCUMBIA, ALABAMA

Kate was pregnant. But instead of being happy, she was worried about the responsibility of raising yet another child. Worried about what calamity might fall on the newborn.

She tried to calm herself by reading. But her mind was consumed by the thoughts of household chores, encouraging Arthur's older boy, James, to study for his end of year exams, and controlling Helen.

Trying to distract herself and allow for some rest, she picked up Charles Dickens' *American Notes* which detailed the British author's trip to America over forty years earlier. The book was far from captivating, but it supplied her with some escape. She read how Dickens, a foreigner, saw America and American culture. As she read on, one passage grabbed her attention:

> "In Boston I went to visit Doctor Howe, who is an expert in the education of the blind. I sat down before a girl blind, deaf, and dumb;"

Kate sat up, her knuckles whitening as she gripped the book with alarm.

> "Her name, I had learned from Doctor Howe, was

Laura Bridgman. She was thirteen years old. There she was, before me, built up, as it were, in a figurative marble cell, impervious to any ray of light or any particle of sound; beckoning to some good man for help, that her immortal soul might be awakened.

The help had come in the form of Doctor Howe. When I met the young lady, her face was radiant with intelligence and pleasure. Her dress, arranged by herself, was a pattern of neatness and simplicity; the work she had knitted lay beside her;"

Kate gasped. "Knitted"?! That girl could "knit?"

She went back two paragraphs to make sure the girl in subject was blind and deaf. Yes, she was—it stated so clearly. Kate read on, her heart beating fast:

"I have extracted a few disjointed fragments of her history, from an account written by Doctor Howe, the man who has made her what she is. Here is an excerpt from that fascinating report:

"Laura Bridgman was born in New Hampshire in 1829. She is described as having been a very sprightly and pretty infant. She appears to have displayed a considerable degree of intelligence. However, when she was 22-month-old she was sickened; her disease raged with great violence during five weeks, when her eyes and ears were inflamed, suppurated, and their contents were discharged. What a situation was hers! The darkness and the silence of the tomb were around her: no mother's smile called forth her answering smile, no father's voice taught her to imitate his sounds: they were but forms of matter which resisted her touch, but which differed not from the

> furniture of the house, save in warmth, and in the power of movement; and not even in these respects different from the dog and the cat."

Kate began to weep. This captured so well what she thought Helen must be experiencing! She went on reading:

> "But the immortal spirit which had been implanted within her could not die, nor be maimed or mutilated; and though most of its avenues of communication with the world were cut off, it began to manifest itself. She followed her mother and felt her hands and arms as she was occupied about the house; her disposition to imitate led her to repeat everything herself. She even learned to sew a little, and to knit."

Kate felt envy bursting in her. Sew? Knit? Could it *be*?! Little Helen could not sit still to learn *any* craft whatsoever! It sounded unreal. Untrue.

> "The opportunities of communicating with her were very, very limited, and the moral effects of her wretched state soon began to appear. Those who cannot be enlightened by reason can only be controlled by force; and this, coupled with her great privations, must soon have reduced her to a worse condition than that of the beasts."

When Doctor Howe first heard of the child he immediately hastened to New Hampshire to see her:

> "I found her with a well-formed figure; a strongly-marked temperament; and her whole system in healthy action. The parents were easily induced to consent to her coming to Boston, and following my visit they came and brought her to me. For awhile she was much bewildered; and after

waiting about two weeks until she became acquainted with her new locality, the attempt was made to give her knowledge of arbitrary signs, by which she could interchange thoughts with others.

"There was one of two ways to be adopted: either to go on to build up a language of signs for every *individual* thing, or to give her a knowledge of *letters,* of which she could, by combination, express herself late on. Teaching her sign for each individual object would have been easy, but very ineffectual; teaching her letters seemed very difficult, but, if accomplished, very effectual. I determined, therefore, to try the latter."

Kate read with growing interest, her hand shaking as she read:

"The poor child patiently imitated everything I did as I began teaching her the letters of the manual alphabet used by the deaf. I performed the action with my fingers, the child feeling my hand with both her hands and then imitating the finger motion.

"It was evident that the only intellectual exercise was that of *imitation* and *memory*. The process had been mechanical and the success about as great as teaching a very knowing dog a variety of tricks.

"But then the truth began to flash upon her: her intellect began to work: she perceived that here was a way by which she could herself communicate anything that was in her own mind to the mind of another. While the result is quickly related here, not so was the process: many weeks of unprofitable labor were passed before it was effected."

Kate came to the end of the excerpt. Dickens went on to summarize the chapter:

> "Such are a few fragments from the simple but most interesting and instructive history of Laura Bridgman. The name of her great benefactor and friend is Doctor Howe. There are not many persons, I hope and believe, who, after reading these passages, can ever hear that name with indifference."

Kate flipped to the following chapter, disappointed to see Dickens went on to write about non related matters. She got off her bed and hurried to Captain Keller's study. "Arthur! Arthur!"

"What is it?" Arthur said, turning from his desk to look at his wife.

Kate, speechless, placed the book before him, opened to the passage about Laura and the incredible Doctor Howe.

Arthur looked at her shaking finger and proceeded to read. Kate watched him as his interest grew, seeing him rapidly devouring the chapter to its end:

> "The name of her great benefactor and friend is Doctor Howe. There are not many persons, I hope and believe, who, after reading these passages, can ever hear that name with indifference."

Arthur looked at Kate, "Well we must write to this Doctor Howe!"

Kate hugged him, "Yes! I know! We must!"

Arthur looked puzzled, "I had never heard of such case." He flipped the book and opened the first page, searching for the year of publication. His heart sank when he saw the year, 1842. He looked at Kate, dismayed, "That was years ago," he calculated, "forty-three years ago!"

Kate nodded, "But we must try anyway, Doctor Howe may still be alive, he might help us with Helen!"

Arthur nodded, "I'll write now to Mr. Bane, my lawyer friend in Boston."

Kate hugged him, "Oh Arthur, there might be hope!"

Arthur put his hand on his wife's rounded belly. "I'll write to him right now!"

BOSTON, MASSACHUSETTS

It was painful for fifteen-year-old Annie to work as a domestic in the boarding house in Boston during the summer. The task of cleaning rooms was tiring, boring, and difficult due to her limited sight.

But she was comforted at least that she wasn't in the almshouse.

One day, a resident noticed the young woman cleaning in the entrance hall, squinting her eyes as she worked. One glance at her red eyes told him the story. "Young lady, are you blind?"

Annie turned to the voice. Then, looking at the ground, said, "Partially, Sir."

"I see. Have you ever met Dr. Bradford of the Massachusetts Eye and Ear Hospital?"

"Sir," Annie said, irritated, "my eyes have been operated on five times now, and with but momentary success each time!"

"But you have never been operated on by Dr. Bradford, young lady. He's a good friend of mine. He is very good. I'll give you a personal note for him."

Annie was hesitant, but agreed to receive the note.

The note burned in her apron pocket. Could it be that this doctor might be different? The thought of seeing well unnerved her.

One afternoon she asked the owner of the boarding house for two hours leave. He gave it to her, and she rushed to the Massachusetts Eye and Ear Hospital.

Dr. Bradford was kind and scheduled an operation for her the following week.

* * *

The operation was successful to Annie's great surprise. After several days of rest in the hospital, she could see better than she had seen since five years old. She could actually *see* printed letters.

It was a true miracle.

Kind Dr. Bradford warned her not to strain her eyes. But Annie, filled with joy, wanted to read everything she could lay her hands on.

She felt invincible.

* * *

Coming back to the school in September, Annie was thrilled. Her eyes worked. True, after an hour of reading the letters might become blurry, but she could *see*. It was a true miracle.

Another miracle was awaiting her in the school. The housemother, Mrs. White, who was always rather scornful of Annie, did not come back for the school year. Instead, she was replaced by a woman of only forty years old by the name of Mrs. Hopkins.

Mrs. Hopkins at once took a liking to Annie,

complimenting her on her dress, which Annie bought with the money she earned during the summer. Annie was shocked to be complimented by the house mother of all people!

Mrs. Hopkins was unaware of Annie's isolation at the school. She regarded Annie like all the other girls in her house. In fact, she found Annie very bright. When Mrs. Hopkins mentioned it to Mr. Anagnos he muttered, "You should have seen that little devil when she came here!"

But Mrs. Hopkins was adamant, "I don't know what she was like *then*, but I assure you, she is one of the brightest girls in your school!"

"We'll see about that," Mr. Anagnos retorted.

One Sunday Mrs. Hopkins baked a cake for the twenty girls in her house. Annie, knowing the school's library was closed, went to help Mrs. Hopkins in the kitchen.

Annie looked at Mrs. Hopkins and started a conversation. "Mrs. Hopkins, do you have any children?"

Mrs. Hopkins looked at Annie, a little taken aback by the question. "I had one daughter. Her name was Florence."

"Oh, I'm sorry to hear that, Mrs. Hopkins."

"It's alright," Mrs. Hopkins paused. "Hepatitis…." She sighed, "She was a very bright young woman. She was sixteen years old."

Annie gulped. Florence was the same age as her when she died. "I'm so sorry."

Mrs. Hopkins smiled sadly.

Annie's curiosity overcame her and she continued to interrogate her companion with unlady-like questions. "And do you have a husband, Mrs. Hopkins?"

Mrs. Hopkins sighed slowly. There was something refreshing about Annie's candor and honesty. "I had," she said slowly, "his name was John. He was a shipmaster. He died at sea three years ago."

Annie went to Mrs. Hopkins and—uncharacteristically of other girls her age—put her hand on Mrs. Hopkins's hand, "I'm so sorry to hear that!"

Mrs. Hopkins nodded.

Silence followed.

"How about you, Annie?" Mrs. Hopkins asked as she cleaned the kitchen, "Do you have any siblings?"

Annie was baffled. In her mind the whole school knew of her desolate state: abandoned, living in an almshouse, her brother dying there. "I had one brother," she said, numbing the pain of her forgotten baby sister and where she might be today. "Only one brother. His name was Jimmie. But he died. He died when I was ten."

"I'm sorry to hear that, Annie. That must have been awful!"

Annie nodded. No one ever expressed such sympathy toward her.

Mrs. Hopkins spoke quietly. "And I understand both your parents died?"

Annie bit her lips and nodded, feeling her cheeks burning with the lie.

Mrs. Hopkins sighed and smiled, "Well, I suppose we

are both free birds, so-to-speak."

Annie smiled. She liked Mrs. Hopkins.

Years later she would write:

> "I wondered at Mrs. Hopkins' good-will towards me. It might easily have collapsed before a student so retractable as I was. My mind was willing and docile, yes, but my spirit carried a chip on its shoulder. Mrs. Hopkins, however, did not think I was quite such a dyed-in-the-wool black sheep as others did. How good she was to me!"

TUSCUMBIA, ALABAMA

Kate checked the mailbox by the entrance to the farm regularly. It was winter and it began snowing. The snow and Christmas decorations only brought so much joy to her heart. She was eager to receive the answer from Mr. Bane in Boston.

When it came, Arthur opened it. Kate looked at him, seeing his disappointed face.

"What?" Kate asked, "What does he say?"

Arthur finished reading the letter and sighed, "Dr. Howe died a decade ago."

Kate put her face in her hands.

Arthur put his hand on her shoulder, "Don't you worry, we'll find—"

Suddenly shouting from the sitting room made both of them jump. Helen was screaming. Martha, too, rushed from the kitchen.

Kate ran to the living room and screamed as she saw smoke. Martha rolled Helen in a blanket on the floor, hitting the blanket with her hands to extinguish the fire, while Arthur rushed and rolled Helen on the floor from side to side. Kate stood frozen in terror. The room was smoky. Helen must have caught fire from the fireplace.

After the fire was fully extinguished, Arthur pulled Helen out of the blanket. She coughed heavily. Martha cried, "I'm sorry Kate! I'm sorry Captain Keller! I was in the kitchen when I heard her screaming—"

Kate wanted to reassure her, but her attention was given to Helen. Her hands were heavily burned and some of her hair was scorched, too. She looked like a scared animal.

Arthur sank into the divan and shouted, "It can't go on this way!"

Years later Helen would write:

> "My poor parents: one day I happened to spill water on my apron, and I spread it out to dry before the fire which was flickering on the sitting-room hearth. The apron did not dry quickly enough to suit me, so I drew nearer and threw it right over the hot ashes. The fire leaped into life; the flames encircled me so that in a moment my clothes were blazing. I made a terrified noise that brought Martha, the cook, to the rescue. Throwing a blanket over me, she almost suffocated me, but she put out the fire. My parents rushed over. Luckily, except for my hands and hair I was not badly burned. My parents were deeply grieved and perplexed."

BOSTON, MASSACHUSETTS

As the end of the school year approached, Mrs. Hopkins was appalled to hear that Annie had no place to go, and was planning on working in a boarding house. "Annie, would you like to spend the summer with me?"

Annie was speechless.

* * *

That summer went by very quickly. The experiences Annie had with Mrs. Hopkins at her home by the sea in Brewster gave her an alternative view of life. There was laughter and gayety among the large Hopkins family. While Mrs. Hopkins herself was a widow, she had a brother, old parents, neighbors and friends. Mrs. Hopkins took Annie with her everywhere, visiting friends, shopping in the quaint local market, taking books from the library, visiting religious revivals. The food was wonderful and Mrs. Hopkins friends and family treated Annie as an equal. One of Mrs. Hopkins's friends taught Annie how to ride horses. Another taught her to sail. She felt like a proper young lady.

* * *

One year turned into the next. Whereas in the previous

two years Annie dreaded the summer vacation, now she learned to wait for it eagerly like the other girls. She finally had a home to visit.

She spent each summer with Mrs. Hopkins, who became a mother figure to her.

In school, she advanced rapidly. Her eyes were better. She could still not read for long periods of time, her eyes becoming watery and painful—but she nevertheless could read real print. She excelled in all her schoolwork.

As the last school year approached, 19-year-old Annie was a woman. A real young woman. And to everyone's surprise she was the best student in her class.

She wished to enjoy her accomplishment, but she couldn't. The end of the school year meant that life outside of her haven would begin. The other girls had comfortable homes to return to. Annie could not live with Mrs. Hopkins in Brewster, as Mrs. Hopkins returned to the school each autumn for her role as a housemother.

Annie could not rejoice in the silly worriless existence of the fellow girls in class. The girls were busy talking about the recent wedding in Washington of President Cleveland to young Frances Folsom, who was only twenty-one years old. Photographs of Frances Folsom's dress appeared in the newspapers, and Annie—the only one in class who could somehow see—was begged by the girls to tell them all she could about the dress.

Annie played along, detailing the white muslin dress, the petticoat with its deep Hamburg ruffle, the scalloped edges of each ruffle. She described the exact look of the delicate Valencia lace, the elbow-length sleeves and the beautiful hairdo, with ringlets at Frances Folsom's temples. The girls drooled as Annie read to them how the wedding was held in the oval-shaped Blue Room on the first floor of the White House; how the 49 year old President donned a tuxedo and white bowtie and how he danced with his young bride to the soft music played by the presidential orchestra.

The girls all dreamed about getting married, though they knew it was almost impossible. Why should a man want a blind wife? But Annie's dreams were different. "One day," she whispered to the other girls, "I shall visit the White House. I'd love to have tea with the President and the new First Lady!"

The girls giggled. Annie recognized their mirth—they were laughing *at* her. She resented not feeling like she belonged, even after six years and trying her best.

Perhaps she indeed did not belong. She had *real* concerns on her mind. The fear of going back to the almshouse was more real than end of school celebrations. She remembered the almshouse clearly: the rats crawling around, the kitchen boss fondling younger women, the shouting of the mad women at night, the straightjackets, the forsaken pregnant girls. The deaths.

Determined to change her lot in life, Annie marched to the principal's office. "Mr. Anagnos! I need to see you!"

Mr. Anagnos was surprised, "Miss Sullivan! Why won't you schedule an appointment and I'll be happy to—"

"Mr. Anagnos, the end of the school year is approaching. You of all people know that I have no place to go when I graduate. I wanted to ask you to hire me."

Mr. Anagnos nearly stuttered, "To... *hire* you?"

Annie nodded.

Mr. Anagnos mumbled, "As *what*?"

Annie drew her chin back, "Why as a teacher, of course!"

Mr. Anagnos sighed and leaned back in his chair and tapped his fingers on his desk. "Miss Sullivan, the school is not a *charity*. We already pay Miss Laura Bridgman in her role as a 'teacher.' We cannot afford to have another—"

"Mr. Anagnos, you have seen my grades, haven't you?"

Mr. Anagnos nodded.

"I can teach, Mr. Anagnos!"

"But what about your eyes?"

"Mr. Anagnos! You yourself say each year in the graduation speech that employers must not discriminate against people with disabilities, and that blind people can be more valuable than regular people."

Mr. Anagnos sighed and stood up. "Even if I had a position, Miss Sullivan—which I do not, mind you—I could not hire you due to your hot temper—"

"I don't have a hot temper!" Annie shouted.

Mr. Anagnos took a deep breath and looked at Annie knowingly.

Annie's chin quivered. "Very well," she mumbled, turned around, and stormed out of Mr. Anagnos' office.

She felt devastated.

She felt defeated.

* * *

The only thing that comforted Annie was Mrs. Hopkins. "Annie, I hear you are to give the valedictorian speech on graduation day."

"Me?" Annie replied, alarmed.

Mrs. Hopkins smiled, "Unless you know of another Annie Sullivan!"

"But why me?" Annie asked.

"You received the best grades in class," Mrs. Hopkins grinned.

Annie gulped. This was going to be a great challenge, but she would conquer it. She was determined to prove that she was worthy. Not less worthy than any of them.

> "I had a mind capable of growth and discrimination. Many of the false ideas I had hugged to my breast while in the almshouse fell away like dead leaves when I was in school, and truer ideas came to take their place. The light of knowledge spread slowly, putting darkness to flight.
>
> Slowly the realization came to me that I could not alter anything but myself. I had to accept the conventional order of society if I was to succeed in anything.
>
> Yet I was heavy with discontent, with pent-up anger against what seemed to me a cruel fate. How was I, handicapped as I was—both physically and mentally—to succeed in the world? My partial blindness, I knew, was insurmountable obstacle to any profession."

TUSCUMBIA, ALABAMA

Kate was in her eighth month of pregnancy. She was anxious. Helen did not offer any comfort. During the previous months she had only become worse. The more attention Kate tried to give her—the more affection and love—the more Helen became unruly and disobedient.

Her temper fits became more frequent.

Once Helen followed her mother to the small pantry room, examining all the various jars in which her mother made pickles, jams and other preserves.

Martha was outside helping in the field.

Helen eventually grew bored in the pantry and left her mother in the room, closing and locking the door behind her.

* * *

It was three hours before Martha returned to the house and released poor Kate from the pantry.

That night Arthur was furious. "We must do something, Kate!"

Kate, exhausted with her pregnancy, said with tears in her eyes, "How about that Doctor Chisholm? He is said to have performed real miracles with blind people."

"He's in Baltimore! I don't intend to travel a thousand miles and three states with that uncontrollable little savage of yours!"

"Arthur!"

Silence followed.

They both said nothing.

Arthur sighed heavily. "I'll write to him and see if he can see us. Something must be done and soon, before some real danger happens to you by that girl!"

> "One day, after I found out the use of a key, I locked my mother up in the pantry, where she was obliged to remain three hours as the servants were away. She kept pounding on the door, while I sat outside on the porch steps and laughed with glee as I felt the jar of the pounding. This most naughty prank of mine convinced my parents that something must be done as soon as possible."

BOSTON, MASSACHUSETTS

Annie spent days in the library, trying to write an appropriate valedictory address. She read the addresses of graduates of past years, but found none of them appealing. She went on to read great speeches by the greatest of orators: Mark Twain, Patrick Henry, Ralph Waldo Emerson and Abraham Lincoln. She wrote several unsatisfactory drafts.

She even spelled the entire speech to Laura. Laura sat attentively, and when Annie was done she spelled, "It was fine but a little too combative."

Annie spelled back, "Combative?"

Laura smiled, "You speak of the 'obstacles' and 'circumstances' which must be fought against. That is too much."

Annie was infuriated, "But the speech is aimed at preparing students for life! We must know what it is like out there! Whenever graduates come back to visit the school, they all say how difficult it is and how impossible to find a job anywhere! The students must know life is a battle!"

Laura sighed. She felt Annie's agitation. She spelled to

her young friend, "Yes, but the donors do not want to hear it. They want to believe that the school 'prepared you for life.' They do not want their felicity of consciousness disturbed."

Annie shook her head. "I will say what I want to say. It is my speech!"

Laura shrugged her shoulders, took the needle and thread and continued sewing.

* * *

The graduation ceremony approached. Mrs. Hopkins was kind enough to take care of Annie's clothing. When Mrs. Hopkins brought a large box into her room. Annie was surprised, "What's in there?"

"Well," Mrs. Hopkins tried to play down her surprise, "I thought you might need some help for the ceremony."

Annie reached hesitantly to the box and opened it. She gasped at the white dress.

Mrs. Hopkins smiled, "Take it out."

Annie's heart beat fast as she unfolded the white muslin dress, seeing the outside petticoat with a Hamburg ruffle. Inside the box there were two elbow-length gloves. Annie murmured, "It's like Mrs. Cleveland's!"

Mrs. Hopkins beamed, "I thought you might want to feel like the school's First Lady."

Annie put the dress down carefully, tears in her eyes, "Mrs. Hopkins!" she said as she hugged her housemother.

Mrs. Hopkins smiled and hesitantly took out a small

box and opened it, revealing a pink sash, rolled in a bundle, along with delicate white slippers. "These..." she murmured, "These were my daughter's... Florence's. She wore these at her high school graduation, the year she.... I want you to wear them for the ceremony."

Annie was speechless.

Mrs. Hopkins smiled and whispered, "We'll make you a queen, Annie! We'll put your hair up, and give you some ringlets! You deserve all the good that the world has to offer, child."

* * *

The ceremony came. Annie sat on the stage at Boston's Tremont Temple Church. For the past six years she attended the five ceremonies, each time sitting in the back of the large hall, not disturbing the pristine event.

But now she was *on* the stage among the graduates. She looked at the many dignitaries in the audience, at the parents and siblings of the graduates. She could distinctly see Mrs. Hopkins's dress in the second row.

She looked at all the happy families in the audience and felt lonely. A few days earlier she received a reply from the almshouse. She had written to the Massachusetts Infirmary, wishing to invite Maggie, whose family name she did not know, but who was known as "the hunchback," to her graduation ceremony. But the reply from the almshouse notified her that Maggie had died.

Annie's heart broke as she was filled with remorse for not having contacted Maggie over the years, even just to let her know she was well.

But she could not think about it now.

Her attention returned to the ceremony. The governor was giving his speech. Mr. Anagnos, who was sitting in front of Annie on the stage, turned to her and whispered, "Get ready."

Annie nodded. Her heart began pounding. She had memorized the speech, but will her memory fail her?

She tried to listen to the speech of the governor, but could not understand anything. Then applause followed. Mr. Anagnos rose and shook the governor's hand. Mr. Anagnos turned to Annie and glared, muttering, "Now Annie!"

She rose trembling and took to the podium. She gasped as she looked at the audience. Past the third row people's faces were blurry. The entire hall was filled, including the balcony.

She tried to smile. She turned to the governor, as she knew she should, "Governor," she nodded to him, "Legislators, Director Anagnos, teachers, faculty and graduates!"

Her heart pounded. She closed her eyes. "Today we are standing face to face with the great problem of life!"

Silence followed. Annie looked around the hall, frightened. Mrs. Hopkins signaled her to raise her voice. Annie nodded.

She shouted, "We have spent years in the endeavor to acquire the moral and intellectual discipline"—she closed her eyes again, remembering the words—"by which we are enabled to distinguish truth from falsehood, receive higher and broader views of duty, and... apply general principles to the diversified details of life."

She looked toward the graduates on stage, feeling

more confident, "And now we are going out into the busy world, to take our share in life's burdens, and do our little bit to make the world better, wiser and happier."

She looked at the audience and remembered to lift her chin up. She thought of Maggie's words, *'Keep your head up, you're as good as any of 'em!'*

The thought of Maggie troubled her. She closed her eyes tightly, trying to suppress the tears.

She shouted, "We shall be most likely to succeed in life if we obey the great law of our being. God has placed us here to grow, to expand, to progress!"

She looked at Mr. Anagnos, who looked at her worriedly, fidgeting with his fingers.

"We have the power to control the course of our lives! We can, by thought and perseverance, develop all the powers and capacities entrusted to us and build for ourselves a true and noble character!"

She saw some people nodding. She nodded too. "Though we cannot see with our eyes, we *can* develop all other powers and capacities entrusted to us. And because we *can*, we *must*! It is a duty we owe to ourselves, to our country and to God!"

She looked down, but felt an invisible hand pushing her chin back up. She exclaimed, "All the wondrous intellectual and moral endowments with which man is blessed might become useless—unless," she paused, "unless he *uses* and *improves* them. The muscles must be used or they become unserviceable!"

She looked at the fellow graduates, her voice becoming more confident as she shouted the words out, "All our faculties must be used: the memory, understanding and judgment must be utilized, or they become feeble and inactive! If a love for truth and beauty and goodness is not cultivated, the mind loses the strength which comes from truth, the refinement which comes from beauty, and the happiness which comes from goodness."

She took a deep breath, "Therefore we must continue to culture ourselves. Self-culture is a benefit, not only to the individual, but also to mankind. Every man who improves himself is aiding the progress of society, and every one who stands still, holds society back!"

Her thoughts drew to her mother.... *'Annie, I want you to make something of yourself!'*

Annie squeezed her eyes. She remembered her mother, lying in bed, coughing blood, *'Make something of yourself, Annie! Unlike your Mama!'*

"The individual is the key," Annie continued, nodding to herself, "the advancement of society always has its commencement in the *individual* soul."

She remembered writing the speech and thinking of the almshouse, "It is by battling *with* the circumstances, temptations and *failures* of the world—"Her voice broke. She coughed—"It is through battling that the individual reaches his highest possibilities!"

She breathed in and looked at the audience filled with many of the school's donors. "For the abundant opportunities which have been afforded to us for broad self-improvement we are deeply grateful." She looked at the governor, "We thank His Excellency, the Governor, and the Legislatures of Massachusetts for the most generous and efficient aid they have given our school."

She looked at Mr. Anagnos, "Director, teachers and"

she looked at Mrs. Hopkins, "housemothers: we enter life's battlefield *determined* to prove our gratitude to you, by lives devoted to duty! True in thought and deed to the noble principles—the principles which *you* have taught us."

She turned to the graduating class on the stage; the girls who so often taunted her. "Fellow graduates. Duty bids us go forth into *active* life. Let us go cheerfully, hopefully, and earnestly, and set ourselves to find our special part, our own mission. When we have found it, let us perform it willingly and faithfully!"

She looked back at the audience and recited the last sentence, suppressing her tears. "Every obstacle we overcome, every success we achieve, will bring us closer to Heaven and make life more as they *should* be. Thank you very kindly."

She returned to her seat on the stage next to her fellow graduates. She did not hear the applause. She did not acknowledge the nods. She did not register the cheers of her friends, the impressed look of Mr. Anagnos or the proud smile of Mrs. Hopkins.

All that she cared for was that she was done with the speech. A feeling of relief enveloped her.

Mr. Anagnos rose to the podium, and—according to the recollections of the other girls—Annie did not hear it herself—said, "Thank you, Miss Sullivan, what an extraordinary speech! What high thoughts!"

He went on to present the diploma to each of the students. When her name was called the large audience gave her a special applause. This time, however, she did notice. It was soothing—in the minutes prior to her name being called, she saw how each student received applause from their family members. She had feared she would receive no applause. But the audience warmed her heart. She shook the hand of Mr. Anagnos and the other teachers. She felt like an adult.

After the ceremony many people shook her hand. Annie smiled gracefully at everyone, feeling like a queen in her white muslin dress and white slippers. One reporter from *Boston Home Journal* asked for the exact spelling of her name, and said he'll refer to her speech in the Journal as it was "worthy of special mention." She blushed and thanked him.

Many of the younger students in the lower grades of the school came to congratulate her. Some dignitaries came to shake her hand as well. She was overwhelmed by it all.

As she shook people's hands she noticed an older couple waiting, not far away, apparently wishing to speak to her.

The old man, Annie noticed, had an impressive tall stature. He was obviously wealthy, wearing a fancy ulster overcoat and a black silk cylinder hat. The lady next to him wore a beautiful blue pelisse cloak, a pearl necklace and a Parisian bonnet. The two of them waited patiently. Finally, when a young girl finished thanking Annie for her speech and left with her mother, the couple approached Annie. The man spoke first, "I do not presume you'll remember me, Miss Sullivan."

Annie squinted her eyes, "Sir? Please kindly remind me?"

The tall man smiled. The lady said, "I believe, Miss Sullivan, that it was my husband who came to"—she whispered—"the *infirmary*…?"

Annie's jaw dropped. "Mr. Sanborn?"

The man smiled, "That is me. And this," he pointed at his wife, "is Mrs. Sanborn."

Annie eyes began tearing, "Mr. Sanborn!" her fine posture dissolved and she became a 14-year-old child, "I am so happy to see you!" She took Mrs. Sanborn's hand, "You have *no idea* what your husband did for me!"

Mrs. Sanborn was obviously pleased, grinning proudly, "Well, having seen you on stage I may have an *idea.*"

Annie tried to speak, but tears gushed from her eyes, preventing any coherent speech. She suddenly realized the long road she had travelled. She remembered Maggie staring at her through the window as she heard the group of men approaching the gate. She remembered her voice, at first betraying her, but then sounding loud and clear as she shouted for the man who might be her rescuer.

Mr. Sanborn smiled at her. His wife embraced Annie as she sobbed, "Oh, you are excited darling."

Annie cried on Mrs. Sanborn's shoulders, "Oh Ma'am!" she wiped her tears, "I don't want to mess your pelisse!"

Mrs. Sanborn smiled, "It is fine, darling. Please do. I am pleased I finally see some fruit of my husband's labor!"

Annie wiped her tears, surprised at her own reaction.

One of the girls from class, who had partial sight, came to her, "Annie, the carriages are going back to school for dinner."

Annie sniffled and gained her composure, "Thank you, Susan. I'll be right there!"

Susan bowed gently and left.

Annie held Mrs. Sanborn's hands and smiled. Mr. Sanborn said, "What a speech, Miss Sullivan, you made us all proud."

Annie nodded and mumbled, "Thank you!" She looked at the entrance doors, "Please forgive me, I must…."

"Go, young lady," said Mrs. Sanborn.

Annie bowed and ran to the doors, shaking her head in disbelief.

* * *

Later, in her room, she thought of the ceremony. She felt a sensation she could not put in words. An odd feeling. Was it pride? Satisfaction? It must have been. It felt good, though foreign.

She began taking her dress off, knowing she only had a few moments before dinner. She could hear the other girls getting excited for the special dinner.

Years later she recalled:

> "Reluctantly I unfastened the sash and smoothed it out on the bed. The sash was Mrs. Hopkins's and I did not know if I would ever wear it again. I placed it lovingly in the box. I then took the dress off. I fingered the little white buttons as if they had been real pearls.
>
> Finally there were the white slippers. It took a lot of will power to remove them. They were the delight of my heart, even more than the white dress with its three ruffles. I had never worn white slippers before. I brushed them with my face towel and put them back in the box, wrapped

up in tissue paper. From the hall I could hear the girls calling me, but I pretended not to hear. The hour was mine and nothing should interfere with my enjoyment. I began crying as I thought of Mrs. Hopkins... How good she was!

Before that dress all I ever wore were the plainest, coarsest cotton garments. But this dress! How lovely it was! It must have cost Mrs. Hopkins a fortune!

The thought of money brought me back to reality. What will be of me? Where I will I go next year? The thought that I might have to return to the almshouse after all stabbed my heart. From the peak of happiness I had climbed to that day I tumbled headlong into a valley of despondency. Hearing the supper bell ringing, I left my room slowly, resolved that nobody would guess that I wasn't the happiest girl in the world, if only for one evening."

TUSCUMBIA, ALABAMA

Arthur hugged Kate on the train station platform. "We'll be fine," he said.

Kate held baby Mildred in her arms and nodded, tears streaming down her cheeks. She looked at Helen, playing with a bell that her father had brought her. The vibration made her laugh with glee. Kate did not mind the other people on the platform, seeing clearly now that her daughter was ill.

Helen, dressed in her red dress, with the red hair bow on her head, looked excited. She knew, from her dress and the excitement in the house, that she was going on a long journey.

Kate looked at Arthur, "I wish I could come with you."

Captain Keller placed his hand on baby Mildred, "You just make sure to rest." He turned to Martha, "Take a good care of them."

Martha nodded.

Arthur sighed, "I sure hope we would come back with good news from that oculist."

Kate tried smiling. She hoped.

Arthur took Helen by the hand and they boarded the train.

The two-day journey was very tiring for Arthur, trying to keep Helen calm and occupied. He tried to explain to a lady who gave Helen a box of shells that the child could not hear her. Nevertheless, the lady spoke to Helen. This made Arthur feel helpless.

To add to his chagrin, Helen chased the conductor around the train, holding to his long coat tails. After Arthur explained to the conductor Helen's peculiar situation, being both deaf and blind, the conductor gave her one of his ticket-punchers. Helen was thrilled, and soon began punching holes in papers, making the most hideous mess around her seat. She was in heaven. Arthur was in hell.

> "To me, as a young child, the journey to Baltimore was very pleasant. I made friends with many people on the train. One lady gave me a box of shells and for a long time they kept me happy and contented. The conductor, too, was kind. Often when he went his rounds I clung to his coat tails while he collected and punched the tickets. His punch, with which he let me play, was a delightful toy. Curled up in a corner of the seat I amused myself for hours making funny little holes in bits of cardboard. During the whole trip I did not have one fit of temper, there were so many things to keep my mind and fingers busy."

* * *

When they finally arrived at Baltimore, Arthur took Helen immediately to Dr. Chisholm's clinic. Arthur was anxious as the famed doctor examined Helen's eyes. Helen found it hard to sit still while the doctor examined her. Arthur tried to stroke her hand as she sat in the doctor's chair.

Finally the doctor sighed and gave Arthur a long speech. Arthur wilted and unwillingly began feeling tearful. The doctor explained the system of miosis and mydriasis, determining that the pupillary light reflex was completely nonfunctioning, and how both the optic nerves and the retina were irreversibly affected by the disease which Helen contracted as a baby.

Arthur tried to restrain himself and only when the respected doctor finished talking did Arthur say, "You are said to be a miracle worker Dr. Chisholm! We came all the way from *Alabama* just for you to tell me nothing could be done with the child?!"

Dr. Chisholm's murmured, "I didn't say that, Mr. Keller."

"Captain Keller," Arthur mumbled, "It's *Captain.*"

The doctor nodded. "I did not say, Captain Keller, that nothing could be done. Something *can* be done with her, but not with her eyes. I'm not a hearing expert. Why won't you go and see Dr. Alexander Graham Bell, he might be able to fit her a hearing device—"

"Dr. Bell? The telegraph man?"

"The tele*phone*, Captain."

"What does he have to do with—"

"Dr. Bell's mother was deaf and so is his wife. This is how Dr. Bell first stumbled on the phonautograph He was trying to create a device that could transmit to a deaf person exterior sounds through a wire."

Arthur sighed and mumbled, "I did not know that."

"He lives in Washington. If I were you, Captain, I would proceed to him."

Arthur wanted to cry as he looked at Helen who was playing all alone with one of the doctor's measuring devices.

> "In Baltimore, my father took me to Dr. Chisholm who received us kindly, but he could do nothing. He said, however, that we should consult Dr. Alexander Graham Bell of Washington, who might be able to help us with his unique inventions."

BOSTON, MASSACHUSETTS

Annie was packing her belongings. All of the students were packing but her lot was different. They had a home to go to and she only had Mrs. Hopkins.

All of the students were leaving later that day, but Annie leaving the following day with Mrs. Hopkins to her house in Brewster.

Annie folded her clothes quietly into her suitcase. Outside the room she heard the girls saying, "Congratulations Lilian!" There were many gasps and giggles of excitement. Annie wondered what that was all about.

Curious, she went into the hallway. She saw the girls huddled in the adjacent room.

Annie tried to be friendly, "Lilian, what should I congratulate you for? A groom?"

Lilian smiled and murmured, "Oh it's nothing Annie!"

Susan protested, "No it's *not*! It's a *big deal*!" she turned to Annie, "Mr. Anagnos asked Lilian to work for the school next year! There's a deaf-blind girl coming, her name's Edith, and Lilian is going to be Edith's *private tutor!*"

Annie felt her heart shatter to pieces. She forced on a smile, "Oh, Lilian! How lovely!"

Her heart beat fast. Lilian *knew* how much Annie was desperate for a job.

Lilian smiled, "Oh, Annie, thank you for saying that! Isn't it exciting?" she turned to the other girls, "Now you all must *promise* me that you'll visit me so I won't be lonely!"

Annie felt fooled. Conned. Tricked. Deceived. She excused herself and left the house. She hurried to the main building, her steps growing faster until she started running to Mr. Anagnos's office. The secretary tried to stop her, but Annie barged in, muttering at Mr. Anagnos who was sitting by his large desk, "How *dare* you?!"

The secretary came inside the room, "I'm sorry, Mr. Anagnos, but she just barged—"

"It is fine, Mrs. Alcott," Mr. Anagnos said and waved his hand for her to leave. He took a deep breath and looked at the glaring Annie, "Yes, Miss Sullivan?"

Annie felt her chest rising and falling, "You… *you*…! I *need* that work! I *need* the opportunity! And you gave it to… *Lilian*?"

"Well, Miss Sullivan, it was not wholly my decision—"

"If I ever end up on the street," Annie said, her chin quivering as she pointed her finger at him, "it will be *your* conscience that should suffer, Mr. Anagnos!"

She turned her back to him, feeling tears welling in her eyes as she ran from his office, from the building, from the cruelty of the world which she could find no words to describe.

* * *

The following day Annie was more composed. Her suitcase packed, she followed Mrs. Hopkins out of the dormitory house. All the students were gone and only a few teachers remained. After attending the last faculty meeting, Mrs. Hopkins could finally leave.

Annie followed her as they walked into the main building and toward the main entrance to the school.

Outside at the bottom of the stairs, a carriage waited to take them to the train station, where they would take the familiar train to Brewster.

They passed by the main office at the entrance, and as they approached the stairs going out the building Mrs. Hopkins told Annie, "I'll be right back. Please wait here."

Annie nodded. Mrs. Hopkins opened her suitcase, took two of the newspapers out, closed the suitcase, smiled at Annie and disappeared into the main office.

Annie stood by the large wooden doors of the institution that sheltered her for the past six years. She walked slowly to the large white pillars at the top of the long staircase, gently caressing the marble texture. She had gone through so much in these six years. She remembered the first time she climbed these very staircases.

She could hear Mrs. Hopkins's voice from inside the office. She heard Mr. Anagnos too.

Annie found herself slowly drawn into the building. She pretended to look at the letters on the bulletin board by the office as she heard Mrs. Hopkins talking.

"The *Boston Home Journal* praised her address," Mrs. Hopkins said, "for being 'worthy of special mention for its felicity of thought and grace of expression. It was emphatically a beautifully original production!'"

"Yes," Mr. Anagnos said slowly, "I have read it."

"And the *Christian Register,*" Mrs. Hopkins continued, "writes 'an altogether earnest, sincere, thoughtful speech, full of wise suggestions, and spoken in tones that vibrated with true feeling and with genuine refinement.'"

"I've read that too, Mrs. Hopkins."

"Well then why on earth can't you give that girl a chance? She *needs* the money! Lilian does not, she has the safety of her well-to-do New Haven family—"

"Mrs. Hopkins, I care for the quality of tutoring for this pupil in question, Edith—"

"That is exactly the point I am trying to make," Mrs. Hopkins continued. "You and I both know that the 'quality of tutoring' could be *higher* if delivered by Annie! She is the best of her class!"

Annie strained her ears but could hear nothing. She took a few steps toward the office door. She heard Mr. Anagnos whispering, "I must care about the smooth operation of this institution and the *obedience* of its teachers to the management. I simply cannot take the *risk* of having an unruly character among my faculty!"

Hearing that, Annie wanted to go in and strike him. He had always been against her from the beginning. She did nothing to deserve his ill treatment.

Mrs. Hopkins said something very quietly.

Mr. Anagnos whispered, "I simply cannot take this

risk. I assure you that I am doing my best to aid Annie in finding an appropriate work as a domestic worker in one of the—"

"Mr. Anagnos," Mrs. Hopkins said, and Annie could hear a chair moving inside, "I believe you are making a mistake, but you are the principal, and I trust your judgment. I do wish you a very pleasant summer vacation. Hopefully the clarity of summer shall restore your fine judgment which might have been clouded by the long winter. Farewell!"

Annie hurried back to the entrance doors.

Mr. Anagnos called after Mrs. Hopkins, "I will not change my mind on this!"

Mrs. Hopkins walked away, "Certainly, Mr. Anagnos, certainly!"

She walked into the large hallway and saw Annie by the building's entrance, Annie pretending not to have heard anything.

Mrs. Hopkins smiled at her, "Shall we?"

BALTIMORE, MARYLAND

Exhausted, Captain Keller boarded the train with Helen toward Washington.

Dr. Chisholm was kind enough to telegram Dr. Bell about the arrival of Captain Keller and his six-year-old deaf-blind daughter.

Dr. Bell with his big white beard welcomed the two at his large Brodhead-Bell mansion on Nineteenth Street.

The doctor was very friendly toward the weary father and daughter and immediately gave candy to Helen. He took Helen by the hand and helped her climb the stairs slowly to his office in the second floor while asking Captain Keller questions about Helen's language.

Arthur was puzzled, "Doctor, the child does not speak!"

"Oh yes she does. You might not understand her language, but she certainly has one. When she wants something, she pulls you, does she not?"

"Well she does, but—"

"And when she wants you to leave her alone, she pushes, does she not?"

Arthur was perplexed, "I do not suppose, Doctor, that you call these *signs* a 'language!'"

"Oh but that's precisely what these signs are, Captain Keller. A language which only our little Helen knows."

They entered the office filled with peculiar devices, receivers, dials and wires. Dr. Bell smiled at Captain Keller, "Welcome to my kingdom!"

Captain Keller nodded and looked at the large patient chair. He expected the doctor to put Helen there, but instead Dr. Bell sat near his desk and brought Helen to sit on his knees. He began touching her hands, giving her things to play with. He pulled out his pocket watch and let Helen pull the back string, making it vibrate. Helen let out a sound of utter joy.

Captain Keller sighed, wondering why Dr. Bell was not examining her *ears*. All the while Dr. Bell seemed to kiss Helen on the head. Arthur was alarmed by the extreme *familiarity* which the doctor allowed himself with the young girl.

It was only a minute later that Arthur noticed the gentle sounds that Dr. Bell was humming. Dr. Bell caught Arthur's questioning look and smiled, "This is how I first spoke to my mother when she became deaf."

Arthur nodded but he did not understand.

Dr. Bell closed his eyes. He hummed various sounds at different pitches into Helen's hair, approaching her skull and ears from different angles.

The doctor then took several tuning forks and bang them against the edge of the table. He watched Helen's expression. Finally, he smiled at Captain Keller.

Captain Keller looked hopeful, "Yes, Doctor?"

"I'm glad to tell you, Captain Keller, that your daughter is very bright!"

Captain Keller looked at him in anticipation, waiting for him to continue speaking.

However Dr. Bell said nothing.

Arthur mumbled, "And can her hearing be restored Doctor?"

"Oh no, that I'm afraid not.... But she is very interrogative, lively... has a healthy physique, you should be very proud of her, going through what she went through, remaining so jovial and merry!"

Arthur sank into his chair, feeling exasperated. "Can't anything be done with her Doctor?"

Dr. Bell exclaimed, "*Much* can be done! If I were you I would send her to the Massachusetts School for the Blind in South Boston, the school of the late Dr. Howe."

Captain Keller looked astonished, "He has a school?"

"Yes, of course! He founded the best school for the blind in the country!"

Arthur sighed, "Well, but my wife would never allow Helen to leave! She barely agreed to send her to an asylum in Tennessee, which is only a few hours from Alabama, not days!"

Dr. Bell nodded. He gave Helen an old key and a portable lock to play with. She took it with joy. "Mind you, Captain Keller," he said, his eyes still fixed on Helen, "that the school in Boston is *not* an asylum, but a truly worthy *school*. Why won't you write to the director, Mr. Anagnos is his name, and ask him for help? Perhaps there's a possibility of him sending a teacher for you all the way to Tennessee?"

"Alabama."

"Yes, of course, Alabama," Dr. Bell said, more captivated by Helen than by her father.

Captain Keller sighed, "Do you think there is any use?"

Dr. Bell looked at him at once, raised his eyebrows and said, "I think, Captain, that you have a brilliant little girl here! Look at how she plays with the key!"

"That she does at home also," Captain Keller added grimly.

"Of course there is 'use' Captain Keller! Her darkness and deafness does not mean she is to be ignored! I beg you to write to Mr. Anagnos at once!" He patted Helen on the head to mark the end of the meeting and helped her rise from his knees, "And do let me know of little Helen's progress, Captain, will you?"

> "Acting on Doctor Chisholm's advice, we went immediately to Washington to see Dr. Bell, my father with a sad heart and many misgivings, I wholly unconscious of his anguish, finding pleasure in the excitement of moving from place to place.
>
> Arriving at Dr. Bell's, I, as a child, at once felt the tenderness and sympathy which endeared Dr. Bell to so many hearts, as his wonderful achievements enlist their admiration. He held me on his knee while I examined his watch, and he made it strike for me. I loved him at once. But I did not dream that that meeting would be the door through which I should pass from darkness into light, from isolation to friendship, companionship, knowledge

and love."

BREWSTER, MASSACHUSETTS

Annie was desperate.

Sitting on the beach in Brewster in late August, she agonized about her misfortune. She hoped for a miracle—even prayed—but nothing happened. The closer the school year got the more anxious she became.

Suddenly she heard Mrs. Hopkins yelling from the trail, "Annie! Annie!"

Annie rose, wiping the sand away, and hurried to Mrs. Hopkins, who was running down the beach.

Annie was worried.

Mrs. Hopkins waved a letter in the air, "Annie! You received a letter!"

"From whom?" Annie asked as she ran to Mrs. Hopkins.

Mrs. Hopkins, panting, gave her the letter.

Annie saw it was from Mr. Anagnos. The letter was open. She looked at Mrs. Hopkins.

"I'm so sorry, Annie," Mrs. Hopkins said, panting, "I couldn't resist myself. I had to open it!"

Annie opened the letter, the bright light making it difficult for her to read. She tried to shade the letter with her other hand, but the light was still too bright and painful for her to focus on the small letters.

"Here," Mrs. Hopkins said and took the letter, reading out loud:

"Miss Annie M. Sullivan.

Brewster, Mass.

My dear Annie,"

Annie made a disgusted face, "He calls me '*My dear Annie*'?"

Mrs. Hopkins nodded excitedly,

"Please read the enclosed letters carefully, and let me know at your earliest convenience whether you would be disposed to consider favorably an offer of a position in the family of Captain Keller as governess of his little deaf-mute and blind daughter."

Annie mumbled, "*What?*"

Mrs. Hopkins grinned, "Wait, he goes on:

"I have no other information about the standing and responsibility of the man save that contained in his own letters: but, if you decide to be a candidate for the position, it is an easy matter to write and ask for further particulars.

With kind remembrances to Mrs. Hopkins,

Sincerely,

M. Anagnos"

Annie's hands shook, "What does the other letter say?"

Mrs. Hopkins held Annie's hand, "It's a family in Alabama. They have a daughter just like Edith, the same age and she needs a private teacher!"

Annie's heart beat fast. She nearly fainted.

"When Mr. Anagnos sent me Captain Keller's letter and asked if I thought I could teach his little girl, I was very sure that I couldn't. I told him I was not trained for that sort of teaching, or indeed for anything! I did not think I was serious minded enough to make a success of it. I also knew that some of my teachers would laugh in their sleeve at the idea of *Annie Sullivan* undertaking any child's education. It seemed like a chapter out of a romantic and rather impossible tale."

TUSCUMBIA, ALABAMA

"To Mr. A. H. Keller.

Tuscumbia, Alabama.

From: M. Anagnos,

Massachusetts School for the Blind, Boston

* * *

My dear Sir,

The case of your little daughter is of exceeding interest to me. Your brief description of her mental activity reminds me forcibly of Laura Bridgman, and I would certainly go and see her, if the distance which separates us were not so great.

I can recommend to you a young lady as governess of your little daughter heartily and without any reservation. Her name is Miss Annie Sullivan. She is one of the recent graduates of this school: but her sight has been for several years steadily improving, so that she is now able to read and write. She is exceedingly intelligent, strictly honest, industrious, ladylike in her manners and very amiable. Her moral character is all that can be desired. You can find the valedictory address that she composed and delivered at the commencement ceremony, in our annual report which I am attaching, on page 125. It can give you some idea of her literary ability.

Miss Sullivan is familiar with Laura Bridgman's case and with the methods of teaching deaf-mute and blind children, and I assure you that she will make an excellent instructress and most reliable guide for your little daughter. If you wish to employ the services of Miss Sullivan, please let me know the terms which you are disposed to offer, and oblige,

Yours very sincerely,

M. Anagnos."

Kate looked at her husband, "She sounds suitable, does she not, Arthur?"

They were in the sitting-room. Kate was rocking baby Mildred to sleep in the cradle. Arthur stood beside her. Helen was playing in the yard, or in the house, it was hard to know as she constantly moved.

Arthur began walking about the room, "We ought not to rush, Kate. It's a hefty expense. People pay 25 dollars per month for a private nanny. Let us see first if Helen's situation might not improve—"

"Improve?" Kate asked, not believing her husband's words. Arthur had been corresponding with Mr. Anagnos for months while Helen's situation was only getting worse! Her tantrums occurred more often and sometimes repeated several times in one hour. She kicked, hit herself, and even bit her mother if she tried to calm her down. "Arthur," Kate said, trying to sound respectful, "I do not think we can wait much longer...."

Arthur looked defeated, "I've heard about another doctor in Washington. I want to take Helen to him to see whether perhaps he can—"

Kate looked at her husband. She understood him. In the past she too could not accept Helen's deafness and blindness as a final verdict. "Oh Arthur," she murmured, "I understand...."

As she spoke, Helen walked into the room with her doll. Her hair was a mess and her dress was filled with dirt. She must have tried to feed the doll dirt as was her hobby recently.

Arthur pointed at Helen, "What's the use of 'educating' her if she remains this way?" he pointed at his eyes, "Something must be done!"

Helen approached the cradle, wishing to put the doll inside. Seeing that baby Mildred was there, she let out a cry of dismay and turned the cradle to its side, Mildred falling out—when Kate reached caught the baby an instant before she hit the floor. Kate screamed, "Helen! What on earth are you doing?"

Arthur banged his fist on the desk, "She can't hear you! She c-a-n-n-o-t h-e-a-r y-o-u!!!"

Kate held baby Mildred in her arms as the baby cried loudly. "Arthur!" Kate cried, "I beg you! Send for that tutor! We can wait no longer!"

Arthur looked at Helen, who played with the doll in the cradle, oblivious to what she had just done. He looked at Kate and clutched his face in his hands.

> "My poor parents... Once I discovered my little sister sleeping peacefully in the cradle. This was my doll's cradle, and I grew angry. I rushed upon the cradle and overturned it, and the baby might

have been killed had my mother not caught her as she fell.

At the time my failures to make myself understood were invariably followed by outbursts of passion. I felt as if invisible hands were holding me, and I made frantic efforts to free myself. I struggled— not that struggling helped matters, but the spirit of resistance was strong within me; I generally broke down in tears and physical exhaustion. After awhile these outbursts occurred daily, sometimes hourly."

BOSTON, MASSACHUSETTS

The months in waiting passed slowly for Annie. She moved back to the school but spent most of the day in the library waiting for the good news from Mr. Anagnos. He told her he was "corresponding" with the family in Alabama, and that in the "meantime" she should "prepare herself."

She tried.

In the library she went over Dr. Howe's documents from fifty years earlier about the education of Laura Bridgman. Dr. Howe wrote much about the importance of schedule and the slow pace of teaching required. Methodology and patience were words that repeated again and again in his records.

Annie read through his documents, her mind often daydreaming. Dr. Howe wrote about pedagogy, the importance of repeating a specific exercise "several days," while making sure "not to weary" the student. He began teaching Laura with raised letters, and only after a while began with the manual language. Annie found that strange. But she assumed Dr. Howe knew better.

Yet she was confused. The manual alphabet seemed more important to her than the actual alphabet, which could be communicated to a deaf-blind person only with raised letters on cards, and not via simple gestures of the hands.

When she tried to consult with Mr. Anagnos he told her only, "Stick to Dr. Howe's *exact* steps and do not deviate from his method, as it is the only one that ever worked."

She agreed. But as months passed and winter came she grew more restless. She spent many hours reading Dr. Howe's records as well as psychology books. Her sight slowly deteriorated. She was anxious to go to the family in Alabama, but Mr. Anagnos only said that the family was not yet inviting a tutor, and that Captain Keller was "taking his time."

Annie looked at envy at Lilian who received Edith in September and spent each day with her. Mr. Anagnos strictly forbade others—most likely referring specifically to Annie—from trying to converse or teach little Edith. Only Lilian was to do that.

Lilian looked happy, even if it was tiring at times.

Annie talked to Laura, hoping to receive her encouragement. Laura only spelled back, "Patience. Trust Mr. Anagnos. Patience."

This was not the encouragement Annie was hoping for.

She felt lonely in the great school, forced by Mr. Anagnos to "read everything possible" on pedagogy, deafness, blindness and child psychology. Lilian did not have to do *any* of that prior to beginning to work with Edith. Yet Annie did not say a word. She did not want to jeopardize her one and only opportunity.

* * *

Finally, in February, the letter came from Captain Keller inviting "Miss Sullivan" to come to Alabama. Mr. Anagnos sent his secretary to retrieve Annie from the library so he could deliver the good news.

Sitting in Mr. Anagnos' office Annie suddenly became nervous. The moment she had been waiting for months had come. "I must get an eye surgery before I leave," she told Mr. Anagnos, frantically, "I want to see well before I go there!"

Mr. Anagnos was impatient, "You had all these months to do so!"

"I know but I must. My sight has become worse, especially my right eye, I can't see—"

"Well go to the hospital today and have it done, I do not want you to delay!"

* * *

A week later, with her right eye a little swollen from the operation, Annie was ready.

The little girls from the first grade gave Annie a doll for Helen. Laura quickly sewed a dress for the doll and added a note for Helen: "To my sister in Christ."

Annie further took in her suitcase some small games from the first grade class: sewing-cards, wool, and some beads.

Mrs. Hopkins gave her new shoes, respectable, black, adult-like. They were a little tight but Mrs. Hopkins assured Annie that they would expand. Annie was grateful.

Mr. Anagnos gave Annie the fare for the three-day train ride along with advice, "Be patient, Annie! Be polite! Be cordial. Remember you represent the school."

Annie nodded. She wanted to hear reassuring words, but that was all she heard from the principal who was glad to get rid of her.

She was extremely nervous about the task she had undertaken. Suddenly the mission of teaching a young deaf-blind girl to communicate seemed insurmountable. She envied Lilian who could have the safety of the school and the advice of teachers around her. She was to have none of that.

Mrs. Hopkins prepared a lunch sack for Annie and came with her to the train. "You'll do fine, Annie."

Annie wanted to cry but she did not.

She climbed unto the train and waved goodbye to Mrs. Hopkins and to Boston, which was her home for the past six and a half years. Who knew when she was to return?

As the train left and Mrs. Hopkins disappeared in the distance Annie began to cry. The tears further aggravated her swollen eye. She felt miserable.

> "How forlorn and weary I was! My eye was swollen. The shoes that Mrs. Hopkins gave me were tight and uncomfortable. I remember how the conductor on the train noticed that I cried a great deal and tried to comfort me. He stopped to ask, "Any of your folks dead, young lady?" His voice was so kind, I could not help telling him a little of my trouble, and he did his best to cheer me.
>
> In Washington I missed the connecting train to take me to Alabama. Learning this, my heart was beating fast, I felt dizzy, my mind became blank.... I spent the night in a small hotel. The tiny hotel room felt like a prison cell. I cried a whole lot and

the tears further pained my eye. The pain, along with the anxiety, made my dreams that night a continual nightmare."

TUSCUMBIA, ALABAMA

Helen, in the meantime, sensed that something was about to change:

> "I guessed vaguely from my mother's signs and from the hurrying to and fro in our house that something unusual was about to happen.
>
> Have you ever been at sea in a dense fog, when it seemed as if a tangible white darkness shut you in, and your great ship, tense and anxious, groped her way toward the shore, and you waited with beating heart for something to happen? I was like that ship, without a compass and no way of knowing how near the harbor was.
>
> I did not know what the future held. Anger and bitterness had preyed upon me continually for weeks and a deep languor had followed this passionate struggle. I was waiting for my harbor. For my teacher."

WASHINGTON, D.C.

Annie grew more and more anxious.

> "When I woke up in that prison-like hotel room I tried to look at the time on my watch, but my painful eye barely cooperated. Finally I saw, to my great distress, that my watch had stopped! I tried to put my new black shoes on but my feet were so swollen that the shoes simply did not fit no matter how hard I tried. I put my felt slippers on and quickly left my room to learn of the time. I found out that I had only an hour before the train left the station.
>
> I rushed to my room, yet then I could not find the way back to it, nor could I remember its number. I had to run all the way to the reception for help.
>
> I barely made it to the train at time.
>
> On the way to Alabama my eye became further swollen from all the crying, and the conductor kindly brought me ice and towels to ease the swelling and the pain. By the time the train slowed down before Tuscumbia, the ache in my heart was sharper than the pain in my flaming eye or in my swollen feet.

Gathering my things together, I longed intensely for my friends back in Boston. The school had never seemed home to me until that moment. The thought flashed through my mind: "Here I am more than a thousand miles from any human being I ever saw before!"

I was not yet 21 years old, but the loneliness in my heart was already an old acquaintance. I had been lonely all my life. I told myself that it was only a change of surroundings, that's all.

But somehow I was not sorry that I had come. I felt that the future held something good for me."

TUSCUMBIA, ALABAMA

"The most important day I remember in all my life is the one on which my teacher, Annie Sullivan, came to me. On the afternoon of that eventful day I stood on the porch, dumb, expectant. My heart begged, "Light! Give me light!"—this was the wordless cry of my soul. The light of love shone on me in that very day: the third of March, 1887, three months before I was seven years old. I consider this day to have been my real birthday."

* * *

Earliest known photo of Annie Sullivan, age 15, C. 1881.i

Reg. No. 48457-458   Age 10
Name Annie Sullivan
48458 James   " 6 Agawam
Hip disease –
From Agawam Feb 22 1876
Condition Weak Eyes.
Examined   March 29   1876
48458 Died May 30. 1876
Discharged   187

Removed
By whom
For Nos.

10 b July 1866 Agawam &
always lived there till sent
here. Fa Thomas Sullivan
b. Ire. No est cant tell if Nat
or pd taxes or if in
service in War. Now lives
in Agawam working as a
farmer for Stephen O'Hearn
Mo Alice d about 2 yrs
ago in Agawam. Sister
Mary 3 yrs old with Aunt
Mary Clarey in Agawam
Sore Eyes. James has Hip
Complaint neither ever went
to School.

THE TEACHER

The ledger in the previous page shows Annie and Jimmie's admission to the almshouse, Tewksbury, in 1876. For your convenience, here are its details:

Reg. No. 48457-458 Age 10
Name Annie Sullivan
48458 James " 5, b. Agawam
Hip Disease
From Agawam Feb. 22, 1876
Condition Weak Eyes
Examined March 29, 1876
[note added later: "48458 (James) Died May 30, 1876"]
Discharged...................
Removed.....................
By whom.....................
For Nos.....................

Age 10, born July 1866, Agawam, and always lived there till sent here. Father Thomas Sullivan, born Ireland. No estate, can't tell if naturalized or paid taxes, or in service in [Civil] War. Now lives in Agawam, working as a farmer for Stephen O'Hearn. Mother Alice died about 2 years ago in Agawam. Sister Mary, 3 years old, with Aunt Mary Clarey in Agawam. Sore eyes, and James has hip complaint. Neither ever went to school.i

Exterior view of Tewksbury Almshouse, 1898. This view of the women's wards shows two brick buildings connected by a covered glass walkway. The chimney stack in the background is where the laundry was located.i

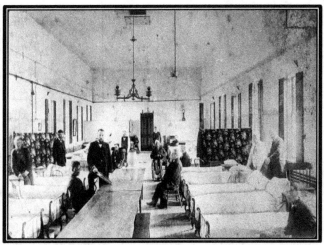

A view of a men's ward at Tewksbury Almshouse, 1898. The rectangular room housed two rows of beds on both sides, and a center aisle with wooden tables.i

View of the main entrance to the Massachusetts School for the Blind (Perkins Institution) in South Boston. c. 1890. Notice the four columns above the entrance.i

A classroom at the the Massachusetts School for the Blind (Perkins Institution) in South Boston. c. 1890. Notice the relatively small group, as well as the piano on the right.

Laura Bridgman, (December 21, 1829 – May 24, 1889). She wore tinted glasses to hide her eyes. Bridgman was known for her ability to sew and knit though she was blind and deaf.

August 26th. 6.

My dear Annie,

Please read the enclosed letters carefully, and let me know at your earliest convenience whether you would be disposed to consider favorably an offer of a position in the family of Mr. Keller as governess of his little deaf-mute and blind daughter.

I have no other information about the standing and responsibility of the man save that contained in his own letters; but, if you decide to be a candidate for the position it is an easy matter to write and ask for further particulars.

I remain, dear Annie, with kind remembrances to Mrs. Hopkins,

Sincerely your friend,
M. Anagnos.

Miss Annie M. Sullivan.
Brewster, Mass.

(See next page)

The letter in the previous page is from Mr. Anagnos, Director of the Massachusetts School for the Blind (Perkins Institution), addressed to Annie Sullivan, offering her the position of governess with the Keller family, August 1886.
For your convenience, here is the full text:

August 26th 1886.

My dear Annie,

Please read the enclosed letters carefully, and let me know at your earliest convenience whether you would be disposed to consider favorably an offer of a position in the family of Captain Keller as governess of his little deaf-mute and blind daughter.

I have no other information about the standing and responsibility of the man save that contained in his own letters: but, if you decide to be a candidate for the position, it is an easy matter to write and ask for further particulars.

I remain, dear Annie, with kind remembrances to Mrs.
Hopkins,
Sincerely your friend,
M. Anagnos.

Miss Annie M. Sullivan. Brewster, Mass.

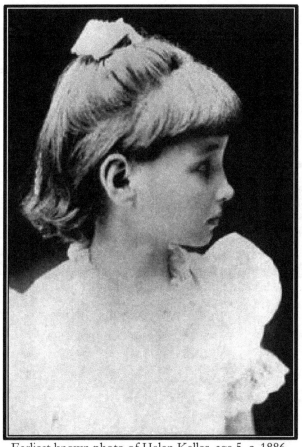

Earliest known photo of Helen Keller, age 5, c. 1886.

Kate Keller and Captain Arthur Keller c. 1887

Helen Keller, age 6, and the family dog, "Belle," c. 1887

Annie Sullivan, age 20, upon graduation, 1886

PART TWO

Based on true documents.

All quotes from letters, diary entries, books and articles are strictly based on the original documents.

"It was evening when I reached Tuscumbia. As I stepped from the train the first person who spoke to me was James Keller, Captain Keller's son, who said Mrs. Keller was in the carriage waiting for me.

I climbed on the carriage. I was surprised to see that Mrs. Keller was a very young-looking woman, only 29 years old. When she spoke, a great weight rolled off my heart as there was such sweetness and refinement in her voice. As we drove to my new home through the little town of Tuscumbia I mused, "This is a good time and a pleasant place to begin my life-work."

We drove through the town, which was more like a village than a town for there were no streets. The main road was lined with blossoming fruit-trees. As we drove I looked at the ploughed fields. There was an earthy smell of spring in the air.

When Mrs. Keller pointed out her house at the end of a long, narrow lane, I became so excited and eager to see my little pupil that I could scarcely sit still. I felt like getting out of the carriage and pushing the horse along faster.

When at last we reached the house, Captain Keller met us in the yard and gave me a hearty handshake. I tried with all my might to control the eagerness that made me tremble so that I could hardly walk. My first question was, "Where is Helen?"

As we approached the porch I saw a child standing in the doorway and Captain Keller said, "There she is. She has known all day that someone was expected, and she has been wild ever since her mother went to the station for you."

I ran up the porch-steps, and there stood Helen by

the porch-door, one hand stretched out, as if she expected someone to come in. Her little face wore an eager expression. She looked healthy—I did not mind the tumbled hair, the soiled pinafore, the untied shoes... all of that, I knew, could be remedied in time—the main thing was that she looked healthy, her body well formed and sturdy, and for this I was most thankful.

Oh, how disappointed I was when the untamed little creature stubbornly refused to kiss me and struggled frantically to free herself from my embrace! Her eager, impetuous fingers felt my face and dress and my bag, which she insisted on opening at once, showing by signs of bringing her hand to her mouth that she expected to find something good to eat in it.

Mrs. Keller tried to make Helen understand by shaking her head and pointing to me that she was not to open the bag; but the child paid no attention to these signs, whereupon her mother forcibly took the bag out from her hands. Helen's face grew red to the roots of her hair, and she began to clutch at her mother's dress and kick violently. I took her hand and put it on my watch and showed her that by pressing the spring she could open it. She was interested instantly, and the tempest was over.

Later, in my small room upstairs, Helen helped me to open my bag, and she was much disappointed to find nothing but toilet articles and clothing. She put her hand to her mouth repeatedly and shook her head with ever greater emphasis as she neared the bottom of the bag.

This was my introduction to that bit of my life."

* * *

Lying in bed, Annie could hear nothing but silence. The house was isolated in the middle of the farm, a long distance from the center of town. Her thoughts were drawn to Agawam, where she spent the first eight years of her life to the time when her father began drinking. She remembered their move, her life with her aunt and uncle, up until her arrival with Jimmie at the almshouse.

There, on the farm in Agawam, there was also a silence such as this. Quiet. Not a sound outside.

At the almshouse, at the school, and at Mrs. Hopkins's home, it was never quiet. This was new for her.

She sat up and got off her bed. The wooden floors under the carpet squeaked as she went to the window. The room in the attic had a slanted ceiling with small storage places under the eaves. The window was crammed between two slanting walls. She looked through it. It was dark outside. After a moment she could make out the yard, the small well house, and the trail leading to the road, next to which the carriage stood.

She felt lonely. So lonely.

She got back into bed, lay under the blanket and quietly cried herself to sleep, afraid to wake anyone with her weeping.

* * *

In the morning, she joined the family downstairs for breakfast. Helen was not sitting on a chair; instead she roamed around the dining hall, picking food from everyone's plates. Annie was puzzled by that, as well as by the fact that no one seemed to care.

Kate smiled at Annie, "How was your sleep?"

Annie nodded, "Very good, thank you." She looked at Helen as she wandered about the room. Helen came and put her hand into Annie's plate, grabbing some scrambled egg and putting it straight into her mouth.

Kate noticed Annie's appalled response, "I'm sorry. I know she shouldn't do it. It's just that she simply won't sit down, you see?"

Annie had a long and harsh reply in her head, but chose to say nothing. She tried to smile at Kate. Captain Keller and 19-year-old James said nothing.

* * *

Later Annie took Helen by the hand and said, "Come Helen, let's begin our first day together!"

Helen pulled her hand back. Annie took again Helen's hand and pointed upstairs, and then at Helen. Helen did not understand but nevertheless decided to follow the strange woman upstairs.

> "Upstairs I gave her the little doll the girls from the school sent her. I thought it was a good opportunity to teach her her first word. I spelled "d-o-l-l" slowly in her hand and pointed to the doll and nodded my head. She looked puzzled and felt my hand, and I repeated the letters, "d-o-l-l."
>
> To my delight Helen imitated each letter very well. Then I took the doll, meaning to give it back to her when she had made the letters all in sequence; but she thought I meant to take the doll away from her, and in an instant she was in a temper and

tried to seize the doll. I shook my head and tried to form the letters with her fingers; but she got more and more angry. I forced her into a chair and held her there until I was nearly exhausted. Then it occurred to me that it was useless to continue the struggle—I knew I must do something to turn the current of her thoughts.

I let her go, but refused to give her the doll. I left her in the room and went downstairs to the kitchen to get some cake. I came back up and held the cake toward Helen's face. She touched it, and then I spelled "c-a-k-e" in her hand, holding the cake toward her. Of course she wanted it and tried to take it; but I spelled the word again and patted her hand. She made the letters rapidly, and I gave her the cake, which she ate in a great hurry, thinking, I suppose, that I might take it away from her.

Then I let her touch the doll again, and spelled the word again, holding the doll toward her as I held the cake. She made the three letters "d-o-l"' and I made the other "l" and gave her the doll. She immediately grabbed it and ran downstairs with it, and could not be induced to return to my room all day."

* * *

At night Annie tossed in bed, turning from side to side. She had finished her first full day and felt it was a *disaster*. She had only managed to teach Helen two words, "doll" and "cake." More importantly, she knew Helen did not respect her. Annie tried to entice her to the room several times but Helen always ran away from her.

Annie stared at the slanted ceiling above her bed. She knew if the situation remained this way, the Kellers might fire her. They had summoned her to help discipline their daughter and to teach her how to communicate, and thus far all she was able to do was to teach her two words and chase her around the yard.

She knew it was only her first day, but her thoughts were drawn to the colossal failure. Helen was rude, uninterested, and rowdy.

Annie's last thoughts before finally falling asleep were of winning Helen over, somehow, somehow....

* * *

The following morning, after breakfast, Annie spoke with Kate, "How do you allow her to eat like *this*, from everyone's plates?"

Kate smiled a sad smile, "Well, I try every now and then to discipline her, you see Miss Annie? But she kicks and hollers and it becomes a very unpleasant scene, you understand? And Arthur cannot tolerate that, so... you see?"

Annie nodded, though she strongly disagreed. She took Helen by the hand, tapping with her hand on Helen's chest, as if to signal that she had something for her. Helen followed her. Annie passed through the kitchen and took some cake with her upstairs.

> "I gave Helen one of the sewing-cards I brought, and completed in front of her the first row myself, with her touching my hands as I sew. I let her feel the card and notice that there were several rows of little holes. She nodded eagerly and began to work delightedly.
>
> In a few minutes she finished the whole sewing-card and did it very neatly indeed! I thought I would try another word; so I spelled "c-a-r-d," and

opened my palm for her to spell it back to me.

She made the "c-a," then stopped and thought for a short moment. She then made the sign for eating. At first I was upset, but then I realized that the two letters "c-a," must have reminded her of our lesson of the day before, "c-a-k-e."

I realized she did not have any idea that "cake" was the *name* of the thing, but it was simply a matter of association, I suppose.

Understanding that, I spelled back "c-a-k-e" and gave her a small slice of cake. She took it in her hand and was pleased of herself.

I then thought of repeating the other word I had taught her. I spelled "d-o-l-l" and began to hunt for it. She followed me with her hands, touching me as I moved about the carpet looking for the doll. She laughed and pointed downstairs, meaning that the doll was downstairs. I then opened the door and pointed downstairs like she did, conveying to her that she should bring me the doll, and spelled it again into her hand, "d-o-l-l."

She started toward the stairs, then hesitated a moment, evidently debating within herself whether she would go. She decided to send me instead. I shook my head and spelled "d-o-l-l" more emphatically, and opened the door for her; but she obstinately refused to obey.

I was at a loss as to what to do. I knew obedience was important for her to learn. Then I noticed she still had a piece of cake in her hand, and so I took it away from her quickly, indicating that if she brought the doll I would give her back the cake. She stood perfectly still for one long moment, her face red; then her desire for the cake triumphed, and she ran downstairs and quickly brought the doll. I immediately rewarded her with the cake. However, I could not persuade her to enter the room again."

* * *

The second day was over. At night Annie once again could not fall asleep. The silence tortured her. Not a road could be heard anywhere, not a horse car, no laughter, not even the tossing of someone in bed. Silence.

Was she heading in the right direction?

Years later she wrote:

> "Oh those first nights—what moods, what doubt, what hopes and hidden fears, what nights of despair and gathering storms of failure."

* * *

The next morning at breakfast Helen was unbearable. Twice she put her hand into Annie's plate. Annie slapped her hand each time. Captain Keller did not condone that. After the first time Annie slapped Helen's hand he coughed politely. After the second time he glared at Annie and said, "Miss Sullivan, I do not presume you wish to starve our little Helen?"

Annie glared back at him, "Captain Keller! I insist on Helen learning the most rudimentary table manners."

At that moment Helen completed a circle around the table and arrived again at Annie's plate and snatched some bread straight from the plate. Annie grabbed Helen's hand forcefully, forcing the bread out of her hand and pushing her toward her own plate, in front of the vacant seat on which Helen was not willing to sit.

Captain Keller coughed, "Miss Sullivan!"

Kate looked at her husband and murmured, "Arthur!"

Captain Keller sighed, "Miss Sullivan. Today is *Sunday*, please allow my daughter to have food from whichever plate she wants." He looked at James eating quietly. He then looked again at Annie, who said nothing, but did not look back at him. "Miss Sullivan, why won't you take the day off today? You are entitled to a day of rest—"

"Captain Keller, I do not need a day of—"

"Well I insist and therefore it shall be."

Kate tried to ease the verdict, "You've been working so hard, Miss Annie. You do deserve a rest!"

* * *

Later, upstairs, Annie was furious. She walked around the room as if in a cage. She knew it could not work this way! Someone had to *teach* and *discipline* the little child!

She thought of Mrs. Hopkins and decided to write to her. She wanted to do so in the previous two and a half days since her arrival, but now—with her "day off"—she could not avoid it any longer. She took out her notebook, placed the ink bottle on the desk, dipped her pen and began writing.

"To: Mrs. Hopkins

Massachusetts School for the Blind

South Boston, Massachusetts

Sunday, March 6th, 1887.

Dear Mrs. Hopkins,

I've been meaning to write to you earlier, but quite frankly, I have been exhausted. I arrived in Tuscumbia three days ago, on Thursday, at 6:30 P.M. Mr. James Keller was waiting for me. He rebuked me for missing the train in Washington, and said somebody had met every train arriving in Tuscumbia for the past two days. I apologized. Mrs. Keller was very kind. The drive from the station to the house, a distance of one mile, was lovely and restful.

When I saw Helen for the first time I was surprised to see that she was a healthy child. Somehow I had expected to see a pale, delicate child—I suppose I got the idea from Dr. Howe's description of Laura Bridgman when he first met her. But there's nothing pale or delicate about Helen! She is large, strong, and ruddy, and as unrestrained in her movements as a young colt! Her body is well formed and vigorous, and Mrs. Keller says she has not been ill a day since the illness that deprived her of her sight and hearing. She has a fine head, and it is set on her shoulders just right."

Annie paused, thinking of how to describe Helen further. There was something about the child that she could not put into words exactly. She thought for a moment and then wrote:

"Her face... it is hard to describe it. It is intelligent, but lacks mobility, or soul, or something. Her mouth is large and finely shaped. You see at a glance that she is blind. One eye is larger than the other, and protrudes noticeably. She rarely smiles, indeed, I have seen her smile only once or twice since I came. She is unresponsive and even impatient of caresses from anyone except her mother. She is very quick-tempered and willful, and nobody has attempted to control her.

The greatest problem I shall have to solve is how to discipline and control her *without breaking her spirit*. I shall go rather slowly at first and try to win her love. I shall not attempt to conquer her by force *alone*; but I shall insist on reasonable obedience from the start!

One thing that impresses everybody is Helen's tireless activity. She is never still a moment. She is here, there, and everywhere. Her hands are in everything; but nothing holds her attention for long.

Dear child, her restless spirit gropes in the dark! Her untaught, unsatisfied hands destroy whatever they touch because they do not know what else to do with things!"

As she was writing these lines she heard steps coming up the stairs. Helen opened her door and searched for her.

Annie muttered, "Go away, your *father* does not allow me to work today!"

Helen felt Annie's face and hands, trying to determine what Annie was doing.

"No!" Annie reprimanded her as she smeared some of the fresh words on the page. She pushed Helen away, "Go away! I'm writing!"

But Helen deliberately came back and felt Annie's hand. This time she found the ink bottle and put her fingers into it, smearing the ink on the table and on the letter. "Helen!" Annie shouted and grabbed Helen's hands. "It's Sunday!" Annie cried.

Helen wrestled with her, trying to free her hands from the tight grip.

"Alright, alright," Annie mumbled and left the table. She opened the drawer next to her bed where she had stored the beads she brought with her. She took out the small bag and opened it on the carpet.

Helen came to the carpet and touched the beads eagerly, noticing the two kinds: the large wooden beads and the small glass ones. She put them in her mouth.

Annie looked at her with pity and sighed. She took a string, tied one end of it, and strung two wooden beads and one glass bead. She repeated this pattern. Helen touched the string, feeling the beads, and then wanted to take it from Annie.

"You want it? Here, it's yours." Annie gave it to her, and held Helen's hand, showing her how she put the beads into the string.

* * *

For the rest of the morning Helen played happily with the beads. Annie tried to rest and read one of the books she found in the library downstairs, but her eyes hurt.

In the evening, Annie finally returned to the letter to Mrs. Hopkins and completed it.

> "Forgive me for the smeared handwriting. This morning Helen came to my room as I was writing to you, and she was very troublesome noticing what I was doing. She kept coming up behind me and putting her hand on the paper and into the ink

bottle. These blots are her handiwork... Finally I remembered the beads I had brought with me, and set her to work stringing them.

First I put on two wooden beads and one glass bead, then made her feel the string and the two boxes of beads. She nodded and began at once to fill the string with wooden beads. I shook my head and took them all off and made her feel the pattern of two wooden beads and the one glass bead which followed. She examined them thoughtfully and began again. This time she put on the glass bead first and the two wooden ones next. I took them off and showed her that the two wooden ones must go on first, then the glass bead. Then she understood. She had no further trouble and filled the string quickly, too quickly, in fact.

She tied the ends together when she had finished the string, and put the beads round her neck, delighted. I then gave her another string and she set to work. However, I had not made the knot large enough in this new string, and when she put it around her neck the beads came off as fast as she put them on; but she solved the difficulty herself by putting the string *through* a bead and then tying it herself around the bead. I thought this was very clever!

She amused herself with the beads until lunch, bringing the strings to me now and then for my approval. Later, in the afternoon, she played in the yard with the children of the servants.

Oh dear, my eyes are very much inflamed. I know this letter is very carelessly written. I had a lot to say, and couldn't stop to think how to express things neatly. Please, Mrs. Hopkins, do not show my letter to anyone.

Yours,

Annie."

Annie laid the pen down and folded the letter. Tomorrow she would take it with Helen to the post office on Main Street. Helen would most likely enjoy the trip.

She lied in bed, feeling, yet again, unaccomplished. At least Captain Keller couldn't force her to hide in her room and pretend she was not tutoring Helen.

She took a deep breath. She thought of Helen. There was something bright in that girl. But as long as Helen did not obey her, and wandered wherever she wanted, Annie could not teach her.

She lay awake, her eyes hurting from the taxing task of writing.

She wanted so badly to succeed.

* * *

The following morning Helen was even rowdier around the kitchen table. Annie refused to allow her to eat from her plate. Captain Keller said, "Miss Sullivan, please!"

"No, Captain Keller!" Annie retorted.

Silence followed. James looked at his father. Arthur's face reddened. Annie continued, "You brought me here, expecting me to *teach* your daughter, but how do you suppose I teach her when she cannot obey even the most *rudimentary* rules?"

Arthur's eyes widened, and he turned from Annie to look straight at his wife.

Kate tried to take his side, "Miss Annie, you have only arrived a few days ago, we do not expect—"

"I must know that I have the freedom to discipline her," Annie said, her voice rising. "Otherwise I cannot see what good can I bring here!"

Helen came back to Annie's plate, and Annie slapped her hand again. Helen retorted, pinching Annie, and proceeded to take the scrambled egg from Annie's plate. Annie again pushed her hand.

Helen fell unto the floor and began kicking. Captain Keller stood up at once, "Would you please let the child eat?"

Annie stood up as well, "I'm afraid, Captain Keller, that you did not desire a *teacher* for your daughter, but an *entertainer*, and that role I am not willing to play!"

Kate, sensing an explosion coming, cried, "Miss Annie, what do you want?"

Annie looked at her, "I want you to leave me alone with Helen and allow me to teach her the most basic table manners—alone—without any interference!"

A long silence followed. Captain Keller was speechless. James watched him with amazement. No one ever dared speaking this way to his father. James tried to discipline Helen before, but his father always forbade him from bothering "the poor child."

Kate looked at Arthur, "Well, Miss Annie, if that is what you want, we shall accommodate you." She stood and placed the napkin on her plate, "I am already full."

James looked at his father. Annie did too. Helen kept kicking on the floor and bellowing a most unbearable cry.

Arthur straightened his jacket, glared at Annie and left the room without saying anything. James followed suit.

Annie was left with the screaming and kicking six-year-old on the floor. She hurried and locked the door to the dining room and said, "Now, Helen, you can kick and scream as much as you'd like. It does not impress me!"

Outside, Kate waited in the sitting room, hearing Helen's horrible cries. Arthur hurried to leave the house and go to town, leaving James to oversee the servants working in the fields.

Kate sat in the sitting room and cried.

* * *

Two hours later, noticing that Annie and Helen did not exit the dining room, Martha walked quietly into the sitting room. "Kate, are you sure that this young Northerner knows what she is doing?"

Kate gulped and buried her face in her hand, "I don't know...."

* * *

"To Mrs. Hopkins

Massachusetts School for the Blind

South Boston, Massachusetts

Monday, March 7th, 1887.

THE TEACHER

Dear Mrs. Hopkins,

I am exhausted, but I nevertheless must write to you. I had a *battle royal* with Helen this morning. Although I try very hard not to force issues, I find it very difficult to avoid them.

Helen's table manners are appalling. She puts her hands in our plates and helps herself, and when the dishes are passed, she grabs them and takes out whatever she wants. This morning I would not let her put her hand in my plate. She persisted, and a contest of wills followed.

Naturally the family was much disturbed, and left the room. I locked the dining-room door and proceeded to eat my breakfast, though the food almost choked me. Helen was lying on the floor, kicking and screaming and trying to pull my chair from under me. She kept this up for half an hour, then she got up to see what I was doing. I let her see that I was eating, but did not let her put her hand in the plate. She pinched me, and I slapped her every time she did.

Then she went all round the table to see who was there, and finding no one but me, she seemed bewildered. After a few minutes she came back to her place and began to eat her breakfast with her fingers.

I gave her a spoon, which she threw on the floor. I forced her out of the chair and made her pick it up. Finally I succeeded in getting her back in her chair again, and held the spoon in her hand, compelling her to take up the food with it and put it in her mouth. In a few minutes she yielded and finished her breakfast peaceably.

Then we had another tussle over folding her

napkin. When she had finished, she threw it on the floor and ran toward the door. Finding it locked, she began to kick and scream all over again. It was another hour before I succeeded in getting her napkin folded.

Only then did I let her out the room and she ran to the warm sunshine. I went up to my room and threw myself on the bed, exhausted. I had a good cry and felt better. I suppose I shall have many such battles with the little woman before she learns the only two essential things I can teach her: obedience and love.

Good-bye, my dear Mrs. Hopkins.

Yours,

Annie.

After finishing writing the letter, Annie read it over. The dim light from the small gas lamp barely illuminated the letters. After having read it, she realized the letter might make Mrs. Hopkins worried. She added below,

> "P.S.
> Do not worry. I'll do my best and leave the rest to—"

She wanted to write "God," but could not bring herself to write that. She wrote instead:

> "I'll do my best and leave the rest to whatever power manages that which we cannot."

She signed again and folded the letter.

That night she fell asleep easily.

* * *

The following morning Annie got up determined. It was her sixth day in Tuscumbia. She sat at the breakfast table, tense and anxious.

Captain Keller seemed to watch her carefully, as if waiting for her to tussle with Helen. But Annie did not. She placed Helen's plate next to hers.

Helen did not want to sit at the table, and got up nervously, waiting to be reprimanded. Annie, however, did not stop her.

Soon Helen was roaming about the room taking from everyone's plates. When she reached Annie's plate Annie did not make a fuss about it, and took Helen's hand and directed her off to the right, where a plate filled with food awaited her. Helen took the food from the other plate, brought it to her mouth gleefully, and then continued roaming about the room.

Kate smiled pleasantly at Arthur, nodding reassuringly. He nodded back, though more hesitantly.

Annie smiled to herself. Obviously the scene yesterday morning has been on everyone's mind. James watched her carefully as well.

After breakfast Annie took some cake from the kitchen. Seeing Kate she said, "Mrs. Keller, could you and I have a walk together sometime today?"

Kate looked puzzled, "Sure. And please, call me Kate. You are now a part of the family and I do not want any formality between us."

Annie smiled, nodded, and took the cake upstairs. On the way she found Helen, who was playing with the family's dog, Belle. Helen was patting the dog on her head rather aggressively. The dog seemed relieved when Annie convinced Helen to follow her and the cake upstairs.

* * *

The morning together was difficult. Annie was restless and could not concentrate. She gave Helen both the beads and the sewing cards to play with, but her mind was focused on the conversation she was going to have with Mrs. Keller. She realized something *had* to be done. She knew she must convince Kate of her new plan.

In the late afternoon, Kate came to Annie's room and was pleased to see Helen playing quietly. "How lovely, Miss Annie, look at her playing like that, so quietly!"

Annie looked at the mess on the floor, at Helen's stubborn face, at the messy hair that Helen would not allow her to comb, and then at Kate. She smiled at the mother politely.

"Well," Kate said, "I think now may be a good time, Helen can play with the children outside and you and I can take a 'walk' as you offered?"

Annie stood up at once, "Splendid, Mrs. Keller—I mean, Kate, I am ready!"

* * *

Seeing Helen playing with the servant's children, Kate let out a long sigh. She and Annie began walking on the trail that led away from the house toward the main road. Annie walked much faster than Kate, but tried to match her pace to her employer's.

In the beginning they said nothing. Annie looked at the large fir trees. Kate smiled and tried to initiate a conversation, "I can't remember the last time I've taken a leisurely walk like this!"

Annie nodded, "It must be hard with the house and the three children."

Kate smiled, "The one child, mostly."

Annie nodded. They kept walking.

Then Kate turned around, "I'd like for us to remain close to the house, if that is fine by you."

"Oh certainly," Annie answered.

"Tell me, Miss Annie, how do you find it here? How have you settled?"

"Oh I find it very nice here, Mrs.—Kate, I find it different than the North, but you have been *very* kind to me, and so is Captain Keller and the rest of the household. I am glad I'm here."

"You are?"

"Of course!"

Kate took a deep breath in, "I'm certainly glad to hear that."

They walked quietly. The gay sounds of the children grew louder as they neared the house. Kate directed them this time passed the house and to a trail leading to the fields. Annie looked around with interest.

Kate, a little anxious, looked at Annie, "Was there anything specific you wished to talk to me about?"

Annie nodded, "Yes, indeed. Kate. I must tell you that I respect your family very much."

Kate's face frowned. She braced herself for bad news. She was right—Annie must want to leave.

Annie did not notice Kate's reaction so she

continued, "And I do think that everyone has Helen's best interests in mind. But I find it difficult to work with Helen in the current surrounding."

Kate remained silent.

They kept walking.

Annie continued, "Unfortunately I feel like I can do nothing with Helen in the midst of the family. I am trying to change her old ways, but being surrounded by her old ways, my control over her is limited."

"Well," Kate said, "I guess we can give you more free reign if that is what you are asking for."

Annie shook her head, "I am thinking that the success of my task will depend on granting Helen and I a greater level of privacy."

Kate looked at Annie, "What do you mean? Is your room not private enough?"

"It is, but… it also isn't. You see, I must make Helen become more obedient before I proceed teaching her further. And for her, knowing that at any moment she can run downstairs and grab onto you, like she did yesterday and the day before—"

"Well that's only natural—"

"Or for Helen knowing that Captain Keller can come in and tell me to let her have whatever she's wanting—"

"Well I can speak to Arthur—"

"Kate," Annie said and stopped walking, "what I am asking is an opportunity to *succeed* at this task. I have *prepared* myself to teach Helen. Yet I cannot do it in the house."

Kate looked alarmed, "What are you proposing?"

Annie hesitated, "What I propose is that for a limited time—a month, say—I will be given a private place, where I can be with Helen alone."

"Alone?!"

"So that she can learn to depend on me!"

Kate began walking, "Let's return, I don't want to be out of reach if anything...."

Annie nodded.

Kate took a deep breath in.

Annie continued, "Kate, I have the interest of Helen in mind! She deserves the *best* that I can give her! And presently she receives but a *fraction* of what I can offer!"

"But you wish to take her away!"

"I—I'm not sure where to, perhaps somewhere here around the farm, where you can visit—"

Kate frowned, "Like the garden house?"

"The garden house?"

Kate pointed at the small cottage at the end of the row of trees, a quarter of a mile away. Annie could not see it.

Kate looked toward the main house, hesitant, hearing the sound of the children. "Here," she said, "let me take you there quickly, not that I think... not that I can...."

Kate led the two of them down the trail and into a small house that stood a quarter of a mile from the main house. They passed by several wooden huts, and Kate explained, "These are the servant's quarters."

Finally, they arrived at the small cottage. Annie followed Kate onto the porch and peered in through the dusty window. She saw a large room, a fireplace, a table, a small bed. "Oh dear! This is lovely, Kate!"

Kate shook her head, "I do not think it is a good idea," she said and walked off the porch toward the house. Annie took a last peek into the house and hurried to follow Kate on the trail. "This can do, Mrs. Keller!"

Kate said nothing. Her mind was cloudy. "I don't want Helen to be separated from me!"

Annie understood Kate's motherly instincts. "You can come and visit daily," she said, "as long as she does not *know* you are there. You can look through the window!"

"'As long as she does not *know* I'm there?!' Miss Annie! She'd be miserable!"

"She'd be given an *opportunity*, Kate. She'd have a *real chance* at beginning anew!" Annie stopped in her tracks. "You brought me here, a thousand miles, to do something. Why did you call me?"

Kate frowned, "Well, for you to help with Helen of course!"

"What do you mean by 'help?'"

"You know what I mean...."

"No, I do not. I want to hear it from you."

"Well to help with... her behavior...."

"What is wrong with her behavior?"

"Miss Annie! Don't torture me!"

Annie said nothing. They walked toward the house. Kate said, "Well, to help with Helen's moods and her tempers."

Annie nodded, "I can do all that, Kate, and I can do *more* than that. I can teach her to communicate! I don't know how long it shall take, perhaps a whole year, but you should eventually be able to converse with her!"

Kate brushed that thought and shook her head.

Annie persisted, "Kate, you could speak to her. Helen is an intelligent child!"

"Annie, you are being very kind but there is no need to—"

"I'm serious! She is very bright! Two days ago I gave her some beads—she showed you the necklace, right?"

Kate nodded.

Annie continued, "She tied the knot herself, wrapping it around the last bead. It was *very clever*! You have a bright child, Kate! She has created her own language of sorts: when she wants you she caresses her cheek, like you do, signaling that she wants you. When she wants food she points to her mouth. She even has a sign for wanting bread, imitating Martha slicing a piece of bread! That is *brilliant*! She is very bright I tell you!"

Kate's face twisted with pain, "Oh stop saying that!"

Annie was puzzled, "Why shall I stop stating the truth?!"

"Because you'll be disappointed that's why!"

They walked silently. Kate sighed, "Miss Annie, you are young and optimistic, but I have lived with her for the past five years since the illness. I had high hopes and the more I hoped, the more—"

Kate's voice broke. Tears emerged in her eyes, "Listen, I want to help you, but please do not fool me or yourself."

Annie wanted to reassure her employer. But she saw that she couldn't.

As they approached the house Kate said, "I'll talk to Arthur about it."

Annie grabbed Kate's hands, "You will? That could be marvelous!"

Kate smiled, "I will."

Annie hesitated. She had a feeling that Captain Keller would not accept the idea. She stopped walking. Kate stopped as well, exhausted from Annie's recurring halts.

"Kate," Annie whispered, "please do not propose the garden house to Captain Keller."

"No? Where else do you—"

"No, let *him* come up with the idea. Tell him that I asked for a private place, and that you fear of not being able to see Helen if you were to find such a house in town for me and her."

Kate measured up the young teacher. She nodded hesitantly.

* * *

The following morning everyone was eating breakfast when Arthur said, "Miss Sullivan, I understand that you are interested in a more secluded dwelling to work with our Helen. Is that correct?"

Annie nodded, "Yes, Captain."

Helen came to her father's plate and grabbed a piece of bread. She was very energetic this morning, going around the table much faster than previously. This drove

Annie mad, but she said nothing.

"Well," Captain Keller said, "I've been thinking about it, and I'm willing to entertain such a plan for a limited time. As long as it is done in our garden house, which is down the trail not too far from the house. You can get the meals from the house."

Annie's eyes shone, "Captain! That would be wonderful!"

Arthur looked at Kate and nodded. She smiled back at him appreciatively.

Annie sat up, the knuckles of her fingers tightening around her fork, "When can we move?"

Arthur said, "Well, we need to clean and arrange it for you. I'll have the young servant, Percy, do it. I suppose you could move there in a few days."

"If I help clean it, Captain, can we move there today?"

Arthur nearly choked on his food.

* * *

In the afternoon, when Captain Keller returned from work, Annie announced to him, "Captain! All is ready. You can come to the garden house and see!"

Captain Keller groaned something undecipherable and followed Annie.

They walked together to the garden house quietly. Annie walked onto the porch. Arthur walked inside, saw the cleanliness and the new arrangement of furniture. He was astonished by the speed. The place was spotless and neat. He opened the closet and saw Helen's clothes folded neatly.

He closed the closet and looked at her, "You sure know how to get something when you want it, Miss Sullivan."

Annie grinned.

Arthur looked around, "Helen might recognize this place, as she has been around here. I'm afraid she'd want to come back home immediately."

"But if we take her on a long journey and only then bring her here, say, after an hour ride, she might think it a different place."

Arthur sighed. "Well, we can do that tomorrow."

Annie tried smiling, "I was hoping for her and I to have dinner here."

Arthur shook his head and mumbled, "You don't give up do you?"

"When it comes to the education of your daughter, Captain, I do not."

* * *

They packed Helen a little suitcase with her dolls, and Kate and Arthur took her on a carriage ride, going around the estate in circles. Finally they stopped near the garden house.

After hugging Helen goodbye, Kate looked at Annie, frowning with fear and worry.

Annie murmured, "Do not worry. I will treat her as my own."

Captain Keller looked at Percy, a servant's son, and said, "You rush back if you need me, you hear me?"

"Yes Sir!"

Kate gave yet another hug to bewildered Helen, and followed Arthur back to the carriage. Annie locked the door behind them.

It was only after the carriage left that Helen began to realize her parents weren't there. Annie tried to hug her but Helen pushed her away violently and began banging at the door. She fell on the floor, kicked and screamed. Percy came from the adjacent room and looked at Helen, banging on the floor. He then looked at Annie, seated on the edge of the bed. "Miss, aren't you going to do anything?"

Annie's eyes were moist, "This is the best thing I can do for her, Percy."

Percy looked at Annie strangely and left to the adjacent room. Soon after Annie called him, "I think it's time to bring us dinner if you please, Mr. Percy."

He nodded and hurried to the main house.

* * *

The following day, exhausted from the previous night's tussle, Annie wrote to Mrs. Hopkins. Helen was playing with the beads on the floor, and every few minutes or so going to the door, as if to see whether her parents were coming. This little gesture broke Annie's heart. She tried caressing Helen, but Helen would push her away each time.

"To: Mrs. Hopkins

Thursday, March 10th, 1887.

Dear Mrs. Hopkins,

It's been seven days yesterday since I arrived. So much had happened. Yesterday Helen and I have gone to live all by ourselves in a little gardenhouse about a quarter of a mile from the Keller homestead. The idea came to me early on: very soon after arriving here I made up my mind that I could do nothing with Helen in the midst of the family, who have always allowed her to do exactly as she pleased. Helen has tyrannized over everybody, her mother, her father, the servants, the little servants' children who play with her, and nobody had ever seriously disputed her will until I came. Like all tyrants she holds tenaciously to her divine right to do as she pleases. If she ever failed to get what she wanted it was not because they wouldn't give it to her, but because of her inability to communicate to her row of slaves what it was that she wanted.

Every thwarted desire has been for Helen the signal for a passionate outburst, and I understand that as she grew older and stronger these tempests became more violent.

As I began to teach her a week ago I was beset by many difficulties. She wouldn't yield a point without contesting it to the bitter end. I couldn't coax her or compromise with her. To get her to do the simplest thing, such as combing her hair or washing her hands or buttoning her boots, it was necessary to use force and, of course, a distressing scene followed.

The family naturally felt inclined to interfere, especially her father, who cannot bear to see her cry. They were all willing to give in for the sake of "peace." Besides, her past experiences and associations were all against me. I saw clearly that it was useless to try to teach her language or anything else until she learned to obey me."

Annie looked at Helen and sighed. She hoped to win her over by love. She hoped, back in the months she was in school, waiting for the letter to invite her to Alabama, that she could simply win the child over with caresses, softness, and affection.

She shook her head and went on to write:

"I had an idea that I could win the love and confidence of my little pupil by the same means that I should use if she could see and hear. But I soon found that I was cut off from all the usual approaches to the child's heart. She accepted everything I did for her as *obvious* and not at all noteworthy, and she refused to be caressed by me. There was no way of appealing to her affection or sympathy or childish love of approbation. It was only her way: she either would or she wouldn't, and that was the end of it.

Isn't life funny Mrs. Hopkins? We study, plan and prepare ourselves for a task, and when the hour for action arrives, we find that the system we have followed with such labor and pride does not fit the occasion; and then there's nothing for us to do but rely on something within us, some innate capacity for knowing and doing, which we did not know we possessed until the hour of our great need brought it to light."

Helen again got up and walked to the door. Annie felt so bad for her little pupil. She took a deep breath and continued writing.

"I have thought about it a great deal, and the more

I think the more certain I am that obedience is the gateway through which knowledge, yes, and love, too, enter the mind of the child. I had a good, frank talk with Mrs. Keller, and explained to her how difficult it was going to be to do anything with Helen under the existing circumstances. I told her that in my opinion the child ought to be separated from the family for a few weeks at least—that she must learn to depend on and obey me before I could make any headway. After a long time Mrs. Keller said that she would think the matter over and see what Captain Keller thought of sending Helen away with me.

Captain Keller fell in with the scheme most readily and suggested that the little garden-house be got ready for us. He said that Helen might recognize the place, as she had often been here; but she would have no idea of her surroundings, and they could come every day to see that all was going well, with the understanding, of course, that she was to know nothing of their visits. I hurried the preparations for our departure as much as possible, and here we are."

Helen returned to play with the beads. Annie looked at her, and then at the bed and table, the large fireplace which she cleaned yesterday. She was pleased with her little victory. Here she knew she could do something with Helen. She returned to the letter and wrote:

"The little house is a genuine bit of paradise. It consists of one large square room with a great fireplace, a spacious bay-window, and a small room where our servant, a 13-year-old boy called Percy, sleeps. There is a porch in front, covered with vines that grow so luxuriantly that you have to part them to see the garden beyond. Our meals are brought from the house by the boy, who also takes care of the fire when we need one; this way I can give my whole attention to Helen."

Annie glanced at Helen, on the floor, and wrote:

"Little Helen was greatly distressed at first yesterday evening, and kicked and screamed herself into a sort of stupor; but when dinner was brought she ate heartily and seemed brighter, although she refused to let me touch her.

She devoted herself to the dolls we had brought with us, and when it was bedtime she undressed very quietly; but when she felt me get into the bed with her she jumped out on the other side, and nothing that I could do would induce her to get in again. But I was afraid she would get a cold, and I insisted that she must go to bed. We had a terrific tussle, I can tell you... The struggle lasted for nearly two hours. I never saw such strength and endurance in a child. But fortunately for us both, I am a little stronger, and quite as obstinate when I set out. I finally succeeded in getting her on the bed and covered her up, and she lay curled up as near the edge of the bed as possible.

This morning she was very docile. Her father came and peeked through the window. Luckily she was playing with the beads. He nodded at me and went on to his office.

She is, though, evidently very homesick. She keeps going to the door, as if she expects someone, and every now and then she would touch her cheek, which is her sign for her mother, and shake her head sadly."

Annie looked at her little pupil. It was time for a lesson. She should teach her a new word. Perhaps the word "key," because she was often looking for the key to the door. Perhaps "mug," because Helen enjoyed drinking milk. Or the word "hat," as Helen needed not to forget going outside with her hat....

Annie sighed. She felt, like Helen, that she too was groping in the dark.

* * *

"To: Mrs. Hopkins,

Friday, March 11th, 1887

Dear Mrs. Hopkins,

It is our third day today in our little piece of heaven. Helen played with her dolls more than usual this morning and would, still, have nothing to do with me.

As to the dolls, it is amusing and pathetic to see Helen playing with them. I don't think she has any special tenderness for them—I have never seen her for example caressing them; but she dresses and undresses them many times during the day and handles them exactly as she had realized her mother and the nurse handle her baby sister.

This morning her favorite doll, Nancy, seemed to have some difficulty about swallowing the milk that was being administered to her in large spoonfuls; for Helen suddenly put down the cup and began to slap the doll on the back and turn her over on her knees, trotting her gently and patting her all the time. This lasted for several minutes. Alas, then this mood passed and Nancy was thrown ruthlessly on the floor while another doll received Helen's undivided attention.

We did manage to have a short language lesson. She knows a few words by now, but has no idea how to use them, or does she understand that everything has a name. I think, however, she will learn quickly enough by and by. As I have said before, she is wonderfully bright and active and as quick as lightning in her movements.

I hope I won't disappoint you, Mrs. Hopkins.

Yours,

Annie."

* * *

"Sunday, March 13th, 1887.

Dear Mrs. Hopkins,

I was so happy to receive your letter of encouragement! How glad I am to have you as my friend. Thank you for your warm words. I was glad to read of your preparation for the spring. All the girls in the house must be so excited.

You will be glad to hear that my experiment is working out finely! I have not had any trouble at all with Helen either yesterday or today. She has learned three new words, and when I give her the objects, the names of which she has learned, she spells them unhesitatingly. But alas, she seems glad when the lesson is over.

We had a good frolic this morning out in the garden. Helen evidently knew where she was as soon as she touched the boxwood hedges and made many signs which I did not understand. No doubt they were signs for the different members of the family.

Her mother came to see her this morning through the window, and was pleased to see Helen was playing quietly. It was heartbreaking for me to beg Mrs. Keller not to come inside. I had asked her, through Percy, to bring me some wool, and she brought us several wool chains. But she expressed her doubt about Helen being able to knit.

I began teaching Helen crocheting and stitching this afternoon. Hopefully she shall prove all the doubters wrong.

You were right, in your letter. I shall write to Mr. Anagnos this evening.

I think of you often and I miss you terribly.

Yours,

Annie."

* * *

"To: Mr. Anagnos

Massachusetts School for the Blind,

South Boston, Massachusetts,

March 13th, 1887

Dear Mr. Anagnos,

It is now ten days since I first saw Tuscumbia, and it seems much longer. I like it here very much and think I shall like better when I am better acquainted. I find Captain and Mrs. Keller very kind people. Helen, my little pupil, is all that her father described her. It is really wonderful the knowledge the little thing has acquired by the sense of touch and I may add the sense of smell for that sense is very acute. I have not been able yet to tell about her taste.

She is remarkably well developed physically. She has an erect frame and a clear rosy complexion. She has never been sick since the terrible sickness which left her as she is.

Helen loves dearly to play in the open air and laughs and frolics with the little servants' children as if she had all her sense. I find considerable trouble in controlling her. She has always done just as her fancy inclined and it is next to impossible to make her obey. However, I think I shall succeed sometime. She can spell *doll*, *cake*, *hat* and *mug* but does not understand the purpose in making the words yet.

I remember you being sick when I left. I hope. Mr. Anagnos, that you are quite well now, but if you are not, the very best thing you can do will be to take a trip South and I am sure one look at nature in all her spring loveliness will restore you. It is perfectly lovely here. All the wildflowers are in bloom and the trees are beginning to leaf and everything looks new and beautiful.

Very respectfully yours,

Annie Sullivan."

* * *

Annie heard a knock at the door. She looked through the window and saw Captain Keller. She walked to the door, thinking of all the progress Helen had made. It had been eleven days since their arrival at the garden house, and she was particularly pleased with Helen today.

Annie exited and closed the door behind her, noticing that Captain Keller had brought the dog, Belle, with him. "Yes, Captain?" she said with the most cordial voice she could muster.

Captain Keller said, "I was thinking that Belle could be company for Helen."

"Captain, I don't think that she needs company, look at her," she pointed at Helen, contently playing with her doll, washing her inside a wash bowl. "Helen is perfectly content."

Captain Keller forced a smile and said, "Nevertheless, I'd like her to have Belle."

"If that is your wish," Annie said and opened the door, allowing the dog inside. She herself remained outside, waiting politely to see if the Captain had anything else to say. The two of them watched through the window as Belle made her way into the room and sat down near the window.

"Interesting," Captain Keller said, "usually Helen knows when Belle is around, she feels the steps…"

"She's preoccupied with the doll. In a moment she'd notice," Annie said all knowingly.

Captain Keller looked worried, "I understood from Percy that Helen is not eating much."

"Helen is eating *fine*," Annie said quickly, "she eats

less than before, perhaps. But in the past, Captain, her eating was more ravenous, now she eats when she *wants*, not out of *impulse*, you see?"

Annie saw the worried look on Captain Keller's face. "I'd like for her to eat!"

"Of course, Captain, but I cannot force food down her throat, can I?"

They looked at Helen, who at that moment lifted her face and looked upwards and then to the sides. She sniffed and began walking toward the smell. She stumbled upon Belle and put her arms around the dog's neck, grinning happily. Then she sat down by Belle and took the dog's claws. She began spelling to the dog on her paws.

Annie burst into laughter. Captain Keller looked at her, dismayed, "Clearly she does not understand your weird hand gestures, not if she thinks that the dog can understand her!"

Annie smiled, "You'll see, Captain. In time she'll understand. She is like a baby now."

Captain Keller looked at Helen spelling into the dog's paw, "Miss Sullivan, I think she must be homesick. She'll have to return to the house soon."

"Captain, we've been accomplishing so much—"

"I see that, and yet," he paused, "the child belongs at *home* with her parents. You can continue what you've started here with us in the house."

"Give me a few more weeks, Captain, please, for *Helen*. Look at her!"

Captain Keller took a deep breath. He nodded, "You have a few more days."

* * *

"To: Mrs. Hopkins,

March 20, 1887.

Dear Mrs. Hopkins,

I was so glad to receive your letter dating March 10th. I was happy to hear of the happenings in the school. Please do tell me how Lilian is faring with little Edith. I only now realize what a difficult task it is to try tutoring a deaf-blind child!

Yesterday Captain Keller brought Belle, the family's dog, to see Helen. Helen was giving her doll Nancy a bath, and didn't notice the dog at first. She usually feels the softest step and throws out her arms to ascertain if anyone is near her. Belle, however, didn't seem very anxious to attract the child's attention... I imagine she has been rather roughly handled sometimes by her little mistress....

The dog hadn't been in the room more than half a minute, though, before Helen began to sniff, and dumped the doll into the washbowl, beginning to feel about the room. She stumbled upon Belle, who was crouching near the window. It was evident that she recognized the dog, for she put her arms round her neck and squeezed her. Then Helen sat down by the dog and began to manipulate the dog's claws. We couldn't think for a second what she was doing, but when we saw her make the letters "d-o-l-l" on the dog's paw, we knew that she was trying to teach Belle to spell!

She is so adorable!

It's been 12 days since we moved into the garden house, and 18 days since my arrival in Tuscumbia. I am happy to report that the wild little creature has finally been transformed into a gentle child!

She is sitting by me now, her face serene and happy, crocheting a long red chain of Scotch wool. She learned to stitch this week and is very proud of the achievement. When she succeeded in making a chain that would reach across the room, she patted herself on the arm and put the first work of her hands lovingly against her cheek.

She also lets me kiss her now, and when she is in a particularly gentle mood she sits on my lap for a minute or two; but she does not return my caresses. Yet the great step—the step that counts—has been taken. The little savage has learned her first lesson in obedience, and finds the yoke easy. It now remains my pleasant task to direct and mold the beautiful intelligence that is beginning to stir in the child's soul.

Already her parents remark the change in Helen. Her father looks in at us morning and evening as he goes to and from his office, and sees her contentedly stringing her beads or making horizontal lines on her sewing-card, and he exclaims, "How quiet she is!"

When I came, her movements were so insistent that one always felt there was something unnatural and almost weird about her. This changed, and her movement is more natural now. I have also noticed that she eats much less, a fact that unfortunately troubles her parents so much that they are anxious to get her home. They say she is homesick. I don't agree with them; but I suppose we shall have to leave our little bower very soon.

Helen has learned several nouns this week: *pin, key, dog, hat, mug,* and *milk.* The latter two, "mug" and "milk" have given her more trouble than the other words. When she spells "milk," she points to the mug, and when she spells "mug," she makes the sign for pouring, which shows that she has confused the words. She still has no idea that everything has a name.

Yesterday afternoon I asked Percy, the servant boy who lives with us, to come in when Helen was having her lesson. I taught him the words I was teaching her too. Him learning the letters pleased Helen very much and stimulated an ambition to excel him. She was delighted if Percy made a mistake, and she made him form the letter over several times. When he succeeded in forming it to suit her, she patted him on his head so enthusiastically! She can be so amusing... Oh Mrs. Hopkins, wish me luck! And do write to me again, your letter brought me so much joy!

Yours,

Annie."

* * *

Annie stood outside the garden house on the porch and listening grudgingly to Kate's and Arthur's compliments.

"Really, Miss Annie," Kate said, "it is unbelievable what you have been able to do with Helen."

"If you think so," Annie said, on the verge of tears,

"then let me continue, here, alone with her!"

Captain Keller smiled, "Miss Sullivan, please! Do understand our position. We are her parents and the child belongs at her home!"

Annie saw that she had no further room for discussion. Any insistence on her part might seem disrespectful. "Alright," she said.

Kate smiled, relieved, and looked at Arthur encouragingly.

"But," Annie added, "I must be able to continue working with her without any interference!"

"Indeed," Kate said, "we would not be in your way."

Annie took a deep breath and looked inside at Helen, quietly sewing. "You must understand that you, her parents," she said, "whenever you allow her to do whatever she likes—to roam around and terrorize the family—are doing her a terrible injustice and disservice!"

Kate nodded, biting her lips. Arthur was less enthused about Annie's remarks.

Annie looked at Arthur, "Captain, the processes of teaching *any* child that everything cannot be as the child wills it, are bound to be *painful* both to the child *and* to the parents. But essentially, it is in the child's benefit!"

Arthur nodded. "Very well. We shall give you a free hand."

Kate joined in, "And we'll help you, Miss Annie. You just tell us what to do."

Annie nodded slowly. She pouted her lips, understanding that the point was as clear as she could make it. She opened the door to the house, "Here."

Kate let out a cry of joy as she walked inside. Captain Keller followed her eagerly. Kate put her hands on Helen's knees. Helen felt the hands, an expression of surprise and astonishment on her face. She then grabbed the hand and let out the loudest hail, uttered from the bottom of her throat.

Annie looked at them and nodded to herself. She did whatever she could do. Hopefully from now it will be easier.

* * *

"To: Mrs. Hopkins

March 28th, 1887

Dear Mrs. Hopkins,

I received your third letter yesterday. Thank you for your encouragement. As to Lilian, I shall write to her this week. I have been lazy about writing. I do apologize.

As to us, Helen and I came home yesterday. I am sorry Captain and Mrs. Keller wouldn't let us stay another week; but I think I have made the most I could of the opportunities that were mine the past two and a half weeks in the garden house, and I don't expect that I shall have any serious trouble with Helen in the future.

The back of the greatest obstacle in the path of progress is broken. I think "no" and "yes," conveyed by a shake or nod of my head, have become facts as apparent to Helen as hot and cold or as the difference between pain and pleasure.

And I don't intend that the lesson she has learned at the cost of so much pain and trouble shall be unlearned. I shall stand between her and the over-indulgence of her parents.

I have told Captain and Mrs. Keller that they must not interfere with me in any way. I have done my best to make them see the terrible injustice to Helen of allowing her to have her way in everything, and I have pointed out that the processes of teaching the child that everything cannot be as the child wills it, are apt to be painful both to the child and to the teacher. They have promised to let me have a free hand and help me as much as possible. The improvement they cannot help seeing in their child has given them more confidence in me.

Of course, it is hard for them. I realize that it hurts to see their afflicted little child punished and made to do things against her will.

Only a few hours after my talk with them, and after they had agreed to everything, Helen and I unpacked upstairs and headed down for dinner. I was nervous to see how Helen would behave, and my fears were not unfounded. Helen took a notion that she wouldn't use her napkin at the table. I think she wanted to see what would happen.

I attempted several times to put the napkin round her neck; but each time she tore it off and threw it on the floor. Finally she began to kick the table. I immediately took her plate away and started to take her out of the room. Her father objected and said that no child of his should be deprived of his food on any account.

I relented, but not without protest.

After dinner Helen did not come up to my room, and I didn't see her again until this morning at breakfast. She was at her place by the table when I came into the dining room. She had put the napkin under her chin, instead of pinning it at the back. She called my attention to the new arrangement. I nodded my head, having her hand feel my head and seeing that I did not object to the new arrangement of the napkin, as long as she had it on. My approval seemed to please her, and she patted herself.

After breakfast, when we left the dining room, she took my hand and patted it. I assumed she was trying to "make up." I thought I would try the effect of a little belated discipline. I went back to the dining room and took a napkin with me upstairs.

In my room I arranged the objects on the table for the lesson as usual, except for the cake, which I always give her in bits as a reward when she spells a word quickly and correctly. I put it on top of the closet where she could not reach it or know it was there.

When Helen came upstairs for her lesson, she felt about the table as she always does. She noticed immediately the absence of the cake and she made the sign for eating with her fingers brought to her mouth. I took the napkin and pinned it round her neck, then tore it off and threw it on the floor, placing her hand on my face as I shook my head disapprovingly. I repeated it again, taking the napkin, pinning it round her neck, then throwing it, then shaking my head. I repeated this performance several times. I think she understood perfectly well, for she slapped her hand two or three times and shook her head as well.

Seeing that she understood, I began the lesson. I gave her a pin and she spelled the name. I proceeded to have her touch and spell *cake, doll, mug, key, hat,* and *box.* She knows twelve words now. After spelling half the words, she stopped suddenly, as if a thought had flashed into her mind, and she felt around the table for the napkin. Finding it, she pinned it round her neck and made the sign for food with her hand, indicating that I should give her cake. You see, it didn't occur to her to *spell* the word, meaning that she still does not make the connection yet between the object and its name... Regardless, I took her little napkin gesture for a promise that if I gave her some cake she would be a good girl. I therefore gave her a very large piece, larger than usual, and she ate it, chuckling and nodding her head approvingly while patting herself.

Spring is here with all its glory. How much I miss you Mrs. Hopkins! The scents in the air remind me of summer and of lying with you on the beach in Brewster. Have you thought of visiting the South? It will be my pleasure to have you visit me. I assure you, you are bound to fall in love with little Helen.

Yours always,

Annie.

* * *

"To Mrs. Hopkins,

April 3rd, 1887

Dear Mrs. Hopkins,

I can't believe it has been a whole month today since I arrived in Alabama! How the time had passed! The great news is that spring is here. We almost live in the garden, where everything is growing and blooming and glowing. Each day after breakfast we go out and watch the men at work in the fields. Helen loves to dig and play in the dirt like any other child. We planted corn, beans and watermelon-seed together in the garden.

She is so funny: this morning she planted her doll in the ground and showed me with her hands that she expected her to grow as tall as I. You must see that she is very bright, but you have no idea how cunning she is!

At ten we come back in and string beads for a few minutes. She can make a great many combinations now, and often invents new ones herself. Then I let her choose which thing she will do next: sew, knit or crochet. She learned to knit very quickly, and is making a washcloth for her mother. Last week she made her doll an apron, and it was done as well as any child of her age could do it. But I am always glad when this work is over for the day. Sewing and crocheting are inventions of the devil, I think. I'd rather break stones on the king's highway than hem a handkerchief!

At eleven we have gymnastics. She likes to run around and we play together.

The hour from twelve to one is devoted to the learning of new words. But let me state it clearly: you mustn't think this is the only time I spell to Helen; for I spell in her hand everything we do all day long, although she has no idea as yet what the spelling *means*.

After lunch I rest for an hour, and Helen plays with her dolls or frolics in the yard with the little servants' children, who were her constant companions before I came.

Later I join them, and we make the rounds of the outhouses around the farm. We visit the horses and mules in their stalls and hunt for eggs and feed the turkeys.

If the weather is fine, Helen and I often ask the servant in charge of the horses to take us by carriage to town. This is usually where I would also drop you a letter at the post office. We then visit some of Helen's cousins. Especially her baby cousin, Ruth. Helen's instincts are decidedly social; she likes to have people about her and to visit her friends, partly, I think, because they always have things she likes to eat.

We are always home for dinner, and later go to my room and do all sorts of things until eight, when I undress the little woman and put her to bed. She sleeps with me now. Mrs. Keller wanted to get a nurse for her; but I concluded I'd rather be her nurse than look after some lazy maid. Besides, I like to have Helen depend on me for everything, and I find it much easier to teach her things at odd moments than at set times.

I recently counted all the words that Helen knew to spell: cake, doll, mug, pin, key, dog, hat, cup, box, water, milk, candy, knife, fork, spoon, saucer, tea, bed, baby, mother, papa. She also personally asked for the words of: eye, finger, toe, and head. I am also proud of her understanding of four verbs, which she can demonstrate after I spell to her: sit, stand, walk and run. Altogether eighteen nouns and three verbs in only one month! Mind you, she still does not make the link that these are actual names, but only sees it as a sort of game. I am proud of her progress, and hope that in due time she shall see that everything has a name and that she can further communicate with other using these words.

Thank you so much for your letters. I am thinking of you often throughout the day and imagine you must be proud of me and of little Helen.

Yours,

Annie.

* * *

Annie sighed. She undressed Helen and helped her into the tub. It was morning. She looked at the expression of excitement on Helen's face. Something changed. Her face brightened since Annie had first met her. Helen's recent request, to know the name of *eye, finger, toe* and *head*, also excited Annie very much.

Helen entered the tub with much pleasure. Annie looked at her and smiled. She was wondering when her pupil was going to understand the meaning of *words*. Annie knew well that this was but a pastime for Helen, and that she still could not make the connection between the funny finger movements and the objects they signified. When Helen would want a cake the natural thing for her was to point to her mouth as if putting an imaginary cake inside. When she would look for her baby sister she would put her thumb in her mouth, imitating little Mildred, even though she knew the word for "baby."

Helen turned her head toward Annie, pointing to the water and looking puzzled, reaching her hand to Annie.

"What?" Annie asked out loud, "You want to know its name? It's water," she spelled into Helen's palm, "w-a-t-e-r."

Helen seemed pleased and continued to play with the water. Annie soaped her head and showed Helen that she should wash her face in the water. After she did, Annie said, "Come, we have to go to breakfast."

Helen did not want to get out of the tub, but Annie took her hand and placed it on her face while shaking her head "no." Helen nodded and stood up. Annie gave her the towel and spoke out loud, "Dry up."

Later they had breakfast. Captain Keller was speaking to James about some biblical passage. Annie could not care less. She was pleased to see Helen eating politely and at the end of the meal folding her napkin. She patted her hand, Helen nodded and patted her own hand as well.

As everyone began leaving the table Annie stayed with Helen, using the opportunity for a little rehearsal. She took some cake from the kitchen and brought it to the table. She handed Helen the butter knife and placed her palm open before Helen.

Helen spelled back into her teacher's palm, "k-n-i-f-e." Annie patted her and gave her a small piece of cake. She then handed her the spoon. Helen spelled back "s-p-o-o-n," and Annie patted her and gave her another small bite. Annie proceeded to give her the copper mug. Helen nodded and spelled back to Annie, "m-i-l-k."

"No," Annie said, irritated, and took Helen's hand

and placed it on her face, shaking it from side to side, "No!" She spelled to her, "mug! M-u-g!"

Helen nodded. Annie grimaced. What an entanglement. These two words, *milk* and *mug*, have become nearly synonymous in Helen's mind.

"Mug, Helen," Annie said out loud, "is the *object*," she let Helen feel it from all sides. "Milk is what you pour *inside*. You can also pour other things into the mug, you see?"

Helen looked dumbfounded. Annie sighed. She took the mug in her hand. "Come," she said to Helen and took her hand.

They walked outside. It was already fairly hot. April in Massachusetts was gloomy and dreary in comparison to Alabama. Annie dragged Helen past the parked carriage, pulling her closer to her so that she wouldn't bump into the carriage. "Here," Annie said as they approached the pump house, "Perhaps this will help you."

They entered the small pump house. It was cooler inside under the wooden trellis. Annie took the handle of the rusty iron pump and lifted it up and down, until water began pouring out. "Here, Helen," she said and gave Helen the mug, "hold the mug under the water." The water coming out was cold. "This is *water*," she said and spelled into Helen's hand, "w-a-t-e-r! Remember asking me in the tub this morning? W-a-t-e-r!"

Helen dropped the mug on the ground. Annie reprimanded her, "Helen!" but then she noticed Helen stood there, frozen. Helen suddenly reached for Annie's hand and opened Annie's palm. She spelled, "W-a-t-e-r."

Annie nodded, "Yes, that's what I've told you—"

"W-a-t-e-r," Helen spelled again, her other hand

under the drizzle of water, "w-a-t-e-r."

Annie looked at her slowly, "Yes, Helen that's what I've been trying to teach you—"

"W-a-t-e-r," Helen spelled again. Then again, "W-a-t-e-r." She fell to the ground and banged on it with her hand, reaching the other hand for Annie. Annie looked at her, puzzled, "You want to know its name? That's the ground, Helen, g-r-o-u-n-d."

Helen spelled back, "G-r-o-u-n-d." She reached her hand to the pump. She touched the pump, and then handed her hand to Annie. Annie spelled into her hand, "Pump, p-u-m-p."

Excited, Helen spelled back quickly, "p-u-m-p!" She then banged her hand against the trellis wall. She touched it, feeling the wooden strips, and then reached her hand to Annie.

Annie shrugged her shoulders, "You really want to know its name? It's unuseful, Helen!"

Helen banged on the trellis wood and stretched her hand to Annie, her palm wide open. Annie spelled, "Trellis, t-r-e-l-l-i-s."

Helen nodded and spelled back, "T-r-e-l-l-i-s." Annie patted her on the hand. "Good." Helen turned to her and suddenly put her hand on Annie's chest, tapping on her teacher's chest and reaching out her open palm for Annie.

Annie laughed, "You want to know my name?"

Helen waited expectantly. Annie thought for a short moment, knowing her actual name did not matter here. "I'm your *teacher*," she said and spelled, "t-e-a-c-h-e-r."

Helen nodded eagerly and repeated the letters

correctly. Annie patted her on the hand and said, "Good girl." To herself she wondered, "Could it be that Helen finally…?"

* * *

"To: Mrs. Hopkins,

April 5, 1887.

I must write you a line because something very important has happened. Helen has taken the second great step in her education. She has learned that *everything has a name, and that the manual alphabet is the key to everything she wants to know.*

In a previous letter I believe I wrote you that "mug" and "milk" had given Helen more trouble than all the rest. She confused the nouns with the verb "drink." She didn't know the word for "drink," but went through the pantomime of drinking whenever she spelled "mug" or "milk."

This morning, while she was washing, she wanted to know the name for "water." When she wants to know the name of anything, she points to it and pats my hand. I spelled "w-a-t-e-r," and thought no more about it until after breakfast. Then it occurred to me that with the help of this new word I might succeed in straightening out the "mug-milk" difficulty.

We went out to the pump house, and I made Helen hold her mug under the spout while I pumped. As the cold water gushed forth, filling the mug, I spelled "w-a-t-e-r" in Helen's free hand. The word coming so close upon the sensation of cold water rushing over her hand seemed to startle her. She dropped the mug and stood as one transfixed. A new light came into her face. She spelled "water" several times. Then she dropped on the ground and asked for its name and pointed to the pump and the trellis, and suddenly turning round she asked for my name. I spelled "Teacher."

Just then the nurse brought Helen's little sister into the pump-house, and Helen spelled "baby" and pointed to the her sister. All the way back to the house she was highly excited, and learned the name of every object she touched, so that in a few hours she had added many new words to her vocabulary. Here are some of them: *door, open, shut, give, go, come,* and a great many more.

P. S.

I didn't finish my letter in time to get it posted last night; so I shall add a line. Helen got up this morning like a radiant fairy. She has flitted from object to object, asking the name of everything and kissing me for very gladness. Last night when I got in bed, she stole into my arms of her own accord and kissed me for the first time! I thought my heart would burst, so full was it of joy!

Isn't she wonderful? I will write more soon!

Yours,

Annie."

* * *

It was already evening when the carriage slowed down before the house and Annie helped Helen out of the carriage, thanked the driver and hurried into the house. She did not want to be late for dinner. She could not wait to share her realizations with Kate. She had spent the whole day with Helen at Helen's aunt and uncle Leila and John in town, observing their little toddler Ruth. New realization came into her mind about how to better teach Helen.

They entered the house and rushed to the dining room.

Captain Keller exclaimed, "Thank God! We thought you were dead!"

Annie bowed, "Captain, Mrs. Keller, James, forgive me. We've been at Leila and John's, visiting with little Ruth."

Captain Keller frowned.

Annie took Helen to wash their hands in the basin, and then quickly came to sit in their seats.

They joined hands, Captain Keller said a short prayer, and they began eating. Annie tried to seem interested in the conversation between the father and son, but her mind was elsewhere. Never before had she found babies so stimulating and the acquisition of language so fascinating! Language was truly a miracle, she thought, and she was determined to emulate that miracle with Helen.

When dinner was over Annie rushed out the dining room with Helen, when Captain Keller coughed and said, "Miss Sullivan?"

"Yes Captain," Annie said and turned around.

Captain Keller walked to her and spoke quietly, "Mrs. Keller and I would like to have a private talk with you later this evening. Perhaps after you put Helen to bed."

Annie's heart began pounding. A talk? What did they want to say? Had she done anything wrong?

Captain Keller said, "We'll be in the sitting room."

Annie nodded and proceeded with Helen upstairs.

* * *

After Helen fell asleep, Annie went downstairs. Captain and Mrs. Keller were sitting on the divans.

"Please sit down, Miss Sullivan," Arthur said and pointed to the chair.

Annie mumbled, "There is no need for such formality, Captain."

Annie looked at Kate, trying to decipher the problem. Kate smiled at her.

Arthur looked at Kate, and seeing she was not going to begin, said, "Miss Sullivan, I wish to understand. Yesterday, and today, you have gone away from the house for the entire day—"

"Arthur," Kate intervened and shook her head, "Miss Annie, let us begin by saying how appreciative we are of all of your wonderful work!"

Annie sat down on the chair, tense.

Kate continued, "Since Helen learned the meaning of words she is highly excited, and I can see the change in her face!"

Annie nodded and murmured, "Her face is becoming so expressive."

Arthur nodded. "Indeed. You are doing a fine work. However, I'm afraid that the lack of schedule and this roaming around is rather unbeneficial for the child."

Annie's eyes grew wider. She waited for Captain Keller to finish speaking. But he added nothing.

She took a deep breath in, remembering Mr. Anagnos and his recommendation regarding her temper. "Captain Keller," she said slowly, "Helen's best interest is always in my mind when I determine the course of her study. Currently, staying in the house is *not* to her advantage. The child wants to be outside, to be in nature, to meet friends—"

"I understand that," Captain Keller said, "but isn't a lesson in a room without distractions more conducive to her progress?"

Annie answered blatantly, "No!"

Captain Keller looked at her, a little astonished.

"Captain, Helen wants to *see* the world, to *hear* everything, and I must serve as her eyes, I must serve as her ears! And the last thing she wants to do is be locked in a room while everything outside is blossoming! Her appetite for knowledge is quite," Annie's eyes became moist, "magnificent! She wants to know the name of everything she touches, she wants to—"

"Which brings me to another point, Miss Sullivan: isn't all this learning burdening the child? I hear you teach her dozens of words."

"Well she *asks* for them!"

Captain Keller smiled, "Well, she can ask for a cold swim in the river in December and I shall not allow it."

Annie took a deep breath and looked at Kate, who was sitting there with a polite smile, unhelpful. Annie looked at Arthur, "Captain," she said, trying to be as polite as she can, "I do not think that it can be 'burdening' for Helen, not as long as she *asks* for it *herself*. On the contrary, during the past three days Helen has been extremely energetic, vivacious, and gay. I see no problem in that—"

"But still," Captain Keller insisted, "isn't it too much for the child?"

Annie looked at him, "I see what you are saying, Captain. And I appreciate your concern. I really do. But I have asked myself again and again, how does a child learn a language? And my only conclusion is that it happens through the *exposure* to language."

Captain Keller looked at her, not understanding.

Annie nodded, "Provided that the child is supplied with sufficient outward stimulus, he is *bound* to learn the language. I've been observing little Ruth, and I see that she already understands a great deal. She does not speak much, but she *understands*, Captain. I asked her, 'Where is your Mama?' and she pointed at Leila. I asked her 'Where is your Papa' and she pointed at John. I asked her many questions, and I saw that before there is *speech*, there is *understanding*. Now, let me ask you, Captain, how many times do you think that little Ruth heard the words 'Papa' and 'Mama'?"

Captain Keller shrugged his shoulders and glanced at Kate, "I assume many times."

Annie nodded, "And I assume *hundreds* of times, if not *thousands* of times. Let me also tell you that not only when she is being spoken *to* does baby Ruth hear words, but also when her parents and other people converse among *themselves* in her presence. She *hears*. Through this absorption in a world of spoken words she will learn to use words independently. She is *absorbed* in words, they are all around her! I must be the *bridge* for Helen, to show her all the words that are around her, do you understand?"

Captain Keller pouted his lips and looked at Annie.

Annie stood up and began to walk around the room, "I must talk into Helen's only ear, which is located here," she pointed at the palm of her hand, "and I must talk to her like I would talk to a regular child, and *trust* that *eventually* all of the information will manifest itself into knowledge. And if you want to help me, you should learn the manual alphabet as well!"

Captain Keller sighed and stood up. He went to the library. Kate smiled at Annie, "Can you teach me all the signs?"

Annie nodded, "Of course! This way Helen could eventually *speak* to you! We shall start first thing tomorrow morning."

Kate smiled, "Good." Arthur returned with a thick report in his hand. "Have you happened to read the report, Miss Sullivan, by Dr. Howe regarding his student Laura Bridgman?"

Annie chuckled, "I 'happened' to read it about a dozen times, Captain."

Arthur nodded inattentively and sat down with the report. "Dr. Howe writes here about the importance of *regular* lessons, of *structure*, of *certainty* for the child."

Annie smiled and walked around, "But he also writes of the importance of allowing the child to *play* and practice *gymnastics* and *rest*."

Captain Keller seemed disturbed, "Miss Sullivan, Dr. Howe's method is *proven*. A daily lesson, repeated regularly each day, enabling the child the structure and confidence of *routine*. These methods, Miss Sullivan, this careful adherence to *structured* pedagogy, enabled Dr. Howe to teach Laura Bridgman how to read! And even write!"

Annie stood behind her chair, clasping the back of the chair tightly, "The child, Captain Keller, ought to have *freedom* and follow her *own* curiosity! Through her own initiative she shall learn much more than in the confinement of a room studying the vocabulary that some 'doctor' saw 'useful' for her!"

Captain Keller looked at Kate, dismayed.

Kate looked back at him and put her hand on his arm, "Arthur, we've been so pleased with the rapid progress Helen been showing in the past month. I personally could have never imagined her sitting so politely by the table!"

Annie tried to conceal her smile, "Captain, give me free reign! I shall overdo Dr. Howe!"

Captain Keller snorted, "Miss Sullivan!"

Annie stood and looked at him, raising her chin and straightening her dress. "Now, Captain, Mrs. Keller, if you'd excuse me, I have to rest before Helen shall lead me tomorrow to who knows where."

Kate looked at Arthur, nodding her head and whispering, "The envelope!"

"Oh yes," Arthur said and stood up, taking out an envelope from the inside pocket of his vest, "This, Miss Sullivan, is for you."

Annie's eyes widened as she looked at the envelope, "Are you *firing* me?"

Kate stood up, "Miss Annie! Never! This is your *salary*!"

Annie blushed, "Oh."

Arthur nodded.

Kate smiled at her, "Thank you, Miss Annie, for all that you are doing with our little Helen."

Annie wanted to say something, but could not find the words. She looked at the envelope in her hand, nodded at the two of them, left the sitting room and hurried upstairs. Her heart was pounding. She was proud of earning her first month's salary. But she was also determined. Determined to prove Captain Keller wrong. She *knew* what she was doing.

* * *

> "To: Mrs. Hopkins,
>
> April 10th, 1887
>
> Dear Mrs. Hopkins,
>
> It's been five days since our water pump episode and I see an improvement in Helen day to day, almost from hour to hour! *Everything* must have a name now. Wherever we go, she asks eagerly for the names of things she has not learned at home. She is also anxious for the children of the servants to spell to her by the fingers, and is eager to teach the letters to everyone she meets. She drops the signs and pantomime she used before as soon as she has words to supply their place. The acquirement of a new word affords Helen the liveliest pleasure. And we notice that her face

grows more expressive each day.

For the present I have decided not to have regular lessons. I am going to treat Helen exactly like a two-year-old child. It occurred to me the other day that it is absurd to require a child to come to a certain place at a certain time and recite certain lessons, when she has not yet acquired a working vocabulary.

I sent Helen away to play the other day and sat down in my room to think. I asked myself, "How does a normal child *learn language?*" The answer was simple: "By *imitation*." The child comes into the world with the *ability* to learn, and he learns of himself, provided he is supplied with sufficient outward stimulus. He sees people do things, and he tries to do them himself. He hears others speak, and he tries to speak.

The important realization is that long before the child utters his first word, he *understands* what is said to him. I have been observing Helen's little cousin Ruth lately. She is about fifteen months old, and already understands a great deal. In response to questions Ruth points out prettily her nose, mouth, eye, chin, cheek, ear. If I say, "Where is Ruth's ear?" she points it out correctly. If I hand her a flower and say, "Give it to Mama," she takes it to her mother. She is so funny! If I say to her, "Where is the little rogue?" she hides behind her mother's chair, or covers her face with her hands and peeps out at me with an expression of genuine roguishness. Ruth also obeys many commands like: "Come," "Kiss," "Go to Papa," "Shut the door," "Give me the biscuit," etc.

And yet, I have not heard Ruth try to *say* any of these words, although they have been repeated hundreds of times in her ears, and it is perfectly evident that she *understands* them. These observations have given me a clue to the method to be followed in teaching Helen language. *I shall talk into her hand as we talk into the baby's ears.* I shall assume that she has the normal child's capacity of assimilation and imitation.

I also decided on another important aspect of my method: *I shall use complete sentences in talking to her.* This is how baby Ruth is being spoken to— with the *assumption* that she can understand! I will therefore use full and complete sentences with Helen, and fill out the meaning with gestures when necessity requires it; but I shall *not* try to keep her mind fixed on any one thing or use short and dumb sentences. I shall do all I can to speak to her like a regular child, make sure to interest and stimulate her mind, and then wait for results."

* * *

"To: Mrs. Hopkins,

April 24th 1887

Dearest Mrs. Hopkins,

It's been two weeks since I have written to you last. Please forgive me for taking so long. I've been so busy with Helen, and at night all I want to do is fall on the bed and sleep! The little girl is quite robust and spirited and has the energy of a lioness!

The new method I have written to you about works splendidly. Helen knows the meaning of more than a hundred words now! And she learns new ones daily without the slightest suspicion that she is performing a most difficult feat! She learns because she *can't help it*, just as the bird learns to fly.

But don't imagine, dear Mrs. Hopkins, that she "talks fluently." Like her baby cousin Ruth, Helen expresses whole sentences by single words. For example, the word "Milk" spoken with a gesture, means: "Give me more milk!"

The word "Mother" accompanied by an inquiring look, means, "Where is mother?"

When she spells the word "Go" she means, "I want to go out!"

I, however, spell to Helen only in *full* sentences. And she comprehends. When I spell into her hand, "Give me some bread," she hands me the bread. If I say, "Get your hat and we will go for a walk," she obeys instantly. I could have otherwise simply stated the two words: "hat" and "walk." They would have the same effect; but the whole sentence, repeated many times during the day, must in time impress itself upon the brain, and by and by she will use it herself. I am certain of that.

We recently began playing a little game which I find most useful in developing her intellect, and which incidentally answers the purpose of a language lesson. It is an adaptation of hide-the-thimble. I hide something, a ball or a spool, and we hunt for it. When we first played this game a few days ago Helen showed no ingenuity at all in finding the object: she looked in places where it would have been impossible to put the ball or the spool.

For instance, when I hid the ball, she looked under

the tray, where the ball obviously could not be! When I hid the spool, she looked for it in a tiny box which could not hold any spool inside. Naturally, soon she gave up the search altogether. But over the past three days she had improved in this game *dramatically*. Now I can keep her interest playing it for an hour or even longer!

She also shows much more intelligence and even a great ingenuity in the search. This morning I hid a cracker. She searched everywhere she could think of without success, and was evidently in despair when suddenly a thought struck her, and she came running to me and made me open my mouth very wide, while she gave it a thorough investigation with her fingers. Finding no trace of the cracker in between my teeth, she pointed to my stomach and spelled "eat?" I assume she meant, "Did you eat it?"

Isn't she adorable?

Friday we went to town and someone gave Helen two candy bars, made of roasted peanuts and honey. Helen was ecstatic. She ate the first one, but kept the other in her apron pocket. When we reached home, she hurried to her mother, who was with baby Mildred. Helen gave the candy bar to her mother and said, of her own accord, "Give-baby-candy!"

Mrs. Keller laughed and spelled back slowly, "No, baby eat–no."

Helen looked puzzled for a moment, and then went to the cradle and gently felt Mildred's mouth. She then pointed to her own teeth, tapping them with her finger, and handed me her hand for me to spell to her the word. I gave her hand to Mrs. Keller, for her to spell to her. She spelled to Helen,

"Teeth, t-e-e-t-h."

Helen nodded and then shook her head in response and spelled "Baby teeth–no, baby eat–no!" meaning: "Baby cannot eat because she has no teeth!"

Oh, Mrs. Hopkins! It is marvelous to see Helen's development day by day!

I will write more soon. Now my eyes are failing me. I shall write to Mr. Anagnos soon, but in the meantime, please send him my highest regards. Please send my love to Lilian, little Edith, and to everyone. I miss the school terribly. Perhaps sometime in the future Helen and I could come visit together.

Yours,

Annie."

* * *

"To: Mr. Anagnos,

Massachusetts School for the Blind

South Boston, Massachusetts

May 8th 1887

Dear Mr. Anagnos,

Your kind letter was duly received and I heartily thank you for the words of sympathy and interest in Helen. I suppose you hear of my little pupil's progress from Mrs. Hopkins. It is a constant pleasure to me to watch Helen's mind unfolding day by day and to see her face light up with the beauty of intelligence.

She is becoming attached to me and I can see that she obeys more from *love* than because she thinks she *must*. She is naturally so imitative, and so easily controlled when away from her parents that I feel sure if she could only be away long enough, she would become a lovely and lovable woman. True, she inherits a quick temper and a good deal of obstinacy, but I think she is learning to control her temper, and if her obstinacy can be turned in the right direction it may serve her well.

I have taught both her parents the manual alphabet. It is good, but I insist with them that I shall be the only one to give her *new* words. It is very trying, however, as they do not pay the slightest attention to my request. Captain Keller sometimes gives her words that it is not well for her to have and that she cannot have the least idea of their meaning. The other day he spelled to her the word "gone." Of course she does not know what it means! You can see how trying it is for me....

Then there is one other thing I want you to know about for it may cause trouble if it continues. Captain Keller has taken into his head to send for Helen whenever he pleases, and of course this interference is very annoying to me and harmful to Helen. This afternoon he sent for her and although she objected to leave her work with me, I was obliged to make her go to visit him in his study. She was not willing to come back and her father would not insist upon it, so we have both had a vacation of sorts for the rest of the day.

I keep her with me about seven to eight hours

every day; but of course I do not keep her *studying* all that time. We walk and play and I do everything I can to amuse and interest her. Mind you, I would not keep her for so many hours were she not perfectly contented to stay with me that long. Whenever she gets restless and I see that she is tired I let her go.

However, Captain Keller's disregard to my time with Helen is very challenging. I know as soon as she goes to him all discipline is at an end. It is aggravating to have one's plans upset and for no good reason. I have written you thus fully, that you may understand perfectly the situation.

Everything is beautiful here except for the weather, which is terribly hot. Yet we have such a quantity of lovely roses all over the place. And we are enjoying strawberries and green peas. Please write to me back, I long for your kind and wise advice.

I am, with highest esteem,

Respectfully yours,

Annie Sullivan"

* * *

It was late afternoon. Annie was happy to see Helen playing with the servant's children. Helen was so energetic even though she walked with Annie all the way to the river and back and played the whole day. Annie, however, was tired. She also had to answer to Mrs. Hopkins's last letter, which she wanted to do for a few days now.

The children were running, playing hide and seek. Annie walked to Helen and took her hand, spelling, "I am going upstairs."

Helen spelled back, "Why?"

"I have to write a letter."

Helen made a sad face, but then one of the children grabbed her arm and she screamed with joy.

Annie smiled and walked into the house. She climbed upstairs and opened the door to her room. It was terribly hot in her attic. She opened the window and took her blouse off, fanning herself with her small feather-fan. She opened the ink bottle and took out new sheets paper from the drawer. She began writing:

"To: Mrs. Hopkins,

May 8th, 1887

Dear Mrs. Hopkins,

I received your last letter from April 26th. I was happy to read of the newly opened kindergarten. I believe with it our school may well be the best in the country. What a great pride!

As to your question, I don't need any more kindergarten materials, thank you. In the beginning I used my little stock of beads, cards and straws because I didn't know what else to do; but the need for them is past at the moment."

She looked through the window and sighed. She wrote:

"I am beginning to suspect all elaborate and special systems of education. They seem to me to be built up on the supposition that every child is a kind of idiot who must be taught to *think*!

I have found, however, that if the child is left to himself, he will think more and better and faster too! Let him go and come freely! Let him touch real things and combine his impressions for himself instead of sitting in class at a little desk while a sweet-voiced teacher suggests that he build a stone wall with his wooden blocks, or make a rainbow out of strips of colored paper, or plant straw trees in bead flower-pots. Such teaching fills the mind with artificial associations. I'd rather encourage the child to develop independent ideas out of his *actual* experiences.

I am proud to write to you that Helen is learning adjectives and adverbs as easily as she learned nouns! Before I arrived, Helen had had signs for small and large that she had made up herself. If she wanted a large object and was given a small one, she would shake her head and spread the fingers of both hands as wide as she could and bring them together as if to clasp a big ball. If she wanted to indicate something small, she would take up a tiny bit of the skin of one hand between the thumb and finger of the other.

The other day I substituted these signs with the words *small* and *large.* Helen at once adopted the words and discarded her previous gestures. I can now tell her to bring me a *large* book or a *small* plate and she would do it!

Also, I have taught her the words *quick* and *slow.* I can now ask her to go upstairs quickly, to walk slowly, etc.

I have also taught her the conjunction *and.* This morning she used it for the first time! We played a game in which I tell her to do things and she performs them. I told her to run to the door and shut it, and she added, "and lock!"

Annie smiled to herself. She was pleased with Helen's progress.

Suddenly she heard steps coming upstairs, the unmistakable thumps of Helen.

Helen came into the room panting. Her eyes were filled with tears. Annie grabbed her hand worriedly and spelled, "What happened?"

Helen spelled, "Dog, baby!"

Annie did not understand. She spelled, "Dog bit baby?" She then realized Helen did not know the word *bit*. She spelled, "Dog do not good baby?"

Helen shook her head and spelled back emphatically, "Dog! Baby!" and showed Annie her five fingers, putting each one in her mouth. She took Annie's arm and pulled her, pointing toward the stairs.

"Alright, alright, I'm coming," Annie said and closed the ink bottle. "What is it?" she thought out loud as she put on her blouse and followed Helen downstairs quickly.

Helen led her out the house, feeling the way with her hand like an expert. She led them into the pump house. There, under the trellis, Annie saw what the excitement was all about.

* * *

An hour later she returned to the room, grinning. She opened the ink bottle and continued writing. It was cooler outside now and a pleasant breeze blew through the window.

"I had to leave just now as Helen came upstairs in a state of great excitement, tears in her eyes. I couldn't make out at first what it was all about. She kept spelling "dog-baby" and pointing to her five fingers one after another, and sucking them. My first thought was, one of the dogs has hurt baby Mildred; but Helen's beaming face set my fears at rest. Nothing would do but I must go somewhere with her to see something.

She led the way to the pump house, and there in the corner was her dog Belle with five dear little pups! I taught her the word "puppy" and drew her hand over them all while they sucked and spelled "puppies." She was much interested in the feeding process, and spelled excitedly "mother-dog" and "baby" several times. She noticed that the puppies' eyes were closed, and she spelled, "Eyes-shut, sleep-no!" meaning, "The eyes are shut, but the puppies are not asleep."

She screamed with glee when the little things squealed and squirmed in their efforts to get back to their mother, and spelled, "Baby eat large!" I suppose her idea was "Baby eats much."

Then she pointed to each puppy, one after another, and to her five fingers, and I taught her the word *five.* Then she held up one finger and spelled, "baby." I knew she was thinking of Mildred, and I spelled, "One baby and five puppies."

After she played with them a little while, the thought occurred to her that the puppies must have special names, like people, and she asked for the name of each pup. I laughed and told her to ask her father. She smiled and shook her head, spelling back, "No, ask mother!" She evidently

> thought mothers were more likely to know about babies of all sorts."

Annie's face beamed. Her eyes became moist and bothered her writing. She loved that girl. She took a deep breath and continued writing:

> "Helen then noticed that one of the puppies was much smaller than the others, and she spelled "small," and I spelled back "very small." This was the first time I spelled to her the word *very.* She evidently understood its meaning correctly, for all the way back to the house she used the word *very* properly: one stone was "small," another was "very small." We entered the house and found her mother and baby sister. She touched Mildred and spelled to me, "Baby–small, puppy–*very* small!"
>
> Soon after, she began to vary her steps from large to small, and little mincing steps were "very small." Oh! She is so funny! As I am writing to you right now she is going through the house, applying the new word to all kinds of objects.
>
> What a joy she is, my dear Mrs. Hopkins! Since I have abandoned the idea of regular lessons, I find that Helen learns *much* faster! I realize most teachers spend much time teaching the child what he does not want to learn! Then they spend even *more* time digging out of the child what they had put into him, for the sake of satisfying themselves that their work was not to waste and that what they had taught had taken root! I think, personally, that it is so much time thrown away! It's much better to assume that the child is doing his part, and that the seed you have sown will bear fruit *in due time.* It's only fair to the child, and it saves the teacher much unnecessary

distress!"

* * *

That night when they laid down to sleep, Annie spelled to Helen, "Helen is clever."

Helen smiled in the dark room and spelled back, "Helen is clever. Teacher is *very* clever."

Annie laughed and spelled back, "Helen is very clever!"

Helen spelled back, "Teacher is very *very* clever!"

Annie kissed Helen on her forehead and shook her head. She was happy.

* * *

> "To: Mrs. Hopkins,
>
> May 16th, 1887
>
>
> Dear Mrs. Hopkins,
>
> It has been two and a half months since I arrived, and I am pleased to tell you that I began teaching Helen reading. I teach her the letters from the little books I brought with the raised letters. I spell to her palm the letter A as she knows it in the manual alphabet, and then have her touch the raised letter in the book. She is very quick. We have reading lessons every day, mostly outdoors by one of the trees.
>
> Each morning, immediately after breakfast, we take a long walk. In the morning the weather is

fine, and the air is full of the scent of strawberries. Our objective point is the Tennessee River, about two miles distant. We never know how we get there, or where we are at a given moment; but that only adds to our enjoyment, especially when everything is new and strange.

Indeed, I feel as if I had *never seen anything until now*! I see things through Helen's mental eyes for the first time. She finds so much to ask about along the way! We chase butterflies, and sometimes even catch one. Then we sit down under a tree, or in the shade of a bush, and converse about it. Afterwards, if the butterfly has survived the lesson, we let it go; but usually its life and beauty are sacrificed on the altar of learning—though in another sense it lives forever, for has it not been transformed into living *thoughts*?

It is wonderful how words generate ideas! Every new word Helen learns seems to carry with it necessity for many more. Her mind grows through its ceaseless activity.

We have a favorite spot near the river, overgrown with moss and weeds. The solitude of the place sets one dreaming. Near it there is a beautiful little spring. There one can get a glimpse of a squirrel every now and then, as the squirrels come to drink from the spring. I tell Helen what I see, and she gets very excited. She named the spring "squirrel-cup," because the squirrels come to drink there. Isn't she adorable? She often asks me when are we going to "squirrel-cup."

In the past she had had opportunities to feel dead squirrels and rabbits and other wild animals, and she is now anxious to see what she calls a "walk-squirrel," which interpreted, means, I think, a "live squirrel."

Each day we return from our long walk at around lunch time, and Helen is eager to tell her mother everything she has "seen." This desire to repeat what has been told her shows a marked advance in the development of her intellect, and I think it is an invaluable stimulus to the acquisition of language.

I ask everyone around her to encourage her to tell them of her doings, and to manifest as much curiosity and pleasure in her little adventures as they possibly can. This gratifies the child's love of approbation and keeps up her interest in things. It is the basis of real communication!

Do not think, Mrs. Hopkins, that she spells fluently. She makes many mistakes in her spelling, twists words and phrases, puts the cart before the horse, and gets herself into hopeless tangles of nouns and verbs. But that is only natural in my opinion—even hearing children do that! I am sure these difficulties will take care of themselves over time.

The important thing is the impulse she has to *share*. She has the desire to tell and communicate and I encourage it as much as I can: I supply a word here and there, sometimes a sentence, and suggest something which she has omitted or forgotten. Thus her vocabulary grows apace, and the new words germinate and bring forth new ideas and they are the stuff out of which heaven and earth are made."

* * *

"To: Mrs. Hopkins,

May 22nd, 1887

Dear Mrs. Hopkins,

Thank you for your last letter and your keen interest in my work! Oh, it grows ever more absorbing and interesting every day! Helen is a wonderful child, so spontaneous and eager to learn. She knows about 300 words now and *a great many common idioms*, and it is not three months yet since she learned her first word! It is a rare privilege to watch the birth, growth, and first feeble struggles of a living mind. This privilege is mine and moreover, it is given me to rouse and guide this bright intelligence.

If only I were better fitted for the great task! I feel every day more and more inadequate. My mind is full of ideas but I cannot get them into working shape. You see, my mind is undisciplined, full of skips and jumps, and here and there a lot of things huddled together in dark corners. How I long to put it in order! Oh, if only there were some one to help me! I need a teacher quite as much as Helen. I know that the education of this child will be the distinguishing event of my life—if I have the brains and perseverance to accomplish it!

I have made up my mind about one thing: Helen must learn to use books—indeed, we must both learn to use them, and that reminds me. Will you please ask Mr. Anagnos to get me from the library Bernard Perez's *The First Three Years of Childhood* and James Sully's *Studies of Childhood*? I think now I shall find them helpful.

We have reading lessons every day. Usually we

take one of the little books to a big tree near the house and spend an hour or two with Helen feeling the raised words in it. We make a sort of *game* of it and try to see who can find the words most quickly, Helen with her fingers or I with my eyes. When her fingers light upon words she knows, she fairly screams with pleasure and hugs and kisses me for joy, especially if she thinks she has me "beaten" in our little game, and that I have yet to "spot" the word myself! It would astonish you to see how many words she learns in an hour in this pleasant manner.

Afterward I use the new words, and sometimes it is possible to tell her a little story about a bee or a cat or a little boy in this way. She knows so many words now! I can now tell her to go upstairs or to go down, to go out of doors or into the house, lock or unlock a door, take or bring objects, sit, stand, walk, run, lie, crawl, roll, or climb. She is delighted with action-words; so it is no trouble at all to teach her verbs. She is always ready for a lesson, and the eagerness with which she absorbs ideas is very delightful. She is as triumphant over the conquest of a sentence as a general who has captured the enemy's stronghold!

One of Helen's old habits, which is strongest and hardest to correct, is her tendency to break things. If she finds anything in her way she tends to fling it on the floor, no matter what it is: a glass, a pitcher or even a lamp. She has a great many dolls and every one of them has been broken in a fit of temper or weariness. The other day a friend of Mrs. Keller, Mrs. Grace Moore, brought Helen a new doll from Memphis and I thought I would see if I could make Helen understand that she must not break the new doll.

I took the doll and made Helen go slowly through the motion of knocking the doll's head on the table. I then spelled to her: "No, no, Helen is naughty, Teacher is sad," and let her feel the grieved expression on my face, as if I was crying. Then I made her caress the doll and kiss the hurt spot and hold it gently in her arms. Then I spelled to her, "Good Helen, Teacher is happy!" and I let her feel the smile on my face.

She went through these motions several times, mimicking every movement, then she stood very still for a moment with a troubled look on her face and spelled, "Good Helen," and wreathed her face in a very large smile. Then she placed the doll aside, gently. Isn't she clever?

Please give my kind regards to Mr. Anagnos and let him see my letter, if you think best. I will write to him tomorrow, as I think we need some special words printed for Helen in raised letters. This could be a delight for her.

I have not forgotten, my dear Mrs. Hopkins, that by the time you'll be reading this letter, you will be celebrating your birthday! Allow me to wish you a very happy birthday! I am attaching a few mirasol seeds as my humble gift. I'm not sure about the weather in Boston and whether they can grow there, but knowing your gardening talent I thought you might like to try planting them. I thank you from the bottom of my heart for the mother-love you have given me, and I wish to send you the same love through this letter. May this year be one of many blessings and joy for you! I also thank you for the correspondence, as it is a pleasure for me to know someone cares about my troubled mind and foolish thoughts.

Yours,

Annie."

* * *

"To: Mr. Anagnos

Massachusetts School for the Blind,

South Boston, Massachusetts,

May 23rd, 1887

Dear Mr. Anagnos,

I hope you are doing well, and the preparations for the end of the school year are not taxing, and even enjoyable. I am pleased to write to you that my little pupil can now read every word she can spell! She spends hours every day finding these words in her books. When she touches a word she knows her face grows radiant, and if by any chance she find part of a sentence that conveys any meaning to her mind her joy is unbounded.

However, it is unfortunate for us to go through two or three books to find a few words with which she is acquainted. And there are many words that she cannot find at all in any of the small books I brought with me.

She became very angry this morning because I could not find her own name being spelled in any of the books, nor the name of her older brother James or her baby sister Mildred. No matter what I tried to do afterwards, she would not touch the book the remainder of the day.

Now if you could have the some of the words she knows printed in RAISED LETTERS on block cards, it would be a great help to us both! I spoke to Captain Keller and he said he would pay for them, if you could have them printed in raised print in Boston. Almost all of the words are the common words that any child her age would use. I am attaching the list. I thank you in advance from the bottom of my heart.

I am, sincerely, your friend,

Annie Sullivan

* * *

"To: Mrs. Hopkins,

June 2nd, 1887

Dear Mrs. Hopkins,

I hope you are doing well. I miss you terribly. I also miss the weather in Boston! Here the weather is scorching. We need rain badly... We are also very troubled about Helen.

She has been very nervous and excitable recently. She is restless at night and has no appetite. It is hard to know what to do with her.

The doctor says her mind is "too active." But how are we to keep her from thinking? She begins to spell the minute she wakes up in the morning and continues all day long. If I refuse to talk to her, wishing to give her some rest, she spells into her own hand! And she carries on the liveliest conversations with herself...!

I gave her my braille slate to play with, thinking that the mechanical pricking of holes in the paper would amuse her and rest her mind. But guess what? Yesterday she came to me with a sheet of paper that she had punched full of holes, and searched my drawer for an envelope! When I asked her what is that, she told me, "Helen write letter!"

What was my astonishment when I found that the little witch was trying to write a letter! I had no idea she even knew what a letter *was*.

True, she has often gone with me to the post-office to mail letters, and I suppose I have repeated to her things I wrote to you and to Mr. Anagnos. She knew, too, that I sometimes write "letters to blind friend" on the slate, that is, I wrote a short letter or two to Laura these past three months; but I didn't suppose that Helen had any clear idea what a letter *was*!

I asked her who was her letter for, and without blinking she spelled to me, "Uncle Frank!" I nearly burst out of laughter, and asked her what she had "written" to Frank (of course she does not know braille yet!)

She replied, "Much words."

I asked her, "Which words?"

She nodded enthusiastically and began telling me all of what she "wrote:"

"Puppy mother-dog–five."

"Baby–cry."

"Hot. Helen walk–no."

"Sun–bad boy!"

"Uncle Frank–come. Helen kiss Uncle Frank."

And lastly: "Strawberries–very good."

What a laugh I had! I told it to her parents, who were unfortunately less enthused, as they are worried about her state.

Helen is almost as eager to read as she is to talk. I find she grasps the import of whole sentences, catching from the context the meaning of words she doesn't know; and her eager questions indicate the outward reaching of her mind and its unusual powers.

Last night when I went to bed, I found Helen sound asleep with one of the small raised letters books clasped tightly in her arms. She had evidently been reading, and fallen asleep.

When I asked her about it in the morning, she said, "Book cry," and completed her meaning by shaking and other signs of fear. I taught her the word afraid, and she said: "Helen is not afraid. Book is afraid! Book will sleep with Helen! "

Oh, the rogue! I told her that the book wasn't afraid, and must sleep in its case, and that Helen mustn't read in bed. She looked very roguish, and apparently understood that I saw through her ruse.

Friends of the family are taking a deep interest in Helen. No one can see her without being impressed with her accomplishments. She is no ordinary child, and people's interest in her education will be no ordinary interest.

I want to write something here that is for your ears alone. Something within me tells me that I shall succeed with Helen beyond my dreams.

Were it not for some circumstances that make such an idea *highly* improbable, even *absurd*, I should think Helen's education would surpass in interest and wonder Dr. Howe's achievement with Laura. Helen has remarkable powers, and I believe that I shall be able to develop and mold them. I cannot tell how I know these things. A short time ago I had no idea how to go to work; I was feeling about in the dark; but somehow I now know, and I know that I know. I cannot explain it; but when difficulties arise, I am not perplexed or doubtful. I know how to meet them; I seem to sense Helen's peculiar needs. It is wonderful."

* * *

"To: Mrs. Hopkins,

June 5, 1887

Dear Mrs. Hopkins,

It is now three full months since I arrived here. The weather, however, was very different then. Now it is intolerable. The heat makes Helen languid and quiet. Indeed, the weather has reduced us all to a semi-liquid state.

Yesterday Helen took off her clothes and sat in her skin all afternoon. When the sun got round to the window where she was sitting with her book, she got up impatiently and shut the window. But when the sun came in just the same, she came over to me with a grieved look and spelled emphatically:

"Sun is bad boy. Sun must go to bed!"

Helen is the cutest little thing now, and so loving! One day she played all afternoon. When she returned to our room before dinner, she spelled to me:

"Legs very tired. Legs cry much!"

She was much interested this morning in some little chickens that were pecking their way into the world. I let her hold the egg in her hand, and feel the chicken "chip, chip." The hen was very gentle and made no objection to our investigations. Oh what was Helen's astonishment when she felt the tiny creature inside! I cannot describe her expression in words.

Besides the chickens, we have several other additions to the family–two calves, a colt, and several funny little pigs. You would laugh if you were to see me hold a squealing pig in my arms, while Helen feels it all over, and asks countless questions—questions not easy to answer either! After seeing the chicken come out of the egg, she asked about the new little piglet: "Did baby pig grow in egg? Where are many shells?"

* * *

"To: Mrs. Hopkins,

June 12th, 1887

Dear Mrs. Hopkins,

The weather continues to be hot. Helen is about the same: pale and thin. But you mustn't think she is really *ill*. I am sure the heat, and not her mind, is responsible for her condition. Of course, I shall not overtax her brain. Unfortunately we are both bothered a good deal by people who assume the responsibility of God and tell us that Helen is "overdoing," and that her "mind" is "too active." Mind you, these very people thought a few months ago that she had no mind at all!

They suggest many absurd and impossible remedies. But so far nobody seems to have thought of anesthetizing or chloroforming her, which is, I think, the only effective way of stopping the natural exercise of her faculties. It's queer how ready people always are with advice in any imaginary emergency and no matter how many times experience has shown them to be wrong, they continue to set forth their opinions, as if they had received them from God Almighty!

I've been trying not to teach Helen new words and let her mind rest in technical and simple tasks. I find that teaching her to write does exactly that: it is repetitive and keeps her mind quiet. I use that odd "square-hand letters" method. Since she cannot see the letter she draws, she uses a frame, like a ruler, with square holes in it, and inside each square hole she writes the letter. I'm not sure if you know what I'm talking about, ask Laura Bridgman to show you. All the letters are based on the shape of a square, and it looks a little odd, but it is readable and can be written in an organized manner. Like anything, Helen learns it quickly.

Regardless, the square-hand letters are only used now as a sort of diversion. It gives Helen something to do, and keeps her quiet, which I think is desirable while this enervating weather lasts.

Recently I taught her to count, and since then she had developed a sort of mania for counting. She has counted everything in the house, spoons, forks, plates.... As I am writing to you now she sits next to me and is counting the words in one of the raised-letters books... I hope it will not occur to her to count the hairs of her head!

If she could see and hear, I suppose she would get rid of her superfluous energy in ways which would not, perhaps, tax her brain so much. Although I suspect that the ordinary child takes his play pretty seriously. A little boy who plays in the nursery is concentrating his whole soul on his imagination too.

She just came to me and spelled, with a worried expression:

"Helen not count very many words."

I spelled back, "No, go and play with Doll Nancy!"

This suggestion didn't please her. She replied:

"No. Nancy is very sick."

I asked what was the matter. She spelled, "Much teeth make Nancy sick!"

Her baby sister, Mildred, is teething, you see?"

* * *

"To: Mrs. Hopkins,

June 15th, 1887

Dear Mrs. Hopkins,

Good Heavens! We had a glorious thunderstorm last night and it's much cooler today! We all feel refreshed as if we'd had a shower!

Helen is as lively as a cricket. She wanted to know if men were shooting in the sky when she felt the thunder. In the morning she asked me. "Did trees and flowers drink all the rain?"

She continues to manifest the same eagerness to learn as in the beginning. Her every waking moment is spent in the endeavor to satisfy her innate desire for knowledge, and her mind works so incessantly. But luckily her appetite, which left her a few weeks ago, has returned! Her sleep, also, seems more quiet and natural. She will be seven years old in two weeks.

She seems to understand about writing letters and is impatient to learn all the letters in square-form so that she can "write Uncle Frank a letter!"

She enjoys punching holes in paper with the stiletto, and I supposed it was because she could examine the result of her work; but her mother and I watched her one day, and saw her imagining she was writing a letter. She kept this up for nearly an hour. She was (or imagined she was) putting on paper the things which had interested her. When she had finished the letter she carried it to her mother and spelled, "Frank letter," and gave it to her to take to the post-office.

She recognizes instantly a person whom she has met, even if only once, and can spell that person's name in an instant. She is fond of gentlemen, and we notice that she makes friends with a gentleman sooner than with a lady.

She is always ready to share whatever she has

with those about her, often keeping but very little for herself. She is very fond of dress and of all kinds of finery, and is very unhappy when she finds a hole in anything she is wearing. She discovered a hole in her boot the other morning, and after breakfast she rushed to her father and spelled, "Helen new boot!"

* * *

Annie jumped out of bed, hearing screaming in the yard. She nearly fell down the stairs, terrified to hear children screaming and recognized Helen's guttural hollers.

As she exited the house she saw Helen wrestling with one of the girls, Viney. Viney was trying to push Helen away from her but Helen was biting and scratching Viney wildly.

"Helen!" Annie shouted, grabbing the hands of wild-looking Helen. Viney fell on the ground and crawled away, crying. Annie spelled into Helen's palm, "What happened?!"

Helen spelled back emphatically, "Viney is bad!" and began kicking Viney on the ground. Annie grabbed Helen and lifted her in the air, bringing her to the stairs of the porch where she held her firmly. Helen fought against her, her arms and legs kicking wildly.

Annie looked back at Viney, "What happened?"

"She…" Viney cried, "she was playing with that glass," she pointed at a large glass bowl on the ground, "she put stones into it and I was afraid the glass would break, so I tried"— she sniffled and wiped her tears—"I tried to explain to her but she did not understand, so I tried to take the glass from her, and she began to bite me...."

Martha, the cook, hurried outside and glanced at Helen crying, "Viney! What have you done!" she slapped Viney and Annie said, "Please, Martha, no! I don't think it was Viney's fault!"

Helen began sobbing quietly in Annie's arms.

Kate came out of the house, baby Mildred in her arms, "What's going on here for God's sake?"

Helen sensed her mother on the porch and flung her hands to her mother. Annie let her go and said, "Helen was fighting with Viney. Apparently Viney was trying to tell her to be careful not to put stones in the glass bowl, fearing it would break. Whatever happened, when I ran here Helen was biting and kicking Viney, and it didn't seem as if Viney was fighting back."

Kate was stunned, she embraced Helen and mumbled, "That is so... I'm so sorry...."

Annie dusted herself off and stood up. Martha walked away with Viney. Annie looked at Mrs. Keller and at Helen, feeling her heart beating fast.

Annie returned to her room, noticing the slippers she had forgot to take when she jumped off the bed, running barefoot downstairs. She fell unto the bed, astonished, troubled, disappointed, hurt.

A few minutes later Helen came to the room. She felt about the bed. Annie mumbled, "Go away Helen!"

Helen tried to kiss Annie but Annie moved away. She then grabbed Helen's hand and spelled, "I cannot kiss naughty girl!"

Helen's face twisted with pain. She shook her head emphatically and spelled, "Helen is good! Viney is bad!"

Annie spelled back, "You struck Viney and kicked and hurt her. You were very naughty, and I cannot kiss naughty girl!"

Helen's lips pouted. She hugged herself and shifted her weight from leg to leg. She then took Annie's hand and spelled, "Helen does not love Teacher! Helen does love mother! Mother will whip Viney!"

"Oh go away Helen!" Annie mumbled, tears in her eyes.

* * *

At the dinner table Annie did not eat anything. Kate tried to encourage her, "Please, Miss Annie, eat something."

"Thank you," Annie mumbled, "but I'm not hungry."

Captain Keller and James were talking about the local news. Annie had no interest in their conversation, nor in anything, really.

Helen felt around the table with her hand, reaching over gently to Annie's hand, finding both resting in her lap. Helen's hands hurried to the plate, finding that it was empty. She spelled to Annie, "Teacher sick! Martha make tea for Teacher!"

Annie spelled to her, "My heart is sad. I do not feel like eating."

Helen began to sob loudly. Captain Keller said, "For Christ's sake, what is going on?!"

Annie exhaled, "I'm sorry. I'd better go to my room. Excuse me," she pushed her chair back and left the table. Helen clung to Annie. Annie tried to push Helen away, but then felt pity and continued walking without resistance.

Captain Keller exclaimed, "Helen!"

Mrs. Keller waved her hand, "Let them go, Arthur."

Upstairs, Annie fell onto the bed. Helen, tears in her eyes, put her arms around Annie's neck and spelled, "I will be good tomorrow. Helen will be good all days!"

Annie felt many emotions stirring in her. She spelled back, "Will you tell Viney you are sorry, very sorry, for having scratched and bit and kicked her?"

Helen's face reddened, and then her frown suddenly turned into a smile as she spelled, "Viney cannot understand finger words!"

Annie shook her head and mumbled, "You little rogue..." she spelled "You and I will go together to Viney and I will tell Viney you are very sorry?"

Helen hesitated for a moment and then nodded.

"You will go with me now?"

Helen nodded slowly.

They went downstairs and passed by the dining room. Annie said, "Helen and I shall go to Viney and apologize for what happened in the afternoon."

Captain Keller's eyes widened, "No daughter of mine is going to go out to the slave's quarter—"

"The servant's quarter!" Mrs. Keller corrected him.

Silence followed. James looked eagerly to see his father's response.

"I forbid it."

"Captain Keller," Annie said, holding Helen's hand, "your daughter today, in a fit of rage, bit, scratched, and kicked Viney. To the best of my observation, Viney did not fight back, fearing the implication of fighting the daughter of her parent's employers. Now, Helen is willing to go and apologize, which I think is the proper thing to do. I have heard of Southern kindness, and I think her offer to apologize demonstrates just that."

Kate stood up and looked at her husband, "I shall go with them."

Captain Keller, stunned, leaned against the back of his chair and waved his hand at them dismissively.

Kate nodded, left her napkin on the table, and walked out the dining room. Annie spelled to Helen, "Mother comes with us to see Viney."

They walked quietly, Mrs. Keller leading the way. It was still warm outside, though the sun had already set. Kate seemed lost in thought. Annie looked at her. She admired her taking a stance.

They reached the servant's huts lit with a dim gas lamp. They heard voices inside the huts. Annie thought she heard a harmonica playing. Percy noticed them through the mosquito door, "Mrs. Keller! Miss Sullivan!"

Silence followed as the father of the family opened the door. Annie knew him as one of the workers in the fields. Mrs. Keller said, "We have come with Helen. She wanted to say something to Viney."

The father invited them all inside. Annie led Helen in front of her. She was surprised to see seven people inside. Viney was sitting in the corner, and her mother pushed her forward to the hut's entrance.

Annie spelled to Helen, "Viney is here."

Helen nodded her head slowly and spelled to Annie, "Sorry."

Annie spelled back to her, "Sorry for what?"

"Sorry for Helen be naughty girl."

Annie said, "Helen says she is sorry for having been a naughty girl."

Viney nodded, and then turned quickly to look at her mother. Her mother said, "Now say you forgive her and that you are sorry too."

Viney said that. Annie spelled it into Helen's hand, while looking at Mrs. Keller.

Helen then reached both her hands forward. Viney hesitated, but then embraced Helen for a quick second.

Helen smiled. Annie spelled to her, "Good girl!"

Helen nodded and spelled back, "Helen good girl!"

Kate looked around the room, "Please forgive us for coming unannounced. Have a pleasant evening." She then led the way out the hut. Some other servants stood outside. As Annie and Helen followed Mrs. Keller to the main house, Annie could hear whispers and sounds of astonishment behind them.

She spelled again to Helen, "Helen good girl. Teacher very happy."

Helen grabbed Annie's arm tightly and nodded.

* * *

"To Mrs. Hopkins,

July 3rd, 1887

Dear Mrs. Hopkins,

Yesterday afternoon I was in my room when I heard Helen screaming and ran down to see what the matter was. I found her in a terrible passion. I had hoped this would never happen again. She has been so gentle and obedient the past two months since we returned from the garden house, I thought love had subdued the lion; but it seems he was only sleeping.

At all events, there she was, tearing and scratching and biting the servant girl, 10-year-old Viney, like some wild thing. It seems Viney had attempted to take a glass bowl, which Helen was filling with stones, fearing that she would break it. Helen resisted and Viney tried to force it out of her hand and I suspect that she slapped the child, or did something which caused this unusual outburst of temper. When I grabbed Helen's hand she was trembling violently and began to cry. I asked what was the matter, and she spelled: "Viney bad!" and began to kick Viney again with renewed violence. I held her hands firmly until she became calmer and her mother came.

At the dinner table she was greatly disturbed because I didn't eat, and suggested that "Martha (the cook) make tea for Teacher." But I told her that my heart was sad, and I didn't feel like eating. She began to cry and sob and cling to me.

Later she was willing to go and apologize to Viney. She and Viney hugged. I was proud of her. In all events, this morning she woke up and has been unusually affectionate. It seems to me there is a sweetness—a soul beauty in her face which I have not seen before. I am proud of my little pupil."

* * *

Helen was ecstatic as Annie opened the small wooden box. They were both in their room upstairs. Annie noticed a letter inside the box, and opened it. She recognized Mr. Anagnos' handwriting:

"To: Miss Annie Sullivan,

Captain Arthur Keller Household

Tuscumbia, Alabama

My dear Annie,

Please find in this package several copies of the list of words prepared by yourself for the use of your pupil. Do accept them for little Helen with much love and my best wishes. Please dismiss Captain Keller's insistence on paying for them, and see these cards as a gift from the Massachusetts School for the Blind.

From Mrs. Hopkins, I follow with a most profound interest your account of Helen's remarkable progress and attainments. I am especially impressed with your insistence on teaching her square-hand-letters. For that use, please find a grooved writing board.

Now, dear Annie, I am going to bother you with an earnest request. I want you to prepare for our forthcoming annual report a brief account of Helen's history and education, giving her age, the cause of her blindness and deafness, her temperament, her natural aptitude, the steps taken and the methods employed in her training, and what has already been accomplished. I ask you to do this for your own sake and for the credit of your alma mater. Pray go right to work and write a little every day until the paper is finished. I thank you for that in advance.

With admiration, I remain,

Sincerely your friend,

M. Anagnos."

Annie shook her head. All this flattery felt strange. '*With admiration, I remain*'?!" She sighed. Helen prodded at the box, eager for Annie to open the many envelopes in the box. Annie opened the first envelope and smiled as she saw Helen's name written in raised letters. She gave it to Helen.

Helen's reaction was almost frightening to Annie: she screamed, tears showing up in her eyes, and she ran with the card downstairs. Annie followed her downstairs, chuckling, as Helen found her mother in the sitting room with baby Mildred.

Kate hugged Helen and looked at Annie, "I did not know this was so important to her, Miss Annie!"

Annie smiled, "Me neither!"

* * *

The following day Annie prepared to go to the post office with Helen. She told Mrs. Keller she had written a thank you note for Mr. Anagnos. Hearing that, Kate said, "Oh would you take a letter from me as well?"

Annie nodded, and Kate said, "It will only take me a minute."

Annie played with Helen in the sitting room as Kate jotted a short letter of gratitude to Mr. Anagnos. She sealed the letter and gave it to Annie.

On the carriage, Annie could not stop herself from wanting to open Kate's letter, wondering whether Mrs. Keller had written anything about her to Mr. Anagnos.

Annie glanced at Helen, who was enjoying the wind, sticking her face out of the carriage window.

Annie gently prodded the envelope and pushed it open. She knew it was wrong, but her temptation was stronger. She took out the short note and read it, her heart beating fast:

"Mr. Anagnos,

I tender Arthur's thanks and mine for your kindness in sending Helen the raised words. I think you never gave anyone a greater happiness. She has been disgusted with her books because she could not find the names of the people she knew, and in fact all the words she knows. She was so excited I thought she would never be willing to go to sleep last night, opening with Miss Sullivan and me all the various envelopes. Thank you for your kindness!

Miss Sullivan seems very pleased and proud of her pupil. She succeeds wonderfully in her teaching.

I am yours truly,

Kate A. Keller"

Annie held the letter to her heart, tears of joy appearing in her eyes. She read the last sentence again, *'She succeeds wonderfully in her teaching.'*

Kate said it before to Annie's face, but never had Annie seen it *written*. Nor was it ever communicated, as far as she knew, to the principal of her school! She put the letter back carefully and wetted the envelope's sealing line. She held Helen's hand tightly and mumbled to herself, "Miss Sullivan *succeeds wonderfully* in her teaching!"

* * *

"To: Mrs. Hopkins

July 31st, 1887

Dear Mrs. Hopkins,

I am so happy half the summer is behind us! It has been nearly five months since I arrived here, and I am so pleased with Helen's progress. Her pencil-writing is excellent. I am teaching her the braille alphabet now, and she is delighted to be able to make words that she can *feel* with her own fingers.

She has now reached the question stage of her development. It is "what," "when" and especially "why" *all day long,* and as her intelligence grows her inquiries become more insistent. I remember how unbearable I used to find the inquisitiveness of children before; but I know now that these questions indicate the child's growing interest in the *cause* of things. The "why," I now understand, is the *door* through which the child enters the world of *reason* and *reflection*.

Helen cannot stop asking: "How does carpenter know to build house?" "Who put chickens in eggs?" "Why flies bite?" "Can flies know not to bite?" "Why did father go hunting?"

Of course she asks many questions that are not as intelligent as these. Her mind isn't more logical than the minds of ordinary children. On the whole, her questions are analogous to those that a bright three-year-old child asks; but her desire for knowledge is so earnest, the questions are never tedious, though they draw heavily upon my meager store of information, and tax my ingenuity to the utmost!

I had a letter from Laura Bridgman last Sunday. Please give her my love, and tell her Helen sends her a kiss. I read the letter at the dinner table and then showed it to Mrs. Keller. She noticed the handwriting and the sentence structure and exclaimed: "Why, Miss Annie, Helen writes almost as well as that!"

It is true. Her writing is wonderful. To the unaccustomed eye all the letters are indeed weird-looking. But as far as square-lettering goes, Helen's hand writing is impressive. I am proud of her.

It might be a while before I write again. Captain Keller's brother, George, hurt his arm and his wife Anna wrote to Captain Keller asking to come. Captain Keller does not want to leave the whole household to Mrs. Keller, and suggested that Helen and I will come with him. I was not interested, but Helen was quickly infatuated with the idea of travelling, and all she talks about is the coming trip, especially the train ride, for which she is terribly excited.

I shall write again when we return.

Yours with love,

Annie.

* * *

"To: Mrs. Hopkins,

August 21, 1887.

It's been nearly a month since I have written to you last. We had a beautiful time in Huntsville, visiting Captain Keller's brother and his wife. Everybody there was delighted with Helen and showered her with gifts and kisses. As not to burden George and Anna, we stayed in the small hotel in town. The first evening Helen walked in the hotel's dining room with me, touching all the guests (with their permission of course) and learning their names. There were about twenty guests, I think.

The next morning we were astonished to find that Helen remembered all of the names, and recognized every person she met the night before.

Our stay lasted two and a half weeks. Helen managed to teach the youngsters there the manual alphabet, and several of them learned to talk with her. One of the girls taught her to dance the polka, and a little boy showed her his rabbits and spelled their names for her. She was delighted, and showed her pleasure by hugging and kissing the little fellow, which embarrassed him very much.

While there she wrote the following letter, her first, to her mother. I am copying it here:

"Helen will write mother letter

Papa did give Helen medicine

Mildred will sit in swing

Mildred did kiss Helen

Teacher did give Helen peach

George is sick in bed

George arm is hurt

Aunt Anna did give Helen lemonade

Dog did stand up

Train conductor did pinch ticket

Aunt Anna will buy Helen pretty new hat

Helen will hug and kiss mother

Helen will come home

Good by."

Isn't this letter *impressive*? Given her age, and the fact that up until five and a half months ago she did not know a word in the world, I think it is quite remarkable of her. And she wrote it all herself! I also began encouraging her to write a diary. Each day she registers a few lines in it.

Since we returned two days ago she has talked incessantly about what she did in Huntsville, and we noticed a very decided improvement in her ability to use language. She has a good memory and imagination and the faculty of association.

How has the summer been for you in Brewster? Are you excited about the beginning of the coming school year? Do tell me everything, Mrs. Hopkins, I enjoy your letters so much!

Yours with love,

Annie."

* * *

"To: Mrs. Hopkins

August 28th, 1887

Dear Mrs. Hopkins,

I do wish things would stop being born! "New puppies," "new calves" and "new babies" keep Helen's interest in the "why" and wherefore of things at white heat! The arrival of a new baby cousin the other day was the occasion of a fresh outburst of questions about the origin of babies and live things in general:

"Where did Aunt Leila get new baby?"

"How did doctor know where to find baby?"

"Did Aunt Leila tell doctor to find new baby?"

Her aunt and uncle have both learned the manual alphabet recently. Oh my, Helen asked them these questions directly! Naturally, her questions were sometimes asked under circumstances which rendered them embarrassing, so I made up my mind that something must be done about this matter. If it was natural for Helen to *ask* such questions, it was my duty to *answer* them.

It's a great mistake, I think, to put children off with falsehoods and nonsense, when their growing powers of observation and discrimination excite in them a desire to know about things. From the beginning, I have made it a practice to answer all Helen's questions to the best of my ability in a way intelligible to her, and at the same time while always speaking *truthfully*. I therefore asked myself, "Why should I treat these questions differently?"

I decided that there was no reason, except my deplorable ignorance of the great facts that underlie our physical existence. It was no doubt because of this ignorance that I rushed in where more experienced angels fear to tread...!

There isn't a living soul here to whom I can go for advice in this, or indeed, in any other educational difficulty. The only thing for me to do in a perplexity is to go ahead, and learn by making mistakes. But in this case I don't think I made any. I took Helen and my botany book, "How Plants Grow," up in the tree house, where we often go to read and study, and I told her in simple words the story of plant-life.

I reminded her of the corn, beans and watermelon-seed she had planted in the spring, and told her that the small corn in the garden, and the beans and watermelon vines had grown from those seeds. I explained how the earth keeps the seeds warm and moist, until the little leaves are strong enough to push themselves out into the light and air where they can breathe and grow and bloom and make more seeds, from which other baby-plants shall grow.

I drew an analogy between plant and animal-life, and told her that seeds are eggs as truly as hen's eggs and bird's eggs—that the mother hen keeps her eggs warm and dry until the little chicks come out. I made her understand that all life comes from an egg. The mother bird lays her eggs in a nest and keeps them warm until the birdlings are hatched. The mother fish lays her eggs where she knows they will be moist and safe, until it is time for the little fish to come out.

I asked her where does baby Mildred sleep, and taught her the word "cradle." I then told her that she could call the egg the "cradle of all life."

Then I told her that other animals like the dog and cow and human beings do not lay their eggs but nourish their young in their own bodies. I had no difficulty in making it clear to her that if plants and animals didn't produce offspring after their kind, they would cease to exist, and everything in the world would soon die. But the function of sex I passed over as lightly as possible. I did, however, try to give her the idea that love is the great continuer of life.

The subject was difficult, and my knowledge inadequate; but I am glad I didn't shirk my responsibility; for, stumbling, hesitating, and incomplete as my explanation was, it touched deep responsive chords in the soul of my little pupil and the readiness with which she comprehended the great facts of physical life confirmed me in the opinion that every child has dormant *within* him, when he comes into the world, *all* the experiences of the human race. These experiences are like photographic negatives, until language "develops" them and brings out the memory-images.

I hope I was not boring in my explanation to you, dear Mrs. Hopkins, but I thought you might like to hear of it. Helen talks nowadays a lot about the "School for the Blind" and about "Auntie" (that is how I call you), and about the "little blind girls" at the school. Now that we have returned from Huntsville she talks of going to Boston! She does not understand it is very far away, and she fancies that it will happen soon. Oh, how I wish she was right! I would give anything to see you and my beloved Massachusetts.

Do write to me and tell me how your summer has been.

Yours,

Annie."

* * *

"To: Mrs. Hopkins,

September 4th, 1887

Dear Mrs. Hopkins,

I must tell you a funny episode which happened this morning. Helen had received a letter this morning from Aunt Anna. She was much pleased with the letter, and after she had asked all the questions she could, she took the letter to her mother, who was sewing in the hall, and "read" it to her. It was amusing to see Helen holding the letter before her eyes and spelling the sentences out on her fingers, just as I had done. Afterward she tried to read it to Belle (the dog) and to baby Mildred. Mrs. Keller and I watched the nursery comedy from the door.

Belle was sleepy and Mildred inattentive. Helen looked very serious, and, once or twice when Mildred tried to take the letter, she pulled the letter from her impatiently. Finally Belle got up, shook herself, and was about to walk away, when

Helen caught her by the neck and forced her to lie down again. In the meantime Mildred had got the letter and crept away with it. Helen felt on the floor for the letter, but not finding it there, she got up and stood very still, as if listening with her feet to Mildred's "thump, thump."

When she had located the sound, she went quickly toward the little culprit and found her chewing the precious letter from Aunt Anna! This was too much for Helen! She immediately snatched the letter and slapped Mildred's little hands soundly! We rushed to her, Mrs. Keller took the crying baby in her arms, and I took Helen and asked her, "What did you do to baby?!"

She looked troubled, and hesitated a moment before answering: "Wrong baby did eat letter! Helen did slap very wrong baby!"

I explained to her that Mildred was very small, and did not know that it was wrong to put the letter in her mouth.

Helen spelled back, "I did tell baby, no, no, much times!"

I spelled, "Mildred does not understand your fingers, and we must be very gentle with baby!"

She shook her head and thumped her forehead, spelling to me, "Baby does not think!"

A moment later she spelled to me, "Helen will give baby new letter!" and with that she ran upstairs and brought down a neatly folded sheet of paper, on which she had practiced some words with my braille slate. She gave the letter to Mildred and spelled to me, "Baby can eat all words!"

I just thought you might like this little story, as it

shows my little witch in all her charm!"

* * *

"To: Mrs. Hopkins

September 18th, 1887

Dear Mrs. Hopkins,

First, thank you for the interest in all of my doings. Sometimes I wonder if it is of any interest to you. Receiving your last letter assured me that it was. Thank you for being my dear friend.

Helen is wonderful, she really is. I kept a record of everything she said last week, and I found that she knows six hundred words! Could you believe it? This does not mean, however, that she always uses them *correctly*. Sometimes her sentences are like Chinese puzzles; but they are the kind of puzzles children make when they try to express their half-formed ideas by means of arbitrary language. She has the true language impulse, and shows great fertility of resource in making the words at her command convey her meaning.

Lately she has been much interested in color. She found the word "brown" in one of the books and wanted to know its meaning. I told her that her hair was brown, and she asked, "Is brown very pretty?" I told her of the different colors, and she then dragged me all over the house and asked for the color of everything she touched! When we were done with the house she suggested that we go the hen houses and barns; but I told her she must wait until another day because I was very tired.

We went and sat in the hammock; but there was no rest for the weary there either! Helen was eager to know "more color!" I wonder if she has any vague idea of color. Does she have any reminiscent impression of light and sound? It seems as if a child who could see and hear until her nineteenth month must retain *some* of her first impressions, though ever so faintly... Helen talks a great deal about things that she cannot know of through the sense of touch. She asks many questions about the sky, day and night, stars and mountains....

But I seem to have lost the thread of my discourse. As we swung to and fro in the hammock, one of her funniest questions was "What color is *think*?"

I told her that when we are happy our thoughts are bright, and when we are naughty our thoughts are darker. Quick as a flash she said, "My think is white! My think is white!"

Isn't she adorable? I attach you the letter Helen wrote for the girls in first grade. Please give it to their teacher or to Mr. Anagnos. Helen labored on it for several hours. I am very proud of her.

Yours with love,

Annie."

* * *

"To: Blind Girls

From: Helen Keller

Helen will write little blind girls a letter

Helen and teacher will come to see little blind girls

Helen and teacher will go in train to Boston

Helen and blind girls will have fun

Blind girls can talk on fingers

Helen will see Mr. Anagnos

Mr. Anagnos will love and kiss Helen

Helen will go to school with blind girls

Helen can read and count and spell and write like blind girls

Mildred will not go to Boston

Mildred does eat letters

Helen does play with Belle

Helen does ride in carriage with teacher

Helen is blind and pretty

Helen will put letter in envelope for blind girls

Good by

Helen Keller."

* * *

"To: Mrs. Hopkins

October 25th, 1887

Dear Mrs. Hopkins,

Helen was very excited to receive yesterday the letter from the first grade girls, and hurried to write them back on her own accord! Her father took it today to send it to Mr. Anagnos. I did manage to copy it for you before Captain Keller sent it. Notice the improvement she had had in the one month since her first letter to them. She does not refer to herself as "Helen" but as "I" and even "me" in the proper places!

"Dear little blind girls

I will write you a letter

I thank you for pretty doll

Mother and Mildred came home Wednesday

Mother brought me a pretty new dress and hat

Papa did go to Huntsville

Papa brought me apples and candy

I and teacher will come to Boston and see you

Nancy is my doll

Nancy does cry

I do rock Nancy to sleep

Mildred is sick

Doctor will give her medicine to make her well

I and teacher did go to church Sunday

Preacher did read in book and talk

Lady did play organ

I did put coins in basket

I will be good girl and teacher will braid my hair lovely

I will hug and kiss little blind girls

Good by

Helen Keller."

* * *

I am so impressed with my little pupil! I am aware that the progress she has made between the writing of the two letters must seem incredible. Only those who are with her daily can realize the rapid advancement which she is making in the acquisition of language. She has begun to use pronouns of her own accord. This morning I happened to say, "Helen will go upstairs." She laughed and said, "Teacher is wrong. Do not say Helen will go upstairs. Say YOU will go upstairs!"

This is another great forward step. Thus it always is: yesterday's perplexities are strangely simple today, and today's difficulties become tomorrow's pastime.

Oh Mrs. Hopkins! The rapid development of Helen's mind is beautiful to watch. I doubt if any teacher ever had a work of such absorbing interest! There must have been one lucky star in the heavens at my birth, and I am just beginning to feel its beneficent influence. I sent Mr. Anagnos my account about Helen for the Annual Report, based on my letters to you. It was very taxing for me to write. My only hope in writing it was that Helen's wonderful deliverance might be a boon to other afflicted children."

* * *

"To: Mrs. Hopkins,

November 4th, 1887

Dear Mrs. Hopkins,

Today it is exactly eight months since my arrival in Tuscumbia. So much had happened!

Helen now uses many pronouns correctly. She says, *you, she, it, this,* and it shows a great improvement in her comprehension of language. She rarely misuses or omits one in conversation. Her passion for writing letters and putting her thoughts upon paper grows more intense. She now tells stories in which the imagination plays an important part.

You might recall that I began teaching her the braille system. She learned it gladly when she discovered that she could herself actually *read* what she had written! This still affords her constant pleasure. She finds writing in pencil very tiring and frustrating, as she cannot read what she had written. Now, with braille, she is ecstatic! For a whole evening she will sit at the table writing whatever comes into her busy brain, and she would then reread to herself with much pleasure.

Her progress in arithmetic has been equally remarkable. She can add and subtract with great rapidity up to the sum of one hundred; and she knows the multiplication tables as far as the fives.

These days there are two future events that excite her and have her waiting impatiently. In a week's time a CIRCUS is coming to town, and Captain Keller had given his permission for us to visit. When I told her, she jumped up and down with excitement, realizing she will meet for the first time in her life many new animals. The second event she is excited about is... Christmas! Yes, I know it is in two months time, but the poor girl never knew what Christmas *was* or what made it so *unique*, and she asks many questions about this strange holiday. I tell her much about it. In turn, she is highly excitable about Christmas and the gifts she might receive from Santa Claus.

Recently Helen began realizing that she is not like other children. The other day she asked, "What do my eyes do?"

I hesitated for a moment, and then told her that I could see things with my eyes and that she could see them with her fingers.

Do you think I answered well? I want to make her feel able and strong, rather than damaged and invaluable.

I think of you often, Mrs. Hopkins! The thought of Christmas without you makes my heart aches.

Yours with love,

Annie."

* * *

"To: Mrs. Hopkins:

November 13th, 1887

Dear Mrs. Hopkins,

We took Helen to the circus, and my, we had "the time of our lives!"

The circus people were much interested in Helen and did everything they could to make her first circus a memorable event. They let her feel the animals when it was safe. She fed the elephants, and was allowed to climb up on the back of the largest elephant! She sat in the lap of the "Oriental Princess," while the elephant marched majestically around the ring.

She also felt some young lions. They were as gentle as kittens; but I told her they would get wild and fierce as they grew older. Do you know what she said in response? "Teacher will take baby lions home and teach them to be good girls!"

Oh my, isn't she brilliant?

She was greatly delighted with the monkeys and kept her hand on the star performer while he went through his tricks. She laughed heartily when he took off his hat to the audience. One cute little monkey stole her hair ribbon, and another tried to snatch the flowers out of the hat in her hand. She laughed hysterically.

I don't know who had the best time, the monkeys, Helen or the other spectators. One of the leopards licked her hands, and the man in charge of the giraffes lifted her up in his arms so that she could feel their necks and see how tall they were.

The riders and clowns and rope walkers were all glad to let "the little blind girl" feel their costumes and follow their motions whenever it was possible, and she kissed them all to show her gratitude. Some of them even cried.

Ever since returning home two days ago she has talked about nothing but the circus. In order to answer her questions about the many animals, I have been obliged to read a great deal in the family's encyclopedia and Captain Keller's copy of Johnson's *Household Book of Nature.* All this made me feel like a jungle on wheels!"

* * *

"To: Mrs. Hopkins,

December 12th, 1887

Dear Mrs. Hopkins!

Thank you for your kind letter and for the beautiful gift! I will give Helen the ring on Christmas morning. I know she would be overjoyed. Thank you for thinking of her!

It's nine months since I arrived here. It's getting cooler, which makes me think of home. I find it hard to realize that Christmas is almost here (in spite of the fact that Helen talks about nothing else!) Do you remember what a happy time we had last Christmas together? It brings me tears to think of it, so I try not to.

Helen is as eager to have stories told her as any hearing child I ever knew. She has made me repeat the story of *Little Red Riding Hood* so often that I believe I could say it backward!

Interestingly, she likes stories that make her cry! But don't we all? I think it's so nice to feel sad when you've nothing particular to be sad about....

I am teaching her little rhymes and verses too. They fix beautiful thoughts in her memory. I think, too, that they quicken all the child's faculties, because they stimulate the imagination.

Helen has learned to tell the time at last by feeling the little arrows by touching them gently. Her father is going to give her a watch for Christmas.

Oh, Mrs. Hopkins! I wish you a Merry Christmas, and a Happy New Year! Let us pray that in the coming year we shall see each other more than in the current one!

Yours with love,

Annie."

* * *

"To: Mrs. Hopkins,

January 1st, 1888

Dear Mrs. Hopkins,

Happy new year, dear!

Christmas week was a very busy one here. Helen has become somewhat famous in the area. She was invited to *all* the children's entertainments in Tuscumbia, and I took her to as many events as I could. I want her to know children and to be with them and around them as much as possible. Several little girls have learned to spell on their fingers and were very proud of their accomplishment.

One little chap, about seven, was persuaded to learn letters, and he spelled his name for Helen. She was delighted and showed her joy by hugging and kissing him, much to his embarrassment! The little princess likes little boys very much!

Saturday the school children put up their tree, and I took Helen to their celebration. She was very excited. There was a present on the tree for each child, and to her great delight she was permitted to hand gifts to the children. She received several presents for herself. She placed them all in a chair, resisting all temptation to look at them until every child had received his gifts.

One little girl named Nellie had a fewer presents than the rest of the children. Helen seemed very much troubled by that for a few moments. Then her face became radiant and she spelled to me, "I will give Nellie mug!"

The mug, Mrs. Hopkins, was one of the presents she received. In fact, it was the gift which afforded Helen the most pleasure. She had chosen her prettiest gift and the one which had pleased her most to give to a little stranger! Such an instance of self-denial so simply and so naturally done, was most gratifying for me to witness as her teacher!

It was also very sweet to see the children's eager interest in Helen, and their readiness to give her pleasure. The celebration began at nine in the morning, and it was one o'clock before we could leave. My fingers and head ached; but Helen was as fresh and full of spirit as when we left home in the morning.

After dinner it began to snow, and we had a good frolic and an interesting lesson about the snow.

Sunday morning the ground was covered with snow, and Helen and the cook's children and I played snowball. By noon the snow was all gone. It was the first snow I had seen here, and it made me a little homesick.

Oh, Mrs. Hopkins, I wish you had been here to witness Helen. It was touching and beautiful to see her enjoy her first real Christmas! She hung her stocking and lay awake for a long time, waiting for Santa. She got up two or three times to see if anything had happened to the stocking. When I told her that Santa Claus would not come until she was asleep, she shut her eyes and spelled to me with an earnest face, "Now he will think I am asleep and come!"

In the morning she was the first one to jump out of bed, and ran downstairs to the fireplace for stocking; and when she found that Santa Claus had filled the stocking, she screamed with glee and woke everyone up.

The ring you sent her was in the toe of the stocking, and when I told her you gave it to Santa Claus for her, she said, "I do love Mrs. Hopkins!"

She received a dress for her doll Nancy, and her comment was, "Now Nancy will go to party!"

When she opened up her own new braille slate which Captain Keller bought she said, "I will write many letters, and I will thank Santa Claus very much!"

It was evident that everyone, especially Captain and Mrs. Keller, was deeply moved at the thought of the difference between this bright Christmas and the last, when their little girl had no conscious part in the Christmas festivities.

In the afternoon, when we came downstairs for lunch, Mrs. Keller held my arms and said to me with tears in her eyes, "Miss Annie, I thank God every day of my life for sending you to us; but I never realized until this morning what a blessing you have been to us!"

Even Captain Keller took my hand and tried to say something, but he could not utter a word. I could see in his eyes he was overwhelmed with emotions. In a sense his silence was more eloquent than words. My heart, too, was full of gratitude and solemn joy. It is a great thing to feel that you are of some use in the world, that you are necessary to somebody. I feel truly fortunate."

* * *

"To: Mrs. Hopkins,

January 9th, 1888

Dear Mrs. Hopkins,

The Annual Report came last night. I appreciate the kind things Mr. Anagnos has said about Helen and me; but his extravagant way of saying them rubs me the wrong way. The simple facts would be so much more convincing! Why, for instance, does he take the trouble to ascribe "educational motives" to me that I *never dreamed of?* My motive in coming here was not in any sense philanthropic... How ridiculous it is to say I had "drunk so copiously of the noble spirit of Dr. Howe" that I "was fired with the desire to rescue from darkness and obscurity the little Alabamian!"

You know, and he knows, and I know, that I came here simply because circumstances made it necessary for me to earn my living, and I seized upon the first opportunity that offered itself, although I did not suspect, nor did he, that I had *any* special fitness for the work!

Captain Keller, however, is very pleased with the Annual Report. Already the report was quoted in two articles that were sent to us. And we received several letters from people greeting us about Helen's success.

P.S.

I received a letter from Lilian last week. She said that Edith is a bright, active child but that she has the temper of a little "tigress." She added that it was very hard to control her because Mr. Anagnos "positively" refused to have Edith punished. What astonished me was to hear of her progress. So far she has learned only a few nouns, but Lilian "intends" to give Edith some verbs "very soon." Poor Lilian—or should I say—poor Edith! I didn't suppose that a more incompetent girl could be found to undertake the education of an unfortunate child than MYSELF; but I think Lilian has me beaten by a head at least!

I hope I do not sound arrogant. But I cannot begin to tell you what Helen's success means to me, given my life thus far. I feel suddenly competent in something!

Mr. Anagnos wrote that he might visit us in March. I do hope he'll come, if only to convince Captain Keller to send me and Helen to Massachusetts for a few weeks to learn in the school. I miss the North so much! And of course, dear, I miss you too terribly.

Yours,

Annie.

P.P.S– I might get to visit Memphis next month! Mrs. Keller's family is from there. I hear it is a great large metropolis, somewhat like Boston! I am very excited about being away from Alabama for a while!"

THE TEACHER

* * *

"To: Mrs. Hopkins,

February 10th, 1888

Dear Mrs. Hopkins,

First, before I forget, Mr. Anagnos wrote and said he will be able to come visit in two weeks. Helen is excited, knowing he is the man who had sent her the grooved writing board and the raised letters cards. Oh, dear, I wish you could have come instead of him!

We just returned last night from a whole week in Memphis! We had a splendid time there, but I didn't rest much. It was nothing but excitement from first to last: family luncheons, public receptions, and all that they involve when you have an eager, tireless child like Helen on your hands. She talked *incessantly*. I don't know what I should have done, had some of the young people not learned to talk with her using the manual alphabet. These young relatives of Helen relieved me as much as possible. But even then I could never have a quiet half hour to myself! It was always: "Oh, Miss Sullivan, please come and tell us what Helen means," or "Miss Sullivan, won't you please explain this to Helen? We can't make her understand...."

I believe half the population of Memphis called on us!

The stores in Memphis were very good, and I managed to spend *all the money* that I had with me! One day Helen said, "I must buy Nancy a very pretty hat."

I said, "Very well, we will go shopping this afternoon."

She had a silver dollar and ten cents. When we reached the shop, I asked her how much she would pay for Nancy's hat. She answered promptly, having done her homework, "Ten cents!"

I asked her in response, "What will you do with the dollar?"

She smiled, "I will buy some good candy to take home!"

Mrs. Keller's brother, Uncle Fred, tried to help me and Mrs. Keller in making a list of words Helen knows. We have got as far as the letter P, and there were 900 words to her credit. Uncle Fred called Helen "a genius." (Mrs. Keller told me later that her brother was the most adamant person in the family in pushing Kate to institutionalize Helen, telling her just two years ago, "You ought to really put that child away. She is mentally defective and it is not very pleasant to see her about!" I felt really happy for Mrs. Keller for proven him wrong!)

Captain Keller has had many interesting letters since the publication of the Annual Report and the subsequent articles in newspapers, now amounting to over a hundred articles sent to us, are all stored in one neat folder Mrs. Keller keeps. But of all the letters that best was from Dr. Alexander Graham Bell!

Dr. Bell wrote that Helen's progress is "without parallel in the education of the deaf," and he said many nice things about her teacher! He wishes for us to visit him in Washington, as well as to visit a school for the deaf there. I am highly interested in seeing their methods of education, hoping I can learn something about their ways of teaching.

Do tell me how you are doing. I miss you terribly.

Yours with love,

Annie."

* * *

"To: Mrs. Hopkins,

March 5th, 1888

My dear Mrs. Hopkins,

Mr. Anagnos left yesterday. It was a pleasant visit for him and for us. He spoke at length with Captain Keller about allowing Helen and myself—possibly with Mrs. Keller as well—to visit Massachusetts. I now realize that he hopes to present Helen as the product of the school to be able to raise more funds for the school. I do not oppose it. We might visit soon, as the graduation ceremony is in the beginning of June. Isn't it the best piece of news you have ever heard from me?

Yesterday it was a year since I arrived in Tuscumbia. A year! Can you believe it? Oh, Mrs. Hopkins! How forlorn and weary I was, nobody, not even you can imagine! I remember how the conductor on the train tried to comfort me. He noticed that I cried a great deal, and he did his best to cheer me.

I remember getting off the train and meeting Mrs. Keller in the carriage. When she spoke, a great weight rolled off my heart, there was such sweetness and refinement in her voice! It is a wonder how much of one's character and disposition is revealed in one's voice. There is no doubt in my mind that the voice is a truer index to character than the face. We learn to control the expression of our features; but very few ever succeed in controlling their voices.

I remember seeing Helen for the first time. How disappointed I was when the untamed little creature stubbornly refused to kiss me and struggled frantically to free herself from my embrace, and when her mother took her away from my bag, which she tried to open in search for food, she began to kick violently. This was my introduction to that bit of my life. I need not tell you, dear, that this has been a hard year; but I do not forget the many pleasant moments in it.

Many times I have lost my patience and courage; but I have found that one difficult task accomplished makes the next easier. Oh, my most persistent foe is that feeling of restlessness that takes possession of me sometimes. It overflows my soul like a tide, and there is no escape from it. It is more torturing than any physical pain I have ever endured. I pray constantly that my love for this beautiful child may grow so large and satisfying that there will be no room in my heart for restlessness and discontent!

And, dear, I am glad that my success has been such a gratification for you personally. I thank you from the bottom of my heart for the mother-love you gave me when I was a lonely, troublesome schoolgirl, whose thoughtlessness must have caused you no end of anxiety...!

I know you feared that my quick temper and saucy tongue would make trouble for me here; but I am glad to be able to tell you, at the end of the first year of my independence, that I have lived peaceably with all men and women here. True, there have been murder and treason and arson in my heart; but they haven't got out, thanks to my strong teeth that have often stood guard over my tongue!

These days nearly every mail brings some article in it about Helen. We even received (I'm not sure if I can tell you that, so keep it a secret for now) an invitation from the secretary of the White House, informing us that President Cleveland had read about Helen and wishes to meet her AND her teacher! Could you believe it?!

Oh, Mrs. Hopkins, it is a blessed thing to know that there is someone who rejoices with us when we are glad, and who takes pride in our achievements from afar. Until I met you, Mrs. Hopkins, I never loved anyone, except my little brother Jimmie. I have always felt that the one thing needful to happiness is love. To have a friend is to have one of the sweetest gifts that life can bring, and my heart sings for joy now, for I have both you and Helen as my dear friends.

Yours with love,

Annie."

* * *

"To: Mrs. Hopkins,

April 17th, 1888

Dear Mrs. Hopkins,

I wonder if the days seem as interminable to you as they do to me. We talk and plan and dream about nothing but Boston, Boston, Boston! I think Mrs. Keller has definitely decided to go with us, but she will not stay all summer. Thank you for your invitation to spend the summer with you. I told Helen about it and you have never seen a happier child! She has never been to the sea, and the thought of swimming in the vast sea has her excited as a two year old.

Yesterday, Sunday, was one of the longest days in my life. There is a big church conference in town, and the Presbytery from around the country came. Captain Keller insisted that we should go with Helen, as he wanted the ministers to see her. I was less than enthused, but had, of course, no say in the matter.

When we arrived at the town's church at nine Sunday school was in session, and I wish you could have seen the sensation Helen's entrance caused among the children. Many of them remembered her handing them their gifts on Christmas, remember? They were so pleased to see her that they paid no attention to their teachers, but rushed out of their seats and surrounded us. She kissed them all, girls as well as boys, willing or unwilling. She recognized many of them by their hands and spelled their names!

After that we were taken to a large room in which the ministers gathered. Captain Keller presented us, and the ministers began pouring me with questions to ask Helen. One of the ministers wished me to ask Helen, "What do ministers *do*?"

I spelled it to Helen and she hesitated for a moment. I could see Captain Keller becoming nervous! But then she spelled to me, and everyone listened attentively: "Ministers read, and talk loud, telling people to be good people!"

Everyone clapped in response and the minister who asked the question put Helen's answer down in his notebook.

When it was time for the church service to begin, Helen was in such a state of excitement that I thought it best to take her away; but Captain Keller said, "No, she will be all right." So there was nothing to do but stay.

It was impossible to keep Helen quiet. She hugged and kissed me, as well as the gentlemen who happened to sit on her other side. She felt about the people in the row in front of us and behind us and couldn't sit still. She must have been excited about all the attention she had received in the morning.

When the communion service began and the wine was poured, she smelt the wine and sniffed so loud that everyone in the church could hear. When the wine was passed to our neighbor, he was obliged to stand up to prevent her from taking it away from him.... I never was so glad as when the service ended!

I tried to hurry Helen out-of-doors, but she kept her arm extended, and every coattail she touched had to converse with her and answer her questions. Her primary question was for that person to give a *full* account of the children he or she left at home. Helen accordingly kissed that person, giving as many kisses as the number of children left at home, asking for her kisses to be given to them! Everybody around us laughed and smiled at her, and from their faces you would have thought they were leaving a place of amusement rather than a church!

Later, Captain Keller invited some of the more important ministers to dinner. Helen was irrepressible. She described in the most elaborate sentences, as well as with pantomime, what she was going to do in the summer when we visit you in Brewster. Finally she got up from the table and went through the motion of picking shells from the beach, and walking on the beach while splashing in the water from the waves (and holding up her skirt higher than was proper under the circumstances...)

Then to my horror she threw herself onto the floor and began to "swim" so energetically that some of us thought we should be kicked out of our chairs!

After dinner we all moved to the crowded sitting room, where I was bombarded with questions. One minister asked me how I had taught Helen adjectives and the names of abstract ideas like goodness and happiness. I had been asked these questions a dozen times now. It seems strange that people should marvel at what is really *so simple*. Why, it is as easy to teach the name of an idea, if it is *clearly formulated* in the child's mind, as to teach the name of an actual object. It would indeed be a herculean task to teach the words if the ideas did not already *exist* in the child's mind. If the child's experiences and observations hadn't led him to the concepts *small, large, good, bad, sweet, sour*, he would have nothing to attach the word-tags to.

I, (little ignorant I) found myself explaining to the wise ministers of the East and the West such simple things as these: If you give a child something sweet, and he wags his tongue and smacks his lips and looks pleased, he has a very definite *sensation*; and if, every time he has this experience, he hears the word *sweet* (or has it spelled into his hand), he will quickly adopt this arbitrary sign for his sensation.

Likewise, if you put a bit of lemon on his tongue, he puckers up his lips and tries to spit it out; and after he has had this experience a few times, if you offer him a lemon, he shuts his mouth and makes faces, clearly indicating that he *remembers* the unpleasant *sensation*. You label it *sour*, and he adopts your symbol!

If you had called these sensations respectively *black* and *white*, he would have adopted them just as readily! But he would mean by *black* and *white* the same things that we mean by *sweet* and *sour*. In the same way the child learns from many experiences to differentiate his *feelings*, and we name them for him–*good, bad, gentle, rough, happy, sad.* It is not the *word*, but the *capacity to experience the sensation* that counts in the child's education.

Many of the ministers thanked me for my good work, which was, I must admit, pleasant to hear. Captain Keller then gave them all the extracts from the report that Mr. Anagnos sent me, and had he had enough, he could have disposed a thousand of them! So proud he was! At the end of the long evening one minister said to him and to Mrs. Keller, "I have lived long and seen many happy faces; but I have never seen such a radiant face as this child's before tonight!"

Today both Helen and I woke up late. So exhausted we were! But Captain Keller's face radiated with pride this morning, so I guess it was worth the trouble.

Do you realize that this is the last letter I shall write to you for a long, long time? The next word that you receive from me will be in a telegram from Washington, and it will tell you when Helen, Mrs. Keller and I shall reach Boston. I cannot wait to see you Mrs. Hopkins! I am going tomorrow to buy a proper dress for our visit to the White House. I am also curious about meeting Dr. Alexander Graham Bell after having heard so much about him. The school for the deaf also interests me greatly. But of all things—I am excited of seeing you! Yes, even more than meeting the President himself!

Yours with love,

Annie."

* * *

It was difficult for Kate to say goodbye to Mildred, but her nurse, Sally, reassured her she would take good care of her. Annie and Helen boarded the train after Helen kissed her father repeatedly and done the same to a reluctant James. Annie looked through the window at Kate saying farewell to her husband, and to Sally, who held little Mildred. Annie's heart ached for Kate.

But as the train began leaving the train station, Annie felt a feeling of excitement she had not felt in a long while.

* * *

Throughout the whole train ride Annie talked to Helen's hand, spelling to her descriptions of the views, the Tennessee River, the cotton-fields stretching to the horizon, the hills, the woods, the crowds of people boarding and disembarking in each station.

They arrived in Washington the following morning. Dr. Bell waited for them in the train station and was very happy to see them. He was not overly interested in Mrs. Keller or Annie, but rather began conversing with Helen very rapidly using the manual alphabet. Helen began giggling instantly. The entire carriage ride to Dr. Bell's house, he and Helen conversed. Kate looked at Annie and whispered, "What are they talking about?"

Annie tried to decipher the hand movements, and was puzzled. "I think they are talking about elephants."

* * *

Helen's diary entry from that day stated:

> "Mr. Bell. came to see us. He talked very fast with his fingers about lions and tigers and elephants. The elephant is a very large animal and his body is very heavy. He walks slowly and shakes the ground. He cannot run because he is too big. He has four very strong legs and a little tail. His ears are thin and his eyes are large and mild. The elephant is not fierce like the lion. He has a long

funny nose and he can move it. Sometimes little children give him candy and he puts it into his mouth with his nose. He has two long and very sharp teeth and they are called tusks. When wild animals hunt the elephant he is very angry and he strikes them with his tusks."

* * *

The following day they went to visit the White House. Annie put on her new purple dress. The three of them were first given a tour in the garden prior to meeting the president. Helen asked many questions, and Annie tried to answer them as best as she could, her heart beating fast about the coming meeting.

Then, at four o'clock, they were taken upstairs to the reception room where they met the 51-year-old President and his 24-year-old wife. Annie nearly stopped breathing upon seeing First Lady Frances Cleveland. She was poised and elegant, and only looking at her made Annie stand a little taller.

President Cleveland greeted them and invited them to sit. Helen spelled to Annie, "Can I touch his face?"

The First Lady looked curiously at Helen's hand and asked Annie, "What is she saying?"

Annie looked at Mrs. Keller uncomfortably, "She asks whether she can touch the President's face."

The President smiled, "Of course she can!"

Annie spelled "Yes" to Helen and led her to the President's sofa. Helen touched the face gently and spelled, "Mustache, large mustache!"

Annie explained what Helen was spelling to her.

"Oh indeed," the President Cleveland laughed. The

First Lady looked at him and said disapprovingly, "Too large of a mustache!"

Mrs. Keller smiled. She too was excited about the meeting.

Helen spelled to Annie, "Black? Brown? White?"

Annie shook her head and spelled back. The president asked, "What? What is she saying?"

Annie's face reddened, "She is asking for the color of your beard, whether it is black or brown."

"Well tell her that it *was* black," the President smiled, "but nowadays it is becoming quite white!"

Annie nodded and spelled that to Helen.

The First Lady leaned forward and touched Mrs. Keller's hand, "You must be so proud of little Helen."

Mrs. Keller nodded, "Oh, I certainly am."

Annie was envious of how calm Mrs. Keller looked.

The President asked several more questions and Annie translated them all to Helen. Her heart kept beating fast, and after the meeting she had to ask Kate what were the president's questions.

The only thing she remembered from the meeting was how when it ended the President and the First Lady escorted them to the stairs leading downstairs. The First Lady, radiant and glamorous, looked at Annie and murmured, "You must be so proud of yourself Miss Sullivan!"

Annie nodded.

"Really," the First Lady whispered and looked at the corridor lined with faces of deceased presidents. "It must be such a pleasure to spend your whole day with Helen." She then whispered, "So much better than being forced into formal and boring receptions!"

Annie nodded. She wanted to say something smart, but could think of nothing. She smiled appreciatively at Mrs. Cleveland, who was only two years older than her.

The President shook Helen's hand, and then Mrs. Keller's and Annie's, summing up the meeting by simply saying, "Wonderful, wonderful. Well thank you very much for your kind visit!"

It was only at night when she realized what happened. She *visited* the White House. She had *tea* with the President and the First Lady!

Helen's diary entry summed up the meeting:

> "We went to see President Cleveland. He lives in a very large and beautiful White House, and there are lovely flowers and many trees and much fresh and green grass around. And broad smooth paths to walk on. Teacher told me about the beautiful river that is very near the gardens. The Potomac River is clear and it is very beautiful when the sun shines upon it. Mr. Cleveland and the first lady were very glad to see me."

* * *

The following day in Washington Dr. Bell arranged for Helen and Annie to visit the capital's well-known School for the Deaf. Mrs. Keller remained in the hotel to rest.

Annie was intrigued to see whether the teachers there had interesting methods of teaching the deaf that she could learn from. Her own knowledge was mostly of education for the blind. She had never before visited a school for the *deaf*.

The school was beautiful, located not far from the Potomac. The school obviously had much money, and the green loans were beautifully kept. The principal arranged for two of the teachers to take Helen and Annie around the school. Annie was happy when both teachers, Mrs. Grey and Mrs. Kline, began speaking with Helen using the manual alphabet. The four of them sat in the large teacher's room, overlooking the garden, in which one of the classes was playing ball.

About a minute or two into the conversation of Mrs. Grey with Helen she said, "My, she speaks well!"

Mrs. Kline followed, conversing with Helen. Annie looked at her face, and saw how impressed she was.

After several minutes Helen asked to meet the children, and they were taken into one of the classes.

The following few hours passed slowly. Annie's face grew more and more concerned as they walked from class to class.

* * *

Upon returning to the hotel in the late afternoon, Annie was exhausted and upset. Mrs. Keller was surprised, "Why, Miss Annie, you look forlorn!"

"Oh Kate, I had a terrible, terrible time!"

Helen wanted to eat lunch. She spelled to her mother. Kate looked at Annie, who was taking her shoes off and groaning. Kate asked Annie, "Shall we go to lunch together?"

"You go," Annie said and shook her head, "I must have a short rest."

Kate nodded, "Of course."

Kate left with Helen downstairs, and Annie tried to close her eyes and rest. Her mind couldn't relax so she got up from the bed, took a pen and paper from her suitcase and began writing, her handwriting rapidly filling the paper:

"To: Mrs. Hopkins,

May 15th, 1888

Dear Mrs. Hopkins,

I did not think I shall write to you before meeting you in four days from now, but I simply must tell you of today's happening. Most likely I shall give you this letter in person. But I must write you a line or I'll go mad. We visited a school for the deaf here in Washington, the visit arranged by Dr. Bell. We were very kindly received, and Helen enjoyed meeting the children. Two of the teachers talked to her using the manual alphabet which they knew well.

Both of them were astonished at her command of language. Not a child in the school, they said, had anything like Helen's facility of expression, and some of them had been under instruction for two or three years! At first I was incredulous, thinking they were just trying to compliment me; but after I had watched the children at work for a few hours, I knew that what I had been told was true. Oh Mrs. Hopkins, it was painful to watch!

In one room some children were sitting and looking at the blackboard, painfully constructing "simple sentences." A little girl who sat next to me had written; "I have a new dress. It is a pretty dress. My mamma made me pretty new dress. I love my mamma."

I watched the teacher as she went around the room to check the sentences the children wrote in their notebooks. She passed by the little girl and looked in her notebook and nodded. I asked the teacher, in passing, if the girl's "new dress" was the dress she was wearing. "No," the teacher replied, "I don't think so, you see, these are *general* sentences."

"General sentences?" I asked.

The teacher explained to me, "Children learn better if they write about things that concern them personally. So we ask them to write general sentences in the first person."

I was puzzled. After a while one of the children noticed us and said, looking at Helen and her eyes, "Girl is blind." The teacher agreed and turned to the blackboard. She wrote, "The girl's name is Helen. She is deaf. She cannot see. We are very sorry for her."

I asked the teacher, "Why do you write those sentences on the board? Wouldn't the children understand if you talked to them directly?" The teacher smiled and said something about getting the "correct construction" of sentences.

Oh, Mrs. Hopkins! It all seemed so *mechanical* and *difficult*, my heart ached for the poor little children! Mind you, these children were *older* than Helen—and *seeing* too—and yet their command of language was so limited!

As we passed from class to class I noticed the same difficulty throughout the whole school. In every classroom I saw sentences on the blackboard, which evidently had been written to illustrate some grammatical rule, or for the purpose of using words that had previously been taught to the class.

I do understand that this sort of thing may be necessary in *some* stages of education; but it isn't the way to *acquire* a language!

Oh Mrs. Hopkins! I see no sense in "faking" conversation for the sake of teaching language! It's stupid and deadening to both pupil and teacher. Talk should be natural and have for its object an exchange of real ideas. If there is nothing in the child's mind to communicate, it hardly seems worthwhile to require him to write on the blackboard, or spell dry sentences about "a dress," "a bird," and "a dog."

From the beginning I have tried to talk naturally to Helen and to teach her to tell me only things that *interest* her, and to ask questions only for the sake of *finding out* whatever it is that she wants to know. The child's eagerness and interest carry her over many obstacles that would have been our *undoing* had we stopped to define and explain everything. It is challenging for every person to try and explain the most common of words. What would happen, do you think, if someone should try to measure our intelligence by our ability to define the most common words we use? I fear me, if I were put to such a test; I should be consigned to the primary class in a school for the feeble-minded!

Instead, I believe in conversing to the child and trusting his innate ability to comprehend profound concepts over time. When I speak to

Helen I do not try to explain all the new words, nor does Helen fully understand everything in the little stories I tell her; but constant repetition fixes the words and phrases in the mind, and little by little the meaning comes to her.

But alas, I must not get into the habit of criticizing other people's methods too severely. I may be as far from the straight road as they.

But I must write to you only that it was painful for me to see. Nothing, I think, crushes the child's natural *impulse* to talk more than these blackboard exercises! The schoolroom is not the place to teach any young child language, least of all the deaf child! He must be kept as *unconscious* of the fact that he is learning words. Language should not be associated in his mind with endless hours in school, with puzzling questions in grammar, or with anything that is an enemy to joy!

I shall see you in four days. That is my only comfort now!

Yours with love,

Annie."

* * *

Annie was extremely emotional when the train slowed down before entering the South Boston Train Station. It was at this station that she got off eight years earlier, at age fourteen, after four years in the almshouse.

It was at this station too that she embarked, a year and two months earlier, on a journey southward to an unknown future.

Yet now she returned a victor.

Fourteen months earlier only Mrs. Hopkins was there to send her off, with lunch box, a pair of new shoes which were too small for her, and a red eye from her operation a few days earlier.

Now on the platform Annie was greeted by Mr. Anagnos, Mrs. Hopkins, several other teachers, two journalists and one camera man. The flash coming out of the magnesium flash lamp startled her. Not even in the White House were they greeted with such ceremony. Mrs. Keller smiled at Annie, and Annie could see Kate was flabbergasted just as she was.

Annie nearly knocked down Mrs. Hopkins when she hugged her, tears filling her eyes. Mr. Anagnos immediately took to Helen and began conversing using the manual alphabet, and Annie had to disturb them to introduce Mrs. Hopkins to Helen. Mrs. Hopkins spelled to Helen slowly, her manual alphabet rather crude, "Nice to meet you, Helen."

Helen spelled back rapidly, and Mrs. Hopkins turned to Annie for help. Annie smiled and the throng of teachers slowed their walk down as Annie translated to Mrs. Hopkins, "She says she loves you and thanks you for the kind gift of the ring that you gave Santa Claus to give her."

Mrs. Hopkins smiled, "Oh, tell her it was my pleasure."

Annie spelled to Helen, who spelled back. Annie said, "She asks if she can kiss you."

"Why of course!"

* * *

It was strange for Annie to climb up the stairs to the *Massachusetts School for the Blind.* Seeing the large four pillars that in the past looked so grandiose and scary now seemed a smaller. Shorter. The White House's pillars were much taller.

The school buzzed with excitement and a large banner was hung to greet Helen, Mrs. Keller, and Annie. Annie could not avoid the odd feeling in her guts that Mr. Anagnos was wishing to make Helen and her mother feel a part of the institution with the annual fundraising event coming two weeks later. But she knew it was for a good cause, and therefore she brushed the thought aside.

They went into the first grade class, and Helen was immediately surrounded by many girls. They conversed with her using the manual alphabet. Helen's face radiated with joy. Mrs. Keller looked at Annie and said, "My, Miss Annie, look how happy she looks!"

Annie smiled, "She's been writing to them back and forth since autumn!"

Mr. Anagnos tried joining their conversation, "Well, Miss Sullivan, finally you can take some rest for your weary fingers!"

Annie smiled politely at Mr. Anagnos.

* * *

"From: Annie Sullivan, Boston

To: Captain Arthur Keller, Tuscumbia, Alabama

Dear Captain Keller,

It has been four weeks since our arrival in Boston. Tomorrow Mrs. Keller shall leave back to Tuscumbia, and I wished to write to you a personal note, letting you know how loved and cherished Helen is. You must be very proud of your daughter, Captain. In the graduation ceremony, to which the wealthiest Bostonians were invited, Helen played a key role. She and I were invited on stage, whereupon she was given a poem in braille to read with her left hand. With the right hand she spelled the exact words into my hand, and I recited them to the audience. Everyone was amazed by her speed and cheerful manners. Mr. Anagnos wrote in his letter to the alumni that "so rapid were the movements of Helen's little fingers, that the three processes of reception, transmission and expression of ideas became simultaneous."

I attach the article, notice also, Captain, how Mr. Anagnos notes Helen's "electric play of gestures and of features," and "eloquence of the whole body." She very much enjoyed the experience and her face radiated. She later told me she heard the great applause of the audience by her feet.

I am also obliged to tell you that Helen felt at home with her friends here. The girls in the class have learned the manual alphabet in anticipation of meeting her. On finding that almost every one whom she met understood her manual alphabet, Helen was overjoyed. With the enlarged opportunities afforded by intercourse with so many different minds, she rapidly gained greater readiness in conversation. She eagerly sought the acquaintance of the children, and entered with delight into their occupations.

I went with her to all of the classes, and Mrs. Keller joined us in some of them. Among Helen's favorite classes was the clay class. Modeling in clay was a great pleasure to her; and, after a few lessons, she achieved a very good degree of success.

The bead-work class she loved and joined in very quickly. Sewing class was easy for her as well. When she was able to use four needles, she was delighted with the thought that she could knit a pair of stockings for you! She told me, "I must knit stockings for Father!"

She was greatly interested in examining the school apparatus, the uses of which she readily comprehended. The maps, typewriters, and physiological models are sources of great pleasure to her.

Mrs. Keller will depart tomorrow to return to Tuscumbia and shall give you this letter. Helen and I will proceed with Mrs. Hopkins to her home in Brewster. Mr. Anagnos insists that in September Helen shall come back to school, if only for a few months. I have referred him to you on this matter.

I assure you, Captain, that Helen is in good hands, and that Mrs. Hopkins and I shall take care of her as if she was none but the Queen of England!

Yours kindly,

Annie Sullivan."

* * *

The summer in Brewster had never been happier. It seemed that since the death of Mrs. Hopkins's daughter a decade earlier, the house had never seen as much joy.

Helen was ecstatic about the sea. Her remarks became the subject of much laughter in the gathering of the greater Hopkins family.

Annie told everyone with amusement Helen's first remark after she swallowed some seawater: "Teacher, who put salt in water?"

In August Mrs. Hopkins commemorated ten years since the death of her only daughter. Annie remembered the 15th of August each summer as a sad day in which Mrs. Hopkins would not say much and leave Annie at home while she herself took the carriage to the Brewster cemetery.

But this summer Mrs. Hopkins felt lighter. At the breakfast table she looked at Helen, delightfully eating her meal, and said to Annie, "I was wondering if the two of you would like to join me in going to the cemetery and laying flowers on Florence's grave."

Annie agreed promptly. To spare Helen any difficulty and save herself from being asked too many questions, Annie simply explained to Helen that the three of them were going to a garden with many stones. Little did she know what would happen.

* * *

"From: Annie Sullivan, Brewster

To: Mrs. Kate Keller, Tuscumbia, Alabama

Dear Kate,

I must write to you the strangest thing. You know how Helen has these instances where she seems to call into use an inexplicable mental faculty?

I had such an experience with her the other day, while walking with her on the beach. I was holding her hand while conversing with Mrs. Hopkins as we walked along the shore. Some children were playing with a ball not far away. Suddenly the ball neared us. I do not recall moving in any way, but Helen immediately spelled to my hand, "What are we afraid of?"

Today another peculiar event took place. Mrs. Hopkins asked Helen and me to escort her to the Brewster Cemetery, where her late daughter Florence is buried, as today marked ten years since her passing. I explained to Helen we were to visit a garden with stones, and left it at that.

You and I know that she does not know much about death. Of course, she had handled dead birds before on the farm. She also was fond of the sick horse Russell which Captain Keller had to put to sleep following the horse's inflammation last November. When asking me to see Russell, I told her that he was *dead.* This was the first time that she had heard the word, I believe. I am inclined to believe she did realize the fact that life was extinct in the horse as in the dead birds she had touched. Since this occurrence I have never elaborated on the meaning of death, nor did I think she understood much about it.

Upon entering the safety of the cemetery I

released Helen's hand and allowed her to wander around near us, while I followed Mrs. Hopkins to the grave. Helen examined one stone after another and seemed pleased when she could decipher a name. Then she came upon the marble slab inscribed with the name FLORENCE in relief. She had never heard of Florence, nor do I think she ever knew that Mrs. Hopkins ever had a daughter. Yet upon touching the stone, Helen froze, dropped upon the ground as though looking for something. She turned to me with a face full of trouble, reaching for me hand. When I handed it to her she spelled, "Where is poor little Florence?"

Naturally, Kate, I evaded the question, but Helen persisted. Then she spelled: "I think she is very dead! Who put her in big hole?" I continued to ignore her questions, and she turned to Mrs. Hopkins and spelled to her, "Did you cry loud for poor little Florence?"

As you can imagine, we hurried to leave the cemetery, all the while Helen continuing with these distressing questions.

Upon returning home she went to play with the dolls that Mrs. Hopkins had given her upon our arrival in the beginning of the summer. Suddenly Helen touched the doll carriage and the doll bed, carried them to Mrs. Hopkins, tears in her eyes, spelling, "They are poor little Florence's!"

Both Mrs. Hopkins and I were at a loss to understand how Helen had guessed all of that!

This evening I encouraged Helen to write to you a letter, hoping to distract her. But alas, she is obviously occupied with thoughts about Florence. I hope tomorrow she shall be more equanimous. Please find her letter attached. Also, please forgive me, Kate, if I had operated wrongly in taking Helen to the cemetery. I thought nothing of it, and wished for both of us to be with Mrs. Hopkins during this delicate day of remembrance. I hope you can understand my predicament.

Yours kindly,

Annie.

P.S.

I wrote this letter last night and we're going to mail it right now. Helen has not mentioned Florence this morning."

* * *

"From: Helen Keller

To: Mrs. Kate Keller

My dear Mother,

I think you will be very glad to know all about my time in Brewster. Teacher and I have a lovely time with many kind friends and family of Mrs. Hopkins. Yesterday we rode for a long time to see all the beautiful things in Brewster. Many very handsome houses and large soft green lawns around them and trees and bright flowers and fountains. The horse's name was Prince and he was gentle and liked to trot very fast.

Mrs. Hopkins' nephew Clifton did not kiss me because he does not like to kiss little girls. He is shy. I am very glad that Frank and Clarence and Robbie and Eddie and Charles and George were not very shy. I also played with many little girls and we had fun.

We came home yesterday in horse cars because it was Sunday and steam cars do not go often on Sunday. Conductors and engineers do get very tired and go home to rest.

I play much with dolls in the house. I put my little babies to sleep in Florence's little bed, and I take them to ride in her little carriage. Poor little Florence is dead. She was very sick and died. Mrs. Hopkins did cry loud for her dear little child. Florence was very lovely and Mrs. Hopkins kissed her and hugged her much. Doctor gave her medicine to make her well, but poor Florence did not get well. When she was very sick she tossed and moaned in bed. Mrs. Hopkins will go to see her soon again.

I do love you and I send my kisses to Mildred. Will Mildred sleep with me in bed when I come home?

With much love and thousand kisses.

From your dear little daughter,

Helen Keller."

* * *

As the end of summer approached, Helen was thrilled about returning to the school for the blind. Walking with Annie on the beach one late afternoon she spelled, "I want to go to school already!"

Annie laughed. "What do you like about school?"

An older couple passed by them on the beach, the older woman smiled at them. The man looked strangely at the finger movements of Helen as she spelled, "I like learning! I like reading! I will read a lot and learn a lot and will be very smart!"

Annie laughed, "You are already very smart!"

Helen shook her head, "No, I will be smarter and smarter, I will go to school, then to high-school, then to university!"

Annie paused, wondering who had taught Helen about university. She did not have to ask, however, as at that moment Helen continued, "Dr. Bell told me in university many people learn together and read and talk much about books!"

Annie laughed again, but something in her heart began to bother her. All this talk about the future.... She felt that with Helen's progress, her parents might soon relieve Annie from her role as Helen's tutor. After all, her duty was to help Helen *communicate*. Now she *was* communicating, was she not? How much further could Annie take Helen?

"What are you thinking Teacher?" Helen spelled.

"Nothing," Annie said, and then felt guilty for not speaking the truth. "About the future."

"Teacher will always be with me, right?" Helen spelled quickly into Annie's hand.

Annie hesitated, "Whatever your parents choose, Helen."

"My parents love Teacher!" Helen said and thought nothing else of it.

Annie nodded to herself. A familiar fear began creeping up her spine.

Helen continued musing, "Teacher will help Helen, and I will learn much. I will learn French, and Greek, and Latin."

Annie frowned, "Why do you want to learn all that?"

"Because all people in university know that!"

"Who told you that? Dr. Bell?"

Helen grinned and nodded.

Annie shook her head, "I thought you only spoke to him about elephants!"

"About elephants and about university and about phone, about many things! Dr. Bell knows much!"

Annie bit her tongue. How much longer could she be useful for her little pupil?

"You are worried," Helen spelled.

"No I'm not," Annie spelled back.

"You are worried that I am not smart to go to university."

Annie shook her head, "I did not say that!" She did, however, find this idea a little silly. She knew of no blind person to have ever gone to university, let alone a blind-deaf person.

Helen's face frowned, "Teacher thinks Helen stupid!"

"No!" Annie spelled back emphatically, "I think Helen is very smart!"

Helen's face brightened up, "You think Helen can be good pupil!"

Annie nodded. "I think," she spelled, "Helen is very good pupil. Helen is brilliant!"

"What is brilliant?"

Helen and Annie in Tuscumbia, Alabama, c. 1887

Annie Sullivan, c. 1888

Helen Keller reading a large braille book, c.1888[i]

First known sample of Helen Keller's square-shaped
handwriting, dated June 17, 1887:
"helen write anna
george will give
helen apple
simpson will shoot
bird jack will give
helen stick of candy
doctor will give mil-
dred medicine mother
will make mildred
new dress."

Helen Keller with Michael Anagnos, Director of the *Massachusetts School for the Blind* (Perkins Institute) c. 1891[i]

Helen Keller and Annie Sullivan, c. 1895

Helen Keller and Annie Sullivan, photograph signed by both of them, notice Helen's square-letters, stating "Helen and Teacher," c. 1895

Helen Keller and her sister, Mildred Keller. Mildred was six years younger than Helen. In this photo they are likely 18 and 12 years of age respectively[i]

Helen Keller conversing with friend and benefactor, Alexander Graham Bell, 1902. It was Dr. Bell who suggested to Captain Keller that he write to Michael Anagnos, Director of the School for the Blind in Boston, about the possibility of getting a teacher for Helen.[i]

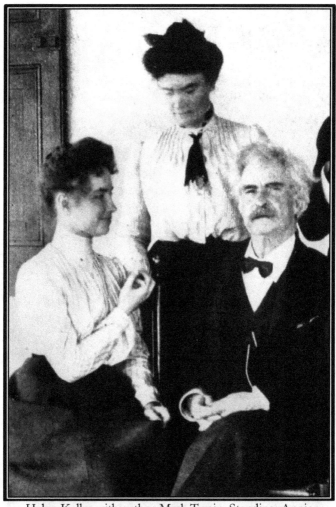
Helen Keller with author Mark Twain. Standing: Annie Sullivan. Mark Twain became one of Keller's best friends, calling her a "Miracle" and her teacher a "Miracle Worker."

Annie Sullivan, c. 1912

PART THREE

A DECADE LATER
1899

Based on true documents.

All quotes from letters, diary entries, books and articles are strictly based on the original documents.

"When I was a little girl I surprised my friends by the announcement, "Someday I shall go to college!" The thought of going to college took root in my heart and became an earnest desire, which impelled me to enter into competition for a degree with seeing and hearing girls. This was in the face of the strong opposition of many true and wise friends."

* * *

Annie paced in the large waiting hall. Behind the door 19-year-old Helen was taking her exam and her teacher of 11 years was tense and moody.

She went over to the secretary, sitting by a desk near the large carved door of the examination room, "Can you at least go and see if she does not *need* me?"

The secretary smiled cordially and said, "Miss Sullivan, all the exams were translated into braille *especially* for Miss Keller. Mind you, this was the first time in the history of Harvard that we have done such a thing!"

"Yes, but there are many *types* of braille," Annie

persisted, ignoring the condescending tone of the secretary, "there's the *English* braille, the *American* braille, and the *New York Point*. And this is especially crucial in geometry and algebra! The actual signs for the mathematical *notations* are different!"

The secretary nodded politely and looked away from her, then stared down at the book in front of him.

Annie sighed loudly and left the large waiting room. It was cold outside, a Massachusetts winter. For the past 11 years she had never left Helen. First at the Massachusetts School for the Blind. Then in New York, in the School for the Deaf. Annie was the one who read to Helen her mother's terrible letter about Captain Keller's sudden death four years earlier. She was the one who defended Helen at the Preparatory School for Harvard, fighting for recognition for Helen's abilities while the Director of the Preparatory School saw her student not only as physically handicapped but also mentally so! Annie was the one to start a fund, along with Dr. Bell, to secure Helen's continued education. She was the one to be cordial to the donors, a thing that she *hated*. She was the one who day after day, year after year, spelled to Helen, translating most of the lessons in her high school classes, since some teachers were unable—or unwilling—to learn the manual alphabet themselves.

For eleven years she sat with Helen in classes, found the proper books for her in the library, translated into her hand for excruciatingly long hours, often into the night when her eyes ached. And now—finally—everything was coming to a climax with these exams: four hours of algebra, four hours of geometry. If Helen failed these exams, Annie knew, her pupil's dream of going to Harvard would be shattered.

She walked outside the building in the cold, but couldn't stand the thought Helen might need her. She quickly hurried back and entered the waiting hall. Her heels echoed in the large hall. She tried a slightly different tactic on the secretary this time. "Please," she said, "can you just go inside, and ask her if there is any *translation* problem. The notation can be—"

"Madam, I must warn you that another interference on your part might result in the suspension of your pupil's examination paper."

Annie's eyes widened. She pouted her lips and glared at the secretary. He was aloof like all the others here at Harvard, who were "kindly willing" to "do the extra effort" as to "allow" Miss Keller to take their silly examinations! Annie despised them with all her heart.

She glared at the secretary, but was wise enough to say nothing. She turned her back to him with passion and walked away. She noticed the paintings on the walls of famous graduates. All were men. She glanced at President John Adams. She passed by Oliver Wendell Holmes. He frowned back at her.

She felt that she did not belong there. Nor, she thought, did Helen.

She exited the hall again, letting the heavy door to slam behind her. She walked out in the cold air, tightening her coat around her for warmth. It was hard not to notice the beautiful campus. Wide green lawns. Tall trees. Grand buildings on both sides of the lawn.

Why did Helen insist on going to *Harvard* of all places? Both *Cornell University* and the *University of Chicago*, having seen Helen's high grades, offered to enroll her without problems!

But no, Helen stubbornly insisted on "Harvard, only Harvard." Not that Harvard had yet allowed women to enroll—Helen was competing for a place in its "Annex for Women." Annie felt degraded in this institution that had to create an "Annex" for women.

She felt, again, that she did not belong there.

Her thoughts turned back to Helen trapped in that examination room, with a braille translation of geometry and algebra that could fail the cleverest *seeing* student. Why? Why did Helen *insist* on making her life so difficult?

But Annie knew her pupil well. In fact, she was the closer to Helen than anyone in the world.

Annie sat down on a cold marble bench overlooking the large lawn. On the left was the magnificent Harvard Medical School. On the right was Harvard Law School. In between the buildings the lawn was tidy with perfectly symmetrical pathways connecting the buildings.

It had been three hours since Helen entered her last exam. Algebra. At noon, after Helen finished the geometry exam, she looked depressed. She did not say much, and Annie could see the fear on her face. Helen did smile, but Annie knew her all too well: the downward slopes at the edge of her smile, the way she spelled into Annie's hand in an agitated way. Annie knew the exam did not go as expected.

Only three days before, they found out the exam were to be written using *American* braille. If Helen only had the courage to step up and refuse to do the examination this way. She knew the mathematical notations of the *British* system.

Of course, they did what they could, and Helen

hurriedly learned the new notations. But even as early as this morning she was still practicing the new method, finding several mistakes in her understanding. Her private math teacher was also distressed. Annie insisted repeatedly that they would protest and *demand* for the exams to be presented in the *British* notation system. But Helen refused to make a fuss about it, not wanting to cause any trouble or appear weak to the faculty, who already doubted her ability to enroll as a regular student.

Despite the cold, Annie felt flushed. She was upset. She was not just upset—she was infuriated.

She looked at her pocket watch and shook her head. She knew what failure in the exams would mean for Helen. It would mean that all the naysayers were right. The Director of the Preparatory Program, who insisted that Helen should take five years to complete the Program before applying to Harvard, rather than the usual three years other students required. Failing would mean that he was *right*. And it would mean that Helen and Annie were *wrong*. Failing would mean that the skeptical articles in the newspapers—those referring to the "deaf-blind girl" as having a "natural limit" to her "mental abilities"—were correct in their forecast. Failing would mean that Helen did not have the capacity to compete with seeing and hearing people. That she had a handicap. A case for pity and feigned sympathy, nothing more.

Annie stood up, straightened her coat, and walked quickly into the waiting hall—perhaps Helen had called for her? She opened the heavy door, walked quickly to the secretary, and questioned him with her face. He shook his head mildly and returned to his book.

She *hated* him.

She *hated* this place!

Tears began to well up, so she turned from the secretary quickly. She kept asking herself why Helen hadn't chosen an easier path for herself? Helen was a great writer. She could have written poems, short stories, even novels, had she not wasted *hundreds* of hours—perhaps *thousands* of hours—studying for the ridiculous exams in Latin, Greek, Geometry and Algebra!

Annie sat in one of the old wooden chairs at the end of the large hall. She sat there quietly, not wanting to go outside—just in case her pupil needed her. She would wait.

Another hour passed.

She thought of Helen, sitting near the desk in that quiet room, only an examiner with her, listening to her typing—typing which she could not *see*! The University insisted that the exams must not be written in braille. They were "willing" to allow Helen to type write rather than print, but braille was out of the question: writing her *exams* in braille might imply that Miss Keller could write *all* her papers in braille while and that was unacceptable for the famed academy.

Annie's thoughts turned, yet again, to Helen not being able to see what she was typing. That, at least, was the good scenario! What if Helen did not understand the actual questions?

Suddenly the large wooden door opened at the end of the hall. Annie jumped from the chair, nearly running. She saw Helen. Helen had tears in her eyes—real tears! Annie embraced her. They hugged, Helen sobbing in her teacher's arms. Annie embraced her firmly, tightening her pupil into her caress. So it was, Annie thought. At least they tried.

* * *

"In 1899 I took my final examinations for Harvard's Annex for Women. The examinations lasted two days. The first day I had Advanced Greek and Advanced Latin, and the second day Geometry and Algebra. The college authorities did not allow Miss Sullivan to read the examination papers to me; so one of the instructors at the University was employed to copy the papers for me into American braille. Unfortunately he did not know the manual alphabet, but only braille. Therefore he could not communicate with me in the examination room, as he did not have the braille slate with him. So I was, alone, trying to understand all that was written in the exam paper. The braille worked well enough in the languages, but when it came to geometry and algebra, difficulties arose.

I was well familiar with all literary braille in common use—English braille, American braille, and New York Point; but the various signs and symbols in *geometry* and *algebra* in the three systems are *very* different, and I had used only the English braille in my algebra and geometry studies. Three days before the examinations I found out that the translation for the examination would be done into *American* braille, and not *English* braille. I sat down immediately and wrote to the University that the signs were unfamiliar to me, asking for clarification. The following day I received by return mail a table of mathematical signs in the American braille system and I set to work to learn the notations. But on the night before the algebra examination, while I was struggling over some very complicated examples, I could not tell the difference between the combinations of bracket, brace and radical.

My math teacher who worked with me for two years was distressed, and so was I. But I decided to do my best, even though I barely had the time to practice the American symbols. During the examinations I was sorely perplexed, and felt discouraged wasting much precious time. In geometry my chief difficulty was that I had always been accustomed to read the propositions in line print or to have them spelled into my hand; and somehow, although the propositions were right before me, I found the braille confusing, and could not fix clearly in my mind what I was reading.

But when I continued to the algebra exam I had even a harder time. The signs, which I had only learned two days before, and which I thought I understood, perplexed me. Add to this the fact that I could not see what I wrote on my typewriter (I had always done my work in braille before). Consequently my work was painfully slow, and I had to read the examples over and over before I could form any idea of what I was required to do. Indeed, I am not sure that I read all the signs correctly. At the end I found it very hard to keep my wits about me."

* * *

The weeks passed. Not a word came from Harvard. Annie checked the mailbox twice a day.

Their rented apartment at 138 Brattle Street,

Cambridge, Massachusetts, was their refuge. But it was also their prison. A walking distance to Harvard, the university of Helen's childhood dreams seemed so close and yet at the same time so far away.

Annie felt sorry for her pupil, but even more so she was sorry for herself. The past decade had cost her much. Her eyes had never been worse. She could read, but not for many hours before the pain would begin. She had also gained some weight of which she was not proud. She looked older than her 34 years of age.

Sitting at her desk, her thoughts turned to when Helen was 14. Helen insisted on learning speech. It was a difficult task, they both knew. They were assisted by a speech expert, but as before, all the real work fell on Annie. She was the one who for hours practiced with Helen, allowing Helen's fingers to touch her face, her nostrils, the tongue and the lips, feel the vibrations of the throat…. Hours and hours, days by days, Annie taught the eager Helen how to make sounds that imitated those of a hearing person.

Helen was somewhat pleased with the result, but Annie was far from pleased. It was a disappointment, really. No one could really *understand* Helen's speech, apart from those who spent many days with her and learned to decipher different sounds.

Annie put her face in her hands. A letter had arrived from Mrs. Keller, wanting to know if there was any news from Harvard, good or bad. Annie sighed. Much like the hundreds of hours trying to teach Helen to speak, this too was a disappointment. Much ado about nothing. The strenuous months—years, really—of preparing for the college's examinations. Was it all in vain?

She took out her pen and wrote quickly.

"Dear Kate,

I'm writing you a brief note. No word from the university with regard to Helen's work yet. Helen is restless and disappointed and I am utterly discouraged. Here is the subject of American pride and fame, clamoring at the door of a nineteenth century university begging for instruction, and getting splendidly snubbed for her audacity! I am so indignant I am left speechless!

Regardless what the news may be, I will telegram you when I find out.

Yours,

Annie."

* * *

When the letter finally came, Annie wanted to tear it apart right at the mailbox. Yet she ran inside, and sat Helen down on the sofa of their small living room. She held Helen's hand and spelled, "Whatever it says, I want you to know that I am proud of you."

Helen nodded her head eagerly and spelled, "Open."

Annie took a deep breath, fear creeping up her spine. She opened the letter. She pulled out the folded paper and glanced at it. She jumped up and screamed.

That same day Helen wrote to her mother.

* * *

"My precious Mother,

Annie encouraged me to write to you right away. I have a piece of news which I know will make your heart glad! I have passed all my preliminary examinations, including advanced Latin!! Latin, dear mother, I have passed WITH HONORS. It seems almost too good to be true, doesn't it? My brain and hands have worked very hard indeed for the last year, the former acting as the dictator and the latter performing the clerk's functions: but, absorbed as I was in my work, I could not suppress an inward fear and trembling, lest I should fail, and now it is an unspeakable relief to know that I have passed my entrance examinations WITH CREDIT! But what I consider my crown of success is the happiness and pleasure that my victory has brought to dear Annie. Indeed, the success is hers more than mine, Mother, for she is my constant inspiration.

Then too the thought that you, dear Mother, will rejoice and be proud of your little girl, fills my heart with thankfulness! I will write more soon, but I just wanted to let you know the good news.

Annie sends her love.

Your affectionate child,

Helen."

* * *

The news spread like wildfire. Newspaper articles featured pictures of Helen with titles as "First Deaf-Blind to Attend College" and "Will She Make It? Helen Keller on Her Way to Harvard."

Requests for Helen's own response to the news filled the Keller-Sullivan's mailbox. Annie encouraged Helen to respond, but Helen declined, spelling to Annie, "What is all this fuss about? Let them come when I graduate, not when I am merely accepted!"

At first Annie agreed. But later she began reading some of the articles and became furious with the misinformation and ignorance of the writers. She also felt a burning hatred towards those who insinuated that it was not *Helen* who was accepted, but her *Teacher*. They hinted that it was not young Miss Keller who was taking Miss Sullivan with her to college, but rather *"Miss Sullivan who drags young Miss Keller along."*

Annie felt disgust, anger and desperation all at the same time. "Helen!" she spelled, "you must write something!"

"But I have never written anything for publication before," Helen spelled back.

"Write but a paragraph or two. Let your voice be heard," Annie spelled back, "So that they know it is *you* who wants this. So that they will get to know *you* through your *own* eyes. You cannot allow all this garbage to be written without your response!"

Helen was contemplative. She folded her hands together, her thumbs caressing one another nervously.

* * *

The following afternoon she worked on a response in her study across the living room. Annie walked around the kitchen quietly, wishing not to disturb Helen's concentration with her steps. She noticed the sound of Helen's typing was louder than usual. In her study, Helen was typing with extra vigor, almost hitting the typewriter.

Annie baked Helen's favorite almond raisin cake. The cake was almost ready when Helen finally exited her study, walking slowly through the apartment with a sheet of paper in her hand to find Annie in the kitchen. Annie took the paper and noticed four paragraphs printed on it:

> "STATEMENT FOR THE PRESS
>
> BY HELEN KELLER
>
> Ever since I set for myself the difficult task of obtaining an education I have heard it said that I should not succeed, but now having passed the entrance examinations into college, I am convinced that I shall go through to the end.
>
> I am not afraid to work. I believe that one reason for my progress in the past has been my capacity for concentration. This is due, of course, largely to my teacher, Miss Sullivan, who interprets for me."

Annie looked at Helen. Helen nodded and mumbled, "Keep reading!"

Annie read on:

> "In university, I am particularly interested in the study of languages, and with the aid of my typewriter, which I have learned to work with ease and rapidity, I hope that I would be able to accomplish as much as any student in the college. I believe I should love to write as well. I have always had aspirations in that direction, but who knows if college life will not develop something else in me? Whatever I become I shall be grateful for this training.
>
> I shall add that I would not be satisfied unless I

take away from the college a B. A. degree. People have said that I should be afraid. I am not a bit. I have been so long nothing in the world, that I have made up my mind I must be something before I die."

Annie gulped and read the last sentence again, "I have been so long nothing in the world, that I have made up my mind I must be something before I die." Was it her little Helen who wrote that? There was so much intensity in this short statement!

Helen felt for her hand and spelled, "What do you think?"

"I think it is excellent!" Annie spelled back.

"No, really, what do you think?" Helen spelled back, her face attuned to Annie's most subtle movements, sensing whether Annie was being sincere.

"I think," Annie spelled slowly, "that you could not have written it better."

A small smile appeared on Helen's face but soon changed into a frown as she spelled, "Let them have it. We will prove all the skeptics wrong."

Annie looked at her 20-year-old student's resolved face. She was her own woman now.

* * *

"To: Miss Mildred Keller, Tuscumbia, Alabama

From: Helen Keller, 138 Brattle Street, Cambridge, Massachusetts

September 15th, 1900

My dear little sister!

You have just turned 14! I cannot believe it! My best wishes for you dearest Mildred! Did you receive the dress I sent you? I promised I will tell you all about my first day in college. My, it was a day full of interest! As you know I looked forward to it for years. The lecture halls seemed filled with the spirit of the great and the wise, and Annie hurried to spell to me the many lectures. I am studying English history, English literature, French and Latin, and by and by I shall take up German and English composition—let us groan! You know I detest grammar as much as you do; but I suppose I must go through it if I am to write, just as we had to get ducked in the lake hundreds of times before we could swim!

In French I am reading "Columba." It is a delightful novel, full of piquant expressions and thrilling adventures, (don't dare to blame me for using big words, since you do the same in your letters!) and, if you ever read it, I think you will enjoy it immensely. You are studying English history, aren't you? Oh but it's exceedingly interesting! We are making quite a thorough study of the Elizabethan period—of the Reformation, and the Acts of Supremacy & Conformity...

For the beginning of the school year Annie and I had four lovely dresses made for us by a French dressmaker, two dresses for each of us. One has a black silk skirt, with a black lace net over it, and a waist of white poplin, with turquoise velvet and chiffon, and cream lace over a satin yoke. The other is woolen, and of a very pretty green. The waist is trimmed with pink and green brocaded velvet, and white lace, I think, and has double reefers on the front, tucked and trimmed with velvet, and also a row of tiny white buttons. Annie too has a silk dress. The skirt is black, while the waist is mostly yellow, trimmed with delicate lavender chiffon, and black velvet bows and lace. Her other dress is purple, trimmed with purple velvet, and the waist has a collar of cream lace. So you may imagine that we look quite like peacocks, only we've no trains...!

Yesterday there was a great football game between Harvard and Yale to mark the beginning of the year, and there was tremendous excitement here. Annie and I went to the game: there were about twenty-five thousand people there, and the noise was so terrific, we nearly jumped out of our skins. It felt as if it was the din of war rather than at a football game! But, in spite of all their wild efforts, neither side was scored, and we all laughed merrily!

I will try to write sooner next time, but do believe me when I am writing that I have no spare time to even think!

Your loving sister,

Helen."

* * *

"To: Miss Mildred Keller, Tuscumbia, Alabama.

From: Helen Keller, 138 Brattle Street, Cambridge, Massachusetts

January 20th, 1901

My dear little sister,

You must think me a villain! I can't think of a word bad enough to express your opinion of me, unless indeed horse-thief will answer the purpose! Tell me truly, do you think me as bad as that? I hope not; for I have thought many letters to you which never got on paper, and I was delighted to get your three letters, yes, I really *was*, and I intended to answer all of them immediately; but the days slip by unnoticed when one is busy, and I have been VERY busy this fall. You must believe that Mildred! Harvard girls are always up to their ears in work. If you doubt it, you'd better come and see for yourself.

When I am a B.A., I suppose you will not dare call me a villain! I am studying English—Sophomore English, mind you, as they placed me with the second year students for some reason! It is hard, very hard at times; but it hasn't swamped me yet.

You asked me if I am studying Mathematics, and the answer is "No!" I am not studying Mathematics, nor Greek or Latin either. The courses at college are elective, only certain courses in English are prescribed. I passed off my English and advanced Latin before I entered college, and I choose the classes I like best. I don't however intend to give up Greek and Latin entirely. Perhaps I shall take up these studies later; but I *have* said goodbye to Mathematics forever! And I assure you, I was delighted to see the last of those horrid goblins!

I hope to obtain my degree in four years; but I'm not very particular about that. There's no great hurry, and I want to get as much as possible out of my studies. Mind you, many of my friends would be well pleased if I would take only two or even one course a semester; but I rather object to spending the rest of my life in college!

Please tell Mother we received the beautiful lace curtains. Annie hung them in the parlor, along with some beautiful pictures. You should come and see how Annie's wonderful artistic skills have transformed our little home.

I must go now as I have to finish my reading for tomorrow. The greatest disadvantage in college is lack of time. I used to have time to *think*, to reflect—my mind and I alone. But in college there is no time to commune with one's thoughts. One goes to college to learn, not to think, it seems.

I hope I made some sense. Do send Mother my love and that I promise to write next week.

Yours,

Your loving sister,

Helen."

* * *

Annie lay in bed, unable to fall asleep.

Months went by and the school year was slowly coming to an end. Annie was at a loss as to Helen's moods. Helen has always been so optimistic and cheerful, but nowadays she seemed more morose than ever before.

Perhaps the workload was too much for her?

Annie proposed to Helen to give up some of the

courses, but Helen stubbornly said "No."

But now it seemed as if her contentment was all gone.

Was it because of the English professor, Professor Copey, giving Helen a nasty remark? Oh, how Annie hated him! Such a nasty remark, and in *English* of all subjects—the subject that Helen loved the most!

Annie still remembered his handwritten comment—how she wished she had not read it to Helen!—it stated so coldly, so plainly:

> "Good, but there was a little too much the rhythm of verse."

Annie could have killed him! Seeing Helen's face wilting was one of the most painful things she had ever seen.

"Rhythm of verse?" Helen spelled back to her.

They were in the student's dining hall. Annie remembered it clearly. They were sitting alone, as they so often did.

Annie did not respond, trying to eat her meal, but Helen did not touch her food. "What do you think he meant? 'A little too much the rhythm of verse?'"

Annie took a deep breath and spelled, "Heaven knows." She did not want to admit that Professor Copey *did* have a point. Helen's tendency was for figurative language, great details, and much attention to the pace of each sentence. She was a master at that. But then—it was very *peculiar*. It was her own unique *style*.

Remembering the professor's comment, now, in bed, nearly half a year later, made Annie's blood boil again. How she detested those university professors, thinking themselves too aloof to answer Helen's questions after class, always excusing themselves for a "lack of time." Always leaving Annie to explain to Helen all by herself. Or at least to *try* to explain.

She tossed from side to side. She could hear Helen sleeping in her adjacent room.

At least she was *sleeping*, Annie thought. Helen had some sleepless nights recently, including some nightmares in which she yelled in her sleep. Annie tried to comfort her, but the situation was odd for them both.

Helen was not willing to tell what her dreams were about. But the following morning Annie heard Helen typing away on her braille slate, most likely pages for her private journal.

Lying in bed, Annie opened her eyes. Perhaps she should read the journal. It might give a clue as to what her student was going through.

She had thought of it before but dismissed the idea. Yet now it seemed almost her *duty* to see that Helen's well being was not compromised. She owed it to Helen. She owed it to Kate. And she owed to herself.

She sat up in bed quietly and got up slowly and made her way to Helen's study. The journal's pages were tucked away in the drawer under the desk with the braille slate. Annie quietly pulled the drawer open. There was a very large pile of papers there. When did Helen have the time to write all that?

Annie felt like a thief. She soothed her consciousness telling herself that it was for *Helen's* benefit. She tried to dub her pupil, but Helen was like a locked chamber. Annie's heart ached; what had happened to her jovial little girl? That thought nearly made her cry. She held the pile of papers in her hand, closed the drawer ever so gently, when suddenly she heard a noise. She froze.

Helen tossed in her room from side to side, but soon Annie could hear that she was back to sleep. Annie hurried out of Helen's study and back to her bedroom.

She turned the bed light on. She grimaced—Helen could read braille with the light off—as she so often did when she was about to go to sleep. But Annie needed the light. Though it was the fingers that would tell her what was written in the long papers punched with endless little holes, and though she did not *need* the light, it nevertheless brought her comfort.

She propped up the pillow and began reading slowly. Her braille reading was rusty—never as good as while she was a teenager in school with the other blind girls. But she could read it, even if not as fast as she would have liked.

Words arose before her, letter after letter. She read the first sentence and paused:

"February 3rd. I am discouraged about writing."

That's it! Annie knew it! It was that damned, good-for-nothing Professor Copey, with his unkind, cruel remarks, that had made Helen overly conscious about that one thing which she had considered her very gift!

Annie went on reading, her heart beating fast:

"I suppose I ought not to give way to such feelings, especially as this is no time for weakness or relaxation; but how can I help it? No one that I know or have heard of has the same slow, halting mind as mine."

Annie moaned quietly and kept reading:

> "My ideas obstinately refuse to flow when I try to write. Oh, how pleasant and interesting literary work would be for me but for this cruel, needless hindrance! As it is, I find it a burden, not a pleasure, and at times I—"

Annie hesitated. Her hand noticed the braille sign appearing twice. It was Dot Six, the one used to capitalize the letter that follows. But there were not one, but *two* of them. She knew what that meant—a capitalization of the *entire* word that follows. She went on to read the word:

"HATE it."

She went back to the beginning of the sentence to understand what she had read:

> "Oh, how pleasant and interesting literary work would be for me but for this cruel, needless hindrance! As it is, I find it a burden, not a pleasure, and at times I HATE it."

Annie took a deep breath in. She felt her eyes moisten. So much was going on inside her poor student's heart—so much that she was unaware of!

She went on reading, reprimanding herself for not having noticed how troubled Helen was!

> "February 4th. I am frustrated. My studies have been marked with no brilliant progress. I have only managed to avoid the shame of being regarded as an utterly incapable scholar. Why is it that more has been done for me than for many a brighter, more deserving person? Year after year gifts have been showered upon me, and I have had splendid opportunities to enjoy the wonderful experiences of travel and society. Many distinguished people have spoken to me kindly,

> even tenderly, as if I were their young sister and not the simple, uninteresting, unpromising girl who stood before them, awed by their brilliancy and oppressed with her own unworthiness!"

Unwillingly, Annie's eyes began to tear up. The page ended. She put it aside and continued to the next.

> "February 5th. It is my ambition to write well; but I think one must have extraordinary ability in order to write at the present time. It seems as if everything one would care to say had been said by somebody else! The fresh joyous creative spirit seems to have died out of literature. Sometimes I feel ideas beating against my brain like caged birds; but they will not sing themselves in words."

> February 6th. Early morning. I had a terrible dream. I was standing on the brink of a great waterfall. Suddenly I saw Annie."

Annie gulped, her finger shaking atop the punched paper.

> "At first I did not recognize her. I thought she was an angel. Suddenly she was swept out of sight, and I dashed forward for I knew she had plunged into the whirlpool! With superhuman strength I seized her and held her fast. In a flash I knew who she was, and my efforts to save her were most frantic. But all was in vain. It seemed as if some unseen power were trying to wrest Annie away from me, and forgetting our past quarrels I thrust my love between her and her destruction. At last, mustering all her strength, she threw herself on the shore; but to my surprise she vanished without appearing to know who I was, or what danger she had been in. I tried calling after her, but she ignored me. I rushed to find her and was

just letting myself down into a cellar by a trapdoor when I awoke.

I awoke with trepidation. It was her ignoring me in the dream that bothered me the most. That was worse than all our quarrels put together!"

Annie couldn't continue reading.

She wiped her tears, but more continued to fall. She reached for her handkerchief. She then drank from the glass of water on her night stand. Her lips were dry. She felt hot, though it was cold outside.

She tried calming her breath, her chest rising and falling. She wanted to think about that dream. Was Helen feeling that she was *ignoring* her? Was Annie *ignoring* her?! That was the worst thing she could have read—she, who had dedicated the majority of her adult life to this child—was seen as if she was *ignoring her?*

Her hand reached for the punched paper. She shook her head disapprovingly as she went on reading:

"February 7th. Night. There are moments when I experience a strange feeling of vacancy both in mind and heart. In my heart there seems to be no feeling—only a void; a vacuum, waiting to be filled by a rush of fresh spiritual life. Tonight I feel the emptiness of heart and the utter want of something essential to self-improvement that often depresses me. What is that something I lack? I repeat this question again and again, tossing from side to side, but in vain. Self-reproach sweeps down upon me each time I reflect on this subject. I know I am not brave or strong or resolute; in fact I regard myself as a failure in all that is highest and noblest in a woman."

Annie felt tears streaming down her cheeks again. She

could not stand the words written there.

> "Not only have I strayed from the way of truth; but I have not performed my duties fully enough or utilized the precious opportunities that have offered themselves to me.
>
> February 8th."

Annie paused. February 8th! That was today! When did Helen write it? Yes, in the morning. She heard her typing before they left to university.

> "February 8th. Melancholy. Yet I cannot cry. Even the tender impulses that have stolen into my soul and made me weep have vanished into indifference. In the past this feeling would have filled my heart with bitterness and despair; now it is a constant trouble that I try to ignore. I wish not to disturb the people I live with and love. But no one can understand or conceive the worry, suspense and irritation I endure. Especially in my futile attempt at writing. If there is anything to alienate me from composition, it is this agonizing slowness, the discomfort caused by the sense of wasted time and the harrowing uncertainty of the result—feelings which fairly make me writhe in my seat as if I were in actual pain! It is this difficulty, and NO OTHER that foils my efforts and frustrates my most ardent wishes. It is this, too, which sours my temper and makes me vicious at times. Not a word of exaggeration in all this, only words that have burnt deep into my soul and wrung secret tears from a smarting heart. And yet there is no one, no one who can understand."

Annie looked on, her finger searching the next sentence. There was none. She reread the last sentence.

> "...And yet there is no one, no one who can

understand."

She put the papers down and straightened up against the pillow. She must do something! Tomorrow they must skip college. Yes. They must go for a trip, just the two of them. "Oh Helen!" Annie thought, "My poor Helen!"

She feared for her student. It could not go on this way. She must find a diversion for her poor student's heart that will take her away from her teacher's harsh criticisms, from the stress of essays and exams. From the loneliness in university. But what?

* * *

Throughout the rest of the school year Annie did her best to divert Helen's attention from her schoolwork. They began hosting guests, including a kind couple who learned the manual alphabet. Lenore and Philip often came to dinners. Annie noticed how Helen would be more cheerful afterwards, and that made her teacher feel more at ease.

Helen passed the end of year exams successfully. Summer was beautiful, and Helen was cheerful.

But as the summer came to an end both women were filled with trepidation about the second school year. Each of the two focused on the other. Annie confided to her new friend Lenore how fearful she was of Helen's melancholic tones, which she had last winter.

Helen wrote to her mother,

> "I really dread beginning my second year on Annie's account. I cannot bear the thought of the

constant and terrible strain upon her poor eyes."

They were both living on an education fund established by Dr. Bell following the death of Captain Keller. Since the death of Helen's father they were very much dependent on support from donors who contributed to the fund. Annie hated it, but she could not see any other way for them financially.

Soon after the school year commenced Annie began seeing Helen falling again into a morose mood. Her journal indicated it ever so clearly:

> "September 25th. It seems as if my separation from the other classmates is inevitable. I have moments of loneliness when the girls pass me on the stairs and in the lecture-rooms without a sign. I have a depressing sense of isolation in the midst of all of them. It's not that I don't understand them, I do understand perfectly how they feel. They cannot speak to me, and they do not see the light of recognition in my face as we pass each other in the hallway. The situation to them must be strange and discouraging. O, how tired I am of being a simple nobody! The terror and anxiety! Why such a life should be mine? Is it all a mockery, or is there a great, unknown fate by which it is decreed that great things shall happen after all because I have lived?"

The words of her student pained Annie.

But now she was determined.

Something *had* to be done.

Helen was not willing to ease her course load and was stubbornly trying to keep up with all the other students.

Finally, one late afternoon, Annie found it: the

opportunity she was looking for.

She was opening the daily letters in Helen's study. Helen was sitting next to her, reading her braille books. Annie went over all the letters when she suddenly saw a letter from the magazine *Ladies' Home Journal*. She detested such journals aimed at women, who assumed women were more idiotic than men, referring to them in a simpler language than the men's magazines would. And yet—something in her was drawn to the letter. She opened it and brought it close to her tired eyes:

> "Dear Miss Keller,
>
> It has come to our attention through Professor Copey of Harvard's Annex for Women that you have a most astonishing literary skill. We are interested in possibly publishing an autobiographical sketch written by yourself in our Journal. We wish to hereby propose to you to write five short essays, each of 4000 words (approximately 8 pages long), to be published in five monthly installments.
>
> For such work *Ladies' Home Journal* is willing to offer 600 dollars for each installment."

Annie nearly fainted as she read the sum. She reread the sentence, bringing the paper ever so close to her eyes to see it was not 60 dollars that was typed there. No. It was indeed 600 dollars for *each* installment. That could mean, she quickly calculated, 3000 dollars! It could secure their future for the days following the end of university when the "education fund" no longer support them!

She turned to Helen, who was quietly studying next to her. She took Helen's hand, ecstatically, knowing this was exactly what Helen *needed*. More than the *money*, this could give her an outlet. A beacon of light!

Helen was puzzled to sense the excitement in Annie's spelling as she read her the letter.

"But," Helen spelled back, "I cannot! With the entire course load, all the homework, how could I have the time to write five more essays! Long essays too!"

Annie shook her head adamantly, "But you would *enjoy* it!"

Helen seemed concerned, "But I don't know how to *write*! I am a *bad* writer!"

Annie clenched her jaw, "You—are—a," she spelled emphatically, "s-p-l-e-n-d-i-d writer!"

Helen shook her head adamantly as well, "You are just saying that because you feel bad for me—"

Annie would have none of that pity-party. "Professor Copey *himself* referred them to you, silly girl!"

Helen paused. She did not know what to say.

Annie spelled again, "Professor Copey!"

She looked at the letter and spelled to Helen, "*It has come to our attention through P-r-o-f-e-s-s-o-r C-o-p-e-y,*" she added, "the annoying fool—"

Helen laughed.

Annie smiled and continued, "'—of Harvard's Annex for Women that you have a most a-s-t-o-n-i-s-h-i-n-g literary skill!"

Helen could not hide her smile, "Do you think he thinks so?"

"Apparently!" Annie spelled back.

"But why did he not say it? All his remarks on my

papers are always so negative! Why did he not tell me—"

"Because he is a stuck up snob!" Annie spelled with vigor, "But a *smart* one nevertheless if he recognizes the truth!"

Helen's face twisted with uncertainty. Annie could see the joy, the fear, the insecurity and the wonder on Helen's face.

"Do you think," Helen spelled, "that I should do it?"

"Do I *think* that you should do it? Do I *think* that you should do it? *Of course* you should do it!"

Helen's forehead tensed, "But Teacher, the workload, I can barely finish reading the *Odes of Horace* for next lesson, and this year is more dense with chores—"

Annie shook her head and spelled, "Helen Keller!"

Helen knew that to be a severe reprimand. Annie rarely used her full name. Annie spelled to her, "Can you please explain to me why does one *go* to university?"

Helen shrugged her shoulders, "To study among the greats?"

Annie thought that her student was so naïve. She spelled, "*And?*"

"And to discuss with the learned the treasures of human knowledge?"

Annie sighed, "And? Why do *most people* go to university?"

Helen did not know what Annie was aiming for.

"Because," Annie spelled, as if talking to a child, "university can help one's *vocation*. So that once one finishes university one can be given great opportunities!"

Helen nodded.

"Fool!" Annie spelled, "This is why you go to university! So that journals can eventually contact you and ask you for what you have to say!"

"But I don't know if I *have* anything to say!" Helen spelled and let out a long moan of desperation.

"Of course you do," Annie spelled, and then repeated, "Of course you do!"

* * *

> "It is with a kind of fear that I begin to write the history of my life—"

Helen paused typing and tried to concentrate. She thought of the sentence again. It sounded awful to her.

> "It is with a kind of fear that I begin to write the history of my life."

She took a deep breath and turned back to her typewriter:

> "I have, as it were, a superstitious hesitation in lifting the veil that clings about my childhood like a golden mist."

She felt the floor under her feet. Down the hall in the kitchen, Annie was cooking dinner. Helen could feel the familiar steps on the wooden floor. The steps of her Teacher. Helen knew she had to tell her story—if not for herself then she must write it for her Annie. Annie deserved the acknowledgement.

But how should she write about the past, most of

which she does not recall?

> "Many of the joys and sorrows of childhood have lost their poignancy; and many incidents of vital importance in my early education have been lost sight of in the excitement of great discoveries."

She went on, hesitantly, wishing to promise the reader that her account will not be boring.

> "In order not to be tedious I shall try to present in a series of sketches only the episodes that seem to me to be the most interesting and important."

She took a deep breath and continued. She could still hear Annie's steps in the kitchen.

> "I was born on June 27, 1880, in Tuscumbia, a little town of Northern Alabama, where I lived up to the time of the illness that deprived me of my sight and hearing. My lovely house was completely covered with vines, climbing roses and honeysuckle. From the garden it looked like an arbor. Its old-fashioned garden was the paradise of my childhood. After my illness I used to be guided by the sense of smell, which would direct me to the violets and lilies. There, too, after my fits of temper I went to find comfort and to hide my hot face in the cool leaves and grass."

She smiled to herself. Not because of the writing— the writing was bad, dull, boring—but because of the memories that began stirring in her. The joy of childhood.

> "What joy it was to lose myself in that garden of flowers, to wander happily from spot to spot, until coming suddenly upon a beautiful vine, I recognized it by its leaves and blossoms. Close by were trailing clematis, drooping Jessamine, and

> some rare sweet flowers called butterfly lilies. But the roses—they were loveliest of all! Never have I found in the greenhouses of the North such heart-satisfying roses as the climbing roses of my Southern home."

She remembered their smell, the soft texture of the petals, the morning dew....

> "These roses were hung in long festoons from our porch, filling the whole air with their fragrance, untainted by any earthly smell; and in the early morning, washed in the dew, they felt so soft and seemed so pure."

Something in the memory made her eyes moist.

Was what she writing any good?

She inhaled deeply. Helen, she told herself, they want to hear of your *life*. Not of the roses! She nodded and placed her fingers on the typewriter, hesitant:

> "The beginning of my life was simple and much like every other little life. I came, I saw, I conquered, as babies often do. I am told that while I was still in long dresses I showed many signs of an eager, self-asserting disposition. Everything that I saw other people do I insisted upon imitating. At six months, I could pipe out "How d'ye," and one day I attracted everyone's attention by saying "Tea, tea, tea" quite plainly."

She bit her lip thinking of what happened next. In remembering the illness she was more tormented for her mother than for herself. It was her *mother* who had to witness what happened.

> "These happy days did not last long. One brief spring, musical with the song of robin and mocking-bird, one summer rich in fruit and roses,

one autumn of gold and crimson sped by and left their gifts at the feet of an eager, delighted child.

Then, in the dreary month of February, came the dreadful illness which closed my eyes and ears and plunged me into the absolute unconsciousness of a new-born baby. They called it acute congestion of the stomach and brain. The doctor thought I could not live. Early one morning, however, the fever left me as suddenly and mysteriously as it had come. There was great rejoicing in the family that morning, but not one, not even the doctor, knew that I should never see or hear again. But during the first nineteen months of my life I caught glimpses of broad green fields, a luminous sky, trees and flowers which the darkness that followed could not wholly blot out."

She heard steps down the hallway. Annie walked in. From her steps Helen knew she was carrying something.

Annie placed a cup of tea and a plate with a cake on the desk. Helen felt gently about the desk and found the cup of tea. It was hot. It smelled like her favorite chamomile tea. She took Annie's hand and spelled, "Chamomile! Thank you!"

Annie spelled back, "And cake."

Helen reached her other hand and felt the plate with the cake. Something about it brought tears to her eyes.

Annie spelled, "Is everything alright?"

"Cake." Helen spelled.

"You don't want cake?" Annie spelled back.

"No," Helen spelled. "It was one of the first words you taught me. Cake."

Annie smiled. She was surprised to see a whole page typed out on the typewriter. She patted Helen's hand and spelled, "You are doing well!"

Helen nodded gently, slowly.

"Continue," Annie spelled and left the room.

Helen heard Annie's steps halting by the door. She closed her eyes and kept writing.

> "Gradually I got used to the silence and darkness that surrounded me and—"

She felt conscious. Was Annie still standing there? She waved her hand at the door.

Annie laughed and walked away from the door, back to the kitchen.

Helen completed the sentence:

> "Gradually I got used to the silence and darkness that surrounded me and forgot that it had ever been different, until she came—my Teacher—who was to set my spirit free."

* * *

She wrote for another hour and produced three whole pages. She took them and walked to the kitchen, following the smell of rice. She loved rice.

She waited by the table. Annie came to her, "What do you have there?"

"Read it and tell me if it is any good."

Annie sat down on a kitchen stool and began reading. It was well written. Actually, she thought, it was *extremely* well written. She finished the first page and continued to the next. Helen's narrative was captivating.

> "I do not remember when I first realized that I was different from other people, but I knew it before my teacher came to me. I had noticed that my mother and my friends did not use gestures the way I did when they wanted anything done, but talked with their mouths. Sometimes I would stand between two persons who were conversing and would touch their lips. I could not understand, and was vexed. I moved my lips and gesticulated frantically without result. This made me so angry at times that I kicked and screamed until I was exhausted."

Annie looked at Helen. It was hard to imagine this polite, gentle, well-mannered girl ever screaming and kicking. Annie smiled, thinking, who would remember that better than herself? She remembered Helen fighting her once in the garden house, even knocking Annie's tooth out. She remembered the blood, and Percy, that servant boy, helping her find a handkerchief and washing it in hot water. That she had not written to Mrs. Hopkins about. No. It would have been too much.

She sighed, looked at Helen, and then went on reading,

> "I understood perfectly when I was naughty, for I knew that it hurt Viney, my friend who was a little older than me, when I kicked her. When my fit of temper was over I had a feeling akin to regret. But I cannot remember any instance in which this feeling prevented me from repeating the naughtiness when I failed to get what I wanted. I was strong and active, and indifferent to consequences. I knew what I wanted and was ready to fight for it, and to fight tooth and nail against everything I did not want."

Annie turned to the third page.

> "One day I had an experience that I remember vividly. I happened to spill water on my apron and I spread it out to dry before the fire, which was flickering on the sitting-room hearth. But the apron did not dry quickly enough to suit me and I drew nearer and threw it right over the hot ashes. The fire leaped into life; the flames encircled me so that in a moment my clothes were blazing. I made a terrified noise that brought the cook, Martha, to the rescue. Throwing a blanket over me she almost suffocated me, but she put out the fire. Except for my hands and hair I was not badly burned.
>
> About this time I found out the use of a key, and one day I locked my mother up in the pantry, where she was obliged to remain three hours as the servants were in a detached part of the house. She kept pounding on the door, while I sat outside on the porch steps and laughed with glee as I felt the jar of the pounding. This most naughty prank of mine convinced my parents that I must be taught as soon as possible."

Annie spelled to Helen, "Where is the next page?!"

Helen frowned, "I haven't written it yet!"

Annie smiled, "I must find out what happens next!"

Helen could not hide her smile, "You think it is not awful?"

"Helen Keller!" Annie spelled to her and found herself simultaneously speaking the words out loud, "This is one of the most captivating personal accounts I have e-v-e-r read! I want the n-e-x-t page!"

Helen smiled. She felt feelings of inadequacy mixed

with hope. Could it be that Annie was telling her the truth?

* * *

The editor of the *Ladies' Home Journal* was thrilled.

> "Was this indeed your own writing? Were you not assisted by others to write it? The descriptions are extraordinary!"

As Annie spelled the letter to Helen, she saw Helen's face lighting up.

It was difficult to say who was happier: was it Helen, who for the first time in over a year wrote an essay which had no red marks on it when it returned?

Or was it Annie, who, looking at Helen's illuminated face, felt a relief that only a mother could understand?

Helen sat down immediately, proudly, to report to the editor that she herself—in fact, and no other—had written the essay.

* * *

It was right before Christmas that Helen received the editor's response:

> "Dear Miss Keller,
>
> Thank you for your letter of clarification. If this is indeed the case we would like to include "AN EDITORIAL FORWARD" to your article, stating:
>
> As the feat may seem almost incredible, it may be

in order to say at the beginning that every word of this story as printed here has actually been written by Helen Keller herself—not dictated, but written by the wonderful girl herself.

Will you approve of such an editorial forward?

Please find attached the check for the first installment, which should appear in the April issue. Please send us the following article as soon as possible, so that we can prepare it for the May issue.

Also, please find attached a check for Miss Sullivan, as a token of our gratitude for her assistance in carrying the correspondence.

Yours sincerely,

Mr. Edward Bok

Chief Editor

Ladies Home Journal"

Attached in the envelope was a check for 600 dollars for the first installment written for Helen Keller, as well as additional 400 dollars for Anne Sullivan.

Both of them were ecstatic.

* * *

"Dearest Mother,

I hope you had a lovely Christmas. I missed you and Mildred terribly.

Yes, I neglect my letters sadly; but the fret and worry about the second "Ladies' Home Journal" article has caused me to feel quite disinclined to write.

If it was not for the prospect of the money, which shall hopefully allow us and you to live cozily in the future, I should quit the whole business! I have succeeded in covering the period of my life up to Annie's arrival in the first article, but there are now challenging and complicated passages to write and I dread "tackling" them. I'm afraid I haven't the gift of keeping the reader's interest from flagging.

But this is a work of love, and the thought of the good that may come out of it gives me courage to go on with this obligation I had committed to.

Do you realize that I am receiving 600 dollars for each article? I already got the first check, you know, and if there are five articles in all, I shall receive three thousand dollars—think of that!

Was it not good in them to let me have the first payment sent right away, in time for Christmas? I did not expect the money so soon! They also sent Annie 400 dollars, because they were pleased that she had persuaded me to write the article!

This led to a great new pleasure in our home: with her money Annie decided to rent a piano and a Pianola! Isn't that lovely? She will now have something to enjoy in the long evenings, when she cannot use her eyes. She taught me to play the Pianola a little, and we have great fun with it!

I told you, did I not, that Lenore and Philip Smith live near here. We see them often, and they are so happy and full of fun, it is good to be with them, and both of them learned the manual alphabet to converse with me directly! Philip has a fine tenor and sings with great animation. Yesterday we had them over and we had much fun with the new piano and Pianola.

I am still in the throes of completing the second "article," so I will make this note very short.

With dear love from Annie,

I am,

Affectionately your child,

Helen."

* * *

Two months passed and Helen was unable to produce the next installment.

Annie and Helen spent frustrating hours in the evenings, trying to put together the article. Both regretted having put themselves in this predicament. Furthermore, Mr. Bok, the editor of *Ladies' Home Journal,* was upset. First came two letters, then telegrams.

Annie tried to read Helen's half-typed pages, but her eyes pained her. She was also fatigued each evening, after having spelled into Helen's hand all the lectures of that day.

Helen was frustrated, unable to put her thoughts together. Many pages lay around her small study, scattered, filled with one or two paragraphs only.

One evening Lenore Smith came by to check on them, as Annie had not spoken to her over two weeks. Lenore, wearing her typical Gibson Girl hairstyle, was alarmed to see Annie distressed. She followed Annie to Helen's study, where papers were thrown all over the desk and the floor. Lenore gasped, "Oh my!"

"I know," Annie lamented. "We put ourselves in a hell of a knot!"

Lenore immediately hugged Helen and spelled to her, while speaking out loud to Annie, "All will be alright!"

The following day Lenore came with a young gentleman, a colleague of her husband Philip. The tall, shy-looking man, stood by Lenore at the door. "This," Lenore said proudly, "is Mr. John Macy. Mr. Macy is a lauded English teacher and editor!"

Annie measured the tall man with the baby face, "May I ask how old are you?"

"Twenty five, Madam!" the tall man said.

They stood at the entrance as Annie inspected him carefully. She did not want any good-for-nothing fellow to come in contact with her cherished pupil. She wished to examine his eyes, and reached up close to his face to an extent that was not wholly appropriate. His eyes were blue, light blue. She thought he probably knew nothing of the world.

Lenore spoke, wishing to ease John's anxiety, "Mr. Macy, Annie, is the editor in chief of the *Harvard Advocate*, you must have seen that paper, right?"

Annie mumbled something unclear.

"Well," Lenore said and smiled an excessively large smile, "shall we take him to Helen?"

Annie sighed, nodded her head and turned around, "Follow me."

Lenore walked inside and smiled back at John who

followed her. Annie entered the messy study. Lenore smiled and spelled something into Helen's hand.

John was not deterred when he saw the messy room. "Well," he said, and surprised Annie with his deep baritone, "this surely looks like a proper newsroom!"

Annie frowned.

"No," John said, "that is a *compliment*, Miss Sullivan. Now, shall you introduce me to Miss Keller?"

Annie felt a little stupid for not having done so immediately. She pushed Lenore aside and spelled something into Helen's hand. Helen immediately grinned and nodded, reaching her hand forward for a handshake.

John shook her hand and Lenore, seeing all was well, said in passing, "I'm sure they'll get along fine!"

Annie pouted her lips. She did not know what to make of the stranger in their house. She looked disapprovingly at Lenore, "Well I must make dinner."

Lenore smiled, and something in her raised eyebrow made Annie feel conscious of her appearance, wearing the kitchen apron. Sensing her burning cheeks she said, "I shall be in the kitchen if you need me."

* * *

Half an hour later Lenore came to the kitchen, "I must go now. I'm sorry, Annie."

Annie waved her hand dismissively, forgetting to thank Lenore for her good efforts.

She assumed the man in the study would soon see the difficult task of even *conversing* with Helen, let alone helping her *compose* an eight-page-essay!

When dinner was finally ready she walked to Helen's study, surprised by the sight: the room was tidy, with four piles of papers organized meticulously on the desk. Yet what was more surprising was Helen holding the man's hand while he spelled to her slowly, looking constantly at handwritten sheet of paper in front of him.

Helen smiled and nodded eagerly, then spelling something back to him. He kept looking at the sheet, ignoring Annie.

"What do you have there?" Annie asked.

John looked at her, "Oh, just a quick list I made to indicate the letters."

Annie came to the desk and took the sheet of paper in her hand, lifting it and bringing it close to her eyes. She saw the alphabet written in a column, with strange drawings near each letter.

John mumbled, "It's nothing, Miss Sullivan, just a list to help me remember the letters." He hesitated, "I find it hard to distinguish between the letters H, U, K and—"

"And P," Annie completed his sentence.

"How did you know?" John asked, astounded.

Annie did not like his tone. How did she *know*? Did he have *any* understanding of the *hundreds* of times she taught the manual alphabet to strangers on their request or on Helen's request, teaching them patiently, whether she wanted to or not? Annie snorted, "These four letters have the same hand shape," she took his hand firmly in hers. The thumb is on the middle finger, but they are distinguished in *orientation.*"

She showed him each of the four signs, forming his

fingers quickly. She then said, "That's H, that's U, that's K and that's P, got it?"

"Oh," John said and nodded slowly, "I see!"

Annie continued quickly, "Similarly but differently, the A and the S—"

"Yes, yes?" John said eagerly, "I had a trouble distinguishing them—"

"—are of the same orientation," Annie continued, "but you must differentiate the *thumb*, which is on the *side* of the *fist* in A, and in *front* in S."

"Oh thank you! Thank you!" John said, and his response surprised Annie.

Annie took Helen's hand and spelled, "Dinner."

Helen spelled quickly, "Can John eat with us?"

Annie took a deep breath in, "If that is what you want."

Helen nodded eagerly.

* * *

That early evening turned into night, as they ate and talked. Later, in Helen's study, John organized the papers together, explaining to Helen about repeated phrases and necessary omissions.

Annie sat with them in the study on the sofa in the corner. Soon she fell asleep. She awoke at midnight when John finally excused himself and left.

She was amazed to see the typed essay. Eight pages.

* * *

"March 3rd, 1902

Dear Mother,

Over a month has passed since we met Mr. John Macy. I have mentioned his name to you, but I shall now explain more of his role. He is a friend of our good friends Lenore and Philip. Lenore arranged for him to visit me when Annie and I could not complete the second article. I liked him instantly; he was eager, intelligent and gentle. He understood my difficulties, and promptly set about relieving me of them. We went over the material I had accumulated, which was in the state of original chaos! Quickly and skillfully he brought the recalcitrant parts to order; and we constructed a tolerably coherent and readable chapter in a few hours. John is an instructor in the English department at Harvard, and is very bright; he is also a writer himself, with a keen, well-stored mind. His advice is most precious to me, so in most cases we hearken to his guidance as to an oracle. I think he enjoys our society, especially the company of Annie, as the two of them laugh a lot together. I believe we have every reason to be fond of him. Even Mr. Bok, the editor of the *Ladies' Home Journal* is fond of him. He wrote back thanking me for the second article, and hailed John as a *deus ex machina* for his help in finally sending the article.

He is one of the noblest men I ever knew—his nature is much the same as Dr. Bell's. Oh, have I told you Dr. Bell has been kind enough to place a *telephone* in our home? Imagine, Mother! Now, is Dr. Bell not lovely?

We have had several parties, and have been out sleighing repeatedly. One night we invited Lenore,

Philip and John to ride with us, and a more gay time I never had! The moon was full, the air fresh and crisp and I enjoyed the crunch of the snow as the sleigh ran over it.

I am sorry Uncle Fred is not well. Please send him my love and my best wishes for a quick recovery.

I must stop now as John has arrived to help us with the third article. I hope you are proud of our progress.

Affectionately your child,

Helen."

* * *

One evening Annie, who had just finished making dinner, walked down to Helen's study calling, "Children, dinner is ready!"

She was surprised to see John in tears. Helen was sitting next to him, waiting in anticipation.

"What is going on?" Annie asked.

John raised his eyes from the sheet of paper and marveled at her, "Miss Sullivan, you are a genius!"

Annie snorted, "What has she written now?"

John handed her the paper. She took it and sighed, her eyes were too tired. They had a long day, as the end of year exams were in the coming week. She tried reading, but frustratingly gave John the paper back, "I'm tired, I'm sorry—"

"Oh of course! Let me read it to you!"

"But dinner is ready," Annie said.

"Of course, pardon me," John said.

Annie spelled to Helen that dinner was ready, and the three of them moved to the small dining room near the kitchen. John brought with him the three pages he had been working on with Helen.

They began eating when John looked at Annie appreciatively and murmured, "How did you know?"

"How did I know *what?*" Annie said, her mouth full with mashed potatoes.

"How did you know she would understand?"

"Understand what," Annie mumbled, "John Macy you are talking in riddles!"

He shook his head, took the paper, cleared his throat and began reading:

> "At first, when my teacher told me about a new thing I asked very few questions. My ideas were vague, and my vocabulary was inadequate. I remember the morning that I had found a few early violets in the garden and brought them to my teacher. She tried to kiss me: but at that time I did not like to have any one kiss me except my mother. Miss Sullivan put her arm gently round me and spelled into my hand, 'I love Helen.'
>
> 'What is love?' I asked."

Annie smiled to herself. She remembered this instance well.

John continued reading out loud, his eyes becoming moist. Annie looked at him strangely. She was not used to men being so gentle or so emotional.

"'What is love?' I asked.

She drew me closer to her and said, 'It is here,' pointing to my heart, whose beats I was conscious of for the first time. Her words puzzled me very much because I did not then understand anything unless I touched it.

I smelt the violets in her hand and asked, 'Is love the sweetness of flowers?'

'No,' said my teacher.

Again I paused to think. The warm sun was shining on us.

'Is this not love?' I asked, pointing in the direction from which the sun shone on us. 'Is this not love?' It seemed to me that there could be nothing more beautiful than the sun, whose warmth makes all things grow!

But Miss Sullivan shook her head, and I was greatly puzzled and disappointed. I thought it strange that my teacher could not *show me* love."

Annie laughed and said, "She wrote that?"

John nodded.

Annie took Helen's left hand and spelled, "Helen Keller, you are a *writer*!"

Helen laughed and continued to eat.

John went on to read the second page,

"A day or two afterward I was stringing beads of different sizes in symmetrical groups: two large beads, three small ones, and so on. I had made many mistakes, and Miss Sullivan had pointed them out again and again with gentle patience. Finally I noticed a very obvious error in the sequence and for an instant I concentrated my attention on the lesson and tried to think how I should have arranged the beads. Miss Sullivan touched my forehead and spelled with decided emphasis, 'Think!'

In a flash I knew that this new word, 'T-h-i-n-k,' was the name of the *process* that was going on in my head. This was my first conscious perception of an abstract idea."

John looked at Annie and spoke passionately, "How did you *know*?"

"Know what?!" Annie exclaimed, "That she could understand?"

"Yes!"

Annie smiled. She was quiet for a moment. She felt John's gaze on her. She took a deep breath, "I once read," she said quietly, "a quote by Goethe."

She saw John nodding eagerly. She went on, "It stated, 'Look at a man the way that he is, and then he only becomes *worse*. But look at him as if he were what he *could* be—"

John interrupted, completing the quote, "—Then he becomes what he *should* be!"

Annie smiled and nodded. Seeing John's anticipation she continued, "It is true in education as well. Treat a pupil the way that he *is*, he only becomes worse! But treat him as if he were what he *could* be, then he becomes what he *should* be. I agree with that wholeheartedly. Why should I have treated Helen as if she was dumb!"

"But everyone else treated her like that!"

Annie snorted, "You are still young, Mr. Macy. But

sooner or later you will understand that what *everyone else* says or does is often the worst compass for one's actions. Doesn't the Bible say, 'Do not *conform* to the pattern of this world, but be *transformed* by the renewing of *your* mind!"

"Of course," John said, "Romans 12:2."

Annie smiled. "You are a learned man, Mr. Macy!"

"And so are you, Annie," John said.

Annie blushed. She said nothing. John coughed, sensing he was acting too familiarly. He went back to the paper and said, "May I continue reading this to you?"

"Oh please do!"

Helen sensed the two were talking. She was happy for Annie—for having someone speaking to her teacher *directly*, rather than using her as a *translator* to reach her student. Helen sensed the tense movements of her teacher, indicating Annie was excited.

John went on to read:

> "For a long time I tried to find the meaning of the word 'love.' In light of the new word, 'think,' I began thinking about it further. The sun had been under a cloud all day, and there had been brief showers; but suddenly the sun broke forth in all its southern splendor."

Annie smiled at Helen. She liked that last phrase. She was moved by the whole passage.

John continued,

> "Again, I asked my teacher, 'Is this not love?'
>
> My teacher replied, 'Love is something like the clouds that were in the sky before the sun came

out.' Then in simpler words than these, which at that time I could not have understood, she explained: 'You cannot touch the clouds, right?'

'Right,' I said.

'But still, you feel the rain and know how glad the flowers and the thirsty earth are to have it after a hot day!'"

Annie suddenly began tearing up and immediately wiped away her tears, embarrassed.

John caught her, "Exactly! That's what I was thinking too! And listen to the rest:

My teacher continued, 'Likewise, you cannot touch love either; but you *feel* the sweetness that it pours into everything. Without love, Helen, you would not be happy.'

Suddenly the beautiful truth burst upon my mind. I felt that there were invisible lines stretched between my spirit and the spirits of others. It was called 'Love.'"

John raised his moist eyes at Annie.

She bit her lip and looked away.

* * *

"I think John likes you," Helen spelled into Annie's hand one Sunday afternoon. They were sitting on a bench near the park. Helen just returned from Church to which she went with Lenore, and felt particularly happy. The exams were finally over. So were the five articles for *Ladies' Home Journal* that received many positive reviews and brought not only money to Helen and Annie, but also a sense of pride.

Annie snorted and spelled back, "He likes you too!"

She then quickly added, "Mr. Macy is a fine gentleman."

"No," Helen spelled, "I think he likes you *very much*."

Annie did not respond. What was all this about?

Helen spelled again, emphatically, "He l-i-k-e-s you! He told me so!"

"No he didn't!" Annie spelled quickly and turned to see Helen's face.

"Well," Helen hesitated, "not in *these* words—"

"What did he tell you!"

Helen smiled, "Why are you so eager to know?"

"Oh you bloody rogue!" Annie spelled and Helen laughed with delight. "Helen! Tell me already!"

"He said," Helen spelled slowly, "'Annie is the most devout teacher you could have ever hoped for, Helen!'"

A small smiled appeared on Annie's face. "*And?*"

Helen enjoyed the conversation and spelled slowly, "*A-n-d* he said that he feels fortunate to have Lenore and Philip as his friends, as without them he wouldn't have gotten to know such two fine ladies!"

Annie grunted. She had hoped for a more specific reference to herself.

Helen continued, "He also said that the articles can be developed into a book!"

"He told me that," Annie spelled and sighed.

"I think he said it because," Helen paused, "because

he wants to have an excuse to call on you more often."

Annie said nothing. She stared at the garden. It was nice that spring had finally come after such a cold and unpleasant winter.

Helen continued, "He said that you too should write your own account, and that both of our accounts can be bound together in the same book."

Annie grimaced. The thought of having to write daunted her. If anything, she wanted to stay away from books, writings, and all other obligations that would add more of a burden to her already tired eyes. The workload that she *already* had, having to read to Helen the textbooks, the mail, and the newspaper headlines was already more than she could take.

She said nothing.

"He said he could help you," Helen persisted.

"Why is this so important to you?" Annie asked, not anticipating an answer.

"You are a very charitable person," Helen spelled slowly.

Annie did not understand. "Charitable??" She spelled and wiggled the question mark sign twice.

Helen smiled cunningly, "And as a charitable person, you must not say no to such a plea from a man in need."

"PLEA?" Annie spelled. She felt her student was fooling with her and on this subject of all subjects! She shook her head disapprovingly. "Enough, Helen!"

Helen persisted, "Why don't we tell him that we'd like to discuss this further? He wants to work on it! Summer is here, and it can give us an excuse to see him more often now that the five articles are over. Would you not want that?"

Annie ground her teeth. "Fine. Tell him what you must. But this was not *my* idea!"

"Indeed," Helen spelled and smiled.

Annie moaned and spelled, "Oh stop being so pleased with yourself!"

Helen laughed.

They said nothing more.

* * *

"You see," John spoke passionately, walking back and forth around the small living room, "the book must serve the reader's thirst for knowledge and supply a *full* comprehension of the miracle called Helen Keller!"

Annie sat along Helen and rapidly spelled to her John's words. By now, after years of lessons and two years of university lectures from morning to evening, she spelled without thinking anything of it. It was as natural as breathing.

John paced passionately. Annie thought that from his enthusiasm and grandeur of speech an outside observer might think he was proposing an amendment to the constitution.

John went on, "Readers wish to have the *entire* picture, and not only see 'Teacher' from the point of view of her 'student,' but also see the 'student' from the eyes of the 'Teacher!'"

Helen nodded eagerly.

"What did the teacher experience," John went on, "was she afraid? Was she always confident? Was she certain of her methods, or were there doubts? One must answer these questions in order to paint a more *whole* portrait of this unique situation."

Annie sighed. It sounded like too much work to her.

"Sigh not!" John said with a wink.

Annie smiled as he continued, "This does not mean crossing through the Red Sea," he went to his valise, "Reading these," he pulled out four thick booklets, "one can see most of the text had already been written!"

It was only when John placed the four thick booklets on the small coffee table that Annie suddenly realized what he had pulled out. "Oh my! The Annual Reports of the Massachusetts School for the Blind! How on earth did you get them?"

John sat down on the opposite sofa, obviously pleased with himself, "One must do some research before embarking on a great endeavor."

Annie shook her head disapprovingly. She leaned forward and took the report at the top of the pile and opened it. She saw John's handwritten comments inside. She looked at him, sighed, and looked again at the booklet. She saw many of John's comments. One of them pointed to a paragraph and stated, "Most amusing story, must be included!" Annie strained her eyes and looked at the small print, reading the first line:

> "I must admit that Helen has a great notion of "primping!" Nothing pleases her better than to be dressed in her best clothes."

Annie smiled to herself, remembering the incident, and how she wrote about it to Mrs. Hopkins. She kept reading, a sheepish smile on her face:

> "The other day I told her to put her hat on and I would take her for a walk. I was changing my dress, and I suppose Helen thought I was dressing up. She rushed downstairs in a great hurry, and showed her mother that she wanted her best dress on. Mrs. Keller paid no attention to her. Hence Helen decided to fix herself. When I searched for her I found the most comical looking child imaginable. She had wet her hair until the water was running in little streams in all directions, and if it did not look sleek nothing ever did! She had also found her mother's powder and applied that in such quantities so that she looked like a ghost. When she had completed her toilet to her own satisfaction she came for her mother's approval with such a self-satisfied air. Of course she found us both laughing as if we would die. You never saw anyone look so comical."

Annie smiled and shook her head. What experiences they had!

She caught John standing above her. Her smile turned into a frown, "But who would want to read *this?* I cannot believe I sent this to the *Annual Report!* It's...."

"Fascinating!" John interrupted. "And it made you smile—isn't that a good thing? Good writing must evoke emotion, Miss Sullivan, and you had done just that!"

Annie took a deep breath and spelled to Helen's hand quickly, "He's talking nonsense."

Helen shook her head and spelled, "Listen to him!"

Annie flipped through the pages of the report, her lips pouting. Her first year with Helen. She put the report down on the table and moved to the next. The second year, 1888. She moved the report aside, revealing the third, 1889. Then she suddenly saw the Report from year 1886, before she met Helen. "Well," she looked at John, happy to find a flaw in his research, "this report is irrelevant!"

John smiled at her nonchalantly and took the 1886 Annual Report, opening it in the very end. He read:

> "One of the most interesting educational occasions that occur each year in our school is naturally the commencement ceremony of our recent graduates. The exercises for the school year just closed took place in Tremont Temple, in the presence of a thoroughly sympathetic audience that completely filled the Temple. These occasions are always of a very high order of merit and fraught with great interest, as well as being the cause of wonder and admiration at the Perfection to which the instruction of the Blind has been brought...."

Annie sighed. This sounded so much like poor old Mr. Anagnos and his pompous, flowery language.

John continued eagerly:

> "The valedictory, by Miss Annie M. Sullivan was worthy of special mention—"

He looked knowingly at Annie. She shifted on the sofa uncomfortably,

> "...for its felicity of thought and grace of expression. It was emphatically a beautifully original production."

John closed the report with a triumphant look.

Helen turned to Annie and spelled, "What is John

saying?"

Annie, who stopped spelling when John began reading, spelled simply, "Hot air."

John leaned forward from his couch and took Helen's other hand, spelling to her, "I read to her the comment made about her valedictory address, 'its felicity of thought,' and 'grace of expression.'"

Helen's face frowned as she spelled in both hands simultaneously, "I did not know that Annie gave a valedictory address!"

John spelled emphatically, "Exactly!" He got up and walked about the room again.

Annie took another deep breath as she spelled to Helen, "It was nothing to write home about or worthy to mention in a *book*!"

John seemed frustrated. He pointed at the Annual Reports, "All the material is here, in these three reports. I can put it all together so that the narrative flows. But there are some missing periods. I understand the reports include some excerpts from letters. Can we get hold of these letters?"

Annie exhaled. Mrs. Hopkins. In recent years their relationship grew colder, though they had spent the previous Christmas together. "I presume," she murmured, "that we can ask for them."

John said, "You must help me do this. You must put your trepidations aside, Annie. This should be a gift that you give to humanity. I envision half a book written by you!"

"But this is Helen's book," Annie protested.

"Well, with a..." John searched for words, "an *annex*,

an *appendix* by her teacher! Not writing it might seem to some people disrespectful of you!"

Annie frowned, "Disrespectful?!"

John looked at her, sat down and took her hand in his hand. "Annie, yield to me. You won't regret it!"

Annie moaned, "I already do!"

* * *

Mrs. Hopkins was happy to send the letters. They arrived in a small wooden package. Annie placed the package on the kitchen table and avoided opening them for a whole week.

It was only when Helen was gone with Lenore to church on Sunday that Annie finally mustered the courage to sit by the small wooden box in the kitchen. She was afraid to open it for some reason. "Why?" she asked herself.

She did not know.

"Oh the hell with it," she said and brought a kitchen knife and opened the wooden seal. So many letters were crammed inside. Was it she who wrote all of them?

Her chin quivered as she tried pulling out the first letter, which refused to yield to her fingers, being pressed tightly against the others.

But finally it did come out. Her handwriting amazed her. Dense. Rapid. As if on a mission. She brought it closer to her eyes and read:

"Dear Mrs. Hopkins,

> I've been meaning to write to you earlier, but quite frankly, I have been exhausted. I arrived three days ago, on Thursday, at 6:30 P.M."

The thought of the journey to Alabama made her heart sink. Only now did she understand just how *lonely* she had been. Thinking of the many tears she had shed on the train overwhelmed her.

She put the letter down and stood up.

She walked to the window. She was surprised by her reaction. These were good letters, weren't they? They were good! They told of good things! The *result* was good, wasn't it? Then why was her hand shaking so?

She felt tears but steeled herself to keep reading.

> "Mr. James Keller was waiting for me. He rebuked me for missing the train in Washington, and said somebody had met every train arriving in Tuscumbia for the past two days."

She snorted. James, that fool. What an unkind welcome!

She went on reading:

> "The drive from the station to the house, a distance of one mile, was very lovely and restful."

She felt tears coursing down her cheeks and muttered to herself, "Enough, enough!"

> "I was surprised to see that Helen was a healthy child. Somehow I had expected to see a pale, delicate child—I suppose I got the idea from Dr. Howe's description of Laura Bridgman when she first came to the school. But there's nothing pale or delicate about Helen. She is large, strong, and ruddy, and as unrestrained in her movements as a

young colt."

She wept. She remembered her first night. Alone in that attic. Alone in the world.

> "Her body is well formed and vigorous, and Mrs. Keller says she has not been ill a day since the illness that deprived her of her sight and hearing. She has a fine head, and it is set on her shoulders just right."

She giggled and sniffled.

> "Her face is hard to describe. It is intelligent, but lacks mobility, or soul, or something."

She remembered the violence with which Helen hit and kicked her. She remembered the blood from the broken tooth in the garden house. But more than anything she remembered the loneliness, the sheer loneliness. She had not a friend in the world. Even Mrs. Hopkins was but a figure to her, a locked chamber. Loving, yes, encouraging, yes, but not a *friend*.

She read on:

> "You see at a glance that Helen is blind. One eye is larger than the other, and protrudes noticeably. She rarely smiles."

How she longed to love that little blind and deaf girl, and how *hard* it was to love her! How almost impossible it was to *relate* to the girl who would push her face each time she came to hug her or kiss her? The girl who two days after her arrival locked her in her room?! That episode, too, she had kept from Mrs. Hopkins. How difficult Helen was! The girl ran away from her as if her life depended on it!

> "She is unresponsive and even impatient of caresses from any one except her mother. She is

> very quick-tempered and willful, and nobody has attempted to control her. The greatest problem I shall have to solve is how to discipline and control her without breaking her spirit."

Annie paused, amazed at the last sentence. She read it again:

> "The greatest problem I shall have to solve is how to discipline and control her without breaking her spirit."

What wisdom she had! What insight! Yes. She was right! Her 21 year old self—no, she was not even 21 then—how did she *see*? How did she *foresee* the difficulty?

Suddenly she realized the enormous weight on her shoulders then. There was too much pressure on the little girl, too much discipline to the extent that the girl would rebel against her for good—and the Kellers would have fired her!

What courage, Annie thought to herself. She was surprised by her own strength.

> "I shall go rather slowly at first and try to win her love. I shall not attempt to conquer her by force alone; but I shall insist on reasonable obedience from the start."

"Yes," Annie mumbled to herself, "Yes!" Now, at age 36, she could see just how brilliant her younger self was.

> "One thing that impresses everybody is Helen's tireless activity. She is never still a moment. She is here, there, and everywhere. Her hands are in everything; but nothing holds her attention for long. Dear child, her restless spirit gropes in the dark. Her untaught, unsatisfied hands destroy whatever they touch because they do not know

what else to do with things."

Over the years Annie remembered Helen's rude behavior. But it was always a dim memory. One not to be touched. Now, suddenly, Annie was at a loss of words, seeing her own handwriting and remembering the insurmountable task of winning over her unruly, savage-like pupil.

She read on, seeing the smeared ink:

> "Forgive me for the smeared handwriting. This morning Helen came to my room and was very troublesome noticing I was writing this letter. She kept coming up behind me and putting her hand on the paper and into the ink bottle. These blots are her handiwork... Finally I remembered the beads I had brought with me, and set her to work stringing them.
>
> First I put on two wooden beads and one glass bead, then made her feel of the string and the two boxes of beads..."

Annie went on to read a whole page she wrote about teaching Helen how to string beads. As she read, she was amazed with her own *patience*. She did not have the same patience now, that was for sure. Far from it! It was incredulous for her to read on. It made her feel tired, exhausted, yet at the same time exhilarated. Her eyes jumped to the end of the letter,

> "Oh dear, my eyes are very much inflamed. I know this letter is very carelessly written. I had a lot to say, and couldn't stop to think how to express things neatly. Please, Mrs. Hopkins, do not show my letter to anyone.
>
> Yours,

Annie."

She went on to the second letter.

Then she continued to the third.

She read about her insistence to move into the garden house so that she and Helen could be alone. She looked at the dates of the letters. She had always thought of the idea to move into the garden house as something which happened a month into her stay, or at least several weeks after her arrival. Now, looking at the dates she realized it was not a week before she had pushed for this idea! She remembered her walk with Mrs. Keller. How brave young Annie was! How courageous! And even more, how wise seeing that this was *exactly* what Helen needed!

Perhaps John was right? Perhaps Helen was right? Perhaps she did do *something* right?

In her heart, all these years, she felt simply *lucky*. She was *lucky*. Lilian was not—she was given Edith, who was a slow child. Helen, however, was *gifted*. She was always eager, active, willing to learn.

But as she read, skimming through the many letters, tears streaming down her cheeks, she thought—could it be that perhaps she *was* worthy of the praise?

She remembered all the times Dr. Bell had asked her to write of her "pedagogy." The mere word made her laugh! She did not have any "pedagogy!" She was just playing by ear, trusting that she would know what to do when the moment comes.

But as she read on, the written sentences proved her wrong. She saw a determined young woman. She suddenly saw *herself*.

She got up nervously and walked again to the

window, afraid of the weird, odd sensation she was feeling.

Yet she felt drawn again to the letters. She hurried back to the table, reading through them quickly, devouring them with her eyes, her mind filled with memory after memory, joy and pain, gratitude and guilt. Yet through them all she saw a young woman, confident, daring, brave beyond what words could describe. She read how she decidedly took Helen to see her baby cousin, Ruth. She remembered observing Ruth for *hours*, trying to understand how she had learned to utter the few words she knew.

Bitterly she remembered Captain Keller's summoning her to the living room—as if she had done something wrong, so wrong—and *reprimanding* her for not having a "proper schedule!" Nonsense! Her *entire day* was dedicated to his daughter! From the very first breath at dawn to the last—from the earliest thought, into the night, deep into her very *dreams*, Annie was *always* thinking of Helen—

Tears filled her eyes as she thought of all she had done. And of how, when Helen's father got into financial troubles, four years into her teaching, he could not pay her any longer. And how she stayed trusting that somehow all would be well. At least she had a roof over her head, and food served on the table! But Captain Keller never explicitly *thanked* her for working without a salary! Captain Keller! The poor old fool! He should have at least acknowledged her sacrifice!

She went back to the letter, reading of her observations of baby Ruth—and remembering bitterly again how Captain Keller quoted Dr. Howe and his stupid report on Laura Bridgman. How much further

Annie was able to push his deaf-blind girl! How hard she had worked!

Bitterness mixed with newly gained awareness filled her mind. She read eagerly:

> "Baby Ruth also obeys many commands like these: "Come," "Kiss," "Go to Papa," "Shut the door," "Give me the biscuit."
>
> And yet, I have not heard Ruth try to say *any* of these words, although they have been repeated hundreds of times in her ears, and it is perfectly evident that she *understands* them. These observations have given me a clue to the method to be followed in teaching Helen language. I shall talk into her hand as we talk into the baby's ears."

"Yes!" Annie shouted, alone in the kitchen, "Yes! Good thinking Annie!"

> "I shall assume that she has the normal child's capacity of assimilation and imitation. I also decided on another important aspect of my method: *I shall use complete sentences in talking to her.* This is how baby Ruth is being spoken to, with the assumption that she can understand. So I will use full and complete sentences with Helen, and fill out the meaning with gestures when necessity requires it; but I shall *not* try to keep her mind fixed on any one thing or use short and dumb sentences. I shall do all I can to speak to her like a regular child, interest and stimulate her mind, and then wait for results."

Tears streamed down her cheeks.

Still, she did not understand *why* she was crying.

She reached for the next letter as she suddenly heard the doorbell. She looked at the clock. It was too early for

Helen and Lenore to return from church.

She wiped her tears away as she went to the door.

She opened the door and was surprised to see John.

"I was just passing by," John said sheepishly, "and I was thinking of calling on you." Seeing Annie's face he said, "That is, of course, if you do not mind."

Annie composed herself, "I'm sorry, Mr. Macy, Helen is not here, but she shall return within, I'd say, an hour and a half."

"Well, I, if you don't... Well, I had thought of visiting with *you* as well—of course, if that is not too presumptuous of me to—"

Annie's eyes grew wider as he spoke, "No. No," she said, and then added, "No! Not at all!"

They stood there for a brief awkward moment before Annie moved aside and said, "Please, come in."

John followed Annie into the living room. They sat down in the opposing sofas. John smiled. Annie thought of something to say.

John got up suddenly and walked to the kitchen, "I'll get us some water!"

Annie stood up, "Oh I'll get it!"

"No," John said as he entered the kitchen, "do not bother yourself."

Annie followed him into the kitchen noticing him standing with his tall frame over the kitchen table looking down at the letters, "Are these what I think...?"

"Yes they are—" Annie said and rushed forward, beginning to put all the letters away in the box.

"No, please!" John said and put his hand on hers, "please!"

She froze.

John took one of the letters in his hand. He looked at the box, crammed with hundreds of letters. "Are *all* of these yours?"

She nodded.

He read quietly, shaking his head slowly from side to side as he read.

She felt exposed. Here was her heart lying on the table, and this man, who she had only known for half a year, was examining her open, bleeding heart like a surgeon.

He finished the first letter and moved on to the next, mumbling, "I hope you don't mind...."

She minded. But she said nothing.

He read and mumbled, "Fascinating...!"

She felt uncomfortable, "Listen," she finally could bring herself to say, "I am not sure if... I was thinking about the book...."

He hummed as he read on and only a moment later looked at her, "You were thinking about the book?"

She did not know what to say. She felt uncomfortable. He was an educated man. A Harvard graduate.

A lecturer.

A man.

"Oh nothing," she said. She stood up and walked to the window. He continued to read. She looked at his back.

It was odd not to have Helen in the house. She looked at the clock, hoping for her to come already. But she knew it would take more time.

She said nothing, looking at him, his fingers gently touching the letters as if they were gold, shaking his head slowly, mumbling to himself repeatedly, "Fascinating...!"

She should have not allowed him inside. Not when she looked like this. She was not properly dressed. She looked at her homely dress with disgust. Her hair was also not made up. And she was crying before he came! He must have seen it, did he not?

She leaned back against the counter, seeing him sifting through the letters.

Suddenly he asked, "Who is Fred?"

"Helen's uncle," she'd say, "Mrs. Keller's brother."

He nodded and continued reading.

She walked closer to him, quietly. She saw him putting his finger to his lips as he read, concentrating. She felt excruciatingly uncomfortable. She was the center of attention. He was reading her *own* letters—almost as personal as a *diary*. She felt almost infringed upon.

At the same time she felt an odd sense of exhilaration. Almost as if she *wanted* him to look through her letters. As if she *wanted* him to know her private thoughts.

Her thoughts snapped into reality when he said, "Who is Lilian?"

"Lilian was a fellow student, she too was given a deaf-blind student—" suddenly she realized what he might be reading. She walked fast to him and snatched the letter from him, bringing it close to her face, reading what she had feared he had read:

> "I received a letter from Lilian last week. What astonished me was to hear of Edith's progress. So far she has learned only a few nouns, but Lilian "intends" to give her some verbs "very soon." Poor Lilian—or should I say—poor Edith! I didn't suppose that a more incompetent girl could be found to undertake the education of an unfortunate child than MYSELF; but I think Lilian has me beaten by a head at least!"

Her cheeks burned with shame, "I did *not*," she mumbled as she walked away with the letter to the window, "I did *not* want you to read *that*!" She suddenly turned around and hurried to the letters, taking them all and piling them together, shoving them into the box.

"Um, Miss Sullivan, I'm sorry, I didn't mean to—"

"It is not your fault!" Annie said, her voice a little too loud, "it's me, foolish me, blabbering about such nonsense! My, such conceit. I'm sorry you had to read this!"

"No, I was—" John hesitated—"I was actually happy, if I may say, to read that!"

She gulped and glared at him. Was he mocking her?

Seeing her eyes he looked down, "I mean, it read as if you realized your accomplishment…." He was at a lack of words, and slowly reached his hand to the box, "May I?"

She did not know what to say.

"I'll just look for that letter. We can omit that line from the book, of course, but what is important here is not this Lilian, but you...."

His hand reached for the box. Annie said nothing. He skimmed through them quickly and found the letter. "Listen to this, listen, please, Miss Sullivan, listen to what you wrote:

> "I hope I did not sound too arrogant. But I cannot begin to tell you what this success means to me, given my life thus far."

John looked at her. "You credited your work as *success*, Miss Sullivan, here: '*I cannot begin to tell you what this success means to me.*' I am happy to read that!"

Annie pouted her lips and lifted her chin, looking at John with a penetrating, assessing look.

He put the letter in the box and closed the lid. He leaned backward on the chair and said, "It would have been a *shame* had you not recognized your virtue!"

She wanted to hate him. She wanted to despise him and his disrespectful pry into her life. She wanted to hate his sweet talk. Her memory was inevitably drawn to poor Sadie, the pregnant girl in the almshouse. "Don't you ever—ever—trust boys, you hear me Annie? They will talk sweet and then act sour, you understand?"

She gulped. She remembered Sadie, poor Sadie, giving birth in the almshouse, and then, a few hours later, breathing her last breath. Sadie was so much older than her, so much more experienced! How old was Sadie? Sixteen? Seventeen?

Her face must have betrayed her thoughts, as John murmured, "Why do you hate me, Miss Sullivan?"

"I—" Annie was at a loss of speech, "why, Mr. Macy! I do not hate you—"

"I'm no fool, Annie—can I call you Annie—" he did not wait for her answer, "I can see in your face that you despise me. Have I done anything to you?"

Annie gulped again, feeling her heart beating fast. She said nothing.

John stood up and neared her. Her back leaned against the counter. John was so tall. "I sincerely mean good, Annie. I admire you. I find in you—" he paused, "I see you as a great woman. One of a kind really."

She wanted to cry. Her face twisted with pain. She remembered the boy. The boy. The boy who had seduced her at the almshouse and then tried to threaten her with a knife. Had it not been for the arrival of the warden, passing by the yard, that boy would have taken her away—

"Annie," John said softly, "do you hear me? I wish for you to know that I'm *for* you: with this book, with Helen, with everything, really, I'm for you—"

Her thoughts turned to her father. She remembered him crying by her mother's bedside. Crying and cursing. "Don't go Alice!" he cried "Don't you go on me!"

"Annie," John took her hand, "All I ask is that you do not have preconceptions against me. Can I ask that?"

Annie nodded, frightened to her bone.

"Good," John said and smiled. He released her hand. He walked away to the living room. He opened the piano cover and sat down.

She remained frozen there in the kitchen. She heard him playing Schubert's *Serenade*. The chords were soft, gentle, almost hesitant, inviting.

Her eyes began to well. She bit her lips firmly, the taste of blood emerging on her tongue. Her chin quivered. His words still echoed in her head, "I wish for you to know that I'm *for* you, Annie."

Could it be?

Could she ever trust him?

She had never been—*never*—with a man. She was doomed to die as an old spinster. She promised Maggie that she would never fall for anyone! Poor old hunchback Maggie! The thought of her brought even more tears. John was playing with gusto now, the melody ever so sweet. She knew the piece. She wished to go and sit next to the man—who dared to hold her hand and speak to her softly—to sit on the chair next to him and play in four hands.

Could she ever allow herself?

Could she ever allow herself to trust?

Would she ever allow herself to be loved?

* * *

"January 5th, 1903

Dear Mother,

Please forgive me for not having written earlier. We were very busy with completing the book, on which we have worked tirelessly for several months. Now, finally, our literary work is nearly done. The book was sent off to the publisher, and we look for the proofs every day. John might have to go to New York to finalize the version for print.

In preparation for the appendix describing Annie's perspective, John read to me the letters which Annie had sent to Mrs. Hopkins when she began to teach me. They shall be included in Annie's part of the book. I know you will think them as wonderful as I do. They show the inborn wisdom and courage with which Annie went to her task. These letters also tell a great deal about your naughty monkey of a daughter, that I have entirely forgotten, and that made me feel, when I was reading it, as if I were making the acquaintance of quite another self.

In university I am taking this coming semester a course titled *The History of Human Thought*. I have began reading in preparation for the beginning of the semester this week. I have now come to the schools of thought that were formed immediately after Socrates's death. I have read the "Apology," "Phaedo," and several of Plato's Socratic dialogues in Greek. They are so interesting, that I can scarcely shut the book to take up other lessons!

I'm pleased that we were able to complete the manuscript and send the book off to the publisher. We have now more of John, our FRIEND, and less of "Mr. John Macy," the EDITOR. Recently John insisted on taking Annie to an eye doctor. She was unwilling, but he convinced her. She said that the only doctor she trusts was Dr. Bradford, who had restored her sight while she was still at school. To the best of her knowledge he had already retired. John tirelessly searched for him, and found that he now lives in retirement in New Hampshire. On John's insistence Annie travelled with him there. Dr. Bradford's examination was not pleasant. His only recommendation was for Annie to use her eyes less, especially in reading small print.

Luckily, with John's help, I am able to complete my school's work. Indeed, without John's assistance, I fear I could not have managed it. I do not know what we should do without him. He is most kind and helpful. He helps me in Philosophy and looks up what I want to know in other subjects; so Annie does not have to use her eyes half as much as she did before. Oh Mother, I must confide to you that John is really very good. And I know Annie is happy. She had told me that John had confessed his love to her. I was so happy for her! If he only remains as considerate and kind as he now is, (and I am sure he will) Annie's happiness is safe and my longing for her peace is satisfied.

Please send my love to Mildred and tell her I shall write soon. Annie sends her love as well.

Your affectionate child,

Helen."

* * *

The romance caught Annie by surprise. She never imagined herself being so docile, so sweet, so optimistic.

But she was.

Happy.

At last.

* * *

"From: Annie Sullivan, 138 Brattle Street, Cambridge, Massachusetts

To: John Macy, 30 West 60th St., New York

April 15th, 1903

Dearest Heart,

I was very sorry to say goodbye to you last week after the pleasant hours we spent together. Yes, I know that you had to see that the prints are satisfactory, but I do miss you. The sense of being at home comes to me so deeply when I am near you that I am always a little shivery when you leave me, as if the spirit of death shut his wings over me, but the next moment the thought of your love for me brings a rush of life back to my heart.

Both Helen and I miss your presence. The evening was very beautiful and I went with Lenore and Helen for a walk. They talked and I thought. Later after Helen had gone to bed I went out on the balcony to say good-night to the fragrant, beautiful world lying so quietly under the pines. There was only the sound of one bird talking in his sleep to break the stillness. Somehow, I felt out of sympathy with the calm loveliness of the night. My heart was hot and impatient—impatient because the repression and self-effacement of a lifetime.

My life seems to me a century long as I look back upon it. I stood in the balcony a long time thinking of you and trying to find a reason for your love for me. How wonderful it is! And how impossible to understand! Love is the very essence of life itself. Reason has nothing to do with it. It is above all things and stronger! For one long moment I gave myself up to the supremest happiness—the certainty of a love so strong that fate had no dominion over it and in that moment all the shadows of life became beautiful realities. Then I groped and stumbled my way back to earth again—the dreary flat earth where real things are seldom beautiful.

Dearest—this is the first letter I have written to you and I am afraid I have said things in it which you will not like. You will say that we have no right to test present happiness by harping on possible sorrow. It is because your love is so dear to me beyond all dreams of dearness that I rebel against the obstacles the years have built up between us. But you will not leave off loving me will you—not for a long time at least!

I kiss you my own John and I love you, I love you, I love you.

Yours,

Annie."

* * *

The joy Annie had when John returned with the printed book was immense. She embraced him at the door and kissed him as she never had. He lifted her up in the air and she laughed, "Put me down, put me down!"

She was happy. So was Helen. And, with the book printed, so was John.

They spent the summer together in a rented house in the quaint village of Wrentham, an hour train ride from Harvard. Annie loved the open air, the fields, and the small village market. It was lovely being away from the city and from the university. Having John by her side, as well as Helen, brought her more pleasure than she could ever put in words. She enjoyed the hot sun, which made her feel nourished after the long winter. It reminded her of her days in Tuscumbia when Helen was but a child. Yet, in the South, summers were unbearable for her. In the North, summers were idyllic. It reminded her of summers with Mrs. Hopkins in her school years. And it even reminded her—with the open fields, and with the houses made of wood—of her forgotten childhood home.

But this was not the time to dwell on old and painful memories. This was the time to create new cheerful ones. With the book out, John skimmed the newspapers each morning, buying all the newspapers in the village grocery store. Finally he found it.

He nearly ran to the veranda, where Helen and Annie sat each morning, and exclaimed: "They've written about us! We are in the papers!"

Annie was not as excited as he was. But Helen was, and soon John began reading them the extremely positive review, both reading and spelling to Helen simultaneously:

> "Helen Keller's *The Story of My Life*, with an afterword by her teacher, Anne Sullivan, is unique in the world's literature."

Annie, relieved by John being the one to spell, laughed, "Unique in the world's literature! Oh my, have they gone mad?"

John laughed, "Listen to this!

> "The delivery of the poor pupil from isolation and

darkness by her good teacher is a fascinating read. Anne Sullivan proves to be a writer of precision and grace."

Annie blushed and fanned her hand by her face, "Oh my!"

John grinned, spelling into Helen's hand, "And this next sentence shows we were right all along about including both of you!

"The double narrative constitutes an absorbing presentation of an astonishing experience."

Helen let out a long sigh of enjoyment, as if she had tasted something delicious. She grabbed Annie's hand and repeated to her, "'Anne Sullivan proves to be a writer of precision and grace!'"

Annie grimaced and spelled back, "Oh enough, I heard it already once too much!"

The following week another, more thorough article was published, written by famed psychologist Joseph Jastrow:

"Miss Sullivan's letters indicate an appreciation of the psychological *and* educational problems involved in bringing up a bright but sightless and silent child, which one would have expected from the result, but which it is most assuring to read in print as a contemporaneous record."

* * *

The day after John rushed again to the veranda, reading to them yet another critique:

"The style is full of force, individuality and charm. It seems to be the style of a practiced writer rather than that of a college girl. In England, where the book was simultaneously published, it is said the book is selling extremely well, and that even the King himself read it with much interest. The fascination in Helen of royalty and commoner alike is easily understood, as her courage and tenacity to leave her mark on humanity, in spite of her overwhelming obstacles, make one ashamed of the ordinary excuses which are offered for failure to make the best of one's opportunities."

John was ecstatic. So was Helen. But Annie took a deep breath and told them, "Contain yourselves. Not all reviews will be good, we must not be swayed with the positive ones, and then be likewise overwhelmed by the negative ones. We should attempt being stoic about—"

John interrupted her, "Why are saying that Nan?"

Nan was his new given nickname for Annie.

Annie smiled and caressed his arm, noticing it was becoming handsomely tanner due to their many days in the sun together. "John, love, you are still young," she taunted him, "you'll see."

"I cannot see any reason why people find any fault in a book"—he looked at the article and quoted—"'*full of force, individuality and charm!*'"

* * *

The following week Annie was surprised one day that John did not join the two of them on the veranda after his return with the newspapers from the village grocery store. Annie found him in their bedroom upstairs. He was slouched on the pillows, holding a bottle of wine in his hand. "John?" Annie asked worriedly. She had never seen him that way.

He said nothing, gazing into space, and pointed at the

New York Post laying on the floor.

Annie bent down and brought the article close to her eyes. She read the article briefly. It was far from being favorable. The last paragraph was the harshest:

> "All of Miss Keller's knowledge is hearsay knowledge. Her very sensations are for the most part vicarious, and yet she writes of things beyond her powers of perception with the assurance of one who has verified every word. The book lacks, therefore, literary veracity. One resents the pages of second-hand description of natural objects, when what one wants is a sincere account of the attitude, the natural attitude towards life of one whose eyes and ears are sealed. If it could have been brought home to her that such likeness in her case could be attained only by the sacrifice of truth; if she could only realize that it is better to be one's self, however limited and afflicted, than the best imitation of somebody else, the book would have proven a more worthy read."

"Oh John," Annie said and sat on the bed.

John said nothing. His eyes were fixed on the bottle.

Annie tried smiling, "Don't take that to heart!"

John muttered, "That lousy journalist pissed on our book!"

"Oh don't make such a Shakespearean tragedy out of it! They'll be wrapping tomorrow's fish and chips with it! Now-now, come and join us on the veranda, the sun is wonderful!"

John mumbled something unclear. Annie pressed, "Come now, I can't understand what you are saying!"

"Leave me alone!" John shouted at her.

"Fine, fine," Annie whispered. She left the room and headed downstairs with a heavy heart.

* * *

"To: The Editor of the New York Post

From: John Macy, Harvard University

Dear Sir,

Having read the commentary printed in your paper regarding the book *The Story of My Life* by Miss Helen Keller, I am obliged to respond to the allegations put forth in that critique. I press you to print my comments as they are brought below.

The commentary leaves the impression that Miss Keller's autobiography is borrowed knowledge and borrowed observation and so perversely misses the very *lesson* of the book. The one hundred and forty pages of her *own* story as told from her *own* viewpoint, are packed with *individual* experiences, much of which no one else in the world *but* Miss Keller ever possessed or ever put into words.

The critic is unabashedly guilty of a kind of *arrogance* of his *own* senses. He thinks that a blind person cannot know what we know through our eyes and ears, or what we *imagine* we know through them. Worse than that, this critic thinks he *knows* what only a deaf-blind person can know.

Having read the critic's attack on her book, Miss Keller wrote the following remarks, addressed to the critic:

"I suspect that if I had confined myself strictly to that which I knew of my own observation, without mingling it with derived knowledge, you would have understood me as little as he probably knows Chinese. Had it occurred to me to build a little tower of Babel for myself and others like me, do you think you would have scaled my castle wall or ventured to communicate with me? Have you ever thought it worthwhile to find out what kind of ideas the silent, sightless inhabitants of this world actually originate in their isolation from the rest of mankind?"

This was Miss Keller's response to the attack. Can one read her book through and not know that if she had *not* tried to be like other people, we should have never heard of her? If her dedicated teacher had *not* made her pupil try to understand the world through the eyes and ears of a seeing and hearing people, we should never have heard of Helen Keller! Undoubtedly, the critic has missed Helen's *life*. No wonder he has missed the truth in her *story* of her life.

The *New York Post* ought to find larger and more human questions in Miss Keller's book, and treat them more intelligently. I have thought it worthwhile to write at this length because there has always been a great deal of ignorance about the simple facts of Miss Keller's education, not to speak of the more complex questions. A review like that in the newspaper breeds even more ignorance than it contains, and you will, I know, grant me the space to remove misconceptions which may stand in the way of a clear vision into the many vast problems of Helen Keller's education.

John A. Macy,

The English Language Department,

Harvard University."

* * *

Regardless of the occasional attacks on the book, the book sold extremely well. Moreover, many letters of support flooded their apartment to which they returned to complete Helen's last year of university. Of the many letters, one especially touched Annie.

She found it so riveting, she dared not read it to Helen nor to John. She knew the letter was right in his assessment, and yet she feared the implications in it.

"To: Annie Sullivan

From: Dr. Alexander Graham Bell

Dear Miss Sullivan,

I have read Helen's book with interest and delight, and, frankly, I was outraged. Why in all the world did you not tell us about those letters to Mrs. Hopkins! They are of the greatest value and importance and contain internal *evidence* of the fact that you were entirely *wrong* when you gave me the idea that you approached the education of Helen "without method," and only acted in everything you did on "the spur of the moment!"

These letters to Mrs. Hopkins, dear Miss Sullivan, will become an educational *standard*. The principles that guided you in the early education of Helen are of the greatest importance to *all* teachers. They are TRUE and the way in which you carried them out shows—what I have all along recognized—that Helen's progress was as much due to her *teacher* as to *herself*, and that your *personality* and the *admirable methods* you pursued were integral ingredients of Helen's progress.

Now what I want to impress upon you is this: it is your *duty* to use your brilliant abilities as a teacher FOR THE BENEFIT OF OTHER TEACHERS.

I don't want to bother you with this thought too much at the present time; but, as soon as Helen has finished with Harvard, I AM COMING FOR YOU.

You must be placed in a position to impress your ideas upon other teachers! YOU MUST TRAIN TEACHERS so that the deaf as a whole may get the benefit of your instruction.

Please keep this matter in mind. What you have done with Helen can surely be done with some of the deaf who are *not* blind! Once we realize that language is acquired by imitation, it becomes obvious that language comes from *without*, not from *within*.

It is ridiculous to expect that a deaf child—or a hearing child for that matter—shall talk or write good English, unless good English has been PREVIOUSLY presented to the child in spoken or written form. And that must be done in sufficient quantity as you demonstrated with Helen. Then—and then only—will the deaf child spontaneously use good English in expressing his *own* thoughts. Once we clearly grasp this conception we can see the cause of the poor English used by the deaf. It makes one sad to see how this principle is persistently violated in all of our schools for the deaf—but you, dear Miss Sullivan, have pointed out the *remedy* and have clearly demonstrated the truth of your position by an illustrious example, namely, your brilliant student!

My best wishes go with you and Helen. Please also congratulate Mr. Macy for his accomplishment—I have also written to him directly to Harvard, thanking him for the part he has played in the production of the book. But in conclusion allow me to repeat what I began with: YOU MUST TRAIN TEACHERS.

Yours sincerely,

Alexander Graham Bell."

Annie's hand shook as she read the letter. Why all these capitalized words? Why was Dr. Bell so insistent?

His remarks were too much for her to bear. He was giving her more credit than she deserved.

And yet—if she had to admit it to herself—and to herself only—he was right. She knew he was right.

And that thought *terrified* her.

She enjoyed being in the shadow of her "brilliant student," as Dr. Bell called Helen. She preferred remaining quiet herself, never to admit that she had a major part in her student's brilliance.

She looked at the letter again:

"These letters to Mrs. Hopkins will become an educational *standard*. The principles that guided you in the early education of Helen are of the greatest importance to *all* teachers. They are TRUE and the way in which you carried them out shows—what I have all along recognized—that

> Helen's progress was as much due to her *teacher* as to *herself*, and that your *personality* and the *admirable methods* you pursued were integral ingredients of Helen's progress."

She hated the trepidation that she felt in her heart—rather, in her *whole* body—the fear of being called to speak to the podium to share her success and to tell of her own genius. The fear that came along with such a calling paralyzed her.

She much preferred criticism than praise.

And she hated that it was so.

She tucked the letter deep inside her drawer. If Dr. Bell asks, she could say she did not receive the letter—or better yet, that her eyes were too tired for her to respond.

* * *

> "February 15th, 1904
>
> Dear Mother,
>
> I am thrilled to write to you the good news. With the money that we had received from the book, Annie and I were able to buy ourselves a home! We had long wanted a home where we could go after my graduation, and where we had vacationed during the summer in beautiful Wrentham, there was a fine opportunity to buy a most pleasant home!
>
> The house is on one of the prettiest village streets, and has many trees around it. Is it not lovely to look forward to living in a home of our own and doing just as we like?

I will write more soon, but I just wanted to let you know the good news. Will you and Mildred come and join us this summer?

Your affectionate child,

Helen."

* * *

Annie burst into a great laughter.

Here was John, her companion of over a year and a half kneeling with a ring in his hand!

"Why are you laughing?" John murmured, taken aback by her response.

"Get up from the floor, John Macy!"

John got up and cleaned his pants, the ring still in his hand.

"You are very kind," Annie said, trying not to laugh, "but you must understand I can't!"

"Can't?" John mumbled. He was still shocked by her response. He had imagined she'd swoon into his arms with a big "Yes!"

Annie took a deep breath. "John, think! What will become of Helen?"

"Why," John protested, "Helen will live with us!"

Annie's face frowned. Was he being serious? She mumbled, "Do you really mean it?"

John frowned, "Annie Sullivan, do you think me mad? Any man in his right mind who would try to separate the two of you is bound for nothing but a colossal failure. Of course she shall be with us!"

Annie gulped, the severity of his proposal slowly sinking in, "But—" she looked for something to say, "but Helen must graduate first!"

"Well we can wait until her graduation and marry then!"

"John I'm eleven years older than you!"

"Ten," John said, "and that does not matter. What matters is what I feel toward you."

Annie felt her dry lips, her heart beating fast—faster than ever before— "John, have you *sincerely* thought about it?"

"Do you think a man goes and buys a ring without properly—no, 'sincerely'—thinking about it?!"

Annie felt her cheeks burning. Had she just been *proposed* to?

* * *

It was six months after Helen's graduation and after she and Annie had moved to their new spacious house in the village of Wrentham, that an article appeared in the Cambridge Gazette on January 16, 1905, with the catching title:

> Helen Keller ALMOST Married!
>
> A Three Cornered Romance Probably Without a Parallel in the History of the World.
>
> HELEN KELLER, the deaf, dumb and blind genius, is nearly engaged and soon will be almost married. She is essential to the marriage contract,

which would never have been made without her! She is to assist at the wedding, and it is one of the conditions of the marriage that she shall always live in the same house with the quite married couple. She will be the most conspicuous figure at the wedding. In fact there would be no wedding without her.

Miss Keller will be, in fact, more nearly married than any young woman who has not actually made her responses and promised at the altar. The real bride is Miss Keller's teacher. For eighteen years she has been an instructor, friend and mother to the famous blind girl. They have been thought of one thought, almost flesh of one flesh, and when the bridegroom-elect dared to propose marriage to the girl's teacher, Miss Sullivan was amazed:

"I cannot marry anyone," she said.

"Why not?" asked the persistent wooer.

"Because of Helen!"

"But you need not be separated from Helen," said the gentleman, "Our home will be hers. You may go on teaching her all your life."

There followed some personal arguments of the sort that all those who have been engaged will remember are most powerful. At their conclusion the teacher said hesitatingly:

"If you will ask Helen, and if she is willing, I will think about it."

The lover sought Miss Keller in her study and made a second proposal of marriage, this time to a gentle arbitrator: Miss Keller put forth her hands and touched those of her caller and was asked the question. In response she immediately replied:

"What did Miss Sullivan say?"

"She spoke of you!" was the answer of quick fingers.

Miss Keller's response was, "Do you love her?"

One hard hand clasp told the story.

Miss Keller smiled, "Does she love you?"

Another unmistakable hand clasp.

"Then," said Miss Keller, "marry, of course, and I hope you will be very, very happy!"

"We want you to be with us always," said the suitor, "You will be as dear and as necessary to Miss Sullivan as you have always been. We would not marry unless your life and hers were to go on just as before."

A grateful mist covered the blind girl's eyes. The pulse in her white throat throbbed with emotion as her fingers spelled, "Thank you, my dear friend. Now please go to Miss Sullivan and tell her that what you have told me has made me very happy and that I will be very unhappy unless she marries you!"

From that moment a new interest had come into the 25 year-old-girl's life. There was a new, beautiful, mysterious element in life, of which she had read, but which had seemed until now very far away and mythical. She talked of the bridegroom. "He is a good, great-hearted man. I know it by the touch of his hands. They are hearty, generous, gentle hands, hands that will never for a moment fail you."

Miss Keller's teacher and friend of eighteen years is Miss Anne Sullivan. Her betrothed is Mr. John

Macy, the son of Powell Macy and Janet Foster Patten, descendants of early New England settlers long associated with Boston's elite. Mr. Macy grew up in Boston and attended the Malden High School. Upon graduation in 1895 he enrolled at Harvard, majoring in English literature. He was one of the honor men in his 1899 class and was a popular fraternity man. In 1900 he received the degree of M.A. and the same year was made instructor in English at Harvard, a position he still holds. Mr. Macy, twenty-eight years old, is the currently the editor of the *Harvard Advocate.*

Miss Sullivan was born in Springfield to Thomas and Alice Sullivan, Irish landowners. When she was five she attracted an eye-disease and was thought of as blind. A priest who was a friend of the family pressured her parents to send her to the Massachusetts School for the Blind. Both her parents have since died. In the Massachusetts School for the Blind an eye operation proved to salvage much of Miss Sullivan's sight. In 1886 she graduated from the School as the Valedictorian of her class, and accepted the position of a tutor for young Miss Keller in Alabama. From that time they have been inseparable companions.

Ever since the announcement was made Miss Keller speaks of the wedding only. Among other questions, she asked her teacher, "Can I be the godmother of your forthcoming children?"

"Perhaps we ought not to talk about that now," came the answer from Miss Sullivan's nervous hand.

"Very well!" came Miss Keller's quick answer, "Oh, how happy I am! I am to have two teachers instead of one!"

* * *

Annie was nervous.

Lenore and Helen helped her put on the tight dress of her choice: a simple, elegant traveller's dress. Lenore tried to convince Annie in the days leading to the wedding to choose a *white* dress. Annie chose a blue one instead: a blue traveller's dress. Lenore felt the color might be ominous, but said nothing.

Now, inside the tight dress Annie could barely breathe.

Her fear—which she had communicated to no one— was that John would disappear, flee just before the wedding.

She could hear the guests in the living room. She breathed, trying to calm herself. She squeezed Helen's hand. Helen grinned and squeezed her hand back, patting it with her other hand.

The guests waited in the spacious living room of the new home in the village of Wrentham. There were only twenty of them. Annie insisted on having a small wedding, and on having it at home.

Mrs. Keller was there, and Mrs. Hopkins too. Philip—who was the best man—was running around, making sure all was arranged for the ceremony. John's parents and siblings were already seated in the many chairs they brought from the neighbors. A few friends of John from Harvard were there too. Mrs. Keller was sad that Mildred was unable to come due to having caught acute laryngitis a few days earlier. Helen reassured her young sister in a telegram that she would tell her all of what took place, as if she was there herself.

All the guests waited patiently. The living room grew hotter in the bright May sun.

Annie was stressed. She wanted everything to go smoothly. When she heard a knock on the door she froze. Was John gone? Were they to tell her the wedding was cancelled?

Lenore opened the door slowly, allowing but for a crease, not wanting anyone in. Her husband, Philip, smiled at her through the crease, and then glanced at Annie—surprised to see the bride wearing a blue dress. Lenore widened her eyes at him at once warning him not to say anything. He coughed and whispered to Lenore, "Is she ready?"

Annie muttered to herself out loud, "As ready as she'll ever be…!"

* * *

"Dearest Mildred,

The newly weds have just left on their honeymoon and I am left here to write to you. Within a few days Mother and I shall return home, and I shall hold your hand and make sure you heal quickly!

Oh dear, I must capture the many impressions I had before they disappear, and by writing them fulfill my promise to you. But do not worry, I shall tell you all in detail when Mother and I come home.

First, the dress. Annie decided to marry wearing a blue travellers' dress, with a white waist, which was absolutely beautiful! I wore a moss green dress, and I stood with the bride. My friend Lenore sat behind me and spelled to my hand what was going on without interrupting the ceremony. John wore a gray frock-coat which was most becoming! The ceremony was lovely and very touching.

Immediately after the ceremony we had luncheon, quite without formality. Annie made the wedding cake herself, as well as the salad and the punch. Mother made many of the other dishes along with Lenore and Mrs. Hopkins who arrived two days earlier. We also had many beautiful flowers around the house, and each of the guests carried away a bunch of carnations as a souvenir of the occasion. There were about twenty persons invited.

The wedding presents were very handsome—a beautiful wooden armchair from Lenore and Philip, a fine French clock with candelabra from Dr. Bell, a large punch bowl with glasses from Mr. Wade, a splendid box of silver containing one hundred and twenty-five utensils from Mrs. Rogers, an immense silver loving cup from John's Harvard classmates, and many, many more. For weeks I was hiding many secrets, my friends told me what their gifts were going to be, and I had great fun trying to keep them, and if a girl ever kept a secret with difficulty, it was I!

Mother had convinced me to come home not for a week, but for a month, and by that allow Annie and John some time alone after the honeymoon. Therefore, you and I shall spend much time together, like we had not had in years, ever since our summer before I entered Harvard!

Mother told me she had taken John aside before

he and Annie left and told him that as Annie was her surrogate daughter, he was now her adopted son. She also told him that he could "abide with us until he behaves unworthily." I reprimanded her for speaking this way to John, but she told me that there are things that only mothers understand. O Mother!

I must stop now and help with making dinner. It is lovely to have Mrs. Hopkins here with Mother and I. She will be staying in the house until the lovebirds return.

Excited about seeing you soon, and sending you my best wishes of a quick recovery, I am

Your loving sister,

Helen."

Helen Keller in graduation from Harvard's Annex for Women (Radcliffe College) in 1904. She was the first person in history with deafblindness to attend and graduate from college and she received her bachelor of arts degree cum laude.[i]

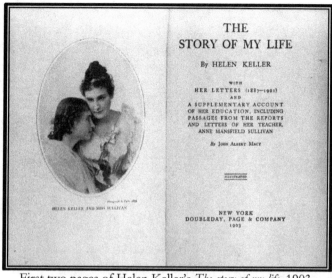

First two pages of Helen Keller's *The story of my life*, 1903.
On the left a photo of Annie and Helen with an inscription
with their names. On the right:
THE STORY OF MY LIFE By HELEN KELLER
with her letters (1887-1901) and a supplementary account of
her education, including passages from the reports and letters
of her teacher, Anne Mansfield Sullivan
By John Albert Macy
Illustrated; New York, Doubleday, Page & Company, 1903

John Macy, two years before meeting Annie and Helen, age 23, 1900.[i]

The house Helen Keller and Annie Sullivan bought in the village of Wrentham, Massachusetts, 1904.

Helen and Annie together, spending time on a tree in their yard. Notice the dog at their feet. Wrentham, Massachusetts, 1904.

Helen Keller conversing by hand with John Macy, Annie Sullivan is standing behind Helen. Wrentham, Massachusetts, c. 1905.[i]

Helen Keller conversing by hand with John Macy, Annie Sullivan is standing behind Macy. Wrentham, Massachusetts, c. 1905.[i]

The last page of a letter from Alexander Graham Bell in Washington, D.C. to Annie Sullivan in Cambridge, Massachusetts, April 2, 1903. This part of the letter is transcribed below:

[…]cause of the poor English used by the deaf. It makes one sad to see how this principle is persistently violated in all of our schools for the deaf - but you have pointed out the remedy and have clearly demonstrated the truth of your position by an illustrious example.

My best wishes go with you and Helen, and in conclusion allow me to repeat - what I began with - YOU MUST TRAIN TEACHERS.

Yours sincerely,
Alexander Graham Bell

John, Annie, and Helen, with a dog, in their house in Wrentham, Massachusetts, circa 1905.

Annie Sullivan dressed in evening clothes, unknown date, most likely prior to a lecture with Helen, c. 1910

Annie and Helen, most likely in a photo for advertisement of their lecture together. c. 1914.

PART FOUR

A DECADE LATER
1914

Annie did not want to return to the empty home again.

Helen stood by her, silently waiting. She knew how hard it was for Annie.

John was gone. For good, it seemed.

The house was cold without him.

Annie opened the large lock and left the door open for Helen to walk inside. She then pulled the two weighty suitcases inside. They were extremely heavy, filled with clothes and memorabilia from their short lecture tour. But the suitcases were not as heavy as Annie's heart, which threatened to drown her in an ocean of pain.

She opened the shutters of the house which once held so much hope for her, for Helen, and for her beloved John. Their safe haven. At least this is what the house used to be. That was in the days before John drank, before he cursed, before he left unannounced only to return weeks later, distraught and reticent, uncommunicative and short-tempered.

Annie had given him so many chances, including

funding a trip for him to go to Europe for several months' vacation on his own—from the money that she and Helen worked hard to earn.

But now she knew—.there would be no more chances.

She knew he would come again. She knew it would be difficult for her not to let him in.

She heard Helen in the kitchen, opening cupboards helplessly. She hurried there and put her hand in Helen's, questioning her. Helen spelled back, "I thought of making us some tea."

Annie nodded and spelled, "Sit down. I'll make it."

Helen tried to protest but Annie's hand was already gone.

* * *

It was only the following morning, when she went through the piles of mail that she found it.

A letter.

From a lawyer.

> "Mr. John Macy has instructed me to inform you that he seeks a marital divorce. In such cases the procedure requires...."

She only read the first two lines before she fainted.

* * *

> "To: John Macy, 30 West 60th St., New York
> From: Helen Keller, Wrentham, Massachusetts

March 4th, 1914

Dear John,

Your letter addressed to me of explanation for the humiliation through which you have put Annie has amazed me and filled my heart with sorrow. I expected your letter to express your remorse, and instead found it unkind and altogether unbrotherly. I feel that you are harsh and unreasonable, and unjust too. You know, John, that you took that apartment in New York because YOU wanted it, not because we did. You knew that we could not be in the apartment as often as you suggested! Your mind does not seem to be as honest and just as it used to be, or otherwise you could not write the way you did.

As to the subject of money, which you brought up in your letter, describing Annie as "ungenerous," I must say a word. You know me well enough to realize that I do not value money any more than you say you do. I have always been willing, glad to share with you, evenly or any way that pleased you, all I had. But do you think it is fair or generous or consistent to say you "hate our money," and in the very same letter to tell us that you deposited a thousand dollars of that "hated" money for yourself?

It is all right for you to have the money. Fine. But it is cruel thus to insult me calling the money "hated" money! You wrote to me, "It was Annie, and not I, that wrecked us." I must say, if it was she, then it was you who DROVE her to it, John.

You are certainly not yourself, or you could not have brought yourself to write as you have, even if we had been in the wrong. Annie has many faults, so have I, and so have you. But we are not irredeemable! I pity your blindness, and I suffer on.

If you ever loved her or me, I beseech you to be calm, fair, kind, and to reconsider what you have said in that letter. You are wrong, John, in thinking that Annie has tried to influence me against you. She never has. She has always tried to make me see how very good and helpful you have been to us both.

Please, please be fair, be just! You wrote: "I can never explain to you what my life with Annie has been like." I remember that in spite of many hard trials in the past we have had happy days, many of them, when we three seemed to feel in each other's handclasp a bit of heaven. Have you forgotten it all? Why should you say such bitter things about my teacher? Have you forgotten all the sunshine, all the laughter, all the long walks, drives and jolly adventures, all the splendid books we read together? Have you forgotten that at times, when we had all been impatient, you would say to me; "If we were not a trouble to each other, we could not love as we do!" Have you forgotten all of that?

I know how imperious, changeable and quick-tempered Annie can be. I have suffered just as much from those failings as you have: but my love for her has never wavered, never will! Perhaps she owes her success to some of those very failings! You know—you have often told me as much—that the education of a deaf blind child is a tremendous strain upon the faculties and the health of the teacher, and that only a FEW can stay with such a child more than a year or two. Only Annie's splendid vigor has made it possible for her to stick to her colossal task during twenty-six years. Think of it!

You wrote to me, "She has never been a wife to me, nor has she done any of the things that a woman might be expected to do." You know, we have shared everything we had with you. You have helped us in all our literary work, and all that has come from it has belonged to you as much as to us. You know, too, that you have dictated as freely as we have what ought to be done with any gains we have had from our work, and we have looked up to you in all our problems, all our difficulties, all our undertakings.

Do you remember that you disapproved of the plan for me to take speech lessons from Mr. Devol? It was due to your objection that I refused to take lessons from him. If you still think I am "dominated" by Annie, as you wrote, this example proves that you yourself have "dominated" me, and I love you nonetheless for it!

Again; Annie does not like my public appearances tours: but she was glad to do it when she thought that some money would take you to Italy and give you the chance you desired for a "true vacation"!

With her bad eyes she could not write to you, and I was the one who had to be told what to type to you. She dictated to me, often with her tears running over my hand! She really felt that she was doing and saying things to make you happy and bring you back to us again well and strong!

And now you say that "she has played a game"— that she has been untrue to you! Be careful, John, what you say.

Believe me, John, from this work the great jury of the world will pass its verdict upon her actions and sentiments and upon yours as well. They will also say that this trouble is my affair; Annie is my affair; you are my affair, just as all suffering humanity is my affair.

You, dear, have every one of Annie's failings, as I can show you from my experiences with you: and your letter has proved that you have more grievous ones than she has! And yet, I still cherish you! When I first read your letter, I thought you had destroyed my love for you. Do you remember how once you said you were a sworn foe to all who brought any charges against Annie?

Does not love—true love—suffer all things, believe all things, hope all things, endure all things? Love suffers long and is patient! It gives without stint, without measure, and asks for nothing in return. It expects only good from the dear one through all trials and disillusionments.

O, John, recall that love, foster it more and more, give up everything for it, and believe me, undreamed sweetness and peace shall come into your life. It shall no longer seem to you "a poor life." I have lived to know that love which is love indeed casts out the ghosts of dead affections, dead hopes, wasted years and disappointed ambitions.

I have unfaltering faith in you. Once you have asked me to trot in the same team with you, and now I ask you to do the same.

This is intended to be my last letter on the subject of your relations to Annie. Please do not think that she wants me to write it. She does not.

Lovingly,

Helen."

* * *

"Leave, leave! We must leave!" was Annie's repeated message to Helen.

Helen was surprised. It was Annie who wanted to stop all the public appearances, banquets and ceremonies in support of the blind and deaf. It was *Annie* who wanted to be "home at last." Yet now the same Annie wanted to leave.

"Where to?" Helen asked.

"Anywhere, anywhere! Anyplace but here! His presence is all around! It suffocates me!"

* * *

They agreed and took on several invitations for lectures and luncheons. Helen was glad to say yes, as it brought them some more money and made them less dependent on the charity of people to which Helen always preferred saying no. She wanted the two of them to be independent and not live on the pity of others. Not now, at least, when she was 34 years old and Annie was approaching 50.

The two of them travelled to several destinations, giving lectures and shaking hands throughout the East Coast. Yet it was in Bath, Maine, that suddenly Annie collapsed.

She entered the bed in the small hotel room and could not come out, too sick to communicate with the world. To Helen her last words were that she most likely had influenza. Then she went into delirium and fell asleep, often waking up coughing, spitting into a cup, and then falling asleep again.

Helen was distressed. Here she was trying to aid her teacher, one handicapped person trying to help another. She was terrified her teacher would die because her student had failed calling for help. Leaving the room she felt her way alone to the reception. She tried explaining to them the situation, but no one understood her signs. She called, "Doctor! Doctor!" but her speech was undecipherable to the receptionist, who in fear called the hotel manager. He, too, did not understand her. Finally, they understood her signs for paper and pencil, and she wrote to them in her square letters, "DOCTOR!!! FAST!!!"

* * *

"To: Mr. Andrew Carnegie

From: Helen Keller

April 21st, 1914

Dear Mr. and Mrs. Carnegie,

I am writing to you both for you are so intermingled in my thoughts that what I have to say goes by right to you both. This is what I want to tell you. I have changed my mind about accepting your gift. When I first refused to let you help me, I was filled with the idea that I could succeed with the limited aid I had received from other friends. I was ambitious to earn my own living. Yet I have just been through an experience which shows me how much I need help.

I was determined to earn a living and by that to make things easier for those that I love. But I did not understand until now that in order to carry out this vocation through public appearances and touring, I should have to lay another burden upon the dear shoulders of those who were already heavily burdened.

The experience which I had last Thursday has opened my eyes to my true position. My teacher and I lectured in Bath, Maine. After the lecture Mrs. Macy was taken ill. There was no one to help us in that dismal hotel, not even an intelligent maid. It was a disconcerting experience.

An overpowering sense of my helplessness came over me. Each new experience in life is an encounter. There is a struggle—a cloud of dust, and we come out of it wiser, and perhaps a little bit crestfallen. I hope I have come out of this tussle a wiser woman. I suddenly understood why our friends had insisted that we should have a competent woman travelling with us.

However, the time seems far distant when we shall be able to employ such an assistant without your help. When I reached home, I found an accumulation of letters which Mrs. Macy had to read to me and answer. I was startled to find out how much she had had to do for me all these years. I felt, as I had never felt before, the necessity of having a secretary to help me with some of my work. It was then that your kind words, as we were leaving your house, came back to me with a sense of great relief: "Remember

Miss Keller," you said, "that we are your friends, and that we shall always be ready to help when you need us."

Dear Mr. and Mrs. Carnegie, I need your help now! I must have a staff for my groping feet. I have great faith in the genuineness of your kindness. Faith, you know, is the evidence of things unseen, though in this case I have had much from you to inspire it.

The mere act of writing to you is already making my burden lighter. I feel anew the capacity to rise and meet my life. You have been so wise and clear-seeing in many things, I am sure that you will be equally wise and clear-seeing in your interpretation of this letter.

Please tell your sweet daughter Margaret that her sweet note has made me happy.

With cordial messages from my teacher and myself,

I am,

Sincerely yours,

Helen Keller."

* * *

Her name was Polly and Annie took a liking to her immediately. The 30-year-old immigrant from Scotland was a no-nonsense woman, and in that way reminded Annie of herself. Even more so, she reminded Annie of her own mother, Alice, who had a thick Irish accent and was always busy.

With Polly helping with the cooking, cleaning, and, within several weeks, with spelling to Helen so that she could respond to the many letters she received, Annie was now feeling much relieved.

But even with the generous stipend supplied by Mr. Carnegie, Helen and Annie found it hard to stay afloat financially. They sold the large house in the village of Wrentham and bought a smaller house near New York, in quaint Forest Hills. Still, creditors were pressing. They needed *income*. Annie, in the past, pressed Helen to write more. But her recent books, *The World I Live In* and *Out of the Dark* both earned dismal money in comparison to her first book, which, these days floundered as well. With the World War they received even fewer donations. Helen was at a loss. Each year that passed left them deeper in debt.

* * *

"June 30th, 1917

Dearest Mother,

I have not written before because we have all been distracted by manifold demands, requests and interruptions. I had a lovely 37th birthday. It was a complete, overwhelming surprise! I had not had the slightest suspicion of the great preparations that were being made by Annie and Polly. I had begged Annie to let us spend the day in a quiet, cozy way, and she had said "All right," and so we did. But the next day, when I went downstairs for lunch, I was greeted with an avalanche of handshakes and good wishes from twenty-seven friends—deaf people who had come to spend the afternoon with me. Before I had recovered my breath, they hurried me out on the lawn, and lo and behold, there stood a screened tent which Annie had fixed up! We chatted, laughed, drank punch, ate, and ate again, and everybody seemed thoroughly happy. I received a shower of presents—handkerchiefs, candies, gloves, flowers and a very pretty chain of pink beads. Poor Annie and Polly were quite tired out with the picnic and with all the demands made upon them. So we all rested afterwards.

This had lifted my spirits as I must admit, Mother, that we have been frightfully "hard up." I don't remember a time since college days when we were so much "up against it." But we shall manage all right. Our credit is good, and people understand.

Speaking of money, John recently tried to contact us. O Mother, I was really disgusted with him! He kept asking—no, dunning Annie for money! Now, you know it is money that I am trying to earn to provide for Annie, Polly and myself, not to waste on John! So I wrote him a letter telling him that if he persisted in coming to the house, we shall move away from here. I begged him to go to work at anything and prove to his friends that the John Macy they once knew was not utterly given over to selfishness and alcohol.

He wrote me back that he would terminate his relations with us and trouble Annie no more. So far he has kept his word. O Mother, I hated to write him such a letter, believe me! But what could I do? I couldn't bear to have Annie treated thus, or to see John's last spark of manhood quenched without an effort to save it. I don't know, though, what Annie will do. After prodding me to tell her what I wrote to him she seemed to feel terribly about it. She said she simply couldn't help it.

She does try hard for my sake to let things take their course, but, well, you know her warm heart and her constant remembrance of what John was to her once.

I will write more soon, but today I'm awfully tired after the surprise. I do hope Mildred's sons are better, and will soon recover entirely. I can't be easy until I know they are all well. Mildred must be worn out with it all. Do send her my love.

With love from us all, I am,

Your affectionate child,

Helen."

* * *

The three women, along with their two dogs, sat in the living room downstairs, going over the mail. This was the daily routine. One might have thought it strange that in the spacious living room the three women must sit so close to one another. But this was how it was, Helen holding hands to both Annie and Polly as Polly read the letters out loud.

Polly went through the usual letters. Helen was famous everywhere. Letters poured from as far as Japan, Russia and Argentina. Her book—the first book—was translated into twelve languages already. If only, Helen thought, this could have been translated into monetary gains.

But the royalties could not support their monthly expenses.

With Annie now 51 years old and almost totally blind, Helen knew that the burden of keeping them secure financially was on her shoulders alone.

This was why, when she heard Polly read the letter from the Hollywood producer, Helen sat up and paid close attention.

Polly read the cordial greetings from the filmmaker, Mr. Miller, and then read:

> "A motion picture film is in my opinion a new form of art. Your life, Miss Keller, is a form of art as well."

Annie smirked and spelled, "Sounds like he wants something!"

Helen hushed her with her hand and mumbled to Polly to keep reading. Polly already understood Helen's unique speech—which took long months for her to become accustomed to. But now, nearly four years since she had been with the two women, she understood Helen's words perfectly clear. She continued reading:

> "The film could show how you have been saved from a cruel fate. Similarly, our nation can be saved from a cruel fate. The distracted, war-tortured world could be saved from strife and social injustices following your example. My suggestion is that we reach the whole seeing world through the medium of Motion Pictures. This is the greatest medium that we have for appealing to the hearts and sympathies of the people, with its 20,000 theaters in the United

States alone. The message of the proposed picture featuring yourself is clear: Your world sees; our world is spiritually blind.

I await your answer and will be glad to discuss the matter further.

Cordially yours,

Francis Trevelyan Miller."

Helen liked the tone of his words. Him mentioning "social injustices" and "spiritual blindness" made her want to hear more.

She turned to Annie and spoke, "What do you think?"

"I think it's nonsense!" Annie spelled and spoke at the same time for Polly to hear, "Nonsense! He sounds too highbrow, as well as oddly sentimental! Besides, I don't like motion pictures!"

"Sure you do!" Helen said quickly. She remembered clearly how Annie and John went several times to the cinema in Boston to see some films featuring Charlie Chaplin, who Annie praised later as 'the funniest man you had ever saw!' Annie also said, 'It takes a genius to know how to tell a story that is both entertaining *and* touching, and Chaplin is a genius!'

Helen hesitated, but then spelled to Annie, "You don't like motion pictures? You did like Charlie Chaplin!"

Feeling Annie tensing, Helen immediately regretted bringing up Chaplin's name. She knew it brought up old memories that she always preferred avoiding for the sake of her teacher's emotional state.

Annie said nothing for a long moment and then

spelled, "Movies hurt my eyes, and the author of this letter sounds like he has no idea what he is talking about!"

Helen nodded, took the letter from Polly's hand, folded it and placed it in her lap. "Go on, Polly," she said, "who is the next letter from?"

* * *

It was only a day later that Helen spoke to Annie in private while Polly was making dinner. "Annie, we are in a dire situation and you know it."

Annie did not reply, but squeezed Helen's hand as if to say, "*And?*"

"I want to see if this filmmaker can make us an offer. Could we reply in the affirmative, wishing to hear more?"

Annie sighed, "I you insist, but I think against it."

Helen nodded her head. "Thank you. Let us see what he has to say."

* * *

The negotiations over the film lasted half a year. Annie was tough with the filmmaker and with his producers from Hollywood, who came several times to their house in Forest Hills for long sessions debating the script, the rights, and the financial compensation. She wanted to get the best royalties possible. And she had many corrections to the script, which she criticized as "too artistic" and "too full of odd symbolism."

Throughout the tough negotiations Annie's thoughts

often drew her, surprisingly enough, to the late Mr. Anagnos. She thought of how the principal of her old school would have done the negotiations: both polite and fierce. He always got his way at the end. And she tried to do the same.

Finally, all the details were agreed upon, and in July Annie, Helen and Polly stepped aboard the train to Hollywood.

* * *

"To: Lenore Smith

From: Helen Keller

August 15th, 1918

Dear Lenore,

Your letter found us way out here among the hills of Hollywood. It did our hearts good to hear from you again, and to have such pleasant news too! How we should have loved to visit you and the children at the camp—It would have seemed much like the old days when we were all so gay and happy together.

You might ask why I am writing to you from Hollywood! Well, well, the unexpected is always happening to us! We were living quietly in Forest Hills, trying to content ourselves with some pleasures and a few opportunities to help others when lo, the winds of destiny blew us out here. Someone came and said, "Why not make a motion picture of the story of Helen Keller's life? It may mean great help and encouragement to the brave boys blinded in this great war."

We looked into the matter, and the die was cast. A contract was signed and we all came here in July. Can you imagine me in a "movie"? I thought I had worked hard enough writing my story, whose rather troubled genesis you witnessed while we were all in Harvard. But here we are trying to pull off a photographic story which doesn't look much like anything that ever befell any of us! Of course Annie and I are no longer as young and fresh as we were, and there must be substitutes in the early part of the picture.

A lovely child is acting my part as a little girl, and we are all charmed with her. Another sweet girl impersonates me when I was eighteen, and she is so graceful as well. However, I can't say much about Annie's substitute! I'm afraid she hasn't the imagination and force required to play the part of such a strong, original, helpful personality as Annie's. But, knowing nothing about "movies," I can judge only from the comments of others on the picture.

O, how anxious I am to have the educational part of the picture "done proud," so that it may help carry further the message of right teaching, devotion, perseverance and love so nobly exemplified by Annie's life!

It is very funny the way the pictures are taken, dear Lenore! You would laugh to see my "make-up"!! I wear a golden tow wig and with all my make-up my face looks like a corpse! They say that it is necessary in order to get a nice effect on the screen. When the electric lights are turned on for the picture, they are hot enough to dissolve the "make-up," and the rumble of the motor that produces them is villainous.

There is everything here to make our stay enjoyable!! There is a pleasant homelike hotel, the hills, the ocean a few miles away and the glorious odors of roses, oleanders, sage and eucalyptus trees! Polly and I ride horseback every morning, starting at sunrise, and I can't give you any idea what a joy it is to me. I haven't had such a sense of freedom and buoyancy in a long time. The riding is splendid for me in every way. Annie, who in the past loved horse-riding, is trying to ride too, and has been out three times. Of course she gets very tired but if she is able to keep it, we think she will feel quite "made over."

We have met interesting people here, among them a few "movie stars." Generally speaking, everybody has been friendly, but in their compliments to me I am often unintentionally left with a defrauded feeling. None of them speaks of Annie as one who deserved special praise. That is, none but one: Mr. Charlie Chaplin. He invited us for dinner and immediately taken to Annie, who was her exuberant, charming self with him. They spoke for a long time, and Polly tried to keep me up with the pace of their conversation. Both Annie and Mr. Chaplin endured much in their lives. When he spoke of his days as a child in an orphanage, Annie began to cry and the two of them spoke in whispers, so Polly told me.

Mr. Chaplin was outraged that Annie had not yet seen his new movie, *A Dog's Life*. He reprimanded her, but soon after he became quiet and asked Annie if she thought he was disgusting. She replied that yes, he was, and that she had always thought of him as a custard-pie thrower! He laughed heartily and insisted on us coming to visit him the following day in his studio to watch his new film.

We came the following afternoon and Annie laughed and cried as she interpreted to me the pictures on the screen. Mr. Chaplin sat by my side and was very pleased. After the movie was over he insisted on showing us another recent film of his, *Shoulder Arms.* We had a great time with him. I wondered about his quick sympathy with Annie, and realized they had both struggled for education and social equality, and as success had crowned their efforts they had poured themselves out in tenderness to the unprivileged. Both are also shy and unspoiled by their victories over fate. So it is only natural that they should understand each other and afford each other the solace of great artists, in a world that is all too often unfaithful to children of genius.

Guess who is also here with us? My mother! She wrote to me, concerned that the movie would depict me as "odd" and turn into a "freak-show," much like some of those vaudeville circus shows. I reassured her that we read the script carefully, but she was still unsatisfied, so we sent for her. She has since been reassured, and is pleased with the production. I am happy she is pleased, as much depends on the film's success. We have been pressed financially, and our creditors are quite unhappy. Yet everyone believes in the success of the picture, and that keeps the creditors quiet and contented because they know they will receive their money eventually.

Annie joins me in sending her love to you and

Philip. Do write again and tell us how you all are. Also hug the children for me. I suppose Sidney is growing tall and learning fast. Mother sends her love as well.

Always affectionately your friend,

Helen Keller."

* * *

"But the reviews were good!" Helen cried to Annie.

Polly said nothing.

Annie sighed. She feared the movie would flop.

Helen had tears in her eyes. She quoted the article that was published a few weeks earlier, "It said," she shouted, "the film was 'one of the triumphs of the motion picture!'"

Annie took a deep breath, and took the article, holding the paper close to her eyes, "But it also states clearly, Helen:

> "All through the photoplay there is symbolism which often can feel daunting. In places it is overburdened with moralizing, and its optimism is sometimes spread too thickly."

Helen did not know what to say or do. Neither did Annie.

* * *

As the weeks passed, Annie, now 53-year-old, drew more and more into herself. Helen knew it was only a matter of time until they would have to sell their house or begin begging for money from philanthropists. The thought of it maddened her.

Each day she waited for a miracle. Each day as Polly read the mail, Helen expected a letter with some great promise. But none came.

One day after Polly read the mail, Helen, disappointed, spelled into Annie's hand, "What was the name of those brothers that offered us to do a vaudeville tour with their company?"

Annie spelled back disinterestedly, "The Weber brothers."

Helen spelled, "Do you think they might still be interested in having us?"

"Why, Helen, you said 'No!'" Annie spelled, tired already at ten in the morning, "Your mother, too, objected fiercely to the idea of exhibiting you on vaudeville."

"Yes," Helen spelled back, "but we must do something. We cannot just sit here and wait for the creditors!"

Annie sighed and mumbled to herself something unclear. She spelled to Helen, "These audiences of vaudeville shows are simple people, ignorant, not our lecture crowd! They would throw tomatoes at us."

Ignoring her comment, Helen spelled, "They offered a thousand dollars a week, did they not?"

"Helen Keller," Annie spelled and sat up, "have you forgotten all your ideals? You said you wanted to only do educational—"

"My ideal is to support us, rather than being dependent on charity!"

Annie sighed, "What will your mother say?! she will strongly disapprove—"

"I am nearly 40 years old!" Helen spelled back adamantly, and then spoke out loud, articulating each word to her best ability, "I AM NOT A CHILD ANY MORE!"

Annie raised her eyebrows. Polly looked at the two of them.

* * *

Helen persisted, nagging Annie several times a day, until Annie snapped at her, "Fine! Fine! We'll do it if that's your wish!"

"Why are you so upset?!" Helen spelled back, feeling Annie's agitated fingers.

"Because I don't want some foolish vaudeville director to tell us what to do, and for them to make hilarity out of you! Do you know who they have on their programs? Fire-eating clowns and sword-swallowers, along with extremely fat people, giants and midgets!"

"They are people too!" Helen retorted, "I shall not be ashamed to be with them on the same stage!"

Annie was frustrated. "The people who go to these shows are *poor* people, Helen, *uneducated*—"

"We can educate them!"

"Helen! They want to be *entertained*!"

"We can entertain them!" Helen insisted, nearly crying.

Annie bit her lips. Helen felt her teacher's hesitation, "You said yourself that it takes a genius to entertain and to know how to tell a story in an 'entertaining and touching way.'"

Annie said nothing.

"Please, Teacher!" Helen said, addressing Annie in the way she knew would attract her attention, "I need your help! We can say yes, and do it our way. Your way! You are a genius—"

"Oh stop it!"

"You are!" Helen said out loud, "We need to earn money someway. They cancelled our insurance because we couldn't pay, and now the bank wants us to sell the house! We need your genius!"

Annie shook her head disapprovingly.

* * *

The Weber brothers agreed to let Helen and Annie appear in one of their shows as a test. The venue was in a remote out-of-town theatre so that if their act failed at least the failure wouldn't be publicized widely.

They had two weeks to prepare their show. Annie was frantic. "I know these audiences," she repeatedly said as she walked around the living room.

"Where from?" Polly asked.

"I just know them!" Annie shouted, "Stop pestering me!"

Polly's eyes widened as she looked down to the sheet of paper she was writing on.

Annie took a deep breath, "Tell me what we have written thus far?"

Polly nodded,

"Helen and Annie come on stage.

Annie: The woman you see in front of you cannot hear nor see. Yet she is one of the world's most famous women. The only way for her to communicate with the world is through a sense which we all take for granted: touch.

(Annie reaches her hand to Helen)

Annie: it is through the touch of her hand that she hears and sees—"

Annie interrupted, "Boring! Boring, boring, boring!"

Polly swallowed and spelled to Helen, "She does not like it."

Helen spelled back, "But *she* wrote it!"

Polly looked at Annie with anticipation.

"We cannot start this way," Annie said. "They want a show. A *show*, you understand?"

Polly nodded though she did not particularly understand.

"We cannot begin by giving them all we have right from the bat!" Annie said as she paced about the room, "How can we entertain them for twenty minutes if we give all we have in the first minute?!"

Polly was silent. She did not bother to spell Annie's frantic mumbles to Helen.

"We must create an *anticipation*," Annie said, "they must be *hungry* to finally see the miracle called Helen Keller! We must make them anxious to see her!" She turned to Polly, "Erase all you wrote. I'll start anew."

Polly, her eyes open widely, said nothing, but did as Annie asked, crossing the whole page and flipping to the other side.

"Good," Annie said in satisfaction. "'Annie comes on stage,'" she dictated, "'and says: 'When I was twenty years old I was a young teacher, when I heard of a girl of the age of six in Tuscumbia, Alabama, who was deaf and blind'—no! No! Erase it!"

Polly did as she was told. This was already the seventh draft.

But Polly knew better than to argue. She spelled to Helen, "She threw this new one too."

Helen nodded slowly. Unlike Polly, she trusted Annie.

Annie sighed, "When I was twenty years old I was but a young and inexperienced teacher, when I heard of a baby who was hit by a devilish sickness!"

Polly wrote it down, Annie nodding to herself as she paced, mumbling, "Devilish sickness sounds dramatic! That is good! 'This devilish sickness left the poor baby without her hearing or her sight!'"

Polly wrote it down.

"The poor toddler was alone in the world. She could not hear nor see her own mother! She was doomed to a life of utter darkness, of no words! No light! No hope!"

Polly wrote it all down.

"I was sent to her," Annie kept dictating, but then said, "No, that's too passive, '*was* sent to her'…"

She paced the room and said, "Yes. Write it down. 'I decided to take the challenge upon myself'—yes! That sounds better. 'Though I did not know whether I shall succeed or, most likely,'" Annie smiled as she felt the drama, "fail, in trying to touch the dormant soul of the deaf-blind child!'"

Polly wrote it all down, and quietly spelled to Helen, "She is happy."

Helen nodded and spelled, "Good."

Annie continued, "'But! Oh my! How shall I even *begin* to try to communicate with her?! *Pause*.'"

Polly looked at her, not understanding.

"Write," Annie said, "*Pause*. So that I shall know to pause."

Polly nodded, keeping her thoughts to herself, and wrote, "Pause!"

"'I had to utilize the chief sense that was at the poor child's disposal: that of touch! For each letter in the alphabet I learned the sign used by the deaf. This letter being A,'" she raised her fist in the air, "'and this is B, this is C, and so forth.'"

Annie paced about the room, waiting for Polly to finish writing, "But how shall the poor child even understand that these are signs that indicate anything in the real world? *Pause*."

Polly wrote obediently, "Pause!"

"'I knew I had to create *associations* in her mind! Each time I gave her a cake, I spelled C-A-K-E into her hand! Each time she was spelled C-A-K-E, she anticipated a cake!'"

Annie became silent and walked back and fro. "Now, we don't want to tire them. By now some of them may shout, 'Bring out the girl!' and 'We paid to see the girl!'"

She nodded to herself. Polly said nothing, neither did Helen.

"Now we shall begin introducing her," Annie said to herself and turned to Polly, "Write down, 'Little did I know, from this humble beginning, that that very girl would grow up to become a miracle! Little did I know that she was to write the bestselling book, *The Story of My Life* as well as three others, including a book of poetry, *The Song of the Stone Wall*.'"

She turned to Polly and mumbled, "Oh erase that."

"Erase...?" Polly asked.

"Erase the name of the book, they couldn't care less about poetry. Write: 'Little did I know that that little girl would meet presidents of the United States, from Cleveland to Wilson! Little did I know that she was to become the dear friend of the inventor of the telephone, Alexander Graham Bell—"

"I think," Polly said, "that by now they would want to see her."

Annie was upset by the interruption, "Of course they would want to see her! This is what I'm trying to do!"

Polly blushed and looked down at the paper.

"Little did I know," Annie continued, "that Mark Twain would one day say, 'The two greatest characters in the 19th century are Napoleon *and* Helen Keller: Napoleon tried to conquer the world by physical force and failed! Yet Helen Keller tried to conquer the world by power of mind—and succeeded!'"

Annie nodded to herself, pleased, "Now, ladies and gentlemen, the woman who had conquered both blindness *and* deafness, the miracle, the shining star to all struggling humanity: Helen Keller!"

Annie rushed to Helen and took her hand, "I think we might be done with the first minute!"

* * *

They worked on the skit from morning till night each day. One of Annie's ideas was that they would allow the audience to ask questions.

At first, Helen objected, "I am afraid I will not know how to answer them!"

Annie wouldn't have it, "You'll know how to answer them, Helen Keller! You've written four books! You are a Harvard graduate for God's sake!"

Helen was not convinced. Annie, seeing the hesitation in Helen's face, said, "We'll write down every possible question you might be asked, and see what a good answer, a witty answer, could be!"

"We can't think of *every* possible question!" Helen protested.

"Sure we can, people are ignorant, Helen! Their questions are bound to repeat themselves!"

They went on to write dozens of pages of possible questions. Polly and Helen were frustrated with the process, but Annie glowed. "We must enter the mind of the everyday layman. He cares not about Harvard and literature," she explained, "he cares about making a living! About the dreadful prohibition on alcohol! He cares about how to bring food to the table, how not to get into trouble! He would ask for your age, your marital status, how do you wash your hands, do you close your eyes when you sleep, that sort of thing!"

The days passed quickly as they filled dozens of pages with questions and what may be the best and wittiest answers for them. Helen grew more and more nervous, and so did Polly.

* * *

When the day finally came, the three of them stood nervously behind the stage at the remote vaudeville theatre, waiting for the cue of the stage manager. Annie spelled into both their hands, "No matter what happens, we should know that we did our best."

Helen nodded. So did Polly.

Annie said to Polly, "When I call her name and the music comes on, push her to come onto the stage!"

Polly nodded. Annie could feel how nervous their maid was, even though Polly was not to come on stage herself.

"Polly," Annie whispered, "thank you!"

Polly nodded her head. It had been a tough month for her becoming a quasi "assistant director" to Annie, while still cooking, cleaning and reading letters to them each morning.

Annie squeezed Polly's hand again, "Thank you!"

The stage manager signed for Annie to go on stage, but in the dim backstage she did not see his sign. He came upset to her, "Now! Now's your sign!"

The announcer announced in the loud speakers, "And now! Miss Helen Keller—to be introduced by her teacher Mrs. Anne Sullivan Macy!"

Annie suddenly felt her heart beating fast. She stepped onto the large stage and felt the bright lights blinding her eyes.

* * *

> "Helen Keller, As Vaudeville Star, Wins Audience By Her Personality
>
> —AN EXTENSIVE COVERAGE—
>
> B. F. Keith, *Theatre News*, May 24th, 1920

The widespread interest in the achievements of Helen Keller was indicated anew in the enthusiastic reception accorded Miss Keller at the Palace Theatre yesterday evening upon the occasion of her first appearance on the vaudeville stage—first, that is, if a preliminary week in the outlying regions be disregarded.

After an act of trained seals was finished the announcer exclaimed: "Now—Miss Helen Keller—to be introduced by her teacher Mrs. Anne Sullivan Macy." Probably every one in the audience had heard some time or other of Helen Keller, blind, deaf and dumb from the age of nineteen months, who after battling with the impossible has learned to read and write; but for most of us Helen Keller was only a dim, far off character featured in magazines or newspapers years ago. Certainly no one had the faintest idea of what a blind, deaf woman, would be doing in *vaudeville* of all places: where the swiftest, trickiest sort of entertainment "stuff with a punch" is provided for audiences whose critical anticipation of entertainment is set to a hair trigger.

Before coming on stage, her teacher, Mrs. Sullivan, introduced her to the audience. Music followed as Keller walked, all alone, unto the stage. It is useless to attempt to describe how she did it but before she had been on the stage two minutes, Helen Keller had conquered the mountain again, and the vaudeville audience at the Palace, one of the most critical and cynical in the world, was hers.

Sullivan began by asking Miss Keller by means of finger-spelling, "Can you tell when the audience applauds?"

"Oh, yes," Keller spelled back, "I hear it with my feet!"

Miss Sullivan repeated Keller's signs to the audience. She then went on to tell the story of how she taught young Miss Keller the meaning of language. With water gushing out of a water pump, she spelled W-A-T-E-R into young Helen's hand and the latter suddenly realized that her teacher's finger-motions were the names of things! The audience listened attentively as Sullivan recalled the miracle.

Mrs. Sullivan went on to describe how Helen had wanted badly to learn to speak. But how could she learn to speak if she could not hear nor see? The audience was puzzled. Mrs. Sullivan proceeded to demonstrate how Miss Keller put her fingers on her teacher's throat, nose and lips, learning to imitate the gutturals, labials, nasals, vowels and consonants. The demonstration ended with Miss Keller suddenly speaking, her voice loud and clear: "I am not dumb now!"

The audience cheered at the unexpected miracle! Dramatic music followed, played by the vaudeville orchestra, as Miss Keller began to speak. Her speech was unlike any ever made before on stage! The audience was transfixed as she spoke, her voice strange, and her manner of speaking carefully articulated—but this too only added to the realization of Miss Keller's triumph. She exclaimed:

"What I have to say to you is very simple: my teacher has told you how a word from her hand touched the darkness of my mind and I awoke to the gladness of life! I was dumb; now I speak! I owe this to the hands and hearts of others. Through their love I found my soul and God and happiness! Don't you see what it means?"

The audience was spellbound, following each movement and gesture with a rare concentration and palpable sympathy. Mrs. Sullivan repeated Miss Keller's words after each sentence. The music reached a peak as Keller shouted, "We live *by* each other and *for* each other! Alone we can do so little; but together we can do so much! Only love can break down the walls that stand between us and our happiness! The greatest commandment is: 'Love ye one another.' I lift up my voice and thank the Lord for the love and joy and the promise of life to come!"

Everyone in the audience was moved by the astonishing accomplishment for a deaf and blind girl who was no longer mute nor dumb! As the music reached its climax Miss Keller raised her right hand and the music halted as she exclaimed, "This is my message of hope and inspiration to all mankind!"

The audience cheered and gave Miss Keller a standing ovation. All beholders saw that before them was a woman who had surmounted unspeakable difficulties. When the applause subsided, Mrs. Sullivan asked: "Would anyone care to ask Miss Keller a question?"

At first people were somewhat dumbfounded, yet soon questions began pouring from around the large theatre. A man with good intentions but scant knowledge of theatrical manners shouted: "Will Miss Keller tell us how old she is?"

There was a murmur of dissent from the audience, which by this time had adopted the deaf-blind marvel as its own. But Mrs. Sullivan quickly spelled the question into Miss Keller's hand, and the latter smiled, brushed her hair and said, "There is no age on the vaudeville stage!"

That brought a gleeful laughter from the entertained audience. Then a lady in the audience stood up and asked "Can Miss Keller distinguish or understand what *colors* mean?"

After the question was spelled to her hand Miss Keller replied wittily, "No, but once in a while I do *feel blue*."

The audience enjoyed her clever remark. Next some person, most likely not a frequent playgoer, cried: "Does Miss Keller believe that she will see and hear in the hereafter?"

The audience at once manifested disapproval of such a personal question. The inquirer was hissed loudly and there were shouts of "Out! Out!" yet Miss Keller smiled, oblivious to the rumble in the audience.

Then one young man stood up asked, "Does Miss Keller think of marriage?"

Mrs. Sullivan translated the question to Miss Keller. "Yes," came her quick reply, "are you proposing to me?"

The audience laughed wildly at her quick response. An intelligent question followed: "Which is the greatest affliction in your view—deafness, dumbness, or blindness?"

Keller replied, "None."

The man did not relent, "What then is the greatest human affliction Miss Keller?"

Keller answered unhesitatingly: "Boneheadedness!"

The audience was hers. Keller managed to answer a few more questions. For the benefit of our readers some of them are brought here:

Question: "Do you close your eyes when you go to sleep?"

Keller: "I never stayed awake to see."

Question: "Who are the most unhappy people?"

Keller: "People who have nothing to do."

Question: "What have you enjoyed most in life?"

Keller: "Overcoming difficulties."

Question: "What is the slowest thing in the world?"

Keller: "Congress!"

Question: "Do you desire your sight more than anything else in the world?"

Keller: "No! No! I would rather walk with a friend in the dark than walk alone in the light."

Question: "What is your idea of happiness?"

Keller: "Helpfulness."

Question: "In your opinion, is there something worse than being blind?"

Keller: "Yes, some people may have their sight, but have no vision. That is indeed worse."

Question: "Does talking tire you, Miss Keller?"

Keller: "Did you ever hear of a woman who tired of talking?"

Question: "What do you think is the most important question before the country today?"

Keller: "How to get a drink!"

The audience laughed uproariously at her witty replies and was moved by her intelligence and observations. This was when, to the dismay of the audience, the act was brought to an end, and Keller bowed gracefully, blowing kisses to all directions.

Undoubtedly, the Keller act was the most intriguing of all the acts of the vaudeville show, which included acrobats, singers, tap dancers and trained seals. Miss Keller's appearance provided an entirely new sort of a sensation on the vaudeville stage, and the general opinion was that it was a strong object lesson in the possibilities of the human mind.

One member of the audience noted that Miss Keller displayed a "pretty wit" and demonstrated "quickness and good-humor that the keenest of experienced monologists might well have envied!"

The producers of the show, the Weber Brothers, stated that "Miss Keller showed wonderful showmanship in the arrangement of the act, for her ability to make an "act" out of what might have otherwise been considered a voyeuristic exhibition, which was far from her intention. She wishes to educate the public about deafness and blindness, as well as bring hope to soldiers having returned from the war." According to the Weber Brothers, Keller receives 1500 dollars per week, "as high a salary as any star in the vaudeville business." She is scheduled for a coast-to-coast tour to begin next month.

Clearly, the woman who though deaf and blind graduated Harvard University, was smart enough to get the idea of vaudeville *before* she even started in it.

—B. F. Keith, *Theatre News*"

Vaudeville advertisement in a newspaper, c. 1922:
B. F Keith's
[…] A BILL OF EXTRAORDINARY FEATURES!
THE MOST REMARKABLE WOMAN IN THE WORLD!
STAR OF HAPPINESS, **HELEN KELLER** IN PERSON,
BLIND-DEAF-AND FORMERLY MUTE
In the Sweetest Story Ever Told. Assisted by Anne Sullivan Macy, Her Life-Long and Devoted Teacher. […]
Two shoes Daily, 2 PM and 8 PM, Seats on Sale One Week in Advance.

Helen and Annie dressed up for a show, possibly vaudeville, c.1920

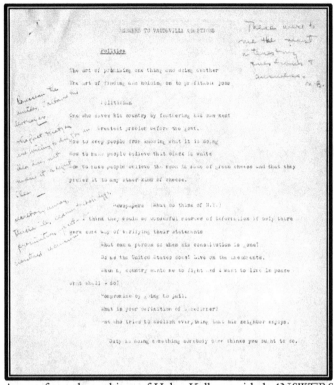

A page from the archives of Helen Keller, entitled *ANSWERS TO VAUDEVILLE QUESTIONS*. Notice the handwritten comments.

Helen seated, Annie standing, c. 1920[i]

Studio portrait of Helen and Annie. This photograph was probably taken as a publicity photograph for a vaudeville tour. Notice their hands held together.[i]

Portrait of Helen, Annie and Polly, with their dog, c. 1925. The photograph is signed by all three with a note from Keller in square-letters: "To Mr. Farringon
with long long memories
Helen Keller."
Below are the signatures of Annie (Anne Sullivan Macy) and Polly (Polly Thomson). Notice the second dog, smaller and black, on the bottom left.[i]

Artistic photograph of Annie, unknown date, unknown photographer, c. 1920

Charlie Chaplin standing behind Polly, Helen and Annie while in Hollywood for the filming of the film *Deliverance* about the life of Helen Keller. Notice how Annie is fingerspelling to Helen, 1918[i]

Annie, Helen and Charlie Chaplin, most likely at his studios in Hollywood. Notice the camera at the back. Helen has her hand on Annie's face, reading her lips, 1918

Advertisement for the film "Deliverance" calling Helen "The 8th Wonder of the World." In the photo, Helen is photographed smelling a rose. 1919 (Full text in the following page)

Full text of the advertisement in the previous page:

The 8th Wonder of the World
Helen Keller
IN THE PHOTO-PLAY BEAUTIFUL-
"DELIVERANCE"
Together with Her
Life Long Friend,
Compannion and Beloved
Instructor
ANNE SULLIVAN (MACY)
Both Appearing
Personally in this
Most Interesting &
Incomparable of
Photo-Plays
DIRECT FROM HER
TRIUMPHANT TOUR
OF AMERICA'S BEST
THEATRES
PLAYING
TREMONT TEMPLE

The house of Helen, Annie and Polly, Forest Hills, New York, in the snow, c. 1930.

Annie sitting in a cushioned chair, Forest Hills, New York, c. 1930.[i]

Annie and Helen as photographed on one of their tours. C. 1930

PART FIVE

A DECADE LATER
1930

"No, no, no!" was Annie's only remark.

Helen felt the hand of the old woman who was her teacher, her friend, her companion. Ever since her mother's death several years earlier, Helen relied more and more on Annie for support.

But Annie did not make it easy for her 50-year-old student. Annie now regarded herself as "an old woman," and all the patience she once had had, if to use her own words, "blew out the window."

They were sitting in the living room, which was not a common occurrence: these days Annie preferred spending time alone in her bed, preferably with one of the dogs curled next to her. Especially with her Shetland collie, Dileas, her exquisite "puff from the creamery of Heaven," as she called him.

But now she was sitting in the living room, dominating the conversation about Helen's upcoming speech, which Helen was extremely nervous about. Helen sat beside Annie, and Polly sat in front of her. On the couch in the corner sat a timid young woman called Nella, who was sent to help Helen with matters relating to the *American Foundation for the Blind*. Nella was quiet, quick and efficient, and often stayed after her paid hours with the three older women. Annie had taken a liking to her, and therefore did not mind her sitting there. "Polly!" Annie barked, "Read the beginning of the speech again!"

Polly began reading.

"Dear Lions…"

Helen waited eagerly as Annie listened, her eyes closed. It was an important speech for Helen. This speech was to be given in a convention with a very large audience, three thousand people. The organization behind the convention, *Lions Clubs International*, was becoming one of the largest volunteer organizations in the country. Furthermore, it was said that in this very convention all the members were to elect the "core mission" of the organization, and direct all their volunteers and money to that cause.

Helen wanted that cause to be *blindness*. For the past few years, she had taken a growing part in the new *American Foundation for the Blind*. In fact, she had become the chief spokesperson for the Foundation. And the Foundation needed money badly. She wanted the *Lions* to support the Foundation, both monetarily as well as with its many volunteers.

Polly went on reading Helen's typed draft:

"…The American Foundation for the Blind is only four years old. It grew out of the imperative needs of the blind and was called into being by the sightless themselves. It is national and international in scope and importance. It represents the best and most enlightened thought on our problems that has been reached so far. It embodies a new—"

"Stop it!" Annie exclaimed to Polly and spelled to Helen, "Why should they even care?!"

"Why should they even *care*?" Helen spelled back, bewildered, "Because it is important!"

"Helen," Annie sighed and spelled, "they have *many* foundations asking them for help. Why should they help your silly little foundation?!"

Helen was frustrated. She appreciated Annie's thoughts, and knew them to be valuable, but she did not like Annie's impatience. "Because," Helen spoke slowly, articulating every word while using the opportunity to practice her speech, "they do not know what it *means* to be blind, and if they knew—"

"Exactly!" Annie said and spelled, "Say that!"

"Say what?" Helen asked, bewildered.

"Say: 'If you were to know how it is to be blind'…. I don't know, say it in your own words, but give them an *emotional* experience before beginning to bore them with unnecessary information about your good-for-nothing Foundation!"

Helen gulped, took a deep breath, and nodded. She rose and made her way to her study, Nella quickly following her with her notepad. Annie tried getting up from the sofa, but the task was challenging for her. Polly reached her arm to help her, but Annie groaned, "Leave me alone Polly! I'm not *that* old!"

* * *

An hour later Annie was laying in her bed when Helen came to her, followed by Polly, with 27-year-old Nella treading behind. Helen spoke to Annie, "Tell me what you think now!" and reached her hand to Annie. Annie took her hand and listened as Polly stood by the bed and read:

> "Try to imagine how you would feel if you lost your sight tomorrow. Picture yourself stumbling and groping at noonday as in the night—all your work, all your independence gone! In that dark hour wouldn't your heart cry out for a friend to teach you how to live in the dark? That is just the kind of friend the *American Foundation for the Blind* will be to all the blind, if people with sight will only give it the support it must have."

Annie nodded her head approvingly, "Bravo," she turned to Helen and spelled, "Bravo!"

Helen looked hopeful.

Annie rejoiced, "Good, Helen, now, what do you want them to *do*?"

"I want them," Helen spelled back, hesitantly, "to donate their money and time to us, to the Foundation!"

"So you are begging for their money and time?"

"Yes—well, not *begging*. I am *offering* them a chance to take part."

"Why should they?" Annie insisted. She did not want to make it easy for Helen. She wanted Helen to be the best. She wanted to either give the best speech in that convention or not at all.

"Why should they? I already wrote," Helen said, "that if they were to become blind, they would appreciate such help!"

"You need to *convince* them. You are offering something *unique*. Don't feel like a beggar! Feel like you are offering them something *valuable*."

"An opportunity?" Helen spelled, and then immediately replied to herself, "Yes, I'm offering them an opportunity!"

"Good," Annie said, "now go develop that idea."

* * *

Half an hour later Helen returned again with Polly at her side and Nella treading behind. Polly read from the new sheet of paper:

> "The American Foundation for the Blind is your opportunity to help those in need. Our Foundation wants to be adopted by you! I know you have other opportunities lying on your table at present, but I hope you will choose the Foundation for the Blind. We are but a new organization of four years old only. And the opportunity the Foundation offers is full of splendid possibilities of service."

Helen was proud of what she wrote. Her hand was reached for Annie's anticipated remarks.

"Better," Annie said. "But there is too much attention on the *Foundation*."

"But that is what I want them to support," Helen spoke, a little tired of even asking for Annie's help to begin with, "I want them to support the *Foundation*! I said it clearly, I want them to *adopt* the Foundation as their own—"

"But a Foundation, Helen," Annie spelled slowly—she was tired as well, but nevertheless felt the urgency Helen was feeling—"is a stranger to them. Where is the Foundation, can they point at it? Can they touch it? Can they see it? The 'Foundation' is something *intangible* for them, elusive!"

Helen did not know what to say. Polly stood silently, and so did Nella.

Annie continued, "For the people in this convention, the American Foundation for the Blind is *you*. It's Helen Keller, that's it. So you want to tell them to adopt *you*."

"But that…" Helen protested, "Does that not sound too personal?"

"It *must* sound personal, dear! You want them to part from their best money and from their precious time, their two most important assets! You *must* speak to them personally!"

Helen nodded slowly, biting her lip.

Annie kept Helen's hand in hers. She spoke to Polly, "Read to me the beginning again."

Polly nodded and read:

> "The American Foundation for the Blind is your opportunity to help those in need—"

"Stop, stop," Annie said. She paused for a long moment and sighed. She spelled to Helen, "Have you heard of the legend describing *opportunity* as a capricious *lady*?"

Helen shook her head, "I heard of *Luck* being a lady—"

"No, no, no, this has nothing to do with luck! There is a legend about *Opportunity* being a capricious lady who knocks at every door but once," Annie spelled slowly, forcefully, "and if the door isn't opened quickly—she passes on! Never to return again!"

Helen smiled. The vigor with which Annie was spelling reminded her of the good old times, before

Annie was sick, before she was always so tired, before she was upset most days. "It is a nice story," Helen spelled back, "where did you read that?"

"A wise old woman told me that once."

Helen was bewildered; she never heard her teacher mentioning 'a wise old woman.' She turned her face to Annie and spoke, "Which woman?"

"Oh stop being such a curiosity shop will you!" She turned to Polly and Nella, "Now go help her with that. It must be personal, convincing, powerful!"

* * *

A week later the speech was ready. Helen wrote four pages, which Annie mercilessly cut to two pages, insisting again and again, "You want them to sit on the edge of their seats, not to get bored for even a second!"

* * *

> "Dear Lions,
>
> You may have heard the poetic legend which represents Opportunity as a capricious lady who knocks at every door but once, and if the door isn't opened quickly, she passes on, never to return!
>
> That is as it should be: lovely, desirable ladies won't wait, you have to go out and grab 'em! (Laughter)
>
> Dear Lions, *I am your Opportunity*, clothed in visibility. I am knocking at your door! I want to be adopted!
>
> The legend about Opportunity being a capricious

lady does not say what you are to do when *several* beautiful Opportunities present themselves at the same door. I guess you are to choose the one you love the best. (Smile) I hope you will choose me. I am the youngest, as the *American Foundation for the Blind* is only four years old. And the opportunity it offers is full of splendid possibilities of service!

Our Foundation grew out of the imperative needs of the blind and was called into being by the sightless *themselves*! (Pause) It is national and international in scope and importance. It represents the best and most enlightened thought on our problems that has been reached so far.

The time has come to regard the work for the sightless as a *whole*, in which the kindergarten, the school, the library, the workshop, the home for the aged blind, as well as sight-loss-prevention are *all* seen as parts of a great *movement* with one goal in view: making life more worth living for the blind *everywhere*! (Applause)

Beside the young blind, for whom existing institutions are supposed to provide, there is a large class of men and women who lose their sight when it is *too late* for them to go to school. Unlike those who are in the dark from childhood—who are pressed hard to find their place in the work of the world—the older man suddenly stricken blind becomes a biblical Samson: bound, helpless, dependent, until a way is found to *unchain* him! (Pause)

Try to imagine how *you* would feel if you lost your sight tomorrow! (Pause) Picture yourself stumbling and groping at noonday as in the night, your work, your independence gone! (Pause) In that dark hour wouldn't your heart cry out for a friend to teach you how to live in the dark?

That is just the kind of friend the *American Foundation for the Blind* will be to all the blind if people with sight will only give it the *support it must have*. Adequately financed, it will help the blind in every emergency of their lives.

To me, as a child, it was but a little word from the fingers of my teacher, a ray of light from another soul touching the darkness of my mind, and suddenly I found *myself*, found the *world*, found *God!*

It is because my teacher cared about me and broke through the dark and silent imprisonment which held me that I am able to work for myself *and* for others! If you care, if we can make the people of this great country care, the blind will triumph over blindness! (Applause)

This is the opportunity I offer you, Lions—to foster and sponsor the work of the *American Foundation for the Blind.* Will you not help me hasten the day when there shall be no *preventable blindness*? (Pause) No little deaf-blind child untaught? (Pause) No blind man or woman unaided? (Pause) I appeal to you, Lions—you who *have* your sight, who have your hearing, you who are *strong* and *brave* and *kind*!—will you not constitute yourselves *Knights of the Blind* in my crusade against darkness?

Thank you!"

[Helen Keller's Address to *Lions Clubs International Foundation Convention*, Cedar Point, Ohio.]

* * *

The four of them returned home triumphant. *Lions Clubs International* had adopted the *American Foundation for the Blind*. Vision loss was adopted as the organization's primary focus. The decision was nothing but historic and they knew it.

As they finally returned from the long train trip to their house in Forest Hills, Polly, Helen, and Nella were exhausted, but pleased. Nella bid them farewell and drove to her home in Garden City.

Annie climbed into bed. She was proud.

She did not say to Helen *why* she was proud. The thought of it brought tears to her eyes.

The thought of the five-year-old, happy little Annie, running around the fields, playing with her baby brother, helping her mother sew and knit, cleaning the house, playing with other children. The thought of that heaven suddenly plagued by the horrible itch, that nasty irritation, burning in her eye which the doctor called Trachoma. The thought of that devilish burn that sat upon her poor good old eyes, the eyes that brought her so much pleasure—the thought of that irritation, of that never-ending itch, of that foam which devoured her eyes—the thought of it being *preventable*!

She cuddled in bed with her two dogs, big Dileas and small Maida, her Lakeland terrier. Tears streaming quietly down her cheeks. She had become more emotional as her age advanced. Now in her sixties she was tired of playing tough all the time.

Stroking both dogs she could not stop her thoughts from wondering: what could life have been like without the mist that covered the world from her?

She remembered herself, five years old, sitting on the porch of their cabin in Agawam. How she itched and itched and how her eyes became worse. She remembered the landlord lady, Mrs. Taylor, saying to her mother, "Your daughter would be so pretty if it were not for her eyes...."

She patted Dileas and Maida, trying to stop the tears. This was her first, most distinct memory: she was on the porch, playing, and she looked up to the landlady coming. Her mother was excited, nervous, as she always was around the rich folks. Annie remembered Mrs. Taylor looking at her and tut-tutting. She must have meant well, saying, "She would be so pretty if it were not for her eyes." But that sentence stung. It stung so hard it never left her. That's when she realized that she was *not* pretty. And that her eyes were to be her curse.

She was cuddling deep under the blankets when Polly came smiling, "I just found a letter which I think you will be very happy about!"

Helen followed her, grinning from ear to ear.

Annie groaned and wiped her tears. What letter could make her "very happy?" Was it a love letter from her good-for-nothing John, who she had been separated from for now 16 years? Or a letter from the father who deserted her when she was nine years old, never to return or contact her again? Or was it a letter from the late Captain Keller, apologizing for having undermined her efforts so many times and not giving her due respect and acknowledgement...?

Annie sniffled and sat upright. Helen joined her on the bed and took her hand. Polly stood and read:

"Dear Mrs. Sullivan-Macy,"

"Wait," Annie said, her voice hoarse, "who is it from?"

Polly looked at the bottom of the letter, "His name is Mr. Charles Beury."

"Beury? I don't know any Charles Beury!"

"He is the President of Temple University," Polly said, "now will you let me read it?"

Annie nodded, chastised.

Polly continued,

"Dear Mrs. Sullivan-Macy,

I am writing to you on behalf of the Board of Trustees of Temple University. As you many know, our University was established over 60 years ago in Philadelphia and is considered one of the finest universities in America. We offer a variety of degrees, including one of the finest medical degrees in the country. We still follow the creed laid out by our founder, Russell H. Conwell, "to give education to those who were unable to get it through usual channels."

Annie snorted and smiled as she spelled to Helen, "Does he want me to enroll? Does he not know I'm too old?!"

Polly cleared her throat and continued reading,

"The Board of Trustees has elected you and Miss Keller, along with Governor Pinchot, as the three recipients of our Honorary Degree of Doctor of Humane Letters."

Annie gasped.

She said nothing, her mouth slightly opened.

Polly continued:

> "We see your accomplishment in the education of Miss Keller one of the greatest accomplishments ever achieved in American education. The Honorary Doctorate is our humble token of appreciation for your efforts of over forty years with Miss Keller, supplying hope and example for teachers around the country and the world.
>
> The ceremony will take place in front of four thousand dignitaries, faculty, students and family members, at the joint Commencement-Founders Day on February 16 of the coming year.
>
> We look forward to your acceptance and to the wisdom you shall bestow with us and with the graduates of the coming academic year.
>
> Yours cordially,
>
> Charles E. Beury,
>
> President
>
> Temple University"

Annie began to sweat and pulled the blanket off. "Oh my!" she mumbled, "Oh my!"

Polly sat by Helen on the edge of the large bed, "Isn't it great news?"

Helen spelled into Annie's hand while pronouncing to Polly, "First the *Lions* adopting us, and now this!"

She tried sitting up straighter, her breath becoming heavy. She was used to *Helen* being given many prizes and acknowledgments. Helen always accepted them—as she should have—knowing what the prizes and acknowledgements mean to fellow people with disabilities which she felt she represented.

But could *Annie* accept such an acknowledgement?

"I can't," Annie said, and then repeated, alarmed, "I can't!"

Polly was confused, "You *can't* what?"

Annie spelled and spoke forcefully, "I can't possibly accept such an honor!"

Helen was taken aback, "Why?" she spoke out loud, "You always say that no one appreciates your work!"

Annie felt a lack of air in the room, "I can't! Now, why did the two of you come to intrude me like this?"

Polly took Helen's hand and spelled, "Let's give her some time, she is excited."

* * *

No matter how hard both Polly and Helen tried to convince her, Annie was unbending. With tears in her eyes she said again and again, "I can't! I can't!"

She did not explain why.

With the help of Polly she wrote a kind letter of refusal. Helen, however, took the letter and hid it. "Think of it further!" she shouted to Annie, "Stop being so righteous! They want to thank you, you cannot stop them from doing it!"

Annie said nothing, each time disappearing in her bedroom, under the blankets, hiding, crying, torn.

* * *

"From: Anne Sullivan Macy, Forest Hills, New York

To: President Charles E. Beury,

Temple University, Philadelphia, Pennsylvania

December 17th, 1930

Dear President Beury,

I received several days ago your very pleasant letter offering me the honorary degree of Doctor of Humane Letters from Temple University. I should have answered it immediately, expressing my deep sense of the honor done me by such a thought, and the sincere regret I felt that such an honor was not for me. But Miss Keller entreated me so earnestly to reconsider my decision that I have carried your letter in my head and my heart for a week with the most genuine desire to catch myself in such a state of mind that I might write and tell you I would accept the degree.

But my decision remains unchanged. I cannot conscientiously accept the degree that you so graciously wish to confer upon me. It is a value to which I do not consider my education commensurate.

All my life I have suffered in connection with my work from a sense of deficiency of equipment. To take pleasure in such a degree as you so graciously wish to confer upon me I should have to feel I deserved it. All the satisfaction that belongs to me—which I derive from the fact that I have discharged my duty towards my beloved pupil Helen Keller not unsuccessfully—I shall realize when Helen herself is honored.

I have much remorse in resisting Helen's pleadings and the kindness of your offer, but one should not be prevailed upon to do something utterly against one's sense of the proprieties.

Please believe me, I am keenly sensible of your beautiful thought of me, especially as it is the first time an institution of learning has wished to recognize my work. Your faith in my fitness for the degree touches me profoundly and my pride is augmented when a mind like yours is moved by an acquaintance with my work to a friendly interest in me.

Since I cannot conscientiously receive the degree, I assure you that your recognition of my dear pupil's accomplishments will bring me real happiness.

I repeat, this letter expresses the perfect sincerity of my attitude towards the Temple University degree, and my gratitude for your wish to honor me.

With very kind regards, I am

Sincerely yours,

Anne Sullivan Macy"

* * *

"What now?" Annie said, feeling both Helen and Polly sitting down on both sides of her bed.

It was a gloomy morning. It rained heavily outside.

Not hearing their answer, Annie took Helen's hand and spelled as she spoke, "What now? If that President

Beury responded, I do not want to read it!"

Something in Helen's hand movement felt odd to Annie.

Helen spelled nothing.

Annie turned to Polly, "What happened? What happened?!"

Polly cleared her throat and said quietly, "We received a letter from Lenore addressed for you and Helen. I just read it to Helen in the living room."

Annie's heart began pounding, "What does Lenore say? Why are you torturing me that way, read it to me already!"

Polly nodded and read,

> "Dear Annie, dear Helen,
>
> I suppose you have already heard. I attach the brief article from the New York Times. The funeral took place yesterday, he was buried at Mount Hebron Cemetery, Upper Montclair, New Jersey.
>
> My heart is with you as always,
>
> Yours,
>
> Lenore."

Annie's heart sank.

Polly went on to read the attached article:

> "Mr. John A. Macy, Author and critic—"

Annie gasped.

Polly's voice broke as she read quietly:

> "—died of heart attack at age 55. Macy died while in Stroudsburg, Pennsylvania, lecturing about

literary matters. Macy graduated Harvard with Honors in 1899. In 1903 he served as the editor of Helen Keller's famed autobiography, *The Story of My Life.* He was the author of several books including *The Spirit of American Literature* (1913), *Socialism in America* (1916), and *The Story of the World's Literature* (1925). He served as a literary editor at William Morrow & Company. He left behind a wife, Mrs. Anne Sullivan Macy. His funeral shall take place today at 4 PM at Mount Hebron Cemetery, Upper Montclair, New Jersey."

Annie, her face completely white, tried to rise from the bed, "We must hurry. We can still make it in time to New Jersey by four!"

Polly could not look her Annie in the eyes, "The article is from a week ago."

"I…" Annie mumbled, "Why didn't he tell me—why didn't they tell me… I'm his wife! I'm his damned wife for God's sake!"

She began sobbing, her eyes wide open as if she had seen a ghost. Helen tried to calm her, stroking her arm, but Annie would have none of it. "Why didn't they tell me!" she snapped at Polly, "Give me that article!"

Polly reluctantly gave Annie the piece of paper, which Annie held to her face, squinting her eyes helplessly, "Oh, John! My John!" she screamed, "My John! My John! My John! Don't you leave me!"

* * *

The following days Annie did not get out of bed. Not even the dogs could lift her spirit. Helen came and sat with her, but Annie said nothing to her. Polly explained to Helen that Annie had feats of temper, crying, screaming, sobbing and then falling asleep. This repeated night and day.

A week later Annie asked for her diary to be found. She had not written in it for years. But now she wanted her diary, fast. Polly was able to find it in one of the drawers. She wondered how Annie, with her eyes, could write.

With trembling hand, not seeing what she was writing unless it was right in front of her poor eyes, Annie wrote a few short lines:

> "Done. The dreadful drama is finished, the fierce struggle that won only despair is ended."

Her eyes streamed with tears, of years of pain and unexpressed love, and more pain. She wrote:

> "His body, once so dear, lies cold and still."

The realization of this unbearable truth shocked her.

> "I have been homesick for many a year for his arms. Now he is dead."

She reminisced about their good years—those which she so often feared to recall—

> "What dreams our marriage held! What tremulous expectations!"

And she allowed herself to hurt the dissolve of their marriage.

> "What clouds of suspicion, of jealousy! What amazing cruelties of looks and tones and sudden denials!
>
> There is more pain than joy in the most passionate love—pain and waste for but a brief ecstasy!"

She felt that now all was gone. Even the faint hope of

rekindling that passionate love which took her by surprise:

> "I was young and foolish, I dared to believe all things possible! My heart still leaps to the whisper of your name, your touch, the first kiss that lived in every kiss..."

She then cried herself to sleep.

* * *

Two days later she added:

> "Oh John! Those vanished golden hours, those warm, loving hands and lips murmuring shy words... One but glances away, and all is gone—all that golden abundance of beauty and joy, of hope, of excitement, of adventure! The sweet blossoms of life's spring-time are now gone past recall!
>
> Gone? No! They flash before me more real than the realities of my mature years."

* * *

Nothing would do. All that Annie would mumble was "Leave me alone!"

She cried to herself, "Die, die, just let me die!"

Her diary stated:

> "Now I wait for death—not sad, not heroically but just a simple death."

* * *

Two weeks later she wrote again:

> "To love and succeed is a fine thing;

To love and fail is the next best;

And the best of all is to fail and yet keep on loving."

* * *

When letters from people associated with Temple University began pouring in wishing Annie's reconsideration, she chose to ignore them.

A new letter arrived from President Beury. As Polly read it to her, Annie began feeling guilty for making such a fuss.

* * *

"From: President Beury, Temple University

To: Mrs. Anne Sullivan-Macy

My dear Lady,

I received your letter from December 17th, in which you graciously but firmly decline the honorary degree which our University wishes to grant you. Please permit me to give you my reasons again, hoping that you will reconsider your decision.

First, I regard Helen Keller as one of the most remarkable personalities now living, and I have always thought that what you have done with her was little, if any, less remarkable than what she was able to do for herself. I am not alone in this feeling: it is the feeling of all who have given your great achievement a moment's consideration.

Another reason why I trust you will accept the degree which Temple offers is this: it gives Temple an opportunity of announcing its wish to encourage rare achievement wherever it may be found, especially when the recipient of its honor occupies a position which makes it unlikely that he can ever do anything by way of return. Allow me to ask you: may it not be that Miss Keller and your many friends more correctly appraise the value of your work than you do?

I hope, too, that both you and Miss Keller will honor me by being my guests when you come to Philadelphia. I live in the country, as most Philadelphians do, but I will place a motor and chauffeur at your disposal and do everything in my power to make your stay in Philadelphia memorable.

Permit me to wish you, both, the compliments of the season.

Yours very sincerely,

Charles E. Beury."

* * *

The kind letter wouldn't do.

Helen tried her best to convince Annie to receive the degree. She also knew Annie's mood was bound to cheer up if she felt such a recognition for her life's work.

But Annie wouldn't listen.

Helen, hoping to convince Annie to accept the honorary degree, sent young Nella to Annie's room. Helen knew Annie liked Nella very much. Perhaps Nella with her young optimism could make Annie say yes?

Nella tried to encourage Annie, explaining to her that if not for herself, she must accept the honor for future generations of educators of the blind and deaf.

Annie was less rude to Nella, but nevertheless her stance was firm. She would not have it.

The days passed. Annie did nothing but stay in bed all day. Her diary, however, began filling, for the first time in decades.

* * *

> "Last night you came to me, John.
>
> I do not know if it was a dream or your spirit presence. I felt your step so near and you were the very same—your manner and the smell of your clothes.
>
> I held your hand so tight and you called me Nan.
>
> I felt the same glad thrill I always felt when you put my hand on your lips and said Hello Nan.
>
> Oh I was so happy because you had come back to me!
>
> We walked in the hill wood and we hunted toadstools and got a basket full that were good to eat.
>
> We walked home through the field and you said, "This is like the old times, Nan!" and the way you said it brought peace to my heart.

I can't tell if it was a dream or a vision. I only know I have been happier today because you called me Nan in the dear old way."

* * *

When the morning came to travel to the ceremony at Temple University in Philadelphia, Helen and Polly got ready. Helen came into Annie's room one last time, spelling into Annie's sleepy hand, "Are you sure you do not wish to come?"

Annie pulled her hand away, not saying anything.

Her dreams and reality mixed together.

Helen came once again, "I asked Polly to call Nella and ask her to come and be with you. Polly and I will spend the night in Philadelphia and come back tomorrow afternoon."

Annie nodded and took her hand away. She wanted to wish Helen a pleasant ceremony. More so, she wanted Helen to shake her and drag her out of bed, to *command* her to come. She wanted someone to fight her, to fight *for* her.

But a few moments later she heard the door to the house closing. She squinted her eyes trying to see the window across her bed. Cold February morning. It was so gloomy—all so gloomy. She closed her eyes and fell asleep again, wishing to drown herself in her dreams, dreams that were so much sweeter than reality.

* * *

Bells woke her up. Bells. Ringing again and again. Along with dogs barking. What was happening?

She suddenly realized it was the door. The door bell. Someone was at the door. Dileas and Maida were barking madly. Who could it be? She got out of the bed and felt dizzy. She made her way down the stairs and shouted at the dogs with her hoarse voice, "Quiet down, quiet down!"

She came to the door and tried peering through the door peep hole. She could decipher a figure, but could not see who it was. "Who is it," she tried shouting, but her voice was scruffy. She coughed and shouted, "Who *is* it?"

"It's me, Nella! I came to be with you!"

Annie grimaced and opened the door. The bright light outside was unbearable. She covered her eyes, "I'm not quite dressed, Nella!"

"That's fine. I brought some croissants from the bakery!"

"Oh," Annie said. She suddenly realized where Helen and Polly were. On their way to Philadelphia. Why did they leave her behind?

She walked into the house, Nella following her and closing the door behind her. Annie sighed and walked to the living room, falling into the sofa. Nella opened the blinds. Annie lay on the sofa, her arm covering her eyes. Nella spoke cheerfully as she walked into the kitchen, "I'm making you some coffee!"

"Thank you," Annie whispered, knowing Nella could not hear her from the kitchen. Her thoughts were drawn to her dreams. What was she dreaming about? All she could remember were the bells. Large bells, ringing. She thought of Liberty Bell, ringing so hard until it cracked.

Nella brought the coffee to the living room and

placed it on the coffee table. She said nothing.

Annie wanted to cry.

Nella said nothing.

The thoughts of the ceremony in the afternoon haunted Annie. "Nella," she whispered, "How long does it take to get to Philadelphia?"

Nella shrugged her shoulders, "About four hours, or five, depends on the traffic and the weather."

Annie sipped a long sip from the coffee. Sweet warmth filled her mouth. She gulped and stood up, still a little dizzy.

* * *

President Beury called Helen and Polly onto the stage. The crowds at the huge Grace Baptist Temple applauded as Helen followed Polly onto the stage. Polly led their way to the table of the honorees, where a large man in a suit sat. He stood up and shook Polly's hand, "Governor Pinchot," he said, "and you must be the famed Anne Sullivan Macy!"

Polly smiled, "I'm Polly, Polly Thomson. Miss Sullivan did not feel well."

"Oh, I'm sorry," said the Governor, and quieted as not to disturb the words of President Beury.

Polly smiled politely. Helen grinned into the air, feeling the reverberation of the large speakers on the stage. Polly looked at the large audience, a little overwhelmed. The Governor leaned toward her and whispered, "4,000 people, not bad right?"

Polly smiled politely and looked away. She began spelling President Beury's words into Helen's hand.

President Beury, his thin white hair shining behind the podium, spoke, "Temple University is proud to grant today two Honorary Doctorates to two people of incredible accomplishments: Helen Keller and Governor Gifford Pinchot. First to speak will be Miss Keller herself. She will be assisted by her interpreter, Miss Polly Thomson!"

The audience cheered, and Polly led Helen to the podium, as she had seen Annie do hundreds of times in their 16 years together. She placed Helen's hands on both sides of the podium, moved the carbon microphone to Helen's mouth, and tapped her hand to indicate to her that she can begin.

Helen spoke, "President Beury and Friends!"

Polly repeated, nearing the microphone, "President Beury and Friends!"

Helen continued, slowly articulating each sentence, with Polly repeating each sentence thereafter:

> "I am proud of the honor which Temple University is conferring upon me. I may even be forgiven a touch of vanity on this occasion, since I am the only one of my particular "sub-species," the deaf blind, that has ever been given a degree by any university in any age of the world, so far as I know."

The audience applauded. Polly touched Helen's hand, indicating for her to pause. Helen smiled at the applause. When it subsided, Polly touched her hand again, as Annie always did. Helen promptly continued,

> "It is natural, is it not,"

Polly repeated her words, and Helen continued,

> "that one who must limp through life should rejoice that the race isn't only to the swift!"

People laughed. Helen's warmth and wit was surprising for a deaf blind person! Helen smiled,

> "I congratulate you, new graduates of Temple University!"

Polly touched Helen's hand for her to wait for the end of the applause. Then Polly tapped her hand again.

> "As you go out into the world, allow me to impart you some of what I have learned in my 51 years on earth. With the Depression plaguing, and after having witnessed the horrors of the Great War, you and I might think that the world is full of suffering. That may be true. But the world is also full of the overcoming of it!"

In the back of the giant hall a door opened quietly, and an older lady, escorted by a younger woman, entered the hall silently.

Helen spoke passionately,

> "As you go into the world, remember, alone we can do so little; together we can do so much. Throughout your life you will be met with many obstacles. But I have learned that when one door of happiness closes, another always opens! The problem is that often we look so long at the closed door that we do not see the one which has just been opened for us."

She paused, allowing her words to sink in.

The audience listened to her and to Polly attentively. So did the older woman standing at the rear.

Helen continued passionately,

> "Remember, as you go to the world, that avoiding danger is no safer in the long run than outright exposure to danger. The fearful are caught as often as the bold. Fear not. Be optimists by choice! No pessimist ever discovered the secret of the stars, or sailed to an uncharted land, or opened a new doorway for the human spirit. Be optimists I say!"

Applaud followed. Helen paused and then continued, feeling the echo of the huge hall and the speakers vibrating each time she spoke:

> "I wish to thank you for this great honor of your Honorary Doctorate of Humane Letters. In a very real sense I feel that you have shown me this distinguished token of your regard, this honorary degree, because you think what I have done may encourage others who have unusual difficulties to overcome. But I also feel that every bit of the usefulness you attribute to me has been unfolded by my teacher Annie Sullivan."

At the back of the large hall, the old woman felt her cheeks burning. Why was Helen talking about *her?*

Helen continued, emotional, articulating each word slowly:

> "Annie has been my lighthouse, and it was in her wisdom that my groping hands found their strength. Together we went through Harvard University. Day after day during four years—"

Helen suddenly began weeping. The auditorium was quiet as everyone sat still.

From the back of the hall, seeing her student crying, Annie stepped forward instinctively, only to pause a second later and freeze in her spot.

Helen gained her composure and continued, Polly repeating her every sentence:

> "In Harvard, Annie sat beside me in the lecture halls and spelled into my hand, word by word, what the professors said. She also spelled to me nearly all the books, word for word, in the same way, for four years."

Helen paused and wiped her eyes,

> "Yet when I received my degree from Harvard's Annex for Women, not a word of recognition was given to my teacher!"

A murmur of dismay passed through the crowds.

Annie felt like an imposter, being there and hearing all that. She reached for Nella's hand and whispered, "I'd like to leave."

Nella nodded and directed them back to the door, but Annie froze as Helen continued speaking:

> "The pain caused me by that indifference, or shall I say thoughtlessness, is still a thorn in my memory. This is why—"

Helen wiped her tears again,

> "—This is why nothing in our life together has made me happier than—"

Helen sniffled,

> "—than your splendid invitation, your honorary degree offered to her! A tribute to her for all that she has done for me for now forty-four years!"

The audience applauded. Some ladies wiped their tears. When the applause subsided, Polly tapped on

Helen's hand.

Annie, at the back of the huge hall, breathed heavily, tears stinging her eyes.

Helen continued:

> "Your earnest desire to honor her also with a degree has made me happier than words could say."

She took a deep breath and continued,

> "That she should refuse to stand with me this day is a grief to me, but her refusal is consistent with her attitude, which she had all throughout the years we have been together."

Helen sniffled, bringing her speech to a close, always remembering Annie's instructions: "Shorter is better, Helen!"

She concluded her speech, looking up, imagining the crowds in her mind's eye:

> "My beloved teacher has closed every door to any recognition that would emphasize her individuality. This is why I can only bow my head, and repeat my thanks to Temple University and President Beury for your beautiful thought of us both!
>
> Thank you all!"

Moved by her speech, the audience gave Helen a standing ovation. She nodded in all directions, and when the applause finally ceased, Polly walked them back to the Honoree's table. The Governor shook Helen's hand as well as Polly's, saying, "Wonderful speech!"

Polly hurried to spell his words to Helen, and Helen grinned and said, "Thank you Governor!"

President Beury took the podium and said,

"Thank you very much, Miss Keller, for your beautiful words. Interesting that you chose to bring up Miss Sullivan in your speech—"

Polly spelled his words into Helen's hand, and Helen nodded.

Annie gripped to Nella's hand. Nella again tried to pull them to the door, but Annie was not moving anywhere. Her head was tilted upwards, hearing each word by President Beury:

"—for I find it terribly unjust that Miss Sullivan found herself, if I may quote her letter to me, "unworthy of the honor." This is what she wrote back in response to the University's plea to grant her the honorary degree. Allow me to read her letter to you. 'Dear President Beury....'"

Annie, as red as could be, whispered to Nella, standing beside her, "Oh my, he isn't going to read the whole damned letter is he?!"

President Beury continued,

"'I received several days ago your very pleasant letter offering me the honorary degree of Doctor of Humane Letters from Temple University. I should have answered it immediately, expressing my deep sense of the honor done me by such a thought, and the sincere regret I felt that such an honor was not for me. But Miss Keller entreated me so earnestly to reconsider my decision that I have carried your letter in my head and my heart for a week with the most genuine desire to catch myself in such a state of mind that I might write and tell you I would accept the degree. But my decision remains unchanged. I cannot conscientiously accept the degree that you so graciously wish to confer upon me. It is a valuation to which I do not consider my education commensurate."

Hearing her words read to the whole audience made Annie nearly faint. She was conscious of not making a sound, but tears streamed down her cheeks, as they never had before. She felt like a child, like an abandoned little child—

"'All my life I have suffered in connection with my work from a sense of deficiency of equipment,'"

President Beury continued,

"...'to take pleasure in such a degree as you so graciously wish to confer upon me I should have to feel I deserved it. All the satisfaction that belongs to me—which I derive from the fact that I have discharged my duty towards my beloved pupil Helen Keller not unsuccessfully—I shall realize when Helen herself is honored.'"

A murmur of disapproval passed through the audience. Even Governor Pinchot thought the humility of Miss Keller's teacher was unjustified.

President Beury continued,

"'I have much remorse in resisting Helen's pleadings and the kindness of your offer, but one should not be prevailed upon to do something utterly against one's sense of the proprieties. Please believe me, I am keenly sensible of your beautiful thought of me, especially as it is the first time an institution of learning has wished to recognize my work.'"

Annie wept quietly at the back of the hall. Nella did not know what to do or say.

"'Your faith in my fitness for the degree touches me profoundly and my pride is augmented when a mind like yours is moved by an acquaintance with my work to a friendly interest in me.

Since I cannot conscientiously receive the degree, I assure you that your recognition of my dear pupil's accomplishments will bring me real happiness. I repeat, this letter expresses the perfect sincerity of my attitude towards the Temple University degree, and my gratitude for your wish to honor me.

With very kind regards, I am,

Sincerely yours,

Anne Sullivan Macy.'"

President Beury folded the letter quietly.

"We did not want to offend Mrs. Sullivan Macy by granting her degree to Miss Keller here without her consent. But let us allow her words to serve as an example for all of us as to how to serve our fellowmen."

President Beury smiled and took a deep breath,

"And now, our next and last Honoree, last but not least, Governor Pinchot. As you may well know, Governor Pinchot is known for reforming the management and development of forests in America and for advocating the conservation of our nation's nature reserves. The Governor coined the term 'conservation ethics.' His leadership put conservation of forests high on our nation's priority list, and for that, among other glowing accomplishments, Temple University is proud to present him our Honorary Degree. Please help me in welcoming Governor Pinchot!"

The audience clapped, though not as eagerly as they did when Helen Keller was introduced. The Governor shook hands with President Beury and proceeded to take the podium. "Before I begin," he said charmingly,

> "My mind is still drawn to that marvelous lady, the teacher of Helen Keller, Mrs. Sullivan Macy."

A murmur of approval passed through the audience, many people nodding their heads with consent. Annie gulped, her eyes widening as if she was under an onslaught.

The Governor looked behind him at President Beury, and then at Polly, who was spelling to Helen.

> "I do not mean to intervene, President Beury, but if I may share my opinion, I do not think it is in Miss Sullivan Macy's *right* to reject the honorary degree!"

Some people in the audience laughed. Almost everyone smiled—that is, everyone but Annie, standing now with her back to the wall near the door, as pale as a ghost.

The Governor continued,

> "I propose, with your agreement, President Beury, and with the agreement of kind Miss Keller, that the *audience* should decide if Mrs. Sullivan-Macy should be granted her degree, regardless of her protest."

The audience laughed and cheered in agreement. President Beury nodded and shrugged his shoulders in slight confusion. Helen, having Polly's quick interpretation, nodded eagerly, enthusiastically, and waved her hands in consent.

The Governor smiled,

> "Why shall we not take a rising vote, to see if the 'House' agrees with conferring the honorary degree upon Mrs. Macy despite her refusal? Who agrees with this proposal?"

Annie's heart stopped beating as she heard the sound of people standing in the back of the hall, in the front, in the middle—women, men, old people, young people. She whispered to Nella, "Take me out of here!"

Nella did not pull, but stood there, knowing it was a crime to take Annie out at this precious moment. The audience around them began applauding. The applause was extremely loud, almost deafening for Annie. On the stage, Helen and Polly too stood up. The choir did as well, as well as all the faculty members.

Annie's eyes widened and she finally could move. She could not say anything, but pushed Nella forcefully to the door. As they left the hall and entered the building's entrance hall, Annie muttered, "Quick! Quick! Get me out of here!"

Nella led them toward the door, when she suddenly said, "Just one moment, Annie!" She approached one of the ushers, an older lady, and said, "Please tell Miss Helen Keller that Nella and Annie were here, and that we shall be at—" she thought for a moment, remembering the hotels she knew in Philadelphia, "we shall be at the Robt-Morris Hotel! Nella and Annie! Please tell her!"

The old usher nodded and searched for a pen, but when she lifted her head Nella and Annie were already gone.

* * *

"From: Helen Keller
To: Lenore Smith
February 18th, 1931

Dear Lenore,

I must write to you a word on what happened in the honorary doctorates ceremony at Temple University two days ago. As you know, Annie had refused to receive the honorary degree, no matter how much pleading we tried. At the morning of our departure to Philadelphia she remained at home. I asked Nella, the kind secretary the Foundation had provided to us, to visit her. Polly and I arrived at the ceremony and were greeted warmly by the university's president, President Beury. After my speech President Beury told the large crowd of Annie's refusal to accept the honorary degree. He even went as far as reading her kind letter of declining the honor! At the ceremony there was another honoree, Governor Pinchot of Pennsylvania, who, when called to give his speech, spontaneously offered that the "House" vote on the matter of whether Annie should receive the honorary degree or not. In a moment four thousand people in the spacious auditorium had risen to their feet and, amid applause, decreed that Teacher's innate modesty should not be permitted to interfere with the purpose of Temple University to honor her! I was delighted!

Little did I know that Annie was in the audience!! After the ceremony we got word that she and

Nella were in fact in the ceremony and proceeded to the Robt-Morris Hotel. Polly and I rushed out from the shaking hands gathering with the university's board of trustees and rushed out to see Annie and Nella. I won't repeat what I said when I got Annie within my arm's reach. She pleaded guilty, saying that the desire to see me honored had proved stronger than her fear of being discovered and punished for her perversity! We hugged and cried for the longest of moments.

Oh Lenore! I wish you would have been there! I was so grateful for both President Beury and the Governor! President Beury had a sense of justice to accord to Annie her true place in education. Even the late Dr. Bell used to say that she was one of the greatest contributors to education—not only of the deaf but also of ALL children. Even Dr. Maria Montessori, whom we met nearly two decades ago, paid a sincere, beautiful tribute to Annie as a "true pioneer" in pedagogy. But you see, Lenore, that all these were comments made in PRIVATE. Now, with the ceremony at Temple, Annie got a glimpse of the public appreciation for all that she had done for me for 44 years, and for education in general.

I shall write more soon, I just wanted to let you know the happy news.

Yours,

Helen."

* * *

"From: Annie Sullivan Macy

To: President Beury

February 23rd, 1931

Dear Sir,

Please forgive me for what I am about to write to you. On the Monday morning of last week, after Miss Keller and Miss Thomson left for the ceremony in Philadelphia, I felt an urge to follow suit. I do not know why I decided to come after all my previous protests. I assume it was seeing my pupil acknowledged publicly that forbade me from missing the ceremony.

I must admit that this unexpected scene of public acknowledgement for my work stunned me and at the same time extremely delighted me. I had the pleasant sensation of thinking that I may after all have been a good teacher.

Please know that I had intended to speak with you after the ceremony, but the kind reference to me moved me so deeply, speech deserted me, and I fled in a sort of panic!

I shall always thank 'whatever powers there be' that I obeyed the call of my heart that day. Thank you again for your kind intentions and warm words, and please forgive me for not having been able to shake your hand and thank you for the great honor you have given us both.

Sincerely,

Anne Sullivan-Macy."

* * *

"To: Mrs. Anne Sullivan Macy

From: President Beury

March 1st 1931

Dear Mrs. Sullivan-Macy,

Thank you for your kind letter of February 23rd. I was delighted and quite pleased when I found out you were indeed present in the auditorium. It was quite like you to quietly and modestly come into our exercises by a side door! Under the circumstances I am glad that you did it that way. The statements and demonstrations made should be conclusive of your worthiness to receive an honorary degree.

With that being said, I wish to invite you again to receive your honorary degree. Would you be willing to honor us with your presence the coming year? I do not wish to insist on it, but certainly after the ceremony we all feel still that you are indeed entitled to the recognition. Will you honor us with visiting the ceremony of 1932 and parting some of your wisdom with the graduating students?

I do not mean to press, but only to express my gratitude and appreciation for your life's work.

Yours warmly,

Charles E. Beury,

President

Temple University"

* * *

It was different at the house in Forest Hills in the months following the Temple University ceremony. Annie was still sickly and often tired, but the 66-year-old woman was more jovial and pleasant than she has been in years. She spent more time in the living room and less time in bed. She even baked a few times, cooking for Helen's favorite cake for her birthday. Helen was as excited as a little girl. They had a splendid time.

Annie was also finally willing to cooperate with Nella, who plead with her to record some of her memories on paper. In the past, whenever Helen would ask her to write her memories, Annie would retort saying, "Why, you already want me dead?"

But now she was softer, milder, and more serene. She still wasn't willing to talk about her years before coming to Tuscumbia, but was finally willing to speak freely of her challenging years with Mr. Anagnos and their conflicting views about Helen's future; about the speech lessons which left both her and Helen frustrated during Helen's teens; about the preparatory program for Harvard and fighting with the Principal of the program; about the years at Harvard and the snobbery and conceit she encountered all around them.... She spoke freely, liberally, as one whose floodgates were finally opened after decades of silence.

But she was reticent when it came to speaking of her late husband John, and completely silent when it came to childhood memories. Nevertheless, whatever she was willing to share was recorded by Nella, who began collecting Annie's memories with personal interest and zeal.

A few months before the 1932 Commencement Ceremony at Temple University, Annie decided to write back to President Beury, consenting to receive the honorary degree.

Helen was ecstatic. Polly was pleased. Nella was eager. But Annie soon realized it was a "mistake, a dire mistake!"

All the powers she had in speech writing seemed to vanish. She fussed and fussed about the speech, thinking of it in bed, in the living room, with the dogs, in her dreams.... She found that she had no concrete idea even two weeks before the ceremony.

She also stressed about being unable to read at the ceremony. Helen tried to reassure her, "You always say that one should speak from his heart extemporaneously, not from written words!"

"Yes, yes," Annie lamented, "but I say it about others, not about myself!"

As the days passed she found it hard to fall asleep at night. And when the dreadful morning of February 15th came, she felt sick to her stomach.

Nevertheless, she entered the car with Polly driving and Helen and Nella at the back, they drove the four-hour drive to Philadelphia.

* * *

They arrived early. Annie climbed onto the stage and walked again and again from the honoree table to the podium, and from the podium to the honoree table. She did not want Polly to assist her. She wanted to at least *seem* to the audience as if she could see. The blurry spots she could see when she squinted barely indicated anything anymore. But she repeatedly walked back and forth, relieved each time she arrived successfully at the podium, clinging to the wooden ledges of the lectern. Then again, each time she arrived successfully at the table of honorees, she let out a sigh of relief.

With Polly's insistence Annie's place at the table was changed from the center seat of the three seats, to the side closer to the podium. Polly also had a word with President Beury, explaining to him the delicate situation. He understood, and said he'd be on guard, offering his hand to Miss Sullivan if needed.

As the large hall began to fill with people, Annie's heart raced fast. She felt her bowels cramping and spelled to Helen, "I feel like I'm about to give birth!"

Helen smiled and reassured her, "Do not worry!"

But Helen's words felt stale. Suddenly Annie was envious of her student, who did not have to *see* or *hear* the crowds, and could just imagine that the best was happening. Annie was now imagining the worst.

Just before the ceremony began Polly helped Annie climb the stage and sit at the honoree's table. She shook hands with the two men who were also to receive the honorary doctorates. She tried to smile, but her face wore a distressed look which betrayed her true fear and trepidation.

Helen, Polly and Nella sat in the front row of the large hall. Helen smiled, excited.

When President Beury finally called Annie's name she rose. She did not hear the applause of the audience. Her goal was to reach the podium. She walked there and bumped into the outreached hand of President Beury.

She shook his hand firmly and pushed him aside, relieved to finally hold the ledges of the podium.

She cleared her throat, and remembered to raise her chin. Who was it that told her that? Maggie's image surfaced from the past and left her, for a short moment, speechless.

'Keep your head up, you're as good as any of 'em!'

People began moving in their seats uncomfortably.

The light shining on her made Annie squint. It hurt her eyes, bringing tears to them. She closed her eyes tightly.

Finally, to everyone's relief, she swallowed and spoke,

> "President Beury, faculty members, ladies and gentlemen,"

She paused, choosing her words carefully.

> "During the long period of time that I have been with Helen Keller, I have been present, and taken part in *many* and *diverse* exercises. May I say,"

She smiled back toward President Beury, as if able to see him,

> "May I say this is the most embarrassing ceremony I have ever attended!"

The audience laughed. Polly translated it all to Helen. Helen beamed.

> "Nevertheless, I am glad to be here, and I sincerely appreciate the distinguished honor conferred upon me by Temple University."

She chuckled,

> "It is foolish trying to thank you, as words would

not deliver my feeling anyway! Yes, I am proud. And humble, very humble, too."

Nella, standing on Helen's other side, spelled into her hand, "She is a natural!"

Helen nodded eagerly.

Annie smiled,

> "I wish to say a word this morning on *education* in the light of present-day knowledge and *need*.
>
> Certain periods in history suddenly lift humanity to an observation point where a clear light falls upon a world previously dark. Everything seems strangely different. Familiar ideas put on new garments. Scholars and thinkers scrutinize events with a new intensity. People look for a sign, a miracle.
>
> I believe we are fortunate to be living in the beginning of such a renaissance."

She thought of the news, of the times. Three years earlier her country was pushed into the worse economic crisis it had ever known. The reports were grim, and the Great Depression was everywhere, penetrating the souls, dampening everyone's spirits. If it wasn't for the aid from The American Foundation for the Blind and Helen's monthly salary as the spokesperson, only God knows what they would have had to do. She continued,

> "Every renaissance comes to the world with a cry. It is the cry of the human spirit to be free. This aspiration is basic in present-day thought. It is manifesting itself in many ways and many places against great opposition.
>
> The Great War proved how confused the world is! And this Great Depression is proving it again. I'm

> afraid we fail to recognize the *gravity* and the *opportunity* of the situation."

She paused dramatically. She pouted her lips, took a deep breath, and, feeling that the audience was with her, she continued:

> "We are afraid. Afraid of ideas, afraid of experimenting, afraid of change. We shrink from thinking a problem through to a logical conclusion. We imagine that we want improvement, but we cling desperately to our chains.
>
> The immediate future is going to be tragic for all of us, unless we find a way of making the vast educational resources of this country serve the *true* purpose of education."

She hesitated. She knew what she had to say was harsh. But she also knew it was important.

> "What is principally wrong with the world is that education currently does not include the teaching of the fundamental meaning of modern day society. Simply put, education, as now ordered, does *not* educate."

Some applause passed through the vast audience, mostly from the graduates themselves. Some murmured. Many were surprised with her words.

Annie continued, raising her hand,

> "Children are simply not taught well! They are told about hatchets and cherry-trees and kings from the 9th century—but they are not told what the money in their pockets means! They are not told what armaments mean! They are not told of the rest of the unseen ideas which cause wars and economic depressions!"

The audience applauded, again, led by the graduates themselves. The old woman behind the podium proved to be rather radical, pioneering with her ideas.

> "In our schools the *wrong* things are predominantly stressed—things *remote* from the student's experience and needs!"

She took a deep breath and raised her chin.

> "What we tend to forget is that in every child born into this world there are *latent* capacities for the development of an individual that shall be an *honor* to the human race.
>
> If my pupil, lacking the two senses that are usually considered the most important, has become a writer of ability and a leader among women, why should we not expect the *average* child, possessed of all its faculties, to attain a far higher ability and knowledge than the schools of today develop? What Helen has accomplished without sight and hearing suggests the forces that lie dormant in *every* human being! Many realize that in our education system there is something *radically wrong*. Our system of education obviously does not *educate*."

Silence followed. Annie sensed the silence and knew it to be good. People were truly listening.

> "Every child begins life an eager, active little creature, always doing something, always trying to get something that he wants very much. Even before he can utter a word, he succeeds in making his desires *known* by cries and grimaces. He invents and devises ways to get the things he wants. In his little world he is *always* the star performer, is he not?"

Some people nodded. Annie continued.

"In the child's little world, is he not the star performer? Of course he is: he is the horse, he is the coachman, he is the policeman, he is the robber, he is the car, he is the driver! He will be anything that requires both *initiative* and *action*. The one thing he *never* voluntarily chooses to be is the grown up man that sits and does *nothing*.

Yet what does our educational system do? It spoils this fine enthusiasm! We impose upon the child the role not of the driver, but of the passenger! We give him no opportunities to exercise his *inborn* creative faculties! We give him no opportunities for the joy of creation!

The child is deluged by us with facts and figures! Naturally, he becomes mischievous and difficult to manage! He is compelled to defy his teachers in order to save his soul!"

Annie was astounded by the silence. Was she talking nonsense? She knew her words to be right, she had *experienced* them to be the truth. But was she preaching to the deaf?

Suddenly she heard Dr. Bell in her head—"Finally, Annie."

"Finally?"

"Finally you are speaking. Tell them. Tell them, Annie!"

The thought of Dr. Bell and his constant nudges for her to share her knowledge pained her. Her eyes became moist. She spoke slowly, loud and clear. She could not see anyone in the audience, but she felt like she was feeling everyone as she spoke:

"No. Our schools do *not* educate. Our schools give no encouragement to reflection, observation and the assimilation of knowledge! They *kill* imagination in the bud! They uproot the creative ideals of childhood!"

A few people clapped. But the sound of the faint applause only highlighted the utter silence in the audience. Polly's eyes widened as she kept spelling to Helen. Was Annie going too far, given the audience and the occasion?

Yet Annie continued, undeterred by the faint applause:

"We forget the child! The child! Isn't the fine soul of the child of far greater importance than high marks? Yet our education system causes the pupil to prize high grades *above* actual *knowledge,* and upon graduating school he goes into his life believing always that the *score* is more important than the *game*!

We try to model our children after a pattern we have in our own minds—a wrong pattern! We deny them any right to wills and natures of their own. We impose our wills *upon* them! We reverse the known laws of evolution: we mark out our own path for the child's development and suppress his spontaneous impulses.

Isn't it funny? We read and talk a good deal about *evolution*, but we seem to be unable to fit these ideas into our system of education. Haven't we followed this mechanical method of education for a good many years now already? And with what result? With what result? Our children leave school doomed to go through life unreceptive, lacking initiative!"

The large hall was quiet. Someone coughed. Annie nodded to herself and said,

> "Do not think that I am turning against teachers. On the contrary, teachers are our future. I have never thought I deserved more praise than any other teacher who gives the *best they have* to their pupils. What earnest effort and consummate ingenuity have I seen teachers expend! I have known teachers to renounce more pleasant jobs in order to devote their lives to what may seem to most people monotonous, uninteresting work! I have watched teachers reduce earth, sea and sky and all that in them to benefit children! With Christ-like love and patience they are ever ready to succor the student.
>
> It is not the teacher's fault. We must all reevaluate our notion of education. In Helen's education I was tempted to have her play the part of ignominious passenger. Yet I had to abandon the conventional system of lessons; arithmetic at nine, language at ten and so on. Regular lessons seemed to *benumb* my little pupil's natural impulses and self-educating instincts. Slowly the conviction formed in my mind that it is the child's prerogative to *take the initiative.* Likewise, it is the teacher's duty to *follow* the pupil's adventures and discoveries as intelligently and as sympathetically as she can.
>
> It is a waste of the teacher's time and of the child's energy to make him *read* when he wants to *build* castles with his blocks, or to make him do *arithmetic* when his whole mind is absorbed in the problem of keeping his boat right side up in the water!
>
> The child will learn more if the teacher lets her

expectations go and turns her attention to the student's own interests. You may think that our students will become unruly and turn into savages. But it is the other way around. Whenever I noticed Helen becoming short-tempered in our lesson, I made it a rule to change the lesson at that very moment. I followed Helen's own initiative in the choice of the next lesson.

Not that I was certain of my ways. At first I had many misgivings as to the wisdom of what seemed a... *haphazard* course."

She bit her lips, stopping the tears that suddenly appeared,

"I had periods of profound melancholy when I thought that my pupil's mind was not receiving proper discipline!"

She sniffled and chuckled,

"I was haunted by the fear that because our work was so *pleasant*, there must be something wrong about it!"

She smiled,

"But, as time went on, my fears faded before Helen's joyous activity. All day long she was receptive! Responsive! Happy! Her delight in everything kept us at a high pitch of enthusiasm, and *enthusiasm makes work succeed*!

Slowly, people began to talk about Helen's amazing progress, and to compare her mental development to that of normal children. Here was a little girl, without sight, without hearing, who was learning faster than most children with all their faculties! It began to dawn on me that my method, or lack of method, might have a broader

> application, might be of value to teachers of all children."

She paused. She was amazed by the silence in the large hall. Were people so interested? Could it be?

> "The more I read the more clearly I saw that my work with Helen offered an answer to many concerns of our current education system, at least a partial answer. I realized that the acceptance of my fundamental idea, that the child should be free, would mean a revolution in education; that it went beyond the schoolroom and met the dawn of a new democracy that shall include all men, women and children. We may fear that word: freedom. But only through freedom can individuals develop *self-control*, *self-dependence*, *will power* and *initiative*."

She leaned closer to the microphone and exclaimed:

> "There is no education except self-education!
>
> There is no effective discipline except self-discipline!"

Her thoughts turned to Helen, six years old, fighting her in the garden house. Helen was violent, truly violent, but Annie *trusted* her. She really *trusted* her. She *believed* in her, though both her parents doubted that Annie could turn their daughter into a person that might add value to this world!

> "All that parents and teachers can do for a child is to surround him with right conditions. He will do the rest. Trust him! And the things he will do for himself are the *only* things that really count in his education!"

She took a deep breath. She knew she could not hold the audience's attention for much longer. She had learned this lesson early on. Helen taught her that.

She smiled, knowing her lesson with her 4000 students was about to end.

> "Yes. The hope of the future lies in the right education of the child. And we must all take an active part: parents, siblings, teachers, grandparents. Let us begin now and apply all that we know to awaken and develop our students, who in their souls have the thirst for knowledge and the will to be free.
>
> Our tendency to place restraint upon our children comes but from our ignorance. Every teacher worthy of the title "teacher" knows that she or he obtain the best results through following the interests of the child and his spontaneous response.
>
> In the future new education will permit the child to truly grow. Real impressions and observations will take the place of learning that is restricted only to books. The child's natural desires and idiosyncrasies will be given wise and sympathetic direction.
>
> Education in the light of present-day knowledge and need calls for some *spirited* and *creative* innovations. May I express the hope that Temple University will continue to carry forward the standard of true education. Let us keep in our mind the meaning of true education. Only when one works *purposefully* and *long* on a problem that one is *interested* in—and in hope *and* in despair wrestles with it in silence and alone, relying on one's *own unshaken will*—only then do we achieve true education!"

She bit her lips.

She raised her chin.

She took a deep breath.

> "I am thankful for this honorary degree and for your kindness. No greater honor can be paid to a teacher than the *recognition* of her work. Today has brought me the happiness of knowing that my work is an inspiration to others.
>
> Thank you very much!"

She was surprised by the roaring applause that she heard. Judging from the silence of the audience during her speech, she feared that she had burdened them with her unwise thoughts. But the applause was unmistakable.

President Beury's firm hand met hers, and she shook his hand proudly. "An astounding speech Miss Sullivan!"

She smiled, and was relieved when he escorted her back to the honoree table. She was a little dizzy. She sat down, but the applause did not subside but rather grew in strength. President Beury took her hand again and shouted in her ear, "They can't have enough of you!"

She rose, smiled, nodded several times at all directions, until, to her relief, the applause subsided.

* * *

Later, in the car, she sat in the front seat. Nella was driving, Polly having admitted that she was too tired to drive. Polly and Helen were spelling to each other in the back. The trunk of their Model T Ford was filled with several bouquets of flowers.

Nella kept shaking her head, "What a speech, Annie, what a speech! You left them speechless!"

Annie, who did not like feigned flattery, protested, "No I did not!"

"Yes you did!" Nella insisted, "Now, we must tell your story! You have so much to tell, so much to teach! People must know your story!" She looked at Annie excitedly, "We must share your life's work with everyone!"

"Look at the road Nella," Annie mumbled, "look at the road."

Polly sighed at the back. Annie turned to her, "Tired, Polly?"

Polly exclaimed, "My, it was tiring spelling the whole speech!"

Annie chuckled, "Try to do it for four years in university, in lectures when you don't know how to begin spelling some of the words...."

Polly frowned, "I would have shot somebody!"

Annie murmured, "I almost did. I almost did."

* * *

Nella's enthusiasm did not subside. On the contrary, the more the months passed, the more eager she was to spend time with Annie. She managed to read every article written about Annie and Helen, and carefully read Annie's old letters to the late Mrs. Hopkins. Nella asked interesting, well-educated questions. Annie, though reluctant somewhat, was willing to answer.

One day Helen came to Annie's room in the early evening. "Nella just left," she said to Annie.

"And?"

"She said she has several chapters ready, but some are

missing."

Annie pouted her lips. Not the same old subject again. "I won't speak about my childhood Helen!"

"Why not?" Helen insisted. She tried to master all her patience and compassion.

"Because I said so."

Helen was not taken aback. "If not for Nella, why won't you do it for me?"

Annie sat up and spelled, "Are you trying to make me feel guilty?"

"No, no," Helen spelled back. She was intimidated, unwilling to show any disrespect to the now-wrinkled palm that had been there for her ever since she understood what love was. She spelled slowly, "I read somewhere that when one has painful memories, and one cannot talk about them, it is useful to try and write them in a journal—"

Annie wouldn't have it, "What makes you think I have painful memories?"

"You told me that yourself!" Helen spelled emphatically, "You said that everything before you came to me was but darkness!"

Annie said nothing, pushing Helen's hand away from her.

* * *

Another time Helen tried again, "What was the name of the priest?"

"Which priest?"

"The priest who convinced your parents to send you

to the *Massachusetts School for the Blind?*"

Annie began cursing, "I never told you that!"

"But you said it to others, it was written—"

"Stop pestering me Helen! You have no manners! Leave me alone will you!"

* * *

A few weeks later Polly left them for a two-month vacation to visit her family in Scotland. It was the first time she had left them, but she had been speaking about the vacation for years.

They hired a maid called Maria to come and spend each day at the house, cooking and cleaning. Nella came almost every day to help with the letters and to spend some time with Annie, always writing down what Annie was willing to share in her notepad. But when Nella was gone, the house felt lonely. The new maid Maria cooked well, but she was no Polly Thomson. Both Helen and Annie missed Polly terribly.

One night Annie was unable to fall asleep, her thoughts wandering to many years before.

To her brother.

To Jimmie.

She turned on the light and took her journal. Not much was written in it during those years. She looked at the last entry, bringing the journal very close to her eyes. It was about John. The words brought her pain and loneliness. She quickly flipped to the next page and began writing:

"Jimmie, my little brother."

It seemed as if it had been ages since she allowed

herself to think of him. Though he had always been with her. She continued writing.

> "I never stopped missing him, though it has been over half a century ago. I remember clearly him hugging me in the almshouse."

Memories stirred in her and before she knew it tears filled her eyes. She closed the journal, cursing, "Oh damn you Helen! I will *not* write!"

But after a moment her hand opened the journal again. She wrote, her handwriting not nearly as beautiful as it used to be.

> "Jimmie. My Jimmie! One morning in the almshouse I was helping him to dress and he began to cry."

Annie began sobbing quietly.

When she could write again she continued.

> "The old woman in the next bed in our ward said, "He was bad in the night and kept me awake all night!"
>
> Both Jimmie and I disliked the creature. I answered rudely, I suppose, because she said, "You are both imps of Satan!"
>
> Jimmie turned to her and began to make faces at her and put out his tongue. The toothless old woman made a horrid sound with her lips and said, "The devil will get you for that, sonny!"
>
> It seems to me that Jimmie tried to stand up by his bed but couldn't. He fell backward and screamed terribly. The matron, or someone else, came and took off his clothes. He pointed to the lump on his thigh which seemed larger than I had ever seen it."

Annie let out a cry, closed the journal, and sobbed quietly for a few minutes. She was embarrassed of herself. Embarrassed of crying like that.

She wept for her brother. She wept for herself.

She was happy that at least Polly wasn't in the house, for her cry might have woken her up. Helen, sleeping in the adjacent room, could of course hear nothing. Annie was relieved for the privacy she had. Good thing the maid, Maria, wasn't living with them.

Annie took a deep breath and opened the journal and wrote, tears still drying on her cheeks,

> "Jimmie kept saying over and over, "It hurts, it hurts!"
>
> The next thing I remember is the doctor bending over him. A few minutes later the doctor came to me and put his hand on my shoulder, "Little girl, your brother will be going on a journey soon."
>
> I immediately understood his meaning, more from the sound of his voice than from the words. Death was not foreign to me. I was perfectly familiar with the idea of death. I had seen my mother lying cold and still and strangely white, and I had seen women die in the ward where we were, and then rolled with their beds into the dead house."

Her chin quivered as she thought of the ten-year-old girl she used to be. And of the doctor. Tears streamed again.

> "As the doctor spoke to me, suddenly an indescribable feeling of terror swept over me, as if sharp cruel fingers gripped my heart. The pain made me kick and beat at the doctor like a little child in a rage. He seized my arms roughly and

> threatened to send me out of the ward.
>
> Instantly I controlled myself. I knew that he could take me away from my Jimmie. They had held that club over my head before, and I had always capitulated and surrendered on their terms."

She shook her head and stopped writing. Why was she writing it? Was it any good—could it serve anyone? This would only bring sorrow to any person who might read this! She mused with giving this to Nella to read. No, poor Nella! Why should she suffer as well?

But her hands were drawn to the journal again, she brought it close to her face and wrote:

> "I must have been sound asleep when Jimmie died, for I didn't hear them roll his bed into the dead house. When I woke, it was dark."

She closed the journal and put her hands on her face. The tears kept coming.

She hugged herself, calming down, as if she was a child.

Only a few minutes later was she able to take a deep breath and open the journal again. She did not know what time it was. Nor did she care.

> "It was night, and I looked near me and saw Jimmie's bed was missing. The black, empty space where it had been filled me with wild fear. I couldn't get out of bed, my body shook so violently. I knew the dead house was behind that partition at the end of the ward. I used to play there a lot with Jimmie.
>
> My whole body trembled. I knew that Jimmie was dead. I can't tell how long that terrible trembling lasted; but it must have lessened; for I got up and

ran to the dead house. I lifted the latch and opened the door. Nobody was awake. The sound of the latch started the trembling in me again. It was dark inside. I couldn't see the bed at first. I reached out my hand and touched the iron rail, and clung to it with all my strength until I could balance myself on my feet. Then I crept to the side of the bed—and touched him!"

Annie dropped the pen and began screaming, sobbing uncontrollably.

She got out of bed and walked to the bathroom. She wiped her tears and blew her nose. She dreaded going back to her bedroom, but at the same time felt an urgency of sorts. She hurried back, opened the journal—the keeper of her secrets—and wrote:

"I touched him. Under the sheet I felt the little cold body, and something in me—"

She sobbed as she kept writing,

"And something in me broke.

My screams woke everyone. Someone rushed in and tried to pull me away; but I clutched the little body and held it with all my might. Another person came, and the two separated us. They dragged me back to the ward and tried to put me in bed; but I kicked and scratched and bit them until they dropped me upon the floor, and left me there, a heap of pain beyond words.

After a while the first paroxysm subsided, and I lay quite still. Maggie, the hunchback, hobbled to me, and bent down as far as she could to lift me up; but the effort hurt her so that she groaned. I got up and helped her back to her bed. She made me sit beside her, and she petted me and spoke tender words of comfort to me."

Annie continued to sob as she wrote, her handwriting almost illegible:

> "Maggie petted me and spoke to me softly. Then I knew the relief of passionate tears.
>
> When it was light, I went to the dead house again; but the attendant wouldn't let me in. She told me to dress myself, and said she would let me see Jimmie. I dressed quickly; but when I reached the door, I was sent to the washroom to wash my face and hands. Then I was made to promise that I would behave myself if I was permitted to see Jimmie. I was put in a chair beside the bed, and they lifted the sheet. The light from the half-window fell upon the bed, and five-year-old Jimmie's little white face, framed in dark curls, seemed to lift from the pillow. Before they could stop me, I jumped up and put my arms around him and kissed and kissed and kissed his face—the dearest thing in the world! The only thing I had ever loved!"

She put the pen away, tucked the journal in the drawer, and covered her face with her hands. She wept silently, totally worn out from the effort of writing these words.

Her thoughts went back to that little girl. How lonely. How lonely she was! Not a soul in the world was left. Her mother, her father, and now Jimmie. Jimmie. Her Jimmie.

She cried herself to sleep.

* * *

In the morning Helen came to see her, but Annie

pushed her away.

At noon, seeing that Annie did not wake up, Helen and Maria came to check on her, concerned for her health. Maria asked, "Miss Sullivan, are you well?"

"Leave me alone. I need the sleep."

The maid slowly spelled to Helen.

Helen, frustrated, took Annie's hand, "At least eat!"

"I don't want to eat! Now go away!"

* * *

It was in the late afternoon that Annie finally got out of bed and ate a little, but did not want to speak to Helen.

She went into her room and firmly closed the door. She opened her journal again and wrote:

"Jimmie.

How I loved him.

They put him in a box.

Then men took the box away.

I rushed after them. The doctor stopped me before I reached the gate. He asked if I would like to go to the burying ground. I begged him to let me go, and he led me to the gate. I had never been out of it since the day when Jimmie and I came to the almshouse with my uncle. We followed the men. They carried the wooden box along a narrow path and soon we came to the burying-ground. It was a bare, sandy field. No trees. There was a hole already dug. I saw the mound of sand and the hole beneath it. Quickly the men lowered the coffin into the grave and began shoveling the dirt upon it. When I heard the sound of the gravel falling upon the little wooden box, I could stand no more, I fell in a heap on the sand, and lay there with my face in the ground. The doctor stood near, talking to the men quietly. When their work was finished, they went away, and the doctor said, "Come now, little girl, we must go back to the almshouse."

I didn't want to leave.

One of the men came back with a few flowers in his hand, and the doctor said, "Look, little girl, the kind man has brought you some flowers for your brother's grave." I stood up, took the flowers from the man, and stuck them in the sand.

Then I was willing to let the doctor lead me away. As we walked back to the almshouse the doctor told me that the reason there had been no service at the grave was that the priest was sick.

But I didn't care.

When I got back into the ward, I saw they had put Jimmie's bed back in its place. I sat down between my bed and his empty bed. I believe very few children have ever been so completely left alone in the world as I was. I longed desperately to die."

Annie wept quietly.

The door to the room opened. Annie quickly wiped her eyes and hid her journal. Helen walked inside slowly. She sat on the side of the bed and reached for Annie's hand. Annie gave her Helen hand reluctantly.

Helen was quick to recognize wet hands. "Were you crying?"

Annie said nothing.

"Please, Teacher!" Helen said, choosing her words carefully, "Please let me in. Let me in! What were you thinking about?"

Annie hesitated.

"Please, Teacher!"

Annie sighed. "Is the maid still here?"

Helen spelled, "Yes."

"Will you send her away?"

"It is not yet seven but if you wish I will."

"Please."

Helen got up and found her way to the kitchen.

* * *

A few minutes later Helen returned. "Maria left," Helen said, "we have dinner on the kitchen counter."

Annie nodded.

Helen, hesitantly, began caressing Annie's hand. Annie wanted to pull her hand away so badly, but didn't.

The dog, Dileas, came by and snuck in between them. Annie, always so happy to have him, said, "No, no, now you go away Dileas!"

She got out of the bed slowly, feeling her fatigued body. She tucked the dog in the corner of the room on his pillow and patted him. She went back to the bed, slowly, afraid of what was to come.

Helen reached her hand and they touched. The mere touch of Helen's hand made Annie want to cry. What was *happening* to her? Was she losing her sanity? She was out of explanation for her miserable state.

They sat there for a long moment, silently.

Helen did not want to say anything.

Finally, Annie spelled slowly, "Have I told you about my brother Jimmie?"

Helen nodded, "Yes, but not much. You said it hurt you to think of him. You said," Helen spelled, remembering the few times Annie had mentioned Jimmie, "that he was the light of your life. That you never loved anyone the way you loved him. You once said that he was mischievous, but in a good way. You said you used to play together a lot, and that you would tell him stories. You said he was a great listener, and that he taught you to be a good storyteller."

"I said all that?" Annie spelled.

"Yes. You said he died when you were ten. That he became an angel. I was young when you told me all that. You never wanted me to mention him again, so I never did."

Annie felt tears collecting in her eyes again, "I don't know what is happening to me, Helen. I am becoming all whiney and peevish!"

Helen said nothing.

Annie took a deep breath. "I don't know why, but I've been thinking about him a lot lately. It might be because I might join him soon."

Helen stiffened at once. She hated when Annie spoke this way. She wanted to reprimand her teacher, but was afraid that if she did, her only opportunity to learn about her teacher's inner world would be lost. So she said nothing.

"I was thinking," Annie said, squeezing her eyes tight to stop the tears, "about his last day, and about the funeral."

"Your parents must have been distraught too," Helen spelled, wishing to show her compassion.

Annie snorted. She realized how little Helen knew.

She wanted to tell Helen of the almshouse. But instantly the familiar old fear clutched her heart. She knew that fear very well. She remembered herself leaving the almshouse at age fourteen, thanks to that divine intervention. She was carrying her small bundle, wearing that cheap calico dress which she thought was beautiful. Her friends from the almshouse—if she could call them 'friends'—followed her.

"Be a good girl," said one.

"Mind your teachers," said another.

"Don't tell anyone you came from the poor-house!" said the third. Everyone nodded and repeated that warning.

One of them told her to come and visit, and the rest retorted, "No, never come back here!"

Later, after saying a painful goodbye to Maggie, the carriage driver, Tim, was very clear with his instructions. He helped her into the train, and then neared his face to hers. "Girl, don't ever come back to this place, you hear me? Forget this place and you'll be alright."

Forget this place and you'll be alright.

Forget this place.

Oh, how hard she tried!

"When I was eight, my mother died," Annie spelled to Helen hastily, afraid she'd regret it, "we began moving from place to place. My father, he drank, he wouldn't—couldn't—take care of us. He left me and Jimmie with our uncle and auntie and he disappeared."

"Disappeared?" Helen spelled. She never heard that. She thought he had *died*. Annie told her several contradicting stories. In one of them it was he who took her to the Massachusetts School for the Blind, escorting her and waving goodbye by the many stairs leading to the large columns at the entrance. Annie told her that story. In another she told her how her father died before she had come to the school in a heroic death, trying to save a woman who was about to be run over by a train.

"Yes," Annie spelled, "he was gone."

The words pained Annie terribly. She paused. "My uncle and aunt couldn't take care of us. Me with my eyes, and Jimmie, he was limping."

"I didn't know that," Helen spelled and immediately felt stupid for her comment.

"Yes," Annie spelled, "Jimmie and I were taken to…."

Annie felt a lack of air, her breath disappearing, her chest crushed by the weight of an unknown rock. " We were taken to an almshouse."

She gasped for air, nearly panting, and added, "A state owned house for the poor."

"With your uncle and aunt?"

"No Helen. Just the two of us."

They sat quietly leaning against the bed's headboard.

"A few months later Jimmie was sick," Annie said, wishing to skip all her memories from the wretched creatures who surrounded her for four long defining years. "One day he couldn't stand up. The doctor came.

The following day Jimmie was gone."

Silence followed. Annie was surprised that she was not crying. "They took him and buried him. My father was not there of course, he had gone. I never saw him again."

Helen nodded slowly. She was afraid to move, afraid to make the wrong comment. Annie never told her any of it. An almshouse? Her father leaving her just like that?

"There," Annie said, "I said it."

Helen nodded. Silence followed, and Helen contemplated what to say. She spelled, "I'm sorry."

Annie's response was quick, "I'm sorry too."

Silence.

Helen spelled, "He must have been very dear to you."

Annie smirked, "Dear? Dear?!"

Helen felt stupid for saying that, but Annie kept spelling, "Dear?! He was all I had, Helen! He was my whole—"

Then the tears came.

They came in a flood.

"He was my whole life! I loved him like I loved myself—no—more! He was my little angel! I remember... I remember the morning after he died, he was in the dead house. When they finally let me in, they lifted the sheet, and the light from the window, it was on his face! Like an angel! My little angel! My little Jimmie! My little Jimmie! My... baby brother! His face was white—"

She couldn't spell anymore, and let out the loudest

roar she ever let out. Her throat felt clogged, a huge lump in her throat prevented from her to speak. She sobbed, her chest rising up and down, all the while Helen holding her hand firmly, at a loss of what to say or do to alleviate her teacher from her unspeakable pain.

* * *

Years later Helen would write:

> "Annie never told me about her past. Only in my fifties did I learn the truth about her life in the almshouse.
>
> Nella was writing a book about her, and I was thankful that such a true, discerning friend should undertake the task.
>
> Polly was abroad on her vacation. Annie asked me to tell the maid to leave early. She even tucked her Shetland collie, Dileas, her exquisite "puff from the creamery of Heaven," off in an out-of-the-way corner. We were alone, just her and me, like in the garden house when I was a child.
>
> We sat side by side and she began telling it all. The terrifying drama of her early years began to unfold in my palm. She was 67 years old: handsome, sensitive, distinguished—a teacher known around the world, a personality to whom the great and gifted had paid high tribute in my presence. And there she was, pouring out a tale of a tragic childhood spent among human beings sunk in misery, degradation and disease.
>
> She confided in me. She knew that for many years I had studied the problems of poverty. She trusted me to understand. I put myself in her place: a young girl, half-blind, lonely, living in that hideous environment.

Then she spoke of her brother Jimmie. I nearly went distracted at the dreadful sobbing with which, after the silence of half a century, she spoke of her brother Jimmie's death in the almshouse.

That night I could not sleep, so keen was the anguish in my soul! I kept dwelling on Annie's love for her brother until I felt it as my own. It seemed to comfort her that both our hearts held his image in equal tenderness.

Only then I understood the desolating memories that had rendered it painful for her to discuss her past. Only then I realized why she always feared speaking of it with anyone.

Another consequence of Annie's narrative was that it gave me a sense of equilibrium. Previously, not knowing much about that part of her life, I had occasionally felt alone and bewildered by some of her peculiarities. Not for the world would I have invaded the secrecy that shrouded her past. Nevertheless, the strangeness was there; something too subtle for words was lacking in our relations to each other.

But after her brave, overburdened soul lay bare before my inner sight, I was conscious of courage of a new quality flowing into me from the fact of Teacher's crossing that awful desert of neglect, becoming the beloved teacher she was to me. As she had dedicated herself to Jimmie in her childhood—especially in those few months in the almshouse—so she devoted herself to me from the young age of 20. She devoted her entire life to me."

* * *

The floodgates were finally open. Annie spoke and cried, cried and spoke. First to Helen, then to Nella, and then to Polly when she returned rejuvenated from Scotland. She spoke and spoke and spoke. Decades of hiding, of shame, of guilt, of fear of exposure—all shed themselves in front of her closest friends, her life companions.

A year later, and after much trepidation, Nella came over with the printed manuscript entitled, *Anne Sullivan Macy: The Story Behind Helen Keller.*

They all sat in the living room, Annie lying on the sofa. It was ten in the morning, and they were all very excited. Nella has been working on the book intensely. Finally, she could read them the result.

Nella opened the thick pile of papers. She revered Annie and wished for the old lady's approval of her delicate work. The thirty-year-old looked at the three older ladies, adjusted her round glasses, and read:

"INTRODUCTION."

She gazed at Annie. She continued reading:

> "Allow me to begin with an anecdote. Mrs. Annie Sullivan Macy and her lifelong student Miss Helen Keller were rarely ever separated. Yet in one of the few times they were apart, Keller wrote her teacher an interesting note:
>
> 'You told me once in a moment of deep sorrow that you thought you would write the story of your life, for it might help to clear up misunderstandings that would otherwise follow you to the grave. I feel sure that if you write this book I shall know you deeply for the first time.'"

Nella looked up. Annie was nodding slowly. Polly

was spelling into Helen's hand. Helen grinned happily and nodded.

Nella looked down at the manuscript and read:

> "Keller went on to write to her teacher, 'That seems a strange thing for me to say, that I shall know you deeply for the first time. After all, we have lived so close to each other during thirty years, but so it is. I have always known that there are chapters in the book of your personality which remain sealed to me.'"

Annie gasped, turned to Helen and grabbed her other hand, "You wrote that to me?"

Helen grinned and nodded.

Annie looked surprised. She waved for Nella to go on.

Nella continued,

> "Mrs. Sullivan never wrote that book. Personally, I find it an irreparable loss to the world that she did not write it while she still had sight enough for the task."

Annie muttered, "'Irreparable loss to the world!' Please, Nella!"

Nella blushed. But Helen, having Polly just translated to her Annie's comment, shouted, "Teacher! Leave Nella alone and let her read!"

Polly smiled, amused. Nella smiled apologetically and waited for Annie's approval. Annie frowned and gestured for Nella to continue, but still quietly mumbled to herself, "'Irreparable loss to the world!' Ah!"

Nella waited a moment and then continued,

> "There are many reasons why Mrs. Macy did not write that book. In the first place, her sight has never been good, and all the sight she has *had* she has given to Helen."

Nella waited for reproach, but Annie said nothing. The silence was her approval. Nella continued,

> "In the second place, she has spent her life since the age of fourteen trying to forget what happened up to that time."

Annie gulped. She felt the nervousness building within her. Should she have not talked to Nella so openly about all that had happened? She wet her lips and whispered, "Go on."

Nella nodded,

> "Though she had tried forgetting all her past, she could not. But she has never *willingly* dwelt upon those harrowing years. When people have come asking for the story of her life (and during the years many have come) she has referred them to Helen. Helen, in her opinion, is all the biography, all the monument she needs or desires."

Annie nodded approvingly. She liked Nella's style. Not melodramatic, but sincere. Above all, she appreciated Nella's yearning for the truth. In that way she reminded her of herself, fighting for the truth to be told, as she so often fought for when she was younger.

Nella continued,

> "During the last few years Mrs. Macy and I used to spend long hours together in their house in Forest Hills, New York. We talked of everything—Shakespeare and Bacon—"

Annie smiled.

> "—the lecture tours, the Keller family, Hollywood, vaudeville, and Helen. On the days when I was adroit we talked about Mrs. Macy *herself*, and it was on one of these that she told for the first time the story of her years in an almshouse. Even Helen had only heard it herself a few days earlier.
>
> Mrs. Macy had hoped that this record would never be written, but long before I knew her, friends of hers had told her that, with or without her consent, the story would be told some day, perhaps after her death. What she had done was too significant to pass unnoticed, however modest her own estimate of it might be."

Annie's eyes watered. She said nothing, not wanting to attract attention to herself.

Nella went on,

> "Anne Sullivan Macy had dedicated her life wholly to one person, and she has been content to remain in the shadow of that person. The one bright thing in her life, as she sees it, is Helen. But this book, as I have had to remind myself a thousand times in writing it, is *not* a book about Helen. Her story has already been told, incomparably, by herself and others. It is time now to talk about her teacher.
>
> Nella Braddy, Long Island, July 1933."

Nella took a deep breath and glanced at Annie.

Annie nodded. Helen sat eagerly. Polly smiled reassuringly at Nella.

Nella began:

> "CHAPTER 1
>
> Out of the vagueness that enwraps the beginnings of Annie Sullivan the following are the first words

that she can remember: 'She would be so pretty if it were not for her eyes!'"

Annie exclaimed, waving her hand around her eyes as if to dry them, "My, Nella, you are not going to make me bawl here on the very first sentence are you?!"

Polly smiled compassionately. Nella did not know what to say. Annie mumbled, "Well, go on!"

Nella continued, reading rather quietly,

"There has never been a time since, that, sooner or later, no matter what was said of her, the dreadful thought was not added. What might she have done, what might she have been—but for her eyes. These eyes were good when she was born, and it was not her fault, nor truly anybody's fault, that they did not remain good. She was but a small atom tossing on the edge of a great movement, and it was inherent in the movement that such things should happen.

Her father and mother had come from Limerick, Ireland, just seventeen or eighteen years after the Great Famine of 1847 which set in motion one of the most extensive migratory movements known to human history.

Annie's mother, Alice, was two years old when the famine came. Annie's father, Thomas, was perhaps a little older. They had both been brought up on stories of starving children clinging to mothers already dead, of men in their madness eating grass by the roadside, of cholera on transport ships, and other horrors too lurid and too terrible to be set down in print."

Annie tut-tutted, shaking her head from side to side. "This *whole* story is too terrible to be set down in print.

Can't you, Nella, just begin with me meeting Helen?"

Nella smiled. Helen, a moment later, said, "Please, go on, Nella."

Nella continued:

> "Thomas and Alice, like most of their countrymen who sought the United States during the years which followed the famine, brought nothing with them—they had nothing to bring. They were both Roman Catholics, and neither had ever been to school; neither could read or write, and neither had been trained to do skillful labor of any sort, in all of which they were no worse off than thousands of their companions, most of whom were to make their livings on farms belonging to better-off American families.
>
> Most of the refugees from Ireland during this period stayed somewhere near the Atlantic coast, dropped there, as one writer put it, "like tired migratory birds." Thomas got work almost immediately in Agawam, Massachusetts—and he and Alice went to live there, where, on April 14, 1866, a child was born by the name of Johanna, or Annie as her parents called her.
>
> The 21-year-old mother, Alice, must have been lonely before Annie came. She was a little more than a girl herself, and she was in a strange country. What relatives she had, and we are not sure of any, were in Ireland. She had tuberculosis, and to add to that, one day she fell against the stove, the stove plunged forward, and she never was able to walk again except on crutches. Thomas had trouble coping with the new difficulties. He was a rough-and-ready out-of-door Irishman who knew only one way to handle

trouble, and that was to drown it."

Annie took a deep breath.

Nella continued.

> "Alice was hobbling about on her crutches now, and was no longer able to take care of a home. She was ill and lame, and there was a child coming. In Annie's memories there is always a child coming. First came Ellen. Then came Jimmie—"

Helen articulated, "I never heard of Ellen."

Annie sighed and said nothing. Her own memories of Ellen were scant. She signaled for Nella to go on.

> "...Then came Jimmie, who had a tubercular hip. Neighbors helped wash clothes and clean the house and cook meals, but they came irregularly.
>
> Little Ellen died of a malignant fever; but all the rest of Annie's life was affected by it, for it was in the midst of it and because of it that she developed that destructive granular inflammation of the eyes known as trachoma. This happened so early that her first conscious memory is the one of which we have spoken; "She would be so pretty if it were not for her eyes," spoken by the wife of the farm owner.
>
> Annie was round and chubby and pink like a cherub, with abundant dark hair like her mother's, and luminous blue eyes—only the eyes were clouded. Her mother was distressed about the eyes. A neighbor advised her, "Wash them in geranium water." And Annie can still see her mother's long thin fingers plucking the geranium leaves. There was not much that the mother could do. Doctors were expensive.

It was not only Annie's eyes that distressed her mother. Annie was not then, nor ever after, what might be called a 'good child,' nor, as many people were to learn, easy to manage. She was blindly and passionately rebellious in the way a child is so likely to be who is surrounded by unhappiness too big for him to handle. No one ever tried to understand her, and the only way her father ever tried to control her was by beating her. This brutal treatment—the beatings were so severe that her mother used to help her hide—might have cowed a different person, but not Annie. The indomitable woman whom the world was later to know was an indomitable child."

Annie wept. Polly and Nella looked at her. She waved her hand for Nella to continue.

"She herself can remember some of her tantrums. Once when her mother left her to look after a loaf of bread which she had put in the oven she burned her hand and dashed to the floor and ruined the bread. Across the years Annie can still hear her mother's voice crying, "Annie, Annie, Annie!" Bread was precious then.

Once in anger she rocked her little sister clear out of her cradle and gave her a cruel scar on the forehead. She got one of her father's whippings in return, but the whippings did not seem to do much good.

Once, on a winter afternoon, a wealthy neighbor came with her little girl in white shoes and white mittens, soft like little rabbits. The neighbor brought Annie a gift, red mittens. Yet Annie intensely wanted the white mittens which the girl wore. "Aren't they pretty, Annie?" her mother asked about the red mittens. "No, I don't want them," she cried. Rage took possession of her, and she threw them into the fire. "What a terrible child!" the neighbor said, with conviction as she hurried to take her girl and leave, "What a terrible, terrible child!"

It was somewhat in the same spirit that she threw whatever she could lay hand on at the small mirror her father used for shaving, and the mirror smashed. "You little devil!" her father shouted. She had been called 'a little devil' before, but always until then in *anger*, not in *fear*. "You little devil! Look what you've brought to this house! Bad luck! Bad luck for seven years!"

The sequence to these memories is uncertain, but bad luck did follow. Ellen, the second little girl, died in May, 1873. Two babies were born a year after year: Mary and Johnny. Mary died several years later while with her adopted family."

Annie mumbled, "Yes? How do you know that Nella?" The thought of her baby sister which was given to some relatives haunted her again and again over the years.

"The Agawam church records and city records show that," Nella whispered.

Annie was quiet. "How old was she?"

Nella closed her eyes, "I believe she was nine."

Annie nodded and took a deep breath, "I was then at the School for the Blind."

Nella nodded.

Silence followed. Eventually Annie said, "Go on, please."

Nella dreaded reading the following paragraph.

"Johnny, however, was not as lucky. His hold on life was so faint that he died two months after his birth. Thomas carried the coffin away on his knees, and Annie was glad to see it go: the baby had spent most of his two months crying: it was a relief for her to be rid of him.

Then came her mother's turn. Alice's sickness—"

"Enough, enough!" cried Annie. "I can't take it anymore!"

Silence followed. No one knew what to say.

Then Annie whispered, "Polly, could you please fix me a drink?"

Polly nodded and said, "I'll fix some for us all, I think we could all use some."

* * *

They read into the afternoon, and kept reading into the evening. They stopped to eat dinner, and then Nella continued reading to them into the night. It was only at four in the morning that they finished reading the book. Nella, in her diary, noted:

"I read the book aloud for Annie, Helen and Polly for eighteen hours—stopping only once for cocktails and once for dinner! We also stopped several times to weep."

* * *

The nearer the time came for the publication of the book the more fearful Annie became. She tried to dissuade Nella from publishing it, but Nella kept referring Annie to Helen, who adamantly insisted on its publication.

A month before the publication Annie cried to Helen, "We must get away! I don't want to be here when it is published."

"Where do you want us to go? To my sister in Alabama?"

"No, no, that's too close! They'll find us there!"

Helen wondered who were "they" who were to "find them." But she said nothing. "Do you want to go to Dr. Bell's daughters in Canada? They'll be happy to have us for some time."

"No, no! I want to go far, *far* away. Let us go to Scotland, to visit Polly's family!"

"But I don't know if they'll have us—"

"Sure they'll have us, you are Helen Keller for God's sake! And they'll be glad to see Polly again!"

Helen was not sure. "What about the University of Rochester, they invited you to receive an honorary Ph.D. in three months and—"

"I don't need these foolish honors Helen!" Annie cried. "Please, Helen, let us go to Scotland. We can stop in Ireland as well! We can search for my family's roots there! Please, Helen, please, for me...."

* * *

Things were arranged, and a week prior to the publication of the book they set sail to Europe. After two weeks at sea they arrived in Ireland.

Years later Helen would write several pages about their journey:

"Annie, Polly, and I took passage for Ireland. Our ship was called the Bally Cotton. Pleasantly I recall our talks with the crew, especially one member who bestowed such thoughtful care on the animals aboard. Annie was impressed by his refinement and his high intelligence concerning not only British politics but also social problems all over the world.

I confess I was worried at the thought of visiting Ireland where we were to try to find traces of Annie's parents. I had read of great beauty in parts of the country, and gratitude had overflowed my heart to Ireland for her daughter who had transformed my life from hunger and thirst to joy and the fulfillment of desire. On our way Annie tenderly spoke to me of her dreams about Ireland which she had since she was a child.

But Annie's distress over the seemingly hopeless poverty that had weighed upon the land for ages was duplicated in my soul. As she dictated to me afterwards, she shrank from "the rusty black shawls of the women, the lagging feet of the men, the gaunt sides of the poor little somber donkeys, the sun which came into Ireland timidly, as if unwilling to look on so much woe." She hated the grim rocks on the hillsides, the bogs from which the people had dragged out peat for their fires, and the wretched aspect of County Clare.

Teacher even began hating England, in spite of herself. Usually she sympathized equally with all the hard-pressed races of mankind. But after visiting Ireland she took to the Irish notion that England was guilty of much of its sorrow. She knew that Ireland's economic woes were not fundamentally different from those of other parts of the world, but just then she was torn by atavistic instincts. She kept saying that no one need tell her she was unreasonable with her hatred toward England, she knew it, but she was held fast as if in a nightmare. She was no longer herself and I was glad when we waved good-by to Ireland and continued to Scotland.

It was in Scotland when the book arrived. All of us read it once again, Polly reading out loud and spelling to me at the same time. This time, however, we were not in New York, but around a warm fire in an old Scottish farmhouse. The fire burned out as we talked far into the night.

Scotland caressed Teacher's spirit as a brooding bird gathers her fledglings beneath her wings. I believe the reason why she found life in Scotland so sweet was her discovery that she was in a warm, kindly world. Many of Polly's friends and siblings came to see us at the farmhouse we were given by Polly's brother, and their sincerity, their responsiveness, their genuine kindness and hospitality were precious to her.

One must understand that for many years Annie Sullivan Macy had been constantly *alert*, *strained*, *on guard*, and it was a comfort for her to relax under the touch of their discerning sympathy.

Though she has been sick for most of the journey, in Scotland she began speaking to me of the life rising up in us which tends to renew itself without us, heals its own injuries, puts hope into our hearts, sharpens our mental vision—"and why cannot all this happen to me as it has done so often?" she said.

She threw herself into lavish entertainment and gaiety. Polly's family visited us often. Dr. and Mrs.

Love, Mr. Eagar, and others spent several days with us. Friends from Inverness, Muir of Ord, and other places all round were always doing something beautiful for us or cheering Annie and imparting to her an affectionate appreciation. It is seldom that I have witnessed such active balm of love. Annie's goodness to the farmers was immense, as it always had been to the lowly, and their rugged but warmhearted hospitality is gratifying for me to remember.

Every morning I stepped out into the garden, and sometimes Teacher walked with me to share the finger-glimpses I caught of the beds of forget-me-nots and anemones, which her ailing eyes could see only dimly. The fascination of Scotland overflowed Annie like a tide, and I shared her feeling that there was no country more captivating, peaceful, or more abundant in sanative influences. That time she was able to be idle and serene in the quiet of the Highlands. She loved to listen to the birds, and she threw out crumbs as they crowded about the door. She renewed her delight in the heather, and in her mind she could picture the splendor of hills and streams which the curtain closing upon her eyes hid from her. Her joy was too great for words in the lanes of silvery birches, rowan trees, whistling larches, and blossoming hawthorn.

However as winter came I realized that Teacher's health was far from improved. I therefore obtained a leave of absence—a sabbatical year—from the *American Foundation for the Blind*. I was determined to leave nothing undone so that Annie might get well. We enjoyed the old farmhouse and if the phrase were not misleading, I should say that I was like a galley slave just released. As a matter of fact I had not had a real vacation since my college days. I had dedicated myself gladly to the activities of the Foundation, but a heavy toll had been exacted from my vitality as well as from Annie's by the myriad of literary work, lectures and interviews, and the uneasy thought of her eyes and health had pursued me for years.

It therefore seemed like a fairy tale when the Foundation sent word permitting us to rest for a year. Then for some days I just lay quietly for hours in the house. I succeeded in gaining an inundation of calm that refreshed my tired brain and to some extent smoothed out my nerves.

But as winter deepened, Annie experienced the beginning of a distressful invalidism. We went to Glasgow at Christmas time and stayed a few weeks, where Annie could receive excellent medical attention. But fate thwarted all efforts to relieve her, and we went back to the old farmhouse in low spirits. She suffered from carbuncles for a year, and Polly, who also deserved a long rest, was constantly nursing her, reading to her, keeping house, and running after my Shetland collie, Dileas, and Maida, the Lakeland terrier, who was always hunting hares or rabbits. After their wild jaunts the two rogues would return, jump on Annie's bed, and share her meals. Dileas, brown with a white collar, white paws, and an adorable pompon brushing the ground, and Maida, black with a funny smoke-blue head and loving, bright eyes, were a comfort without which Annie declared she could not have dragged through the winter.

In the early spring Teacher was able to take a few steps with me among the violets, harebells, and daffy-down-dillies which she touched just as I did, and she spelled to me, "What a blessing it is for us, Helen, to walk through our Gethsemane and feel its abundant blossoming!"

During those intervals of convalescence she invited Polly's family to our house, and the sunshine of their geniality and the comfortable dew of their understanding sped golden hours for us all. But there was in my heart an inescapable foreboding of what was to come."

* * *

Annie grudgingly returned to America with Polly and Helen the following summer. She was not well. She was 68 and had all kinds of illnesses at once. Bronchitis. Influenza. Then her arthritis bothered her. And, of course, her eyes.

New York flooded them with the usual correspondence and visitations. Annie was morose, ever so morose.

One day she called for Helen in the evening. "I want to dictate a letter to Lenore."

Helen nodded, and helped Annie to walk slowly and follow her down the stairs to Helen's study. As they walked, Annie spelled to her, "Look at who is helping who now."

Helen caressed her teacher's hand.

* * *

"Dear Lenore,

I know I haven't written to you in years, but I do wish to thank you for our lifelong friendship. I am now old and infinitely sickened of many things. I've come to the period of my life when I prefer the pleasure of reflection to the fatigue of action. I've become reminiscent and resigned."

Helen added four question marks in brackets, signing them "H.K."

Annie took Helen's hand from the typewriter and spelled, "What are you doing?"

"Nothing!"

"Don't think me a fool, Helen, you are editing my letter!"

Helen laughed with glee and said, "I'm just improving it!"

Annie shook her head disapprovingly and spelled, "Write what I tell you!"

"I am dictating this letter to Helen. She is laughing in her sleeve at me."

Helen added in brackets,

"(no I'm not! H.K.)"

Annie continued spelling,

"Helen's cheerful attitude is tiring and burdening. She is also alarmingly healthy. The food, drink, and cold weather in Scotland had made me ill, but Helen has insides made of cast iron fastened down with hoops of steel, leaving her as healthy as a bull."

Helen inserted parenthesis,

"(It was Annie's own fault that she got sick, she insisted on drinking unboiled water! H.K.)"

Annie kept spelling,

"In a few months Helen and Polly are to speak in Boston at Symphony Hall. I don't know whether I shall go or not. I am almost blind now. I feel old and helpless. Otherwise I might visit. I do so want to see you and the family. Perhaps, if I ever make up my mind to have another eye surgery, and the operation is a success, I may feel different. At present I only long to die out of my difficulties, but with Helen's indignation even this isn't permitted!"

Annie smirked at herself and waited for Helen to insert her remarks. She did not. Annie continued spelling,

"I wish I could believe that we suffer into a better world, but I don't. I often doubt if life is worth the suffering. Maybe this is an illusion, as so many other things are—maybe all things. Perhaps the only peace is in yielding up one's will. But no. This kind of victory doesn't appeal to me. You know me all too well to know that.

Please send the children my love. I do hope we shall meet again.

Yours,

Annie."

Helen did not like the tone of the letter.

Similarly, she did not like when a few weeks later Annie called her to her bed. "I want you to help me with something important."

"What?"

"Could you bring your typewriter in here?"

Helen nodded. She returned carrying the heavy typewriter and placed it on the small desk that Annie rarely used. She reached her hand backward to Annie.

Annie spelled, "Type: Anne Sullivan Macy—Last Will and Testament."

Helen's hand shook. She turned to Annie, not knowing what to say. Annie spelled back, "Please. Please. I did not want to ask Polly. Please."

Helen nodded, her chin suddenly quivering.

Annie took a deep breath. "My portion of the house in Forest Hills," she spelled slowly, "I give and bequeath to my beloved friend and pupil, Helen Keller."

Helen typed the sentence slowly, breathing in as tears began streaming down her cheeks. She noted how her teacher spelled, "friend and pupil" and not "pupil and friend." This little change touched her beyond words. She contemplated the words, "My beloved friend and pupil."

Annie took her hand and spelled, "The trust fund which was set up for me by the late Dr. Bell, I give and bequeath to my dear Polly, in consideration of her great services to Helen Keller and myself during many years."

Helen typed slowly, then reached her hand again.

"My pearl necklace and my personal documents to Nella."

Helen nodded and typed.

Annie sighed, "Finally, my other necklaces and other pieces of jewelry I bequeath to Mildred Keller and to her two daughters."

Helen typed and cried.

Then Annie said, "That's it. Come now and let me hug you."

They hugged in Annie's bed for a long time. Helen felt the frail arms of her once strong and mighty teacher. Helen's pain was unbearable.

* * *

Yet Annie managed to hang on. Another year passed. Annie's sight was gone completely. She insisted on having an eye operation. The doctors advised otherwise. Annie cried and begged, and finally one doctor was willing to perform the operation, explaining to the stubborn 69-year-old that the situation would most likely not improve. She cried to him, "I'm already blind, it can't get any worse than that!"

The doctor operated on her one remaining functioning eye.

Unfortunately, the doctor was correct in his prediction.

* * *

She was brought back home from the hospital, quieter than ever. She did not speak much, and spent all of her days in bed. When Helen's birthday came, they spent it all in Annie's room. Helen later wrote:

> "We spent my birthday in her room, and the cheerful face I wore hid a presentiment that it would be my last birthday with her. She told me

that she would have to take strenuous measures—to put herself into a different frame of mind to continue living somehow.

Her words, however, did not deceive me. I knew that she had begun to die. Instinct told me that as soon as she realized she would never see again, she would lose interest in living. She was a silent woman now, and passionately as I yearned to communicate with her, I was checked by an indefinable fear of breaking open the door she had closed."

* * *

One day Annie surprised Helen and Polly when she came downstairs, gripping firmly to the railing, "I want to be with the two of you."

Polly helped her to the sofa, where she lay like the good old days. She listened to them as they spoke excitedly about a visitor who came the day before, from Japan. Polly said to Annie, "Mr. Takeo wants Helen to come to Japan and educate the government about incorporating blind and deaf people in the workforce!"

Annie was excited, spelling to Helen while she spoke to Polly, "You *must* go to Japan!"

Helen smiled and spoke, "Hopefully, one day, Teacher."

Annie pressed on, spelling adamantly, "Promise me that after I am gone you and Polly will be light-bringers to the handicapped of Japan!"

Helen mumbled something and spelled, "We will try, Teacher."

In the afternoon Nella came to visit. Annie kissed and hugged her, which surprised Nella, as Annie was often distant and more inhibited than Helen and Polly. But Annie spoke with gayety, "How is the book faring, Nella?"

"It is selling very well, Annie, I receive requests for interviews with you all the time!"

Annie chuckled, "Ask them all where they were forty years ago!"

Nella tried to smile, but she was taken aback by Annie's frail body. Annie looked extremely weak.

Nella helped Polly go over the piles of letters. These days letters came from around the world, and their quantity amazed both Helen and Polly. Polly and Nella divided the dozens of letters between them. Each person first read the letter to herself, then summarized it to Helen and answered her questions. This way no time was wasted, as Nella and Polly took turns reading each letter to Helen and then taking her instructions. Annie was proud sensing the scene about her. Her pupil was giving orders.

Then Nella gasped at one of the letters, "This is so sad!"

Annie turned her head to her, "What is?"

"There is a baby girl," Nella said while spelling to Helen, "deaf-blind, who was abandoned in a hospital in Louisville...."

"In Kentucky?" Annie asked.

"Yes," Nella said. "The head of the maternity ward is asking her for recommendation for a suitable institution for her."

Annie exclaimed, "Let her come here!"

Polly rolled her eyes as she spelled to Helen, amused, "Annie wants the baby! God help us!"

Silence followed. No one knew whether Annie was serious or not. Annie was frustrated she couldn't see their faces, "What? We can have that baby!"

Helen put her hand on Annie's, "That is so kind of you, Teacher. But I will refer them to the Foundation, we can find a suitable family—"

"I want that baby!" Annie shouted. Silence followed.

"Yes," Annie said, "you might think me mad, but who else can take care of that baby? With the three of us, and with your help, Nella, we can save that poor baby girl!"

Annie's eyes began to water, "We can save that little girl! We can save her I'm telling you!"

Helen was afraid of Annie becoming too excited in her frail physical state. "Teacher," she spelled, "why won't you rest a little…."

"You are not listening to me!" Annie spelled vehemently as she shouted, "I am serious! I can teach her! We can put her cradle in my room, we can all take care of her together!"

Polly, wishing to dissuade the conversation, said while spelling to Helen, "Annie, that is a good idea!"

Nella turned to Polly with bewilderment, and so did Helen. Polly continued, "I shall write to that hospital right now."

"Oh please, Polly," Annie cried, "please do!"

* * *

The following days, to everyone's surprise, Annie kept mentioning the baby and all the things they could do with her.

Helen's heart sank.

* * *

Years later Helen wrote:

> "One day we read of a neglected deaf and blind baby, who was in Louisville, Kentucky. The thought of imparting light and the music of joy to the little one went through Annie as if the flame of immortal youth had entered her tired body. It was only after many an unwilling argument that we who knew of her failing health induced her to give up the idea of adopting the baby. But her darkness throbbed with the hidden fire of that longing, and she would often remind me of all the deaf and blind children throughout the world waiting for deliverance. "Hold out your arms to them, Helen, forget yourself in them! Be faithful to their cause! There may be a wall between you and them, but hammer it down, stone by stone, even if you are broken by the effort. That, Helen, will be your true memorial to me."

* * *

Annie's deterioration was difficult to watch.

> "One day Teacher tried coming downstairs, and once she reached the bottom floor she became dizzy and collapsed. We half carried and half led her back to her room upstairs and put her to bed. She cried to me, sobbing, "I am trying so hard to live for you!"

With Promethean will she fought back pain and lassitude so that she might give whatever assistance any part of my work needed, in counsel or suggestion. Although the oil of light was low in her tired body, the flame of her inner life was burning clearer and higher.

But next day she was taken to the hospital in an ambulance. In the hospital Annie was carefully examined, and the doctors and nurses were most kind to her. She remained there for a month. One day after my daily visit she said, "The doctors and nurses are so good to me here."

I said to her that I was so pleased to hear it.

She nodded and whispered, "Helen, lying here in the hospital I feel that I am at the Feet of God."

After a month, when all that was possible had been done for her, we accompanied her home.

In the days that followed it seemed as if my heart would stop beating. Teacher would shift from mood to mood. She would yield to despair and much of the time did not seem to care that Polly and I were full of anguish. She kept talking to me about the Angel of Death coming for her soon and we should have everything in order at his arrival. Then, regardless of what she had just said, she would ask about my work and what good news I heard from my appeal letters for the Foundation."

* * *

She enjoyed being back with her dogs. Helen and Polly came to her room many times a day. Nella did too. Even Lenore came to visit from Boston. On Helen's request even her sister, 50-year-old Mildred, came from Alabama. Annie was not very talkative, however.

She spent her days in bed, in darkness, caressing her dogs, pouting her lips, as if waiting for something.

One day they summoned Maria, the old housemaid, to help Polly, who was exhausted taking care of both Annie and the house.

Upon hearing Maria's voice in the room Annie began screaming for Polly.

Helen recalled:

> "We invited old Maria to relieve Polly, and Annie somehow got the impression that this meant that Polly was going to leave us. She jumped out of bed and staggered pitifully after Polly crying, "Polly, oh, Polly, don't go!"
>
> Polly caressed her and coaxed her back to bed saying, "I am only going downstairs to get you a cup of tea!"
>
> Turning to me, Annie spelled, "Will you two come with me to Scotland next spring? I should be at peace there! I felt that lovely land was cuddling down in me, Helen. Will you two take me there next spring?"
>
> I promised.
>
> My last memory of Teacher as I knew her was an evening when she was fully awake. For some reason she insisted on coming downstairs. We tried to convince her not to, but she insisted. Nella and Polly helped her downstairs.
>
> We sat and we spoke like in the good old times. Annie was laughing while Nella told her about the rodeo she had just been to. Polly was tired, and it

was Annie who spelled to me all of what Nella was saying. She spelled to me the entire story. How tenderly she fondled my hand!

Her dearness was without limit, and it was almost intolerable. Beautiful was her touch—the creative flame from which sprang the joy of communication and the power love, binding me forever to her."

* * *

"Polly," Annie whispered, "Polly!"

It was night. Polly rushed to Annie's room. "What's wrong?"

Annie murmured, "Nothing. I was just lonely. Is Helen asleep?"

"Yes, do you want me to wake her up?"

"No…. Let my baby sleep."

Polly sat on the edge of the bed.

Annie smiled. She inhaled deeply which hurt her ribcage. Her face twisted with pain. "Oh Polly," she whispered, "we've been together for so many years"

Polly smiled, "Twenty."

"Twenty years?! Oh my… where has all the time gone by?"

Polly smiled and put her hand on Annie's thin hand.

Annie mumbled, "Twenty years! Oh my…."

She dozed into sleep.

When she woke up she moved her hands around, "I cannot see! I cannot see!"

Polly, who was half asleep in the chair next to Annie's bed, said, "Shhh, I'm here."

"Mama?" Annie asked.

Polly's eyes filled with tears. She wondered what to say. "Shhh," she said, "I'm right here."

Annie fell asleep again.

* * *

In the morning Polly phoned Nella and asked her to come and help. Helen was beside herself, pacing around the house, unable to sit still. They were all taking turns by Annie's bedside.

In the early evening Annie woke up and said, "Water."

Polly quickly handed her a cup. She helped her drink.

"Tell Helen," Annie whispered.

"Wait," Polly said, "I'll call her, she told me to—"

"No," Annie said, "let her rest. Tell her that I love her."

Polly nodded. She rarely cried, but now she could not help it. She sniffled, "I will tell her."

"Oh…" Annie said, "I'm so tired."

She fell asleep again.

* * *

She woke up in the middle of the night. "Polly?"

Polly, drowsy, cleared her throat, "I'm right here."

"Could you," Annie whispered, "write for me?"

Polly nodded, turned the small light lamp on and said, opened the drawer and took out paper and a pen. "I am writing Annie."

Annie nodded. She said nothing.

Polly, thinking Annie had not heard, said, "I am writing."

Annie nodded, "I heard you."

She breathed heavily. "I wanted," Annie whispered ever so quietly, "I wanted…."

"You wanted?" Polly asked and neared her ear to Annie's mouth.

"I wanted… to be… loved."

Polly nodded, "You wanted to be *loved*?"

"Yes," Annie whispered. "Are you writing?"

Polly, having forgotten about the paper in her hand, said, "Of course." She wrote down:

"I wanted to be loved."

Annie's chin quivered. She closed her eyes with pain.

Polly, troubled, said, "Perhaps you should rest now Annie."

"No. Write down. I wanted to be loved. I was lonesome. Then… then…" she choked with tears. She swallowed, "Then Helen came… into my life. I wanted… her… to love me… and I loved her."

Polly nodded and wrote it down.

"Then," Annie whispered, "you came, Polly, and I loved you. And we were always so happy together."

Polly nodded.

Annie coughed. It was difficult for her to speak. She continued, "My Polly! My Helen!"

She began weeping.

Polly said nothing, choked with her own tears. She took Annie's hand and held it firmly.

Annie said, "Dear children, may we all... meet together... in heaven...."

Polly wrote it down.

Annie fell asleep. Polly, sensing the moment was of importance, went and woke Helen up. Helen sprung up as if anticipating Polly's hand the whole night.

Polly returned quickly to the room. Annie was alarmingly quiet. Polly brought her ear to Annie's face, and was relieved to hear that she was still breathing. Helen rushed in. Polly spelled to her all that Annie said. Helen cried and put her hand on Annie's hand.

The touch must have woken Annie up. She mumbled, "John? John is that you?"

Helen spelled to her, "It is me, Helen."

"Oh...." Annie said slowly, not bothering to spell back.

She fell into delirium, mumbling out of sleep, "John, John...."

* * *

Two hours later she woke up. It was four in the morning. She exclaimed: "Good-bye John Macy, I'll soon be with you! Good-bye! I loved you!"

Polly and Helen tried soothing her. She fell asleep

again.

* * *

In the morning they were all exhausted. Annie woke up and asked for water. Polly gave her a drink and then brought a little porridge to her mouth. Annie refused to take it, pushing the spoon away, "Don't take him away from me!"

"Don't take who?" Polly asked. She knocked on the floor for Helen, who was back in her room, to get up. Helen rushed into the room and searched for Polly's hand.

Polly spelled, "She is saying 'Don't take him away from me!'"

Helen felt helpless. She did not want to tire Annie by spelling into her hand. She put both her hands on Annie, but Annie suddenly screamed, "Jimmie! Jimmie! Don't take him away from me! Jimmie!"

Polly caressed her head, "Shhh... Annie.... Shhhh..."

"My Jimmie," Annie cried and sobbed, choking on her own tears, "I'll lay these flowers by your face, little brother! Don't take him away from me! I love him! He's all I've got!"

She cried and cried. Helen and Polly caressed her. Soon her tears subsided and she fell asleep again.

"Did she say anything?" Helen spelled to Polly desperately.

"Yes," Polly spelled back, dazed. She repeated Annie's words and then wrote them down.

* * *

In the afternoon Annie woke up again, and smiled. Nella was in the room. She hurried to the corridor and shouted, "Polly!"

Polly came upstairs. Nella held Annie's hand.

Annie whispered, "Polly?"

Polly hurried into the room, "Yes, yes, I'm here!"

Annie whispered, "Polly will take care of Helen, yes?"

"Very good care of Helen," Polly said and smiled at Nella.

Nella smiled back grimly. She had never seen a person dying. She asked Polly, "Shall I call Helen?"

Polly said, "She'll be here in a second, she heard me running."

As if on a call, Helen rushed into the room and frantically searched for Polly's hand. Polly spelled to her and reassured her all was well.

Annie murmured, "As the years go on Helen's speeches won't be so brilliant. No. My guiding hand won't be there to take out what should be taken out."

Polly nodded. Helen couldn't hold it any longer. She burst in tears and shouted, "Teacher! Teacher!"

Annie cried, "Come here, my little Helen, come here!"

She hugged Helen's head, caressing her hair with all the power she had left. She whispered, "Thank God I gave of my life that Helen might live! God help her to live without me when I go!"

These were to be her last words.

* * *

On the paper near the bed, later to be revered by generations to come, were written Annie's last words as written by Polly:

> "I wanted to be loved, I was lonesome. Then Helen came into my life, I wanted her to love me and I loved her. Then later Polly came and I loved Polly and we were always so happy together, my Polly, my Helen. Dear children may we all meet together in heaven.
>
> Good-bye John Macy! I'll soon be with you, good-bye, I loved you!
>
> My Jimmie, I'll lay these flowers by your face, don't take him away from me, I loved him so he's all I've got...
>
> Polly will take care of Helen. As the years go on her speeches won't be so brilliant as what people will think but my guiding hand won't be there to take out what should be taken out.
>
> Thank God I gave of my life that Helen might live. God help her to live without me when I go."

* * *

Polly, her hand trembling, called an ambulance. Nella tried comforting Helen, who breathed heavily and moved her lips silently, as if in a trance.

The paramedics came into the house, followed Polly to Annie's room, and a few minutes later left the room with Annie's feeble body lying on the stretcher.

Nella drove Helen and Polly to the hospital.

Polly arranged everything, from the location and time

of the funeral service to the cremation procedure. She spoke on the phone from the hospital for nearly two hours, while Helen was hugged by Nella.

After having finished with all the arrangements, Polly came to Helen in the hospital hallway and touched her shoulder, spelling to her, "We need to release an announcement to the press."

Helen wiped her tears and nodded. "I'll do it."

Polly spelled, "Are you sure? I can just write a sentence and have the secretary here wire it—"

"No, I'll do it," Helen insisted and stood up, "I can do it."

Helen and Nella found a typewriter, and together they wrote the brief statement:

> "For fifty years Anne Sullivan Macy, my beloved teacher, has been the light in my life. Now she is gone and the darkness that covers me has fallen upon her; still the light of her love shines amid the encircling gloom, and we are happy."

She signed, using the square-alphabet Annie had taught her 49 years earlier:

> "Helen Keller."

* * *

"MRS. MACY IS DEAD; AIDED MISS KELLER

The New York Times, October 21st, 1936

Mrs. Anne Sullivan Macy, who for nearly fifty

years was the kindly, patient and brilliant teacher of Miss Helen Keller, the famed blind and deaf, died yesterday at their home in Forest Hills. She had been suffering from a heart ailment, which became acute this Summer. Mrs. Macy was 70 years old.

Mrs. Macy taught Miss Keller to read, speak and know the world about her by use of her fingertips. Their lifelong devotion to each other was internationally famous and one was seldom seen or heard of without the other. Blindness, which had shadowed the child Anne Sullivan's life and which she had conquered before she met Miss Keller, had returned to darken her last days; Miss Keller, familiar with the darkness of blindness, had to aid her teacher, by that Miss Keller becoming the teacher and Mrs. Macy the pupil.

Miss Keller paid this tribute to her deceased teacher: "For fifty years Anne Sullivan Macy, my beloved teacher, has been the light in my life. Now she is gone and the darkness that covers me has fallen upon her; still the light of her love shines amid the encircling gloom, and we are happy."

Miss Polly Thompson, Miss Keller's secretary, said yesterday to the press that Miss Keller was "bearing up magnificently" under her loss. During the last week Miss Keller was almost constantly at Mrs. Macy's side. Mrs. Macy's last words were: "Oh, Helen and Polly, my children, I pray God will unite us in heaven."

Mrs. Macy, so long the link to light for Miss Keller, lost the sight of her eyes due partly to a cataract, for which an operation was performed in May of last year, but thereafter she was able to distinguish only light and color with it. She could no longer read or guide her beloved Miss Keller, who, despite her own handicaps, devoted herself to her friend.

Unlikely Beginnings

Mrs. Macy was 21 years old when she met Helen Keller. Born in Agawam, Massachusetts, on April 14, 1866, the daughter of Irish immigrants, Thomas and Alice Sullivan, Mrs. Macy suffered the loss of her mother when a young child. For a year or two she was supported by poor relatives, but at the age of 10 she was sent to the State Infirmary of Massachusetts.

She was already partially blind and at the infirmary two eye operations were performed, but her sight did not improve. She was led to believe that Mr. Frank B. Sanborn, chairman of the State Board of Charities, might be able to aid her. She pleaded with him and he arranged for her entry into the Massachusetts School for the Blind in Boston, where lived Laura Bridgman, blind and deaf, who had been trained there.

Valedictorian of Her Class

Mrs. Macy entered the Massachusetts School for the Blind in 1880, made there a brilliant scholastic record and learned to study with her fingers, and later, after two operations had restored her sight, to use her eyes. She learned the manual, or finger, alphabet, to be able to talk to Laura Bridgman. In 1886 she graduated as valedictorian of her class.

Not long after her graduation Helen Keller's father, Captain Arthur Keller, wrote to the institution asking for help for his daughter. Miss Sullivan was chosen to be her teacher and, after familiarizing herself with the details of her new work, went to Helen's home in Tuscumbia, Alabama.

The two, who were to mean so much to each other until Mrs. Macy's death yesterday, met first on March 3, 1887, three months before Helen turned 7 years old. Miss Keller said later that it was "The most important day in all my life."

Working carefully, so as to bring Helen under some sort of discipline without breaking her spirit, Mrs. Macy began spelling words into her hand. With no understanding of what they meant, Helen began repeating them. The teacher persisted, spelling the word 'doll' when she gave the child a doll, 'bread' when she gave her bread and 'candy' when she gave her candy.

Teaching Along New Paths

One day Mrs. Macy tried to teach Helen the difference between a *cup* and the *water in* the cup. She took her to a pump, pumped water over one hand and spelled *water* into the other hand. Helen at last understood; she realized that everything had a name and that she had a way, the finger alphabet, of calling the names. She pointed to Miss Sullivan, who spelled back to the eager child, "*Teacher.*" Indeed, "teacher" she was to be to the close.

Mrs. Macy educated Helen, always using finger spelling, but treating her like any other child. Several years later, as a teen, after preliminary lessons in articulation, Helen learned from Mrs. Macy to converse and even speak from a platform.

Together they prepared for Harvard University and in 1900 Helen passed triumphantly her entrance examinations, entered The Harvard

Annex for Women and in 1904 was graduated *cum laude*.

Throughout all these years Mrs. Macy was with Helen, spelling into her hands the words of the textbooks and the books of required reading. Miss Keller's career thereafter brought her more and more into the public eye. She became famous as an author, raised great sums for the blind and traveled extensively. She was everywhere acclaimed, and Mrs. Macy went everywhere with her.

"My own life," Mrs. Macy said once, "is so interwoven with Helen's life that I can't separate myself from her."

Honorary Doctorate

In 1931 Mrs. Macy received an honorary degree of Doctor of Humane Letters from Temple University, but declined it. Nevertheless, the following year she was willing to receive it, and gave the commencement address at Temple. Temple University President, Mr. Charles E. Beury, described Mrs. Macy's address as "brilliant" and "thought-provoking."

In 1933 a biography was published about her life, authored by Mrs. Nella Braddy Henney. At the time of publication Macy fell ill, healing in seclusion in Scotland, while Miss Keller nursed her. Mrs. Macy's blindness grew more pronounced and on her return from Scotland she said: "It's not the big things in life that one misses through loss of sight, but such little things as being able to read. And I have no patience, like Helen, for the braille system, because I can't read fast enough. Helen is and always has been thoroughly well behaved in her blindness as well as her deafness, but I'm making a futile fight of it, like a bucking bronco."

The University of Rochester, the Roosevelt Memorial Association, and other institutions have wished to give Mrs. Macy honorary doctorates and awards, but she declined.

Mrs. Macy was married to John Albert Macy, author and critic, in 1905. Mr. Macy died in 1932. There are no immediate survivors. Her funeral service will be conducted at 2 P. M. tomorrow at the Park Avenue Presbyterian Church. After the service, cremation will take place, in accord with Mrs. Macy's wish, at the Fresh Pond Crematory, Queens."

* * *

Back at home, the doorbell did not stop ringing. Flower bouquets came by the dozens, and messenger boys from the post office and Western Union brought hundreds of telegrams from people expressing their condolences, from unknown blind and deaf around the world, to Charlie Chaplin, to First Lady Eleanor Roosevelt who wrote, "Dear Helen, both the President and I were distressed to hear of your teacher's death and we realize what her loss means to you. You have our deep sympathy. Yours, Eleanor."

Polly, exhausted from going to the door every other minute, placed four baskets for flowers near the door and a bag for telegrams on the door, with a note: "Please do not disturb! Mail to the bag, flowers to the baskets. Kindly, the grieving family."

Mildred, who had visited just two weeks before, telegrammed that she was on her way.

Lenore hurried to come from Boston to join Helen, Polly and Nella in the house. But no one spoke much that evening. Each of the four women preferred to remain alone with her memories.

* * *

The following day Polly helped Helen dress in black for the funeral. Nella drove them and Lenore to Manhattan, where the service was to be held in the Presbyterian Church on Park Avenue. On the way Helen and Polly fretted in the back seats.

Helen spelled, "We should have postponed the funeral a day so that people could come from afar."

Polly spelled, exhausted both emotionally and physically, "It is not good to wait. And people can pay their homage later."

Helen was not convinced. "I don't want the church to be empty. We should have telegrammed the Foundation and asked them to send a bus with some of the New York Chapter members. We should have waited for Mildred to come. She would have wanted to be present for the ceremony...."

Polly patted her worried friend on the hand and gazed out of the window. They drove on the Queensboro Bridge into Manhattan. Polly spelled, "It will be alright, Helen. Annie would have not wanted a big service anyhow."

Helen nodded. Polly was right, but still—she wanted her teacher to receive the respect she deserved.

As they crossed Lexington Avenue Nella slowed down. A policeman, standing by an impromptu police barrier, slowed down the traffic and directed people north and south. Nella rolled her window, "We need to get to the Presbyterian Church!"

"I'm sorry Ma'am," said the policeman, "it's clogged with people. You'll need to park here and walk."

Polly wouldn't have it, she leaned forward and exclaimed, "Excuse me, officer! We need to get to a funeral!"

"I'm sorry Ma'am," the policeman said and pointed at the crowds, "so do all the others here."

Polly looked behind the police barrier and gasped. Helen spelled to her, "What is happening?!"

* * *

"HUNDREDS PAY TRIBUTE TO MRS. MACY, TEACHER OF HELEN KELLER

New York Herald Tribune, October 22, 1935

Services for Mrs. Anne Sullivan Macy, for 49 years the devoted teacher and friend of Helen Keller, were held yesterday at the Park Avenue Presbyterian Church, Manhattan. Mrs. Macy died on Tuesday at her home in Forest Hills. She was 70 years old. The church was filled to its full capacity and hundreds stood in the streets outside, paying their last homage.

The quartet of Marble Collegiate Church opened the service with 'Nearer My God To Thee.' Describing Mrs. Macy as the "great emancipator," the Rev. Dr. Emerson Fosdick, who delivered the eulogy, said that "the consequences of her work will be a shining beacon to people all over the world for generation after generation."

The reverend continued, "We stand in awe of her great achievement. We see that her outstanding qualities and characteristics were her deathless and indefatigable friendship, and her craftsmanship that enabled her to do a beautiful piece of work for the satisfaction of doing it that way. She was truly a great artist."

With Miss Keller at the service was her secretary, Miss Polly Thomson, and several close friends. There were many blind men and women among the twelve hundred people who attended. The choir sang Dvorak's "Going Home," one of Macy's favorite selections, and the organist played Schubert's Serenade, "Ständchen."

After the funeral procession passed down the middle aisle of the church, behind the black-robed ministers came twelve honorary pallbearers preceding the coffin, which was blanketed with pink roses and ferns. They were followed by a very emotional Helen Keller and her secretary Polly Thomson. Then, according to her wishes, Anne Sullivan Macy's body was taken to Long Island for cremation.

Nation-wide Radio Commemoration

The Columbia network announced yesterday that a nation-wide radio broadcast would be dedicated to the devotion and self-sacrifice of Mrs. Macy, to be broadcasted tonight at 8 PM over the Columbia network.

* * *

The days were dreary. Helen wished to travel to Scotland, and Polly arranged their travel as soon as they were done with the arrangements.

A mysterious plea came forth, and it was unclear who had initiated it. It was not Helen herself, nor Polly, though both supported it. Someone, some said the First Lady herself had convinced the Bishop of the National Cathedral in Washington to intern Annie's ashes there.

It was a unique proposition, as no woman was ever buried there in her own right: only wives of famous Americans, admirals and presidents.

* * *

"Mrs. Sullivan Macy, Teacher of Helen Keller, Brought to Rest at National Cathedral

Washington Herald, 2nd November, 1936

Before the sightless eyes of Helen Keller, her lifelong companion and pupil, the ashes of Mrs. Anne Sullivan Macy were committed yesterday afternoon to a crypt in the columbarium of Washington Cathedral. In the burial service, Bishop James E. Freeman said it was an honor to the Nation's Capital to have the ashes of such great teacher.

Bishop Freeman continued: "The Cathedral honors itself in giving sepulture to Mrs. Anne Sullivan Macy. Among the great teachers of all time she occupies a commanding and conspicuous place. She was a bringer of light to one in darkness. Possibly no recorded service bears comparison with her supreme accomplishments. The touch of her hand did more than illuminate the pathway of a clouded mind—it emancipated a soul!"

Miss Keller was accompanied to the cathedral by Miss Polly Thomson, her secretary, as well as several friends. She sat in the front row close to the chancel, where Miss Thomson interpreted the service to her by the touch of her hand.

Representatives of the American Foundation for the Blind, the Columbia Institute for the Blind, the Polytechnic Institute and the National Education Association were among those present. Twenty-five young men and women came from Gallaudet College, where the government gives higher education to youths who are deaf and dumb.

Miss Thomson's fingers translated Bishop Freeman's words: "In bringing light and understanding to the mind of Helen Keller, Mrs. Macy gave the world one of the rarest women of our generation."

Of the honor given to her beloved teacher by placing the urn containing her ashes in the National Cathedral, Miss Keller said: "I feel that a nobler tribute could not be paid to her whose love and resourceful mind brought liberty into my dungeon of silence."

Only Miss Keller and close friends were present when, after the public chapel service, the urn containing the ashes of Mrs. Macy was placed in the columbarium adjoining the chapel. Mrs. Macy is said to be the first lady to be buried in the National Cathedral unassociated with marital distinction."

* * *

Helen was relieved to climb on board the ship to Scotland.

Finally, she could be alone with her thoughts.

Years later she wrote:

> "Once the ashes had been placed in the National Cathedral in Washington D. C., Polly and I took passage for Scotland, where her brother generously received us into his home so that I might recover my equilibrium.
>
> I have never lost faith in personal immortality, but Teacher's departure so disorganized my life that many months passed before I could reorient myself. I felt powerless. It was as if the fire of Teacher's mind through which I had so vividly experienced the light, the music, and the glory of life—had been withdrawn. There was still the wonder of language which she had left in my hand, but the mysterious battery from which it had been kindled was withdrawn.
>
> So also was the irreplaceable stimulus that comes from day-by-day living with a unique individual, one who had kept all the shadows—ever pressing down—from closing in upon me.
>
> I had not then sufficient inner light to beat the shadows back on my own."

* * *

The months in the dreary winter of Scotland found Helen Keller depressed and beaten down. She was 56 years old and yet she felt like a child, abandoned, deserted.

Polly tried to entertain her. She did everything she could to lift Helen's spirit, yet deep inside she regretted listening to Helen and crossing the ocean to go to Scotland. In New York at least they had Nella, and Lenore, and the Foundation and many visitors who could sooth Helen's aching soul.

The more the months passed the more solemn and withdrawn Helen became. Polly feared that the jovial Helen she had known for twenty years was disappearing. She feared she was letting Annie Sullivan down.

And that thought troubled Polly beyond words.

This was why Polly, upon opening the letters that Nella forwarded and seeing a letter from Japan, was excited.

She spelled to Helen, "There is a letter from the gentleman who visited us in Forest Hills, the man from Japan!"

Helen was nonresponsive.

"Helen," Polly glanced at the letter, "he shares his condolences, again," she read through the long letter. "He had written several times, he says, and wishes for us to follow on his earlier invitation."

Helen sighed. "I do not have the power to travel."

Polly ground her teeth. What would Annie say?

She tried again, "He begs us to come and educate the government about incorporating blind and deaf people into the workforce and opening schools for the blind and deaf!" Seeing Helen's disinterest Polly said, "Annie would have liked that!"

Helen turned to Polly, "Yes," she spelled back, "she would have liked that."

Then, after a moment, Helen spelled, "She made me promise, that we shall go to Japan. That we should be light bringers to the handicapped there!'"

"Yes!" Polly said and smiled, "Yes!" Personally, the last thing Polly wanted was to travel. But she wanted her Helen of twenty-years *back*. If going to Japan would be what would bring the old Helen back, then Polly was willing to hop on a ship tomorrow.

Helen looked reminiscent. She spelled to Polly slowly, hesitantly, "'Hold out your arms to them,' Teacher told me. 'Forget yourself in them, and be faithful to their cause... That will be your true memorial to me, Helen!'"

Helen got up and spoke—it was the first time she had articulated words in months—"We need to go to Japan. It will be my tribute—our tribute—to Teacher!"

* * *

> "The year before Annie died, Mr. Takeo Iwahashi, the head of the work for the blind in Japan, came to see us in our house in Forest Hills. He was studying American methods of solving the problems of the blind. He had a command of English that amazed us. Blind himself, full of poetic fire and enthusiasm, he urged me to come over to Japan and pour sunshine into the hearts of the struggling blind. I told him of Annie's condition—she was too ill to see him and

remained in her room upstairs—and I said I could not think of leaving her. The following day, when she heard of our interview with Takeo and saw how impressed we were by his noble personality she said, "Here is a unique opportunity that you must not miss, Helen!"

"But I simply can't go without you," I answered, "and since you can't accompany me, I shall not accept the invitation."

Teacher insisted. "I beg you to promise me that after I am gone you and Polly will be light-bringers to the handicapped of Japan."

After her death I couldn't think of going anywhere. But I did not forget my promise to Teacher. In my darkness I remembered her words. We decided to set sail to Japan. Indeed, it was not until after Polly and I had made our voyage there that a spark of self-activity finally began to illumine the void for me.

When I disembarked the ship on the shore of Japan, I felt as if Teacher's loving hand was held out to me. We were welcomed by Mr. Takeo Iwahashi, government officials, other distinguished personages and the press. My work began with a rush which lifted my mind above personal suffering: conferences with high dignitaries on the correct process of rehabilitating children without sight or hearing, press interviews, a garden party at the Imperial Palace in Tokyo at which we were received by the Emperor and Empress, and speeches at institutions for the handicapped.

Takeo and his wife took us to villages nestling among the hills. We ate Japanese meals sitting on our heels with what grace we could, and we slept in the houses of those who entertained us.

I felt close to the faith of the Japanese as they scattered incense, lighted their "spirit-sticks," and worshiped at the family shrine. Our forms of belief were different, but I loved the warmth with which the people cherished their departed dear ones and anticipated their reunion. I felt Teacher's presence with me everywhere. There was also the intense love of beauty around me which I had known in Teacher.

Takeo worked indefatigably translating my messages of encouragement into Japanese, explaining to me the ignorance of the seeing public concerning the blind as "cursed." Thanks to him I met with less trepidation the questions asked by those who wanted to create paths of inner light to darkened minds and stunted lives.

I knew positively that Teacher was with me, and I felt her presence still more every day. This expansion of Teacher's work to far lands and the rebirth of her presence in my life are the most treasured souvenirs that I gathered on that trip."

This, however, was just the beginning.

The following decade Helen, along with Polly, both in their sixties, visited China, France, Greece, and Italy. Everywhere they went they brought with them hope for the blind and for the deaf, establishing new foundations and organizations for the handicapped, bringing publicity and encouraging financial support to the foundations already in existence in each country. They visited New Zealand and the Philippines. After Helen turned seventy years old they visited Australia, Korea, South Africa, Zimbabwe, Egypt, Israel, Jordan, Lebanon and Syria. They also visited Brazil, Chile, Mexico,

Panama, and Peru. Everywhere they went Helen saw her teacher in the hands of others, and heard Annie whispering to her spirit: 'Hold out your arms to them, forget yourself in them, be faithful to their cause—there may be a wall between you and them, but hammer it down, stone by stone.'

As Helen approached her eighties and Polly was in her mid-seventies they travelled to Burma, India, Indonesia and Pakistan, bringing light and raising awareness of the plight of the deaf and blind. They visited Germany, Portugal, Spain, Canada, Denmark, Finland, Iceland, Norway, Sweden and Switzerland. By the time Helen was 80 years old she visited 39 countries. In her diary she referred to her efforts around the world as "further growth of the tree of Teacher's life in me."

In her last years Helen wrote and published a book dedicated to Annie, simply called "Teacher: Anne Sullivan Macy." In it she wrote,

> "In my many speeches, with emotion that almost choked utterance, I thanked people for recognizing the source from which I had drawn my strength. Thus it is that Teacher ever journeyed with me to all places where new tests were laid upon me, and after all the years, still shared with me all the joys.
>
> There was such virtue and such power of communication in Teacher's personality that after her death they nerved me to endure and persevere. I was gripped by the might of the destiny she had mapped out for me, it lifted me out of myself to wage God's war against darkness. Of course there is always a choice between two courses, and, shocked out of all security, I might have let go any further activity, but Teacher

believed in me, and I resolved not to betray her faith."

Helen concluded the 224-page-memoir about her teacher with the following words:

"Conscious of her being alive with me, I have sought new ways to give life and yet more life to men and women whom darkness, silence, sickness, or sorrow are wearing away. And at times it seems that God is using her, who touched my night to flame, to kindle other fires of good. Advancing in years and knowing that I shall be glad to get rid of my worn-out body, I yet experience new birth and youth in the soul of Teacher. The certainty that her creative intelligence and truly human quality of mind do not perish, but continue their vivifying work, sweetens my loneliness and is like the warm spring air in my heart."

This book was to be her last.

At age 88, on June 1, 1968, Helen Keller died in her home.

EPILOGUE

When one visits the National Cathedral in Washington D.C., one can hear whispers of visitors from around the world. Many are the languages spoken in the tall cathedral. Walking to a wide wall, near an arched chapel, one can see an old brass plaque on the wall. The letters on the plaque are embossed—in fact, along with the embossed letters are also the dots of the braille alphabet. Through the tinted hue around the dots one can easily grasp how often these braille letters were felt by the numerous blind visitors, who among the millions of seeing visitors in the decades that passed, came to pay tribute to those buried in the columbarium behind that chapel.

If you ever visit the National Cathedral, you may close your eyes as you put your hand on the cold brass plaque and feel the letters sticking out, as so many did before you, paying their respect:

> "INTERRED IN THE COLUMBARIUM BEHIND THIS CHAPEL ARE
>
> HELEN KELLER AND HER LIFELONG COMPANION
>
> ANNE SULLIVAN MACY."

CODA

May 22nd, 1887

"Dear Mrs. Hopkins,

I want to write something here that is for your ears alone. Something within me tells me that I shall succeed with Helen beyond my dreams... I cannot tell how I know these things. A short time ago I had no idea how to go to work; I was feeling about in the dark; but somehow I now know, and I know that I know. I cannot explain it; but when difficulties arise, I am not perplexed or doubtful. I know how to meet them; I seem to sense Helen's peculiar needs. It is wonderful. **I know that the education of this child will be the distinguishing event of my life, if I have the brains and perseverance to accomplish it.** Yours,

Annie."

-THE END-

One of the earliest known photos of Annie with Helen, ages 21 and 7 respectively, c. 1888

Annie speaks into a dictaphone, a recording device, while simultaneously Helen fingerspells to Annie what to say into the machine.

Annie accepting an Honorary Degree from Temple University, Annie is in the center, Polly is second from left, Helen is third from left; the four men unidentified, most likely Temple University professors, 1932. Notice how Annie is smiling, holding the honorary degree in her hand.

Annie and Nella Braddy Henney sitting in living room in Forest Hills, New York. This photo was taken at the time when Nella was writing Annie's biography.[i]

MRS. MACY IS DEAD; AIDED MISS KELLER

Teacher and Famous Blind and Deaf Pupil Associated Since They Met in 1887.

SHE KEPT IN BACKGROUND

In Recent Years Her Sight Failed and Younger Woman Heroically Looked After Her.

Mrs. Anne Mansfield Sullivan Macy, who for nearly fifty years was the kindly, patient and brilliant teacher of Miss Helen Keller, noted blind and deaf woman, died yesterday at their home, 71-11 Seminole Avenue, Forest Hills, Queens. She had been suffering from a heart ailment, which became acute early this Summer. Mrs. Macy was 70 years old.

Mrs. Macy taught Miss Keller to read, speak and know the world about her by use of her fingertips. Their lifelong devotion to each other was internationally famous and one was seldom seen or heard of without the other. Blindness, which had shadowed the child Anne Sullivan's life and which she had conquered before she met Miss Keller, had returned to darken her last days, and Miss Keller had to become the teacher and Mrs. Macy the pupil.

Miss Keller yesterday paid this tribute:

"Teacher is free at last from pain and blindness. I pray for strength to endure the silent dark until she smiles upon me again."

Miss Polly Thomson, Miss Keller's secretary, said yesterday that Miss Keller was "bearing up magnificently" under her loss. During the last week Miss Keller was almost constantly at Mrs. Macy's side. Mrs. Macy was in a coma from Thursday until she died. On Wednesday she said: "Oh, Helen and Polly, my children, I pray God will unite us in His love."

Mrs. Macy, so long the link to light for Miss Keller, lost the sight of her own right eye in 1929, due partly to a cataract, for which an operation was performed. In May, 1935, a cataract operation was done on her left eye, but thereafter she was able to distinguish only light and color with it. She could no longer read or guide her beloved Miss Keller, who, despite her own handicaps, devoted herself to her friend.

Pupil Guides Teacher in Braille

As early as 1932 Miss Keller had commenced to teach Mrs. Macy to read Braille. But the Braille system had damaged since Mrs. Macy taught it to Miss Keller and the teacher found it difficult.

When it became known that year that Miss Keller, who had been led

MRS. ANNE S. MACY
New York Times Studio Photo.

in Cambridge to prepare her for Radcliffe College and finally Helen passed triumphantly her entrance examinations, entered Radcliffe and in 1904 was graduated cum laude.

Throughout the college course Mrs. Macy was with Helen, spelling into her hands the words of the textbooks and the books of required reading. Miss Keller's career thereafter brought her more and more into the public eye. She became famous as an author, she traveled, she was everywhere acclaimed, and Mrs. Macy went everywhere with her.

"My own life," Mrs. Macy said once, "is so interwoven with my Helen's life that I can't separate myself from her."

Honored by Foreign Lands

When Mrs. Macy's sixty-seventh birthday was celebrated Miss Keller proposed a toast:

"Here's to my teacher, whose birthday was the Easter morning of my life."

In 1931 Mrs. Macy received the honorary degree of Doctor of Humane Letters from Temple University and the Order of St. Sava from the King of Yugoslavia.

In 1932 she became an honorary fellow of the Educational Institute of Scotland. Mrs. Macy stayed in seclusion for several months in 1933 in Scotland while Miss Keller nursed her. Mrs. Macy's blindness grew more pronounced and on her return from Scotland she said:

"Helen is and always has been thoroughly well behaved in her blindness as well as her deafness, but I'm making a futile fight of it, like a bucking bronco. It's not the big things in life that one misses through loss of sight, but such little things as being able to read. And I have no patience, like Helen, for the Braille system, because I can't read fast enough."

Early this month the Roosevelt

"TEACHER"

On a day nearly fifty years ago HELEN KELLER, the blind and deaf child whom ANNE SULLIVAN had undertaken to teach, had put into her hand (literally) the key to the universe. Mrs. MACY, whom ANNE SULLIVAN came to be, tells of the day of the miracle when HELEN, with a new light in her face, learned the word for "water";

Suddenly turning around and pointing to me she asked my name. I spelled "Teacher."

To the end of that miracled companionship which ended yesterday morning she was "Teacher." She literally "spelled the world into HELEN'S hand."

The story of Mrs. MACY'S own life—of a half-blind child, lonely and neglected in an almshouse, who was transplanted to the Perkins Institute for the Blind, and as a young woman was then transported fifteen hundred miles to teach a child deprived of both hearing and sight—is one of a triumph over a dark and sordid environment and terrible poverty. But it takes on a Promethean significance in its relation of how she brought light to one in a double prison of darkness and silence and liberated her spirit. She deserves a place among the world's greatest teachers. HELEN KELLER said in a letter about what she "saw" from one of our tall buildings, which was as a "giant shaft groping toward beauty and spiritual vision," that until we have looked into darkness we can never know what a divine thing vision is. Mrs. MACY in giving vision to eyes that could never literally see performed a divine service in which others than her blind pupil shared.

The lamp which, as the emblem of Prometheus, was borne through the "divine gloom" of SHELLEY'S line should be hers as well who carried the torch that lighted the way of this child into glorious womanhood—the torch of hope across "the night of life" and bore it most triumphantly—and will even beyond the grave carry it to the far goal of Time. For what this teacher has done for one prisoned soul cannot be forgotten, and may now be repeated for others.

Black and white newspaper cartoon by cartoonist Fay King, titled: "Fay King Mourns Death of Helen Keller's Friend." First frame: Drawing of Annie and Helen: "For fifty years the Perfect Teacher and her Perfect Pupil were together"; Second Frame: Annie teaching Helen her first word: "Anne Sullivan was 21 and Helen Keller was 7 when they first met in 1887: learning the first word (Doll)"; Third Frame: Anne's grave, her name and the years 1866-1936 written on the headstone, along with the wreath labeled as "the world".

Inside Cover of Helen's memoir about Annie: Teacher: Anne Sullivan Macy. Below the photograph is Annie's name and the years 1866-1936

Helen and Polly. Polly died eight years before Helen, in 1960. She, too, is burried in the National Cathedral in Washington D.C.

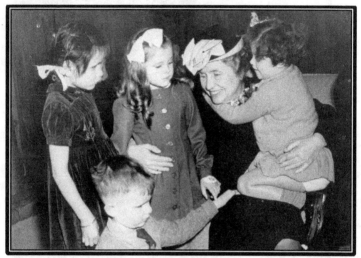

Helen visiting blind children in one of her global tours

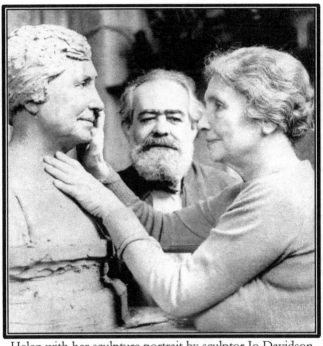
Helen with her sculpture portrait by sculptor Jo Davidson

Helen with First Lady Eleanor Roosevelt, reading the lips of Roosevelt's face with her hand

Helen meets President John F. Kennedy in the White House. This was in the year following Polly's death (1961) and Helen is assisted by her personal secretary Evelyn Seide. The other representatives are from Lions Clubs International.

Helen fingerspelling to young actress Patty Duke who played her role in the film *The Miracle Worker*, 1962. Helen is 82 years old in this photograph. She died six years later.

The National Cathedral in Washington, D.C., where the ashes of Helen, Annie and Polly are interred.

The brass sign at the National Cathedral in Washington, D.C., by the chapel in which the ashes of Helen, Annie and Polly are interred. The sign states in English and in braille (notice the faded hue of the brass around the braille letters): "HELEN KELLER AND HER LIFELONG COMPANION ANNE SULLIVAN MACY ARE INTERRED IN THE COLUMBARIUM BEHIND THIS CHAPEL."

PHOTO CREDITS AND NOTES

[i] Image courtesy of American Foundation for the Blind.

[i] Image courtesy of Public Health Museum, Tewksbury, MA

[i] Image courtesy of Public Health Museum, Tewksbury, MA

[i] Image courtesy of Public Health Museum, Tewksbury, MA

[i] Image courtesy of Larry Melander

[i] Image courtesy of Samuel P. Hayes Research Library, Perkins School for the Blind, Watertown, MA

[i] Image courtesy of Samuel P. Hayes Research Library, Perkins School for the Blind, Watertown, MA

[i] Image courtesy of Samuel P. Hayes Research Library, Perkins School for the Blind, Watertown, MA

[i] Image courtesy of Samuel P. Hayes Research Library, Perkins School for the Blind, Watertown, MA

[i] Image courtesy of Samuel P. Hayes Research Library, Perkins School for the Blind, Watertown, MA

[i] Image courtesy of Pach Brothers, Cambridge, MA

[i] Image courtesy of Samuel P. Hayes Research Library, Perkins School for the Blind, Watertown, MA

[i] Samuel P. Hayes Research Library, Perkins School for the Blind, Watertown, MA

[i] Image courtesy of Samuel P. Hayes Research Library,

Perkins School for the Blind, Watertown, MA

[i] Samuel P. Hayes Research Library, Perkins School for the Blind, Watertown, MA

[i] Image courtesy of Samuel P. Hayes Research Library, Perkins School for the Blind, Watertown, MA

[i] Image courtesy of Samuel P. Hayes Research Library, Perkins School for the Blind, Watertown, MA

[i] Samuel P. Hayes Research Library, Perkins School for the Blind, Watertown, MA

[i] Image courtesy of Samuel P. Hayes Research Library, Perkins School for the Blind, Watertown, MA

[i] Image courtesy of Samuel P. Hayes Research Library, Perkins School for the Blind, Watertown, MA

CLAIM YOUR GIFT!

Thank you for purchasing this novel. For a special behind-the-scenes e-book, including historical background on which *The teacher* was based please visit:

Books.click/Teacher

* * *

This e-book companion includes group discussion ideas, unique photographs and much more!

JOIN OUR ONLINE BOOK CLUB!

Book club members receive free books and the hottest pre-release novels. To join our exclusive online book club and discuss *The teacher* with likeminded readers, please visit:

Books.click/MoringBookclub

* * *

We look forward to see you in our bookclub family!

RATE THIS BOOK!

We thank you for taking a quick moment to rate this book online. Let others know what you thought at this easy link!

Books.click/TeacherRating

The author has requested that we include the following personal email address below. Readers are invited to contact author Marcel Moring directly at the following address. The author attempts to answer each and every email from dedicated readers.

AuthorMarcelMoring1@gmail.com

NOVELS BY MARCEL MORING:

My India

The Survivor

The Holocaust

Innocence

The Teacher

After the Storm

The Revenge

CPSIA information can be obtained
at www.ICGtesting.com
Printed in the USA
LVHW081955131022
730651LV00015B/894